Human Rights:

THE ESSENTIAL REFERENCE

Human Rights:

THE ESSENTIAL REFERENCE

Carol Devine

Carol Rae Hansen

Ralph Wilde

Daan Bronkhorst

Frederic A. Moritz

Baptiste Rolle

Rebecca Sherman

Jo Lynn Southard

Robert Wilkinson

Edited by Hilary Poole

ORYX PRESS

The rare Arabian Oryx is believed to have inspired the myth of the unicorn. This desert antelope became virtually extinct in the early 1960s. At that time several groups of international conservationists arranged to have 9 animals sent to the Phoenix Zoo to be the nucleus of a captive breeding herd. Today the Oryx population is over 1,000, and over 500 have been returned to the Middle East.

© 1999 by The Oryx Press
4041 North Central at Indian School Road
Phoenix, Arizona 85012-3397

Produced by The Moschovitis Group, Inc.
95 Madison Avenue, New York, New York, 10016

Executive Editor:	Valerie Tomaselli
Senior Editor:	Hilary Poole
Design and Layout:	Annemarie Redmond
Copyediting:	Elizabeth H. Oakes
Proofreading:	Carol Sternhell
Index:	AEIOU, Inc.

Published simultaneously in Canada
Printed and Bound in the United States of America

ISBN 1-57356-205-X

Library of Congress Cataloging-in-Publication Data

Human rights: the essential reference / Carol Devine . . . [et al.].
    p.   cm.
  Includes bibliographical references and index.
  ISBN 1-57356-205-X (alk. paper)
  1. Human rights.   2. United Nations. General Assembly. Universal
Declaration of Human Rights.   I. Devine, Carol, 1967–   .
  K3240.4.H847   1999
  323—dc21   99-24395

∞ The paper used in this publication meets the minimum requirements of American National Standard for Information Science—Permanence of Paper for Printed Library Materials, ANSI Z39.48, 1984.

TABLE OF CONTENTS

Preface   vii

PART ONE:
HUMAN RIGHTS BEFORE 1948   1
CHAPTER ONE:
A History of Human Rights Theory   3

PART TWO:
THE UNIVERSAL DECLARATION OF HUMAN RIGHTS   57
CHAPTER TWO:
An Overview of the Universal Declaration of Human Rights   59
CHAPTER THREE:
An Analysis of the Universal Declaration of Human Rights   73

PART THREE:
THE CONTEMPORARY HUMAN RIGHTS MOVEMENT   117
CHAPTER FOUR:
An Overview of the Human Rights Movement   119
CHAPTER FIVE:
Governmental Organizations   133
CHAPTER SIX:
Nongovernmental Organizations   149
CHAPTER SEVEN:
Human Rights Activists   179

PART FOUR:
CONTEMPORARY HUMAN RIGHTS ISSUES   227
CHAPTER EIGHT:
Contemporary Human Rights Issues   229

APPENDIX ONE: Timeline   275
APPENDIX TWO:
United Nations Documents   277
Further Reading   295
Index   297
Contributors   312

PREFACE

The Universal Declaration of Human Rights of 1948 is broadly recognized as the starting point for the modern human rights movement and is itself the quintessential human rights document. According to Dr. H.V. Evatt, the President of the UN General Assembly in 1948, "millions of men, women, and children all over the world, many miles from Paris and New York, will turn for help, guidance, and inspiration to this document."

In keeping with the centrality of the Universal Declaration, we have organized *Human Rights: The Essential Reference* into sections that consider human rights before the Declaration, the Declaration itself, and the post-WWII human rights movement. Part 1 traces the evolution of our modern concept of human rights, beginning with the Classical World and ending with the Second World War and the establishment of the Universal Declaration. Part 2 provides a comprehensive look at the Universal Declaration itself: the first chapter discusses the history of the declaration, what went into writing the draft, how it works, and what it can (and can not) do; the second chapter explores each of the thirty articles individually, discussing the legal history, philosophy, and—most revealingly—the legal and social relevance of each article to contemporary problems and issues.

Part 3 takes us into the present day. Chapter 4 leads off the contemporary sections with an investigation of the post-1948 human rights movement. Chapter 5 details the work of intergovernmental organizations, particularly the United Nations, in furthering the human rights cause, and Chapter 6 looks at the activities of nongovernmental organizations such as Amnesty International, Human Rights Watch, and many others. Chapter 7 is a mini-biographical dictionary of individuals who have had a significant impact on human rights. The inspiring stories that make up Chapter 7 include some of the "superstars" of the human rights movement, such as Peter Benenson, the founder of Amnesty International and South African president Nelson Mandela. We also profile some of the less celebrated but no less heroic individuals who have struggled (and continue to do so) for improved human rights, such as Egyptian author Nawal El Sadaawi and José Zalaquett, who was an instrumental member of the National Commission for Truth and Reconciliation in Chile.

Finally, Part 4 presents short essays on some of the most pressing contemporary human rights issues, from AIDS to the trafficking of women and girls, and from the importance of independent judiciaries to the safety of human rights workers. Although it is impossible to cover every single issue affecting human rights in the modern world,

Part 4 offers a broad survey of activities and concerns that touch the most highly developed nations of the world and the least.

The topics and organizations covered in these pages, particularly in the contemporary sections, are in a process of flux and evolution. The writing of this book began in the spring of 1998 and ended in December of that year, and information is accurate up to that point.

Contributors to this volume came to us from vastly different backgrounds, interests, and much-valued viewpoints. This mix of professional writers, scholars, and human-rights workers offers a unique blend of high levels of scholarship and vital doses of real-world experience. Daan Bronkhorst of the Dutch section of Amnesty International, who served in both authorial and advisory capacities in this work, merits particular mention for his insightful commentary and good humor.

PART ONE

Human Rights Before 1948

The Golden Rule *by Norman Rockwell. Inscribed with "Do unto others as you would have them do unto you,"*
the mosaic was a gift from the United States to the United Nations (UN Photo/M. Grant).

CHAPTER ONE

A History of Human Rights Theory

The history provided here presents a snapshot of the pivotal eras and moments in the history of Western civilization that helped to shape our twentieth-century conception of human rights. It begins with the philosophers and rulers of ancient Greece and concludes with the aftermath of World War II when the United Nations established the Universal Declaration of Human Rights. The declaration, created in 1948, marks the point at which Western countries officially placed human rights on the international agenda.

1. The Greek Tradition

"The real difference between democracy and oligarchy is poverty and wealth . . . . Oligarchy is when the control of the government is in the hands of those that own the properties; democracy is when, on the contrary, it is in the hands of those that do not possess much property, but are poor."

—Aristotle, *Politics*, III, 1297b 6ff

The ancient Greeks were the first civilization to develop a clearly articulated and coherent body of thought that ultimately affected modern concepts of "human rights." Although they were not the first to consider the nature of justice, they broke new ground in their evaluation of the individual and the relationship between lawgivers and those they ruled.

The Individual in Society and Law

At first "the Greeks" were a mere collection of city-states with diverse governments, military styles, and social mores. Later, they included cities on the Peloponnesus (the southernmost landmass of present-day mainland Greece) and hundreds of overseas colonies along the Mediterranean that Plato called "frogs around a pond." Greeks shared a common language, religion, and literature, along with comparable political societies, and forged a consensus that lets us celebrate their legacy—including the enduring importance of the individual—twenty-five thousand years later.

Greek religion and political culture provided the antecedents of claims to universal law that undergird our modern conception of human rights. Early Greek cosmologies viewed humanity as existing within the transcendent harmony of the universe, stemming from the divine law (*logos*) and linked to human life in the law (*nomos*) of the *polis*, the city-state. Indeed, as early as 700 B.C.E. the poet Hesiod boldly and decisively warned nobles that anyone who harms Justice (the virgin Dike, born of Zeus) by "casting crooked blame" could be avenged by Zeus. Around the same time the reintroduction of writing allowed people to read their laws instead of hearing the "god-given" decrees of their monarchs. Although these written edicts may have been harsh, they gave citizens a clear concept of their rights under law.

Later, the Sophists[1] pointed to major differences in morals and human law (which began in Greece as a public arbitration to settle compensation due to injuries) and rejected the claim that human law necessarily reflected any universal law. Taking humanity as "the measure of all things," they saw law, justice, and morality as stemming from human reason alone.

Early Greek Law and Participation in Politics

In practical terms, however, nothing approaching a modern concept of rights was introduced until Solon (638–559 B.C.E.), whose name survives as a synonym for "legislator." Solon codified the laws and is credited with erecting the basis for the first democracy in the city-state of Athens. Although not truly democratic, Solon did end aristocratic control over government and replaced it with the limited rule of perhaps one thousand wealthier male citizens. By 458–457 B.C.E. all citizens but the lowest property class could vote, and even the highest office was open to more than half the citizens. Soon thereafter, councilmen, administrative officials, and even the six thousand jurymen were paid for their service, involving the poor in politics for the first time. Solon also introduced the right of appeal

---

[1] Sophists were members of a pre-Socratic school of philosophy in ancient Greece. Ultimately, they were disparaged for self-serving and overly subtle reasoning.

to the Assembly meeting and added a second council, composed of one hundred men from each of the four tribes, to check the activities of the Areopagus council.

All was not idyllic in Greek law, of course, for competing ideas often held sway, and oligarchy and democracy alternated on the political stage. Furthermore, military needs both swept away rights and expanded the ranks of citizens. Draco (late 600s B.C.E.), another prominent legislator in Athens, wrote his own code of laws. His code punished even trivial crimes with death, and we remember his law as "draconian," or exceedingly severe. Still, Draco underscores the Greek commitment to developing law and refining government to meet the needs of the times, which would inspire similar efforts by the heirs to the Greek tradition.

Greek Philosophy

In fifth-century Athens, Plato (427–348 B.C.E.) looked beyond the law of the city-state in search of a more permanent and unimpeachable source of justice. In his *Republic*'s (400 B.C.E.) utopia, Plato argued that justice prevails when the state reaches ideal forms ordained by its philosopher-kings and is unrelated to the *nomos* of the *polis*. His concept of the common good contains an unusual defense of equal rights for women and a universal moral standard for human conduct, in war or peace, equally applied to Greeks and foreigners.

Plato moved beyond Socratic concepts (such as "the good," "virtue") to a theory of ideas. His historic importance lies with his political works, especially those such as

Plato as portrayed by Raphael in the painting, School of Athens *(CORBIS/Bettmann).*

Politicus (the "Statesman") and *The Laws*, which emphasize wisdom, courage, sobriety, and justice as the key human virtues in a state of laws. Plato believed that if people regulated their inward selves by following these indicators of wise living, then the state itself would exhibit less injustice toward other citizens because of each individual's self-control.

Aristotle (384–322 B.C.E.) argued that society need not rely only on philosopher-kings. He considered humanity to be moral, rational, and social, and he judged his law by how well it promoted these innate qualities. His *Politics* evaluated values such as virtue, justice, and rights and showed that they are best preserved in a mixed government (not a pure democracy, oligarchy, or tyranny) with an economically strong body of citizens.

Soon after Plato and Aristotle, a new philosophical ideal, stoicism, came to the

Greek Society

While the Greek tradition provided the intellectual and practical grist for the West's gradual evolution of human rights, Greek society fell far short of meeting contemporary concepts of individual rights. Even the Athenian "democracy" of the 440s B.C.E. would be considered such in name only today. The classical *polis* never included women, slaves, foreigners, or those who could not prove that both their parents had been citizens. The silver mines seem to have digested slaves insatiably, and war consumed an inordinate share of the Peloponnesus' sparse resources. Women, living in a markedly homosexual society, one in which homosexuality was viewed with much more tolerance than in contemporary western societies, were forbidden from entering any public sphere except religion. Only in Sparta were women citizens given daily and legal freedom in recognition of their biological function in producing citizens.

Gradually, with the growing individualism of the Hellenistic age and the demise of the city-state, the lot of women and slaves improved. The minority Sophist view that slavery was not natural and that a slave could be "free in his own mind" came to be supported by the Stoics, who argued that slaves should at least be properly treated. Given what they saw as a capacity for virtue in slaves, social status was irrelevant. When Alexander's conquests weakened the city-state, the lot of women improved considerably. Their educational, social, and legal status improved, and marriage contracts began enforcing monogamy, sometimes forbidding boy-lovers or concubines. Nevertheless, girl babies were still exposed (left out to die), and although Stoics denied the moral and intellectual inferiority of women, they still encouraged them to remain at home and raise families.

fore. Unlike Plato and Aristotle, who emphasized the individual and his innate capabilities, Stoicism held that people must be free from passion and calmly accept all occurrences as the unavoidable result of divine will. The Stoic school was founded by Zeno of Citium in Cyprus (335–263 B.C.E.). The Stoics believed in the existence of a natural law, the *jus naturale*, born of the *lex aeterna*, the cosmos' law of reason. Man's reason tied him to the cosmic order and put all under a universally valid moral law.

Stoics taught that all humans shared a spark of divinity and that the earth and cosmos belonged to one indissoluble process. As such, humans must live consistent with the laws of nature, under the guiding principle of reason.

A classic example of this natural law principle was that of the playwright Sophocles' character Antigone (in the play *Antigone*, 441 B.C.E.). She defied the new king Creon's command forbidding funeral rites for her brother Polynices because she was determined to obey the higher laws of the gods. This pitting of the state's decrees against the superior demands of universal morality was played out as law versus nature. This contest is reborn repeatedly throughout the Western world's long journey toward a modern concept of human rights.

While Greek philosophers lent weight and grace to the oratory of the Greek *polis*, they never guaranteed humane conduct by the state. They did greatly enlarge the sphere of politics; indeed, the word philosophy originally meant something like "devotion to uncommon knowledge" and did not enjoy widespread recognition until the time of Plato. The real genius of their contribution lay in their in-depth study of law, the state, and moral conduct, as well as their belief that both common people and their leaders must bear responsibility for ensuring justice and the common good under a universally valid moral law.

Eventually, from the 330s B.C.E. on, a new sort of culture sprang up in both Greece and the Hellenized eastern Mediterranean, wherein all those who spoke and behaved as Greeks could be part of the new Greek culture. This Hellenizing allowed the conquering Romans to comfortably adopt and transmit many of the Greek ideals that survive through Roman law today.

2. Roman Foundations

In terms of its impact on human rights, Rome owes a large debt to the Greeks. Not only did Greek Stoicism influence Roman law and ultimately the development of natural law, but it introduced a belief in universal rights for all. Rome added its own unique contributions in law and politics to the base of Greek philosophy. These contributions included professional justices, the use of precedent in judicial cases to determine subsequent decisions, extensive written codes of law, and standards for assessing the legitimacy of law and tradition. Rome also effectively broadened the concept of citizenship, introduced a belief in equal rights for women, and elevated freed slaves to high positions of authority.

Roman Law

Greek Stoicism influenced Roman law development and in turn is acknowledged for helping introduce the concept of natural law. In concert with the *jus gentium* (the law of nations), natural law inspired the notion of universal rights for all human beings, which extended beyond Roman citizenship rights. During much of Rome's history the law was viewed as supreme, surmounting even the emperor. Law was strengthened by another legacy of Stoicism, the enlightened tolerance and humanity portrayed by playwrights such as Seneca, whose works later influenced Europe.

Two figures who helped develop Rome's sophisticated law are etched today in the marble frieze high above the U.S. Supreme Court's mahogany bench: Octavian and Justinian. Octavian (63 B.C.E.–14 A.D.), Caesar Augustus, was the first emperor of Rome. He restored order to the republic, giving justices a new professional, authoritative role and supporting their decisions of previous cases in determining the outcomes of new disputes. This adherence to precedent, rather than arbitrary acts by rulers or justices, is one of the vital principles of the U.S. court system and a bulwark of efforts to institutionalize human rights in law. Then as now, precedent helped build legal integrity and inspired public confidence in the court and in its protections.

Justinian (A.D. c.483–565) codified Roman law and published *Corpus Juris Civilis* (Body of Civil Law). Because of its coherence, it became the basis for modern civil law. Justinian's works, in addition to his prodigious efforts to root out corruption and make the law more understandable and accessible, inspired the term justice. He also helped set standards for judging the legitimacy of laws and traditions, a vital precursor for effectively implementing human rights today.

The Individual Versus the State

From the outset, a tension emerged between the individual and the state that anticipated similar political competitions as the West journeyed toward a modern consensus on human rights. In the early Roman republic (400s B.C.E.) the tension between the individual and the state took the form of a struggle for political power between the patricians (i.e., wealthy aristocrats) and the plebeians (i.e., everyone else but slaves, including small landholders, peasants, and wealthy men attempting to inject themselves into government). Election to government posts was open to all citizens—freeborn adult males—but the system was weighted so that the rich held the most influence. Real power still lay with only a few families.

It took two hundred years before male citizens achieved full equality. The key victory occurred in the 4540s B.C.E. when plebeians forced the publication of the Twelve Tables, the ancient Roman laws. Henceforth, Roman civil law, its penalties, and its processes were known to all citizens. Gradually, plebeians gained magistracies and the first plebeian consul (the highest office in the republic) was elected in 366 B.C.E. Freedmen's sons were admitted to the Senate (the republic's most important deliberative body) in 312 B.C.E., and in 287 B.C.E. decisions of the *Concilium Plebis* were given the full force of law. Nevertheless, wealth was still essential in standing for office, and few plebeians ever achieved individual political power.

Citizenship and Civic Duty

The Romans were geniuses in co-opting citizens of conquered territories, and later even barbarians, into peaceful, tax-paying citizens. Roman citizenship was extremely valuable since it offered protection. Under the republic, citizens could not only vote, but they could appeal a criminal charge to the assembly. Later, citizens could appeal to the emperor. Citizens living within Rome's extensive borders also benefited from the *pax Romana*, the years of peace not achieved again by such a large percent of humanity for nearly two thousand years.

Unlike modern citizenship, which includes ample individual rights, Roman citizenship weighed responsibilities more heavily. Taxes and military service were the main duties. Octavian created the first inheritance tax in 6 B.C.E., to pay for the legions' discharge settlements. Emperor Caracalla (A.D. 188–217), also short of money, doubled the inheritance tax in A.D. 212 just before proclaiming citizenship for all free inhabitants of the empire. Although motivated by tax revenues, Caracalla's grant was remarkable in foreshadowing modern enfranchisement, a cornerstone of human rights today.

Although the Romans were successful in incorporating peoples from diverse races and ethnic backgrounds as citizens, many modern rights were not even foreshadowed during Roman times. The more arbitrary handling of citizens dates from the founding of the empire in 27 B.C.E., ironically called the "restoration of the republic."

Roman political history provides early evidence of the trade-off between upholding citizens' rights and preserving the state's stability. Subsistence farmers had their land confiscated in the first century B.C.E. when it was given to discharged soldiers, forcing about half the peasant families of Roman Italy—perhaps one and a half million people—from the land. Half a million men also served in Rome's civil wars, leaving many families bereft. Displaced poor flooded into the cities, where they lived in squalid tenements, unsuccessfully competing with slaves for limited jobs. Even in the city of Rome rents were exceedingly high, with the poorest living in miserable conditions. Recognizing that the rioting of starving poor people was as dangerous to the state as veterans without land, Octavian began distributing regular grain rations. Three quarters or more of people in Rome subsequently depended on free grain. Emperor Trajan (A.D. 52–117) introduced allowances for children in 100 A.D., the same year he devalued coins.

Slaves, Women, and Children

The Roman concept of natural law clearly legitimized slavery, antithetical to human rights today given our concern with freedom, equality, and liberty. Slavery was essential to the economy and a handy manner of dealing with some conquered peoples, as well as a deterrent to rebellion from others.

Slaves were valuable, worth between 2,000 and 8,000 sesterces (400 a year was needed for subsistence), but this did not guarantee humane treatment. Domestic slaves who saved sufficient funds, or those who enjoyed special favor from their masters, could gain their freedom and become citizens. This remarkable feature of Roman society differed from Greece, where freedom could be revoked. Some slaves ultimately rose even higher; during Emperor Claudius' rule (10 B.C.E.–A.D. 54) he allowed ex-slaves to become his ministers and advisers. Although urban house slaves were treated rather well, many farm slaves, working often in chains, suffered terribly; their lot when old or ill was uncertain. The forty thousand Spanish mine slaves faced the worst conditions. Rural slaves composed the masses in the major slave risings against intolerable working and living conditions. Spartacus' rising in 73 B.C.E. took eight Roman legions (about eighty thousand men) to subdue.

Our current belief in equal rights for women is also rooted in the Roman period, during which their status improved. Free women in Rome lived better than in classical Greece, where only highly educated and accomplished courtesans enjoyed the ability to own private property, travel unaccompanied, engage in commerce, or interact on a fairly equal basis with men. Roman women suffered restrictions however. The Roman father (*paterfamilias*) held impressive power, including the right to custody of children after a divorce (the first recorded case of divorce was 235 B.C.E.). By the first century B.C.E., however, the most common marriage was *sine manu*, or without authority, so the wife remained part of her own family and was not formally under her husband's authority. Women were thus able to achieve some independence after marriage, although the widespread practice of marriage immediately after puberty for women almost always put women under the sway of a much older and more accomplished man. By the late republic many women were highly educated.

The legal status of children was carefully defined, but elements of their care were often cruel. All children had equal rights of inheritance. Children six and under were not legally responsible for their actions; boys under fourteen and girls under twelve could not marry or be guilty of adultery. It was customary for the father to recognize his child; if he did not, it could be exposed. In poor families, unwanted children, especially sick babies or girls, were exposed, and the *paterfamilias* could sell his own children into slavery or kill them, though this was rarely done.

Rome's Legacy

The legacy of the Roman Empire was rooted in its administrative and legal accomplishments. The Romans learned to admirably administer a hundred million people with runners, a stylus, and papyrus—instead of telephones, computers, and e-mail. Their genius lay in how they treated people, not just their own citizens, but conquered peoples whom they embraced. Relatively color-blind, their law theoretically set impartial standards, adhered to precedent, was known to the people, and constrained even the emperor; however, the law did not always fulfill its promise.

With Christ's teachings, a new faith and a new way of life in the empire were born. Although Christianity was viewed for some time as but one of the many tolerated "cults," after two hundred years its potent force was viewed as a major threat. Subsequently, many of the virtues of the Christian culture began to infuse Roman politics, culture, and law.

3. The Judeo-Christian Tradition

"He who destroys one soul is considered as if he had destroyed a world, and he who saves one soul as if he had saved a world."

—Talmud (Sanhedrin 37)

"Blessed are those who hunger and thirst for righteousness, for they shall be satisfied . . . . Blessed are the peacemakers, for they shall be called the sons of God."

—Matt. 5:6-9

The contributions of the Judeo-Christian tradition to our modern conception of human rights are rooted in the fundamental principle of Judaism—and subsequently Christianity—that humankind was created in God's image, and therefore every person has a divine link to the Creator. A traditional Jewish aphorism illustrates this tie: "Whenever you come across a footprint of man, God stands before you." According to the Judeo-Christian tradition, every person—even a slave—has innate value, worthy of respect, simply by virtue of being human. Christianity also shares with Judaism and Islam a belief in one universal and personal God, Creator of the Universe, to which each human may appeal and a belief in God as the highest source of values for humankind, above the dictates of the state. Together these concepts fundamentally influenced the development of Western human rights theory.

Judaism

The belief that God is equally concerned with the slave as with the master underpins the concept of the brotherhood of mankind. For thousands of years Judaic theologians have advised that, since every person is fashioned in God's image, the best way to love God is to love thy neighbor (Lev. 19:18). With that love, however, comes responsibility: as Job says in the Old Testament, "If I have rejected the cause of my manservant or my maidservant when they brought a complaint against me, what then shall I do when God rises up? Did not He who made me in the womb make him?" (Job 31:13-15). Each person is deserving of respect and dignity because each person is, at least in a small way, godlike. For many people this reasoning alone provides a complete defense for human rights. Torture, executions, and other human rights abuses, for example, are an affront to humankind because they are an affront to God.

The Book of Isaiah lays out God's challenge to humanity. It reads, "Learn to do good; seek justice, correct oppression; defend the fatherless, plead for the widow" (Isa. 1:17). Judaism puts great emphasis on the importance of working toward a more just world. In the words of Jewish sage Hillel (c. 1st. century B.C.), "If I am for myself alone, then what am I? And if not now, when?"

Christianity

According to Christian belief, the teachings of Jesus Christ fulfill the prophecy and injunctions of the Old Testament. Emphasizing generosity and relief for the oppressed, He instructed, "Give to him who begs from you, and do not refuse him who would borrow from you" (Matt. 38:42). Christ's life story is one of willing sacrifice on behalf of a fallen world. His teachings on behalf of the weak, lame, sick, widowed, orphaned, poor, and the disenfranchised continue to serve as a model for many contemporary human rights activists.

The heart of Christ's message is love. The love of Christians for each other, called *agape* in Greek, is the essence of Christian action and was the original meaning of "charity" in English (from the Latin *caritas*). Love and charity are described by St. Paul in 1 Corinthians as the greatest of the "theological virtues."

Although directed primarily toward God, love and charity are also owed to our neighbors and ourselves as the objects of God's love. The loving nature of God was highlighted in the Old Testament, but only in the New Testament is it clear through doctrine that love constitutes the essential nature of God (e.g., 1 John 4:8). The Old Testament commandments that human beings should love God (e.g., Deut. 6:5) and their neighbors are linked by Christ (Mark 12:29-31). Indeed Christ demanded that love become a "new Commandment" (John 13:34). In New Testament times widows, for example, were recognized as deserving the charity of their fellows (Acts 6:1). They acquired, like virgins, prerogatives and a recognized position in the church (1 Tim. 5:3-16).

The Christian Legacy of Rome

Because it was the one integrated structure left intact after the Western empire's fall in 476, the Christian Church was able to preserve much of what had been Rome: Latin, the language of the church, was the precursor of all "romance" languages today (Italian, French, Spanish, Romanian, Portuguese). Christian monasteries gathered, restored, and copied Christian, as well as pagan, texts.[2] A large number of Latin texts survived in monasteries until

---

[2] Cassiodorus (490–585) created his own monastery at Vivarium in Italy. He brought his own collection of manuscripts and encouraged his monks to collect others. Many credit him with inspiring similar efforts elsewhere.

the ninth century, when Charlemagne's archivists gathered them and reproduced the copies that exist today. As a result Latin survived as a critical part of Western culture; indeed, most of the thirty-five thousand books published before the year 1,500 were in Latin, and it remained the language for scholarship for another four hundred years.

Of vital importance for human rights was the nature of the books that were saved. The interweaving of Platonism (see Section 1) and its focus on human rights with Christian thought go back to Clement of Alexandria (c. 150–215) and Origen (c. 185–254). Of greater impact on theology and rights theory was the thought of Saint Augustine of Hippo (354–430), who was radically influenced by Platonic doctrines. The authority accorded to his works by the Roman Catholic Church throughout the Middle Ages helped secure a permanent place for Platonic views in Latin Christianity. Strong Platonist influences continued into many English theological writings through the nineteenth century. Similarly, the church applied Roman law to civil contracts, marriages, and wills, thereby preserving some of the best of the ancient world's civil protections of rights.

Judeo-Christian Contributions to Human Rights Theory

Judeo-Christian philosophy offers other important antecedents to the development of human rights theory, such as the conviction that the authority of God is higher than any secular one. In the Old Testament, for example, Daniel was thrown into the lion's den because he defied a law prohibiting prayer: thus, Daniel's obligations as a citizen were trivial compared to his obligations as a Jew. Similarly, in early Christian times, those who witnessed to Christ's life and resurrection often faced hardships for their faith, even death. Those who remained steadfast in their faith against the state, especially during the persecution directed by the Roman Emperor Diocletian (284–305), were soon given honors by the Church as martyrs. (From the earliest times, martyrdom, or the "baptism of blood," was equivalent to normal baptism.) Martyrs were venerated as powerful intercessors for the faithful who lived later. This long-held belief in God's sovereignty over the state is so fundamental in both Jewish and Christian faiths that many religious martyrs throughout the centuries have given their lives in pursuit of human rights goals.

Clearly, the Judeo-Christian tradition fundamentally shaped our modern conception of human rights. Indeed, its philosophical contributions are manifold: the indivisible link between humans and their Creator, the all-embracing brotherhood of mankind, the responsibility of each individual to work toward a more just world, and the supremacy of spiritual authority over secular power. These ideas are so fundamental to our understanding of human rights that it is difficult to imagine what the human rights movement would be today without their inspiration.

Slavery

As in most premodern societies, slavery was an accepted part of ancient Jewish life, and a mitigated form was tolerated by the Mosaic Law (Exod. 21:1-11, Lev. 25: 44–55). However, Jewish tradition established an elaborate code of rules regarding the proper treatment of slaves. The Talmud says bluntly, "Whoever acquires a Hebrew slave acquires a master for himself." The rules included:

- Slaves must be given their freedom after seven years;
- Slaves could not be made to wash their masters' feet, put on their shoes, or carry them; and
- Masters may not eat fresh bread while their slaves eat stale bread, or sleep on a soft bed while their slaves sleep on straw.

Not surprisingly, the standards of treatment for non-Hebrew slaves were less generous, but there were still rules; for example, a master could not force a slave to be circumcised against his will. Like the modern Geneva Convention, which promises safety to prisoners of war, the Talmud affirms that even the lowliest have inalienable rights.

In New Testament times, slavery was an integral fabric of the social system whose abrupt removal would have plunged the Roman empire into chaos. Not surprisingly, there is no explicit standard of treatment for slaves described in the Gospels, but the equality of all children of the Heavenly Father, along with the Golden Rule and Christ's focus on the downtrodden, offered key principles governing Christian conduct. Saint Paul, who recognized neither freedom nor slavery in Christ (Gal. 3:28, 1 Cor. 12:13, Col. 3:11), did not condemn slavery but tried to give both slaves and masters a new Christian spirit of charity, which ultimately helped abolish the institution of slavery itself. Saint Paul's teachings, without the force of law, had great impact on Christian slaves and masters until at least the third century, for Christian masters and slaves shared sacraments as well as sufferings, and sometimes even martyrdom together.

Christian teaching eventually opposed slavery on many grounds: it violates human dignity by treating another human being as chattel; violates a human's rights to liberty of conscience, the stability of family, and the integrity of body and soul; and promotes cruelty in the mind of the owner.

4. English Traditions of Rights and Law

Following the fall of the Roman Empire, Judeo-Christian traditions gradually influenced many institutions throughout Europe—including the monarchy and ruling class in England. By the end of the feudal era, the English were the first to restrict the rights of the absolute monarch,[3] long before continental Europe seriously challenged the "divine right of kings." Before human rights could be enjoyed by the public, there had to be checks on absolute monarchs as well as assemblies of peoples legislating for the common good.

The Magna Carta

This effort began in the early thirteenth century with the Magna Carta, a strategy of English barons to protect their purses and traditional liberties from the rapacious King John. That this process ultimately benefited the common man (and woman) was a happy accident, for it was the intention of the barons to benefit only themselves.

By all accounts King John brought the Magna Carta or "Great Charter of Liberties" upon himself. After losing to the French King Philip II at Bouvines (1214), John tried to recoup his financial losses by demanding scutage (paid in lieu of military service) from the barons who had not fought against Philip. They refused to pay and insisted on a reconfirmation of Henry I's Coronation Oath (1100), which limited the king's financial demands. John refused, but the rebels' fortuitous capture of London strengthened their hand significantly, and John was forced to acquiesce on June 15, 1215.

The result was the Magna Carta, the first dent in an armor of monarchical absolutism that would prove resilient on the continent for five hundred years. King John authorized handwritten copies of the Magna Carta to be distributed for public reading in each of England's counties. He committed himself as well as his "heirs, for ever" to grant "to all freemen of our kingdom" the rights and liberties enumerated in the Magna Carta. He also agreed not to impose major taxes without permission of a "great council" representing the barons and to stop hiring mercenaries (who had to be paid!) if his barons refused to fight. Thus, King John placed himself and England's future sovereigns and magistrates within the rule of law.

Part of the Magna Carta's ultimate value to the cause of freedom was the use of the phrase "any freeman" (instead of

---

[3] "Absolutism" originated with French jurists in the late 1500s. It held that the religion of the monarch would become the religion of the land: *cuius regio, eius religio.*

"any baron," as it had originally read) in describing the beneficiaries of the charter. This minor change helped expand the Charter's protections, even though there were relatively few "freemen" in England in the 1200s, as the majority were serfs. This term ultimately encompassed all the English, although most were not actively involved in or much protected by politics for seven hundred more years. Only the last clause, which established a council of tenants-in-chief and high clergy to enforce the Charter, could have greatly restricted the king's authority. The council never exercised its power, because Pope Innocent III annulled the "shameful and demeaning agreement, forced upon the king by violence and fear." The civil war that followed ended only with John's death in October 1216, but the Magna Carta endured after political realities overcame the pope's injunction.

Its precedent is significant in another way also. More than seventy years later, King Edward I invited bishops, barons, and town officials to meet with him in an effort to help fund another war against the French. From that "parley" or "parliament" began the tradition of the monarch consulting his leading subjects on key issues, and subsequently the beginnings of a constitutional government that restricted royal authority.

The Petition of Right

As the first major step in delimiting the power of British monarchy, the Magna Carta led to many constitutional developments in the centuries that followed. Of particular importance to the history of human rights was the Petition of Right (1628). This second pivotal step, which reduced royal privilege, occurred because of major dissatisfaction over King Charles I's fiscal policies. In 1625 he demanded a forced loan from landowners without Parliament's consent. The next year he further alienated the aristocracy by imprisoning seventy-six gentlemen for refusing to pay. In response, Parliament refused to agree to these levies unless he implemented fiscal reforms. Charles responded by convening three Parliaments in four years; each was dissolved because it refused to grant him funds without reforms.

Parliament ultimately agreed to a tax, but only after Charles accepted the Petition of Right in 1628. It laid down four principles: no "loans" without the consent of Parliament; no "gentlemen" who refused such loans would be arrested, and no imprisonment was to occur without just cause; no soldiers were to be housed on the citizenry in order to save the crown money; and no martial law could be imposed in peacetime.

In the short term, instead of settling any issue, the petition merely angered Charles I sufficiently that he dismissed Parliament for eleven years and tried to raise money in unorthodox ways. The result was the English Civil War of the 1640s, which Parliament eventually won. (Charles was executed for treason in 1649.) Nevertheless, stiff precedent had been set, and Parliament insisted that subsequent monarchs adhere to these key restrictions on the monarch's power.

Puritanism provided the philosophical underpinnings of Parliament's conflict with the throne, and this philosophy would help to shape the development of civil, political, and human rights, particularly in the United States. Puritan belief insisted that the monarchy was under the rule of God, and that individuals were obliged to stand against a monarch who acted otherwise. This duty of individuals to oppose monarchical power was exported to new North American settlements; and a particularly Puritan style of self-rule, including the traditional town meetings of New England, developed there.

The English Bill of Rights

Ironically, with the restoration of the Stuart monarchy in 1660 the stage was set for more conflict, ushering in the last major governmental battle in this period. King James II, who reigned between 1685 and 1688, aroused the ire of Parliament and his public by attempting to reestablish the primacy of the Roman Catholic Church, despite Parliament's laws and the Protestant Church of England's (Anglican) opposition. However, this monarch was also chronically short of funds and dependent upon Parliament to vote them. Parliament's opposition to new taxes and fear that Catholicism might be reestablished were the impetus to the Glorious Revolution of 1688.

When riots forced James II to flee into exile, Parliament was free to invite William III and Mary II (daughter of James II), prince and princess of Orange, to be crowned. After their coronation, Parliament passed "an act declaring the rights and liberties of the subject and settling the succession of the crown" on December 16, 1689. This English Bill of Rights required that the succession would pass through Mary's line, provided that the heir professed Protestantism. Through this Bloodless Revolution, or The Glorious Revolution, the English formally ended the "divine right of kings." This political compromise ushered in a new era of toleration, in which William and Mary forswore oppression of King James II's Roman Catholic supporters.

Parliament achieved a decisive victory over the crown with the bill, by insisting on choosing a monarch as well as dictating his or her religion. It reiterated the principle that the monarch must not raise funds without parliamentary approval. It broke new ground by requiring that parliamentary elections be free and that Parliament's actions could not be questioned or impeached in any court other than Parliament, thereby requiring Parliament to police itself, which ultimately helped establish its legitimacy. Finally, Parliament reiterated its injunction against the monarch keeping a peacetime standing army without Parliament's consent.

The value of the English Bill of Rights lay with its clarification of existing law and its itemization of freedoms from monarchical infringement. Because the bill checked the absolutist tendencies of monarchs, it also restricted the overreach of both powerful nobles and senior officials of the crown, who often took their own initiatives in the name of the crown. Most importantly, it reminded Englishmen that they had the right to petition the king, that they could (if they were Protestant) bear arms for their defense, that they need not face excessive bail, fines, or cruel and unusual punishments, and that they enjoyed the right to a jury trial in capital cases, as well as the right to seek redress of grievances and amendment of laws.

By contrast, the bill's impact on religion was scarcely better than the king's. Protestants were allowed to worship and could establish teaching centers, although Anglicanism remained the established church and only its followers could hold office. By contrast, Roman Catholics faced discrimination. Not only could they not hold the throne, but like Dissenters,[4] they could not hold government positions. The 1689 Toleration Act, which promoted religious toleration, somewhat improved the situation.

In sum, the significance of this period in English history for the development of modern human rights was twofold: the Magna Carta initiated the first effort to check the absolute power of the monarch and encouraged subsequent monarchs to work with their barons, who ultimately evolved into a parliamentary body. This effort was finally successful some four hundred years later with the English Bill of Rights and the Glorious Revolution, when the absolute power of the monarch in England was broken.

5. Natural Rights and the Social Contract

Prominent seventeenth-century philosophers who helped define the ideological battleground between the English Parliament and its monarch through 1689 included John Locke (1632–1704) and Thomas Hobbes (1588–1679). On the continent, Jean-Jacques Rousseau (1712–78) dramatically influenced thought and action in the late Enlightenment[5] (see Section 6), and ultimately provided intellectual fodder for the French Revolution. Together, these three had the most profound impact on European notions of a person's natural rights and the social contract that he or she entered into with the state. Theorists believe that when the political debate shifted from taxation, property, and religious intolerance to seventeenth- and eighteenth-century liberal concepts of equality for all, the foundations of modern human rights were truly laid. These social contract philosophers challenged kings who failed to meet their natural law obligations to protect their subjects, and the shift from natural law as "duty" to natural law as "right" began.

---

[4] Dissenters were Protestants who dissented from the Church of England.
[5] The Enlightenment began in Paris during the eighteenth century but soon spread to much of Western Europe. It sparked an effort to apply principles of reason to studies of human nature.

The Benefits of Absolutism: Thomas Hobbes

The English Civil War helped make Thomas Hobbes "the thundering theorist of absolutism," even though his state was the least absolutist in Europe. Two years after Charles I's execution for treason, Hobbes described the natural condition of humanity as war, or "everyone against everyone." In *Leviathan* (1651) Hobbes argued that England could only be saved if it became a powerful state: "that great Leviathan . . . to which we owe . . . our peace and defense." Hobbes had supported Charles I, arguing that citizens should give up their rights to the absolute monarch in exchange for protection from "that state of nature," where war made life "solitary, poor, nasty, brutish, and short." Hobbes further argued that if the monarch failed to protect his citizens or actually imperiled them, the social contract was null and void. Hobbes' works were viewed as so revolutionary that he had to flee France's absolutist Roman Catholic state. Yet by grounding the monarch's authority on natural rights, Hobbes ushered in three hundred years of debate about the liberal basis for human rights—what we now call "first generation rights."[6]

Limiting the Monarchy: John Locke

Locke agreed that a social contract existed in which the ruled had to give up some rights in return for protection. Unlike Hobbes, however, he argued that individual rights, including property ownership, were best protected when Parliament limited the monarch's capacity to interfere with individual lives. Moreover he believed that people's liberty and innate rights stemmed from nature, not from the sovereign's grant.

Locke's legacy in buttressing the case for what later became human rights theory was substantial. Locke believed in religious tolerance and argued passionately for the right of Englishmen to fight tyranny as they had done against Charles I. Locke expected that natural laws would be discovered that would undergird future human law around which society could be ordered. He believed that humanity, thereby, could improve future social conditions. Perhaps most importantly for human rights development, Locke argued that everyone (except slaves) had the right to life, liberty, and property. Furthermore he viewed marriage as a social contract in which both parties were equal (although he also expected that women should defer to their husbands). Locke carried these beliefs into support for freedom of the press, educational reforms, the study of the family as an institution, and the separation of political

---

[6] Infused with liberal individualism, first-generation rights emphasize economic and social doctrines of laissez-faire. They can be described in terms of "freedom from . . ." rather than a "right to . . ."; for example, freedom of the press is considered a first-generation right.

powers, all ideas as important to England's constitutional development as to America's.

Property Protection and Rights for the Masses

In the 1600s "freedom" was most often linked with protecting property. Locke, friend of some of the landowners who forced James II into exile in 1688, argued for limiting kingly power so that, "The end of government ... should be the good of mankind." Hobbes agreed that the "chief end therefore of men uniting into Commonwealths, and putting themselves under Government is the preservation of their property."

The Glorious Revolution of 1688 was a vindication of the gentry's new power over the high nobility in Parliament. The king named loyal aristocrats to the House of Lord's hereditary seats, but generally untitled, wealthy landowners (gentry) were elected to the House of Commons. During the English Civil War most of the 1,200 titled nobles supported the king, while the gentry controlled Parliament. The gentry, although still a small percentage of the population, grew significantly in the 1500s through land purchases financed by families who rose through law, army service, or commercial enterprises. As their economic fortunes increased, so did demands for political power, especially in the wealthier south of England. Their focus continued to be on protecting their economic assets.

England's growing commercial interests abroad, partly financed by merchants recently elevated to the gentry, boosted the well-being of the common man and woman. Unlike on the continent, where much of the trade brought in luxuries for the absolutist monarchs and their courts, England's ships carried consumer goods that made life easier for many. Cotton textiles, carpets, tobacco, furs, chocolate, sugar, tea, and rum flooded in—greatly adjusting consumption habits, as well as lowering the price of "luxuries" so that the expanding middle classes could afford them.

After the Civil War and the Restoration,[7] even greater international trading wealth again expanded the size of the gentry. Not surprisingly, Parliament responded by aggressively supporting English commerce and manufacturing, at the cost of human rights. Not only did the slave trade (just beginning to be questioned by natural rights theorists) prove lucrative, but property became such a political preoccupation that Parliament passed, without debate, a law in 1723 that added fifty attacks on property that could entail the death penalty, although it was rarely used.

The Social Contract: Jean-Jacques Rousseau

In France, Rousseau's writings became a bridge between the early and mid Enlightenment, which was preoccupied

---

[7] Cromwell died in 1658 and his incompetent son Richard abdicated. While General Monk restored the monarchy that same year, the Stuarts, in the person of Charles II, did not return until 1660.

with reason, and the late Enlightenment, which focused on people's passionate nature, hailing instinct, spontaneity, and emotion. Enlightenment philosophers also linked human freedom to the economy, lauding the work of Scottish political economist Adam Smith (1723–90). (Smith argued that a free man's efforts to better his condition contributed to the good of the whole, and that a laissez-faire policy for government was vital, as it should offer only minimal interference with economic forces.) These works helped undermine the authority of the French monarch and contributed to the French Revolution (see Section 8).

Unlike Locke, Rousseau argued in *The Social Contract* that man surrendered his natural rights to the "general will" in order to find security and order. (Locke felt that Parliament could best protect individual rights by limiting the monarch.) He defined "general will" as that of a community of citizenry of equal political rights. These citizens could live peacefully, unmenaced by monarchs with imperial ambitions. Rousseau concluded that "men are born free yet everywhere they are in chains." Unlike Voltaire and others who hoped to reform monarchs through enlightenment, Rousseau argued that a citizen's sovereignty comes through his search for freedom, not as a gift from the ruler or God. Both Locke and Rousseau justified revolution if the contract was broken.

Rousseau was a deist, meaning he acknowledged the existence of a God based on reason, but rejected revealed religion. He believed that God was a "watchmaker" who had created earth and humans

according to nature's laws and left to human beings the ability to discover knowledge. Rousseau believed that primitive people embodied essential goodness, but that in order for humans to be happy, they would have to develop new political, social, and family institutions. Exiled by the Paris Parlement (not a legislative body, as was England's Parliament, but a court), because his works offended the church and the king, he soon after was forced to flee to England, abandoning his children in a Geneva orphanage.

Railing against the preoccupation with private property, Rousseau charged that civilization had corrupted man's goodness and disrupted man's harmonious primitive state by evolving levels of wealth. Only a republic, like his native city of Geneva, might offer its citizens freedom by virtue of its simplicity and size. At base, Rousseau was always dubious of elected government because poorly chosen representatives could strip away freedoms. He saw some hope in direct democracy by enlightened citizens, led by executives separate from but subordinate to the parliament.

The Impact for Human Rights

In the short term the impact of natural rights philosophy was minimal amidst the significant impact of the rest of the Enlightenment's philosophy and practices. Despite the potency of these arguments, only a very small minority acted upon these principles. The vast majority of all classes remained believers in old patterns of behavior and religion. It took the combined strength of the Enlightenment, the American revolutionary success, and shifting economies to bring these ideas and issues to mass awareness. Only then did natural law as "right" have a direct impact on politics.

6. The Enlightenment

"What is the Enlightenment?... Dare to know!"
—Immanuel Kant

Unlike the origins of natural rights philosophy, which altered few lives at the time, the Enlightenment's impact was far more significant immediately, due to its direct challenge to the era of Absolutism. The contrast between Enlightenment and Absolutist philosophies was so profound that it ultimately called into question virtually every aspect of European society. Although the Enlightenment began in Paris, its impact soon spread throughout Europe and to North America.

Linking Liberty, State Economics, and Politics

Enlightenment philosophers (called *philosophes*) emphasized a deep belief in freedom as well as a conviction that human beings should be ruled by their own laws, not by rulers made such by the accident of their birth. The *philosophes* tried to bring light and progress through human reason applied to studying man's nature. Breaking with tradition, the *philosophes* wanted to enlighten the literate masses. They were strong proponents of children's education as well as of intellectual development throughout life. Voltaire (1694–1778) and Montesquieu (1689–1755) are considered two of the four most influential *philosophes*, along with Diderot, editor of the *Encyclopedia* (see box), and Rousseau

(see Section 5). Montesquieu was born Charles-Louis de Secondat (1689–1755) and inherited the title of baron de Montesquieu as well as presidency of Bordeaux's noble parlement, its provincial sovereign law court. Voltaire was born Francois-Marie Arouet (1694–1778) and was the most widely read of the *philosophes* because of his sarcastic, witty style. Imprisoned in the Bastille for mocking one of the king's family, he took the name "de Voltaire." Voltaire and Montesquieu were both Anglophiles—contrasting England with France, they celebrated England's limitations on the king's power, her press freedom and commercial successes that benefited the common man, and her relative religious freedom.

The third or late stage of the Enlightenment, which linked ideas of freedom to state economies, had the most

Drawing of Voltaire by La Tour (CORBIS/Bettmann).

direct impact on evolving concepts of natural or human rights. Adam Smith's work in England best typified this contribution; his book *The Wealth of Nations* (1776) squarely supported workers and farmers, arguing for high worker wages, the free labor movement, free markets and competition, few tariffs, and an emphasis on the production of consumer goods that would benefit the majority. His laissez-faire approach called for a hands-off policy by government toward commerce. Other important Enlightenment beliefs that foreshadowed modern government and citizens' rights included popular sovereignty, the conviction that rulers had a direct responsibility for citizen welfare, and the separation of governmental powers. The *philosophes* opposed despotism, as well as religious bigotry, slavery, and torture. Nevertheless, while Voltaire, Montesquieu, and Diderot accepted

divorce, they still refused to accept female equality.

Foreshadowing a modern human rights debate, some *philosophes* (including Voltaire) argued that morality—especially notions of how to treat fellow humans—might vary across cultures. Similarly, foreshadowing another twentieth century disagreement over which type of pluralistic society best promotes individual rights, the *philosophes* disagreed on the impact of differences in history and circumstances. For example, Voltaire believed Montesquieu was wrong in assuming that England's political institutions could successfully take hold in France.

Voltaire and Montesquieu also disagreed over whether French parlements could balance the power of the absolute monarch. Montesquieu's patent of nobility surely helped persuade him that they might, but Voltaire saw the parlements as protecting little more than their pocketbooks. Voltaire was convinced that only a British-style House of Commons with elected representatives and enlightened monarchs could protect the public from the aristocrats' self-interest. Montesquieu's two years in England also made him a devotee of Parliament, quite different from the French law courts or parlement. He lauded its "intermediate power," which prevented England from slipping into absolutism or republicanism. In his estimation, republicanism, the concept of a government without a monarch, was chaos. Montesquieu also believed in the enlightened monarch (combining the order of the monarchy with greater protection for the individual), as long as established constitutional safeguards existed, especially the separation of powers into legislative, administrative, and judicial functions. Like Voltaire, Montesquieu argued that sovereignty of the monarch stemmed from the people, not from God.

Montesquieu's writings also foreshadowed many ideas about human rights and government existing today. In Montesquieu's satire *Persian Letters*, he portrayed nature as encompassing a universal standard of justice applicable to all humans. He also rigorously examined the morality of slavery, arguing that it was against natural law because all are born free and independent as "the liberty of each citizen is part of public liberty."

Differing Enlightenment Views on Religion

Although many *philosophes* did not consider science and religion incompatible, they did question rigid church "truths," thereby challenging doctrinal authority. Subsequently, they questioned state churches and called for a secularization of politics. Voltaire was most bitter and vehement in his attacks on the Roman Catholic Church, which he believed blocked personal and intellectual freedom in France. As a deist Voltaire believed that God's creation operated according to scientific laws. (His was a religion developed through his reason; he disowned the established church.) He argued, "Almost everything that goes beyond the adoration of a supreme being and of submitting one's heart to his eternal order is superstition . . . the fewer superstitions, the less fanaticism; and the less fanaticism, the fewer calamities." Although he attacked the church's bureaucracy as unnecessary and restrictive to personal liberties, he also believed that religion was essential because it offered hope, thus making life bearable. It regulated human behavior where even the absolute monarch did not go: "If God did not exist, one would have to invent him. I want my attorney, my tailor, my servants, even my wife to believe in God, and I think that I shall then be robbed and cuckolded less often." Unlike Diderot (see box), who believed that humanity's innate goodness made the church superfluous, Voltaire saw religion as a public service because it promoted proper behavior through morality. As such, free, rational, and personal expressions of religion contributed to human progress.

An Enduring Legacy

The Enlightenment's contribution was reinforced by cultural changes, such as the expansion of educated inquiry beyond the upper classes, the decline of an absolutist religion, and a broader, international culture. These cultural shifts also fueled a growing consensus for the legitimacy of natural rights.

Although the *philosophes* themselves were not revolutionary, their legacy certainly was. Not only did Diderot's *Encyclopedia* bring the sum total of knowledge in the sciences, arts, and trades to the middle classes (see box), but religious bigotry, torture, and slavery were condemned, while constitutionalism, popular sovereignty, and individual liberty were lauded. The stage was now set for these ideas to leap from philosophy to politics—in the American and French Revolutions.

The *Encyclopedia*

Denis Diderot (1713–1784) is best known for his mammoth *Encyclopedia*, the *philosophes'* greatest achievement. At the project's heart was the belief that all knowledge was rational and followed the laws of nature. As such, all could be evaluated against these laws, including politics and society. Thus humanity became the centerpiece of the *philosophes'* inquiry, and they believed that by learning more about man in the world they would improve it. The *Encyclopedia* took over twenty years to complete, from 1751 on, and included some sixty thousand articles with 2,885 drawings in twenty-eight volumes. This was the first attempt to collect and expiate knowledge collected from all sources.

The *Encyclopedia* revolutionized knowledge in the West and fundamentally altered perceptions, including attitudes toward individual rights. Although the Spanish Inquisition inhibited sales through fear, as the police did in Portugal, copies entered middle-class homes (such as those of officials and lawyers) all over Europe and even North America. With its enthusiastic articles about popular sovereignty, representative government, and republics, the *Encyclopedia* implicitly challenged the absolute monarch. French authorities tolerated the earlier volumes but banned the seventh after there was an attempt on the life of Louis XV. Despite obfuscation concerning ecclesiastical satire, the Pope attacked the *Encyclopedia* in 1759.

After Russia's Empress Catherine the Great purchased the *Encyclopedia*, she sought out the works of Montesquieu and Voltaire, and even invited Diderot to Russia. Following their lead, she established a school for the daughters of the aristocracy, authorized the first private printing presses, and encouraged book publishing. Likewise, Joseph II of Austria set up a centralized system of education through the university level, doubled the number of lower schools in Bohemia, and authorized texts in six languages in the West; in so doing, he fundamentally altered perceptions, including attitudes toward individual rights.

7. The American Revolution, the U.S. Constitution, and the Bill of Rights

"We hold these truths to be self-evident, that all men are created equal, that they are endowed by their Creator with unalienable Rights, that among these are Life, Liberty, and the Pursuit of Happiness."

—U.S. Declaration of Independence

English constitutional development (see Section 4), natural rights theory (see Section 5), and the Enlightenment (see Sections 5 and 6) were the intellectual antecedents for the United States' war of independence and its subsequent constitutional development. They ushered in a new era, with the role of man and state radically different from the past. By joining into civil society, people could now protect their basic rights: the right to life and the right to liberty. These conceptualizations culminated in the U.S. Bill of Rights and the Declaration of the Rights of Man and of the Citizen (see Section 8). In concert with America's pioneer egalitarianism, these ideas helped forge a solid and rigorous Declaration and Constitution that have endured for over two hundred years, handbooks for individual liberty and other essential rights that have been emulated around the world ever since.

English Intellectual Antecedents

Through the Petition of Right of 1628 and the Habeas Corpus Act of 1679, the U.S. Constitution benefited from the legacy of the Magna Carta: "No freeman shall be arrested, or detained in prison or deprived of his freehold . . . except by the lawful judgment of his peers or by the law of his land." Similarly, Habeas Corpus[8] is still a vital human rights protection recognized in the U.S. Constitution, as well as in the Anglo-American legal tradition, and has been adopted by many others outside it.

The English Bill of Rights of 1689 and John Locke's *Second Treatise* (in *Two Treatises of Government*, 1690) are regarded by today's human rights theorists as key documents highlighting a liberal understanding of human rights. Locke's argument that individual natural rights could best be protected from a rapacious sovereign through a separation of powers (legislative, executive, and judicial) was included in the U.S. Constitution of 1776 and in France's Declaration of the Rights

---

[8] In law, Habeas Corpus is one of a variety of writs that may be issued to bring a party before a judge or court, having as its function the release of that party from unlawful restraint.

of Man of 1789. Similarly, the English Bill of Rights' focus on property rights is also enshrined there.

America's Liberal Environment

In many ways the geography and environment of the colonies made Americans liberals, just as the doctrines discussed above justified that philosophy. Social mobility existed to an unprecedented degree. The thirteen original colonies together were several times the size of England, with virgin land either free or so inexpensive that humble families lived far better than wealthier cousins in England. If local neighbors or magistrates proved oppressive, there was always room to move on. With no aristocracy to artificially restrict society or the market, uniquely egalitarian farm communities sprang up everywhere. (Only in older seaports and historic settlements did an oligarchy of merchants and landowners develop along English lines.) With an often severe shortage of labor, common builders, artisans, and even unskilled laborers enjoyed substantial wages. Some individuals who indentured themselves for five to seven years or more to pay for their passage and training went on to become millionaire planters, owning hundreds of acres of prime land and many slaves. Opportunity existed everywhere for those who worked hard; most married young and had large families. In that free and easy climate, it was hard to imagine that the individual was not king or that the petty taxes and restric-

tions of the British colonial government had much impact. With England so far away, it soon became reasonable for many to consider it right to resist unjust laws in the name of liberty.

The Immediate Cause of Rebellion

America's open rebellion was an economic protest overlying an ideological one. The immediate cause of dissatisfaction was similar to what had led to English reforms: unfair taxation. In an attempt to increase crown revenues and force the colonies to pay for more of their own defense, Parliament passed a Declaratory Act in 1766 allowing England to tax the colonies as it wished, and in 1767 Parliament imposed duties on imports of English tea, paper, and other products. American protests and calls for liberty encouraged English reformers in Parliament but did not change British policy. The Tea Act of 1773, which allowed the East India Company to ship surplus tea to America at reduced prices, enabled Britain to collect its tariff in America. Although pleased by lower tea prices, the colonists considered this tariff unacceptable and resented its impact on the lucrative smuggling trade. On December 16, 1773, Americans dumped the offending tea into Boston harbor. Parliament responded by blockading Boston's port until Massachusetts repaid the merchants and government for the lost tea. In September 1774 representatives met in the First Continental Congress to discuss making the break from England. Open fighting began in April 1775.

The power of the pen was at least as potent as that of the sword. Thomas Paine's (1737–1809) *Common Sense* (1776) attacked the king aggressively; it reflected Enlightenment thought, especially Rousseau's "social contract" prescriptions. The impact of Paine's document, which circulated in 100,000 copies, was profound, and helped persuade the delegates to the Second Continental Congress to adopt Thomas Jefferson's Declaration of Independence on July 4, 1776. Shaped in part by the writings of Locke, the Declaration offered a new social contract based upon basic natural rights doctrines. Jefferson called his country a "free people claiming their rights as derived from the laws of nature and not as the gift of their Chief Magistrate." Jefferson's inspirational document, influenced by the works of Montesquieu as well, promoted early concepts of rights around the world.

Religious toleration was also a vital aspect of the Declaration and sprang from America's religious antecedents: entire colonies set up with that concern at their base, such as Maryland's Roman Catholics and Massachusetts' Puritans. Even if this had not been the case, the very number of different religious sects made an established religion with strict doctrinal conformity almost impossible in the United States.

By October 19, 1781, Lord Cornwallis, commander of the British forces, was forced to surrender. Despite obvious strength stemming from a population of some six and a half million people and a robust army of 190,000 in the colonies, England had let its vaunted fleet degrade and its armed forces were poorly led; French support for the colonists tipped the balance. Nevertheless, George III's government took two more years to recognize the United States.

America's Revolutionary Legacy

The American Declaration of Independence was the first civic document that met a modern definition of human rights. It asserted universal rights that applied to the general population, included legal as well as moral obligations, and established standards for judging the legitimacy of the state's actions. It was truly modern in arguing that Americans possessed "inalienable rights" and that government authority derived from the consent of those it governed. The Declaration also asserted that the people could limit state power if their human rights were abridged: if governments violated the "unalienable rights" to "life, liberty, and the pursuit of happiness," then the people could rebel. The U.S. Constitution, drafted by the Constitutional Convention of 1787 and signed on September 17, produced a new government of the United States upon ratification in 1789. The Preamble to the Constitution clearly suggests that the ultimate authority of government rests with the people alone. The actual grant of power by the people to the Congress, the president, and the courts is set forth in the seven articles that follow. It not only divided power between three federal branches but it also distributed government between national and local authorities. Through broad congressional powers, supported by the Supreme Court, a limited number of amendments, and precedents set through custom, the U.S. Constitution and its Bill of Rights (the first ten amendments in 1791) remain a living legacy.

Subsequent amendments were ultimately required to more broadly ensure that all Americans enjoyed full civil or human rights. These included the Thirteenth Amendment, which abolished slavery (1865); the Fourteenth Amendment, which defined the rights of citizens (1868, although untaxed "Indians" were still not counted for the apportionment of representatives, and voting was restricted to males over the age of 21); the Fifteenth Amendment, which allowed black men to vote (1870); the Nineteenth Amendment, which allowed woman suffrage (1920); the Twenty-Third Amendment, which allowed the presidential vote for the residents of the District of Columbia (1961); and the Twenty-Fourth Amendment, which barred a poll tax in federal elections (1964).

America's successful revolution was unique in that it virtually swept away ineffective institutions and replaced them with a new form of government based on reason. No Europeans and few Latins could ignore this profound experiment. Indeed, within very short order America's example fueled the French Revolution.

8. The French Revolution and the Rights of Man

"Liberté, Egalité, Fraternité!" ("Liberty, Equality, Brotherhood!")
—watchwords of the French Revolution

The French Declaration of the Rights of Man and of the Citizen in 1789 was the Enlightenment effort's second major achievement in politically promoting natural rights. Buoyed by America's successful independence struggle, the French Declaration boldly stated that "men are born and remain free and equal in rights," while arguing that the "aim of every political association is the preservation of the natural and imprescriptible rights of man." It described those rights as "Liberty, Property, Safety, and Resistance to Oppression."

Foreshadowing the U.S. Bill of Rights, the French Declaration forbade only actions that could be injurious to society: "Whatever is not forbidden by law may not be prevented, and no one may be constrained to do what it does not prescribe." It also offered human rights guarantees: protection from arbitrary accusation, arrest, detention, and punishment; the presumption that every person is innocent until declared guilty; freedom of thought, speech, and religion; assurances that taxation would be equitable, based on means to pay, and that the citizenry could "supervise its use, and determine its quota, assessment, payment and duration;" and finally, since property was "a sacred and inviolable right," no one was to be deprived of it unless by legally established necessity and means.

American and English Influences

The American Revolution was the direct antecedent to the French Revolution. Intimate ties linked the two movements, dating back to geopolitical commitments made by France. The French Declaration, written by George Washington's close friend and comrade-in-arms, the Marquis de Lafayette (1757-1834), derived from the finest writings of the century. It was born of John Locke's natural rights concepts, ideas of the leading French *philosophes*, and Rousseau's general will and citizen sovereignty philosophy. It also celebrated property rights as enshrined in English Parliamentary law and the works of the physiocrats.[9] Individual, liberal protections against lawless or arbitrary monarchical, judicial, or police acts were borrowed from Voltaire, and the belief in universal natural rights was at least in part a concept dear to the Jacobins.[10] The Declaration reinforced and extended the freedoms enshrined in the American Declaration and began a new age in continental Europe.

Causes of Rebellion

The genesis of the French Revolution rested with repressive, doctrinaire monarchical policies that betrayed natural rights in the French social contract, even at the price of economic dislocation. Louis XIV's effort to uproot religious heresy, for example, displaced a large community of Huguenot (French Protestants) manufacturers, artisans, and merchants who were a vital force for economic innovation. Fleeing to Prussia, England, and the English colonies, they significantly robbed French industry. (By contrast, accommodations with religious nonconformists in England had led to vital economic innovation in England, as well as many new wealthy who eventually entered Parliament and helped reform it.)

Many elements of instability existed in pre-revolutionary France besides religious discord. The rigid tax system, Louis XVI's indecision at key moments, and rising popular discontent were all factors. The most immediate cause was clearly a gigantic public debt and a bankrupt treasury, born of seventeenth and eighteenth century wars, intervention in the U.S. revolution, and sheer waste. Even the French monarch's refusal to let his clerics and nobility give him advice finally tipped the balance for the nobles, such that they became leaders of the rebellion against him. Their frustration was joined to that of the

---

[9] Physiocrats were philosophers who emphasized natural philosophy or the study of the natural or material world.

[10] Jacobins were radical republicans (leftists) during the French Revolution. Their cause was founded in 1789.

business and professional classes, who believed that they could better themselves in a "just" society.

The French Estates-General[11] metamorphosed itself into the National Assembly in 1789, proclaimed the Rights of Man, and began to write a new constitution. This process initiated a democratic revolution in the heart of absolutist Europe. It took twenty years, during which all of Europe was affected. For the next one hundred years, reverberations of the French Revolution continued to swell. Indeed, until World War I preoccupied the continent, all of Europe attempted reform through democratic principles. In essence, this occurred because rulers in the late eighteenth and early nineteenth century failed to respect principles of freedom, principles that had been central to natural law philosophy from the beginning. Promoting natural or human rights became the cause of Europe's revolutionaries precisely because their leaders denied those rights.

With the breakdown of the National Assembly's constitution and the beginning of hostilities between revolutionary France and the more conservatively led regimes in Prussia and Austria, France spiraled toward crisis. Although the military's success by 1794 saved the new French republic from foreign threats, it also offered Napoleon Bonaparte an entrée. He took power in 1799 and ruled France as absolutely as his monarchical predecessors until the European powers defeated him in 1814–15.

The Revolutionary Legacy

Unlike the successful American experiment, the French Revolution led to a military dictatorship as well as a monarchical restoration, but true progress still occurred. The majority of the population, the French farmers, certainly benefited from the death of noble property privileges and a rather substantial distribution of noble and church-held lands. This stabilized French society and made the revolutionary legacy irreversible, despite the restoration. Guilds were repressed in the towns, opening up trade more evenly to those who had talent, not just birth ties. As other old monopolies and legal corporations were removed, opportunities sprang up for the motivated and savvy.

Only the Roman Catholic Church offered successful resistance to the tide of republicanism. Although the church lost its lands in 1790 and its clergy became state salarymen, the church remained aloof from the centralized bureaucracy. The effort to democratize the church never succeeded, for its leadership clearly stemmed from apostolic succession[12] and not from free elections by the citizenry. As such, when the Civil Constitution of the Clergy was passed in 1790, it fomented a

---

[11] This weak legislative body in France, beholden to the crown, was called briefly in 1789, for the first time since 1614.

[12] Roman Catholics believe that the power and authority of a bishop derives from the apostolic succession of men anointed by God in a direct line from Saint Paul.

break in French society that has yet to heal. Napoleon's Concordat of 1801 may have made peace with the Pope but it failed to resolve the controversy in France.

Ironically, wiping away monarchical and aristocratic privilege did not fully free French citizens. A centralized bureaucracy added insult by making military service obligatory. First conceived as an emergency measure when the revolution tottered in 1793, it nearly killed the economy and culture through disastrous levees by Napoleon. Meanwhile, elected legislators were so rarely able to speak their minds that their contribution for at least twenty years after the revolution was nil. Likewise, although women played a prominent role in the protests in the cities, they were not specifically included in the "Rights of Man."

Nevertheless, the revolutionary legacy and its impact on human rights endured. Subsequent rulers no longer could base their justification on God or on purely their own authority. France's rulers needed to rouse loyalties, inspire support, and entice obedience and sacrifice from a majority of the citizenry if they were to successfully govern. Such was the legacy of the revolution and the Rights of Man—a public that knew it was free and a public willing to fight for its rights. The example was surely not lost on the rest of Europe, even after the disastrous struggles necessary to control Napoleon's imperialist aims.

This lesson was a vital one, but at base the struggle over the American and French revolutions was intrastate, against arbitrary authority, not yet a broad acceptance of the rights of each citizen, let alone each human being worldwide. What occurred in the United States and France certainly had a moral and political impact on the rest of Europe, but specialists in eighteenth-century international law noted that individual states still had to interpret their governmental obligations toward their citizens or resident aliens. In fact, it wasn't until late in the nineteenth century that a few international lawyers argued that human rights should be a legitimate interstate subject of diplomacy, and not until the twentieth century did human rights actually became so.

9. The Natural Law Critique

"Natural Rights is . . . Nonsense Upon Stilts!"
—Jeremy Bentham

Despite its tremendous impact in inciting the American and French revolutions, the concept of natural rights—or human rights as we know them—was not without its critics. Initially, irreligious or deist[13] liberals eschewed natural rights because they associated it with

---

[13] "Deist" was originally opposed to "atheist" (one who denies or disbelieves the existence of God) and interchangeable with "theist," even at the end of the seventeenth century.

religious orthodoxy imposed with the heavy hand of absolutism. Other liberals espoused natural rights but correctly saw that these "inalienable" rights could conflict with each other. Ironically, these early criticisms of natural rights theory, and later of liberalism and utilitarianism, led to reforms that benefited the natural rights of many. When it became clear that the poor were suffering mightily due to industrialization and few controls over laissez-faire capitalism, government-led social reforms in defense of human rights began.

Rethinking Natural Rights Theory

In England, significant attacks were made on natural rights theory. John Locke's *Essay Concerning Human Understanding* (1690) questioned the possibility of ever reaching universally valid knowledge. Specifically, his criticism of innate ideas led him to a belief in linking all knowledge to individual experience, especially experience gained through personal sensation and reflection. David Hume (1711–76) reinforced Locke's epistemological questions[14] and found new difficulties in reaching certainty in key questions. In general, Locke's efforts promoted a major rethinking of the law of nature by emphasizing individualism. His restatement of natural law emphasized individual rights as opposed to individual responsibilities toward society. Locke argued that before government existed, human beings were "free, independent, and equal in the enjoyment of inalienable rights, chief among them being life, liberty, and property."

Other leading theorists found additional aspects of natural rights problematic. Edmund Burke (1729–97) and David Hume, conservative on philosophical and political issues, agreed with the liberal English legal critic Jeremy Bentham (1748–1832) in questioning natural rights. Burke and Hume were motivated by a distrust of the public, fearing that if too many believed in natural rights they might rebel. Bentham, on the other hand, argued that the "law of nature" could produce only imaginary rights. Rights, he wrote, were the "child of law; from real law come real rights." Further, he stated that "natural rights is simple nonsense; natural and imprescriptible rights, rhetorical nonsense, nonsense upon stilts." Hume agreed with Bentham by stating that natural law and natural rights were unreal metaphysical phenomena.

The Outcome of Natural Law: Edmund Burke

The Irish-born political theorist Edmund Burke's belief in natural law was compromised by fear of "the swinish multitude." By the 1760s the public had agitated for electoral reform, some of the men even calling for universal male suffrage. (Interestingly, none of the major contemporary male philosophers addressed women's rights except John Stuart Mill in *The Subjection of Women* [1869].) A worried

---

[14] Epistemology is the division of philosophy that investigates the nature and origin of knowledge.

Burke focused on keeping England's society and government stable. He preferred the "mixed Constitution" (in which the House of Lords, the House of Commons, and the monarchy mutually checked each other) as "an isthmus between arbitrary power and anarchy." Burke was a zealous supporter of political parties, seeing them as the basis of representative government and political order. Burke viewed the loyal Parliamentary opposition as vital because it afforded legitimacy to the state, even when policy generated significant disagreements.

Burke, who believed in natural law but who denied that natural rights could be derived from it, criticized the Marquis de Lafayette for creating a "monstrous fiction" of human equality in his Declaration of the Rights of Man and of the Citizen. In *Reflections on the Revolution in France*, Burke argued that the Enlightenment's pure theory of rationalism could undermine any nation's evolution by eroding the social structure. He worried that if monarchical order and noble privilege were undercut, in France they would lose their capacity, with the church, to hold the society stable.

Laissez-Faire: Adam Smith and Jeremy Bentham

Liberals also believed that limits must be placed on state authority, particularly in economics, in order to preserve individual liberties. Many liberals supported Adam Smith's (1723–1790) theories, particularly laissez-faire, a doctrine of noninterference by government. Smith argued that a free economy would ensure private interests and that these would serve the public by creating more wealth. He concluded that if the market were allowed to follow its natural course, a freer, more egalitarian society would emerge, with new classes raised up.

Along with laissez-faire theories, the philosophy of utilitarianism, which argued that the greatest happiness of the greatest number should be the guiding principle of conduct, suggested a standard for judging the impact of the state on individual welfare. Jeremy Bentham, utilitarianism's most proud exponent, argued in 1776 that laws should be evaluated for whether or not they insured "the greatest good for the greatest number of people." Later his views were even more pronounced: "Every law is an evil, for every law is an infraction on liberty." His views were more extreme than others such as Lafayette, who argued that "the enjoyment of the natural rights of every man has for its limits only those that assure other members of society the enjoyment of those same rights; such limits may be determined only by law." Utilitarianism helped the individual and the state respond to these criticisms by evaluating the worth of government. For the first time, at least implicitly, an objective standard could be used to assess whether society's natural rights were being met.

This debate in England was important because of the very real fear of societal breakdown—especially if a military leader seized power from elected officials. Into this struggle moved the press. With reformers demanding much greater press freedoms, specifically libel laws that would allow criticism of the government, politics began to generate considerable public interest. Philosophical societies sprang up to educate people about their rights; several hundred printing presses published a plethora of political tracts; and by 1790 fourteen daily London newspapers openly targeted government figures. This was the first time that ordinary people, not in Parliament, had an impact on politics.

Debates about natural rights clearly did not advance individual human rights by themselves. Societal revolution through technological advances had a more direct and lasting impact. Technological improvements, increased international trade, improved agricultural practices, better roads and canals, the growth of a middle class, and urbanization all improved standards of living. With greater and more diversified wealth, more people had the strength and leisure to effectively assert their demands over government, thereby promoting individual rights.

Natural Law Critiques and Social Reforms

It became clear that pure liberalism and utilitarianism could have unfortunate consequences for the natural rights of the masses. Specifically, the poor were becoming too poor because of the Industrial Revolution's tendency to drive skilled workers' wages downward. This encouraged Bentham's supporters to advocate government-led social reforms, particularly education for poor children. By the 1850s most British middle-class citizens supported a government role in alleviating poverty. Edwin Chadwick (1800–90), a friend of Bentham's, produced the *Report*

on the Sanitary Condition of the Laboring Population of Great Britain (1842). This brilliant research analysis significantly influenced policy, including a persuasive plea for a government response after cholera attacked poor London neighborhoods. In large part due to Chadwick's work, Parliament passed laws encouraging the inspection of rooming houses. Soon after, Parliamentary commissions began asking experts to assess living and working conditions for Britain's masses, including health, water quality, and mining.

John Stuart Mill was a vehement defender of both liberty and of natural rights founded on utility, notions that have helped set standards for judging a state's ability to protect human rights. Later Mill recognized the discontinuity between the liberal aspiration for self-development and the effects of laissez-faire economics on the human condition. He became a forceful advocate of government social reform policy. He was always a great believer in the free individual bettering himself, but in later life he supported women's rights as well as employment unions pressing for better labor conditions. Gradually, as with Mill, the liberal movement shifted from laissez-faire to concern for social and economic justice.

Thus, probably for the first time in England, government social policy, philosophy, and the middle classes combined to promote charitable protections for the poor. However, before that charity could turn into a "right" for better working and living conditions, capitalist economic power had to be balanced by government regulations protecting workers and allowing their fair representation in government.

10. Universal Suffrage and Early Feminism

"It seems that life is not easy for any of us. But what of that? We must believe that we are gifted . . . and that [our goals], at whatever cost, must be obtained."

—French scientist Marie Curie, winner of two Nobel Prizes, who was not admitted to the French Academy of Science because she was a woman.

Universal suffrage was grounded in a belief in the right of all humans to help govern themselves. Male philosophers, as we have seen, rarely developed a theory of civic rights that included women. As such, it wasn't until the late 1700s that the societal and political climate had changed enough for women philosophers to publicly address the issue. Early impact was made by Olympe de Gouges (1748–93), a French playwright who promoted women's rights during the French Revolution. Her opus, *The Declaration of the Rights of Woman* (1790), criticized the French Declaration of the Rights of Man and of the Citizen for failing to promote women's needs and prerogatives and argued that their rights were equal to men. At the same time, Mary Wollstonecraft (1759–97) argued in *A Vindication of the Rights of Women* (1792) for women's equality in social issues as well as educational and political. Although these early writers were intellectually influential, it wasn't until the tide of socialism was felt broadly that their ideas were carried forward into the mainstream.

The Beginnings of Universal Suffrage

During the early 1800s, the growing middle class found a philosophy that matched its enthusiasm for human progress and growing economic clout: liberalism. Liberalism reflected the Enlightenment faith in science as a means for human progress. These liberals gradually shifted their focus from the earlier preoccupation with the abstract rights of man to the prerogatives of citizens, born of constitutional guarantees, enshrined in law, and protected by the state.

These middle-class liberals, male only at first, expected their representatives to protect their property rights from kings and aristocrats. However, they also wanted broader electoral rights to match their newly acquired wealth and property status. The turning point in Britain came in 1831–32, when massive demonstrations led by skilled workers forced enactment of the first Reform Act of 1832, almost doubling the male electorate. (About 20 percent of adult males could vote, which was a higher percentage of voting males than in France, Spain, the Netherlands, or Belgium.) The second Reform Act of 1867 enfranchised many others but still excluded domestic servants, adult males without a fixed residence, sons living with parents, and agricultural workers. The third

Reform Act of 1884 enrolled two million more men, mostly agricultural workers, but the categories above were still without a vote as were women. Nevertheless, these acts dramatically increased political party participation and led to expanded franchise on an incremental basis.[15]

Female French socialists attempted to work the same magic that liberals had with male suffrage in England. In the same year as the Great Reform Bill, a group of Saint-Simonian prosuffrage, proworker women established a newspaper, *La Tribune des Femmes*. They argued that "the emancipation of women will come with the emancipation of the worker." The paper's supporters also established an institute to educate poor women and promote job skills.

Other socialist women established another newspaper with a republican editorial slant in 1836–1838, which lobbied for female civil and political rights. Similarly, Flora Tristan (1801–1844) was one of the first Europeans to link socialist reformism with feminism in the late 1830s. Denied her inheritance from her Peruvian father by the French government, which declared her illegitimate because it would not recognize her parents' Spanish marriage, Tristan became a lifelong feminist and suffrage advocate. She had significant impact arguing for female emancipation, equal pay for equal work, and union retreats, where industrial accident victims could recuperate and where workers trained for more skilled jobs.

Women's Suffrage in the Nineteenth Century

In the nineteenth century women all across Europe were subordinate socially, economically, and legally. They could not vote (unlike in the United States, where some states gave women the franchise before 1900), they could not attend universities, and they had little control over their own inheritances, their own salaries, or the family's finances. Very few women were educated in the higher-paying professions such as law or medicine, and if they were, they faced extreme discrimination in employment. Conditions for less-educated women were far more difficult. In general, women earned half of what men did for the same jobs, and real wages actually fell from about 1800 to 1850 as mechanization increased and guild restrictions ended. Women were often the first to be unemployed as trades were mechanized, with some job categories—such as hand-loom weavers—losing as much as three-quarters of their real income between 1805 and 1833. Wages, in general, were highly volatile, with "starving seasons and starving years" facing many.[16]

These appalling conditions occurred in an era when government was still ruled

---

[15] See the discussions of the Reform Acts in John Merriman, *A History of Modern Europe: From the Renaissance to the Present* (New York: W. W. Norton and Co., 1996).

[16] See Merriman's discussion of suffrage, especially in England and France.

Suffrage protest outside the British Parliament, circa 1910 (Library of Congress).

by laissez-faire economics. Government, thus, provided few if any safeguards for workers, and the lack became an acute impetus for political reforms. Bereft of protection from above, middle-class women (and a few men) began to agitate on behalf of the poor as well as themselves.

The foes arrayed against women were formidable. Both ends of the English political spectrum united to deny them. Moderate republicans argued that women couldn't understand politics, and extreme-ly conservative parties opposed women's rights on principle. Even Queen Victoria called demands for equal female rights "mad, wicked folly." Revolutionary social-ists from Roman Catholic states opposed female suffrage, fearing that women would support religious candidates. In France the

rising middle class had so restricted the birthrate in order to preserve property that opponents of women's rights saw the vote as both a dangerous "liberation" of women and the death knell of world power status. Only mainline socialist and worker parties, as well as most unions in Europe, viewed female suffrage as vital in raising wages and improving working conditions.

In the United States, suffragists were often equally aggressive on ending slavery, and these abolitionists, as they were called, received male support on slavery but ran into stiff obstacles on a broader franchise. Women gained more rights after the Civil War with industrial expan-sion and the growth of cities. Moving into positions as bookkeepers, factory workers, sales clerks, typists, stenographers, and telegraph and telephone workers, they helped promote American industry while advancing themselves in new technologies. Women began to open their own businesses in increasing numbers and entered law and medicine, although even professional wages still lagged behind those of men. Suffrage leaders such as Anna Howard Shaw and Carrie Chapman Catt employed quiet persuasion to pursue their aims, while a younger generation of women, led by Alice Paul, mirrored the demonstrations of the British.[17]

British Women Lead Europe

The worldwide suffragist movement reached its zenith in England. In 1864, after much agitation, women were allowed to vote in municipal elections, and in 1870 they were granted county and parish council suffrage. It was another nineteen years, however, before the first International Congresses on Women's Rights and Feminine Institutions in Paris, one hundred years after the French Revolution. Even then, British women were still the only Europeans who had made significant and measurable progress on the issue of suffrage.

By the late 1890s the numbers of British women agitating for a further expansion of women's rights was formidable. A quarter million signatures were presented to Parliament on a reform petition, and the International Women's Suffrage Alliance encouraged like-minded bodies in many countries to do the same.

The Suffrage Legacy

During the first World War most supporters of women's suffrage put aside their fight for the vote and threw themselves into supporting the war against Germany. By 1915 European women held over one million jobs previously restricted to men. At war's end, due to the massive loss of life, many women kept their jobs, having proven their competence. As their economic clout grew, bars to university and professional ranks weakened and broader suffrage became easier to achieve. As a result, this liberal concept, the most central to citizens' rights, was cemented in British and American politics and served as an inspiration throughout Europe.

Without the right to vote, women had to encourage, cajole, demonstrate, and obfuscate to gain economic and political clout and social protections. With the vote—achieved on a national scale in England, the United States, and several other countries by 1920—they had the legal right to be heard in citizens' forums, regardless of their socioeconomic status; they could vote to change policies that discriminated against them as well as support policies and politicians who promoted their cause. Discrimination still existed, especially in labor law, but the symbolism of the vote was impossible not to recognize. It fundamentally changed society, and human rights advanced another important step.

---

[17] See Howard L. Hurwitz, *An Encyclopedic Dictionary of American History* (New York: Washington Square Press, 1970), pp. 719-720.

A New Era of Suffrage Protest

Dismayed by the slow progress of women's suffrage in Britain, Emmeline Pankhurst (1858–1928) ushered in a new and effective era of prosuffrage agitation. Founder of the Women's Social and Political Union in 1903, she and her associates broke shop windows on London's pricey Oxford Street, bombed the house of Liberal Party head David Lloyd George (1863–1945), spilled acid on the putting greens of Peers, and went on extended hunger strikes for women's rights. They were arrested and beaten by police and brutally force-fed during their hunger strikes. Among the women was Alice Paul, who later helped reinvigorate the American cause through Pankhurst's means. Pankhurst and her fellow protesters—mostly middle-class educated women—finally broke through middle- and upper-class English reserve and began to swing the weight of public opinion over to their side. English women were granted the right to be elected to local government in 1907, and in 1910 Parliament debated a bill to grant the vote to single women owning property [it died under the influence of Prime Minister Herbert Asquith (1852–1928)]. In one of the saddest cases, a protester carrying a "Votes for Women" banner at the 1913 Epsom Derby threw herself in front of one of King George V's horses and was killed.

11. The Labor Movement

That the labor movement began in Britain is entirely appropriate. Britain led the world during the first phase of the Industrial Revolution, until 1870. Industrialization's worst excesses led to such abysmal poverty and human rights abuses that the government was jolted into real reforms. These reforms would not have occurred as thoroughly or rapidly if organized labor had not protested, rioted, marched, sang, and voted.

The Need for Reform

The result of industrialization was a complete transformation of English industry and society. Where handwork was once leisurely, individual, and of high quality, now millions toiled in often unsafe conditions for minuscule wages, crafting inputs to uniform goods. Workers became nameless in cavernous, dim, airless factories, instead of faces with names in local hamlets. Where fairly robust adult men previously tended to monopolize most skill categories, now even children under five crawled in dark mines fourteen hours a day, barely able to earn daily bread. In sum, a largely uncontrolled environment existed within which massive profits could be generated quickly by exploiting labor.

Ironically, Britain's success in advocating individual liberty in pursuit of private interests was seen widely as contributing to England's phenomenal industrial success. Laissez-faire economics, a doctrine of noninterference, soon became a vital tenet of liberals in destroying potential impediments to industrialization locally. Unfortunately, many theorists and members of Parliament could not even estimate the negative effects their policy of noninterference in business would have on the common people's rights and living conditions.

The Plight of Women and Children

Women were central to large-scale industrialization and were primarily employed in textiles (22 percent) and in domestic service (40 percent) in England, although they also worked in the leather trades, iron production, building, and mining in the 1850s. In France, women held 35 percent of all industrial jobs and about 50 percent of textile jobs. Domestic workers labored as many as eighteen hours a day. Jobs in industry did not have much shorter days, but domestics ate better, were more literate, and were more often able to marry up socially. Because wages were low, hundreds of thousands of European women supplemented their earnings as prostitutes.

Many families and many single women earning low wages were forced to send their children to work. Children earned one-quarter of what men did, and factory work was often dangerous. In the 1850s, almost a third of all workers were boys under twenty-one, while about 28 percent of girls between ten and fifteen worked.

Without adequate wages for women (and men), nineteenth-century living conditions were often horrific. A general sent to heavily industrialized Manchester in 1839 when the government expected riots from unemployed workers said that it was "the entrance to hell realized!" An American visitor to Manchester wrote in 1845: "Every day that I live I thank heaven that I am not a poor man with a family in England." Conditions only gradually began to improve in Western Europe after 1850 when real wages[18] rose.

The Beginning of the Labor Movement

Workers reacted to this horror by organizing. In England around 1815 more than a million had already joined "friendly societies," about ten tousand of which existed in 1803 and about thirty-two thousand in 1872. Germany and

---

[18] Real, as opposed to nominal, wages take into account inflation and a devaluation of currency and can be compared over time.

France had comparable movements, most of which did not enroll women. Soon real trade unions were established in England, growing rapidly after the Combination Acts of 1799 and 1800 (which prohibited organizing) were repealed in 1824. These unions worked aggressively for better wages, working and living conditions for their members, but their membership only encompassed roughly 20 percent of England's most highly skilled workers. Trade associations, especially those led by women, created burial societies to finance funerals and help members when they were sick. Even Sunday schools taught reading to some two million children in England by about 1850. By 1914 a million workers were unionized in Italy, 2.6 million in France, 1.5 million in Germany, and 3 million in Britain, although the majority were still not unionized.

Organized labor was first moved to active protests in England. Protest leaders such as Francis Place (1771–1854) helped make the period of 1820–1850 volatile. Considerable progress in organizing occurred between 1829 and 1836, with the founding of the first national union (spinners) in the latter. (Only about 7 percent of union members were women because women were discouraged from joining.) Later, in Germany and France, they were even more militant, especially during the "June Days" of 1848 in France and the Paris Commune of 1871. During the Paris Commune women achieved important recognition and positions based on their contributions in the struggle. The better-educated artisans such as seamstresses, tailors, printers, and shoemakers led the fight

and shared newspapers and workers' tracts with the illiterate.

The Legacy of European Labor Reform

When middle-class and workers' rights legislators grew sufficiently numerous in the English Parliament, they were able to usher in social welfare improvements. These included broader voting rights for men (and ultimately women), labor reforms (especially restricted hours for children and women, as well as schooling for children), and some health and safety protections. Later, after many protests, petition drives, mass demonstrations, and some violence, the expanded franchise led to even greater reforms, including controls on unsafe working conditions, recognition of organized unions, and food and housing relief for the poor and unemployed. It was not until 1875, however, that the Trade Union Act ended most restrictions on British unions.

British feminists as well as evangelical Protestants worked hard to improve working conditions for children. Parliament passed a law in 1833 that required owners to set up part-time schools in factories that employed children, although standards and inspections were minimal. The Factory Act, passed the same year, restricted daily working hours for young children to eight hours; in 1847 legislation was passed that limited the workday to ten hours for women and older children. In 1841 the French government passed its first law affecting relations between firms and those they employed, with a focus on child labor. Children were banned from working on Sundays and holidays, as well as at night. Children under the age of eight were prohibited from factory employment, and children between eight and thirteen were restricted to eight hours a day, while those between thirteen and sixteen could work twelve hours a day. The law was notoriously difficult to enforce.

Radicals and socialists induced the French Chamber of Deputies to effect substantial reforms between 1890 and 1904, including the elimination of internal worker passports in 1890; strike arbitration and the prevention of night work for women in 1892; employer liability for industrial accidents in 1898; ten-hour maximum workdays for children and women in 1904; one weekly day of rest required and a minimum age for factory workers; government inspections of workplaces; worker compensation laws with retirement benefits; and finally, medical care for families.[19]

Despite these successes, the lot of European workers remained meager. After World War I, European economies already reeling from war were severely strained by new costs: economic disruptions caused by returning soldiers, changes in trade patterns, exhaustion of key resources, failures of firms unable to return to normal after the boom years, mammoth rebuilding projects, long-term health care and pension costs, and others. These economic changes strained the individual as well as the family,

and left fruitful room for socialists and Marxists to gain new converts.

U.S. Labor Movement

Until large influxes of immigrants concentrated in America's coastal cities in the late nineteenth century, the United States escaped the horrific sweatshops that proliferated in Britain. Instead, U.S. labor was somewhat protected by frontier conditions, as well as a relatively small population and higher values placed on labor. Nevertheless, American industrial leaders seemed nearly as indifferent to the human rights of their workers as were the Europeans. In frustration, early American labor emphasized strikes, which often became violent in later years. They were broken by federal troops and injunctions used by nervous management and government officials. Trade unions rejected socialist principles for improving workers' conditions under capitalism; as such, socialist and Marxist parties never gained prominence in the United States.

The first reform efforts began with workers organizing for a ten-hour day in the 1830s; previous workdays were "sun-up to sun-down." In 1840 President Martin Van Buren issued an Executive Order establishing ten hours as the workday on all U.S. government projects. Soon after, New Hampshire passed the first state law mandating ten-hour workdays; Pennsylvania followed with a ten-hour day, sixty-hour week, in six types of industries. In the 1850s, Massachusetts,

---

[19] Many statistics in this section are drawn from the labor reform discussion in Merriman.

Connecticut, Rhode Island, Ohio, California, and Georgia enacted their own reforms. The next big success for American labor occurred as a result of *Commonwealth v. Hunt* (1842), when the Massachusetts Supreme Court established the legality of labor unions, previously considered conspiracies.

In the wake of the Civil War and growing industrialization, industrialists such as J. P. Morgan became infamous for reducing costs and expanding profit by exploiting labor, ushering in nearly seventy-five years of violent strikes; most were broken by presidential authorization of federal troops. The "long strike" of coal miners in 1874-1875 was soon followed by the 1877 railroad strikes, which were the first nationwide actions taken against wage cuts and sparked riots in Pittsburgh, Chicago, Baltimore, St. Louis, and San Francisco. Some of the most violent strikes in American labor history occurred in the lead and silver mines of Coeur d'Alene in Idaho in 1892.

American labor waited until the twentieth century for comprehensive reform efforts that began to equate labor organizing and influence as a human right. They were aided in these efforts by individuals such as Terence Vincent Powderly (1849–1924), who headed the largest body of the period, the Knights of Labor (1879–1893),

viewed strikes as outmoded and advocated public arbitration and labor bureaus. Samuel Gompers, first president of the American Federation of Labor (AFL), ran the organization from 1886 to his death in 1924, except for one year. The AFL stressed organizing skilled workers, collective bargaining, higher wages, shorter hours, and improved working conditions. One noteworthy success was President Theodore Roosevelt's intervention in the Anthracite Coal Strike of 1902 on behalf of the public through arbitration, which significantly strengthened the hand of the United Mine Workers. The Clayton Antitrust Act (1914) also benefited organized labor when it declared that labor unions were not be considered unlawful combinations in restraint of trade. Similarly, the Norris-LaGuardia Act of 1932 allowed labor the full freedom of association without interference by employers. Nevertheless, broad government action was not taken before several tragedies occurred. Most notably, the Triangle Shirtwaist Company fire in New York (1911), in which 146 workers died, mostly women and girls on the upper floors, provoked revised building codes and revisions in the labor laws. As a result, the International Ladies Garment Workers Union helped eliminate sweatshops in the shirtwaist trade.[20]

---

[20] See Hurwitz, "Labor Unions," 25ff.

12. Socialism and Marxism

"Only by obedience to the state can man attain freedom!"
—Georg Hegel

Socialists responded to the horrific poverty of the masses toiling in factories and sweat-shops by developing an alternative view toward natural or human rights during industrialization. Unlike liberals, who believed that economic advancement should ultimately lead to broad improvements in living standards and political equality, socialists quite rightly noted that the liberal emphasis on laissez-faire economics and few limitations on property rights generally benefited only those with substantial capital and land holdings. As a result, they argued for rights not yet produced by capitalism: universal suffrage and the vote for women, education and health care for all, the prohibition of child labor, as well as health and safety standards and workplace inspections.

Leading authors who ultimately shaped the socialists' human rights agenda included historians such as Georg Wilhelm Friedrich Hegel (1770–1831); Karl Marx (1818–1883), who wrote about the stages of history and pushed for an international agenda; Marx and Friedrich Engels (1820–1895), who together attacked liberal interpretations of human rights; French anarchist Pierre-Joseph Proudhon (1809–1865), who argued against property rights; as well as Marx, Engels, and August Bebel (1840–1913), who discussed women's unequal status.

The March of History: Georg Hegel

The socialists were heavily influenced by a new approach toward principles of historical study, called historiography. Historical philosophers such as Hegel argued that development over time was unique. Historians responded by trying to explain progress in human society, thought, and action, instead of looking for an unaltered natural and human order. As such, they were open to the possibility of societal evolution.

Hegel carried that evolution to the extreme. He saw all history as progressing toward the maturity of the "world spirit," with only one nation as bearer of that spirit in any stage of history. Hegel was convinced that Prussia in Germany was destined to dominate Europe and saw it as the fourth stage in human history (after the Oriental powers, the Greeks, and the Romans). The impact of Hegel's doctrines was profound, especially in Germany. Hegel idealized the nation-state and contributed to German nationalism that reached extreme heights before and during the World Wars. Earlier, the Russian czars and Austria's Prince Metternich (1773–1859) had also been deeply influenced by aspects of Hegel's philosophy, using him as a justification for their tyranny.

On Stages in Human History: Karl Marx

Karl Marx was a disciple of Hegel's notion of historical evolution, and ultimately became, along with Engels, the most influential philosopher to address this new developmental history. Marx interpreted Hegel's "world spirit" as the dialectic movement of society, and he borrowed Hegel's ideas of the class struggle. Marx believed that both would inevitably lead to Communism. Marx's argument for stages in human history satisfied both the embittered labor activist and the angry suffragist. Marx's manifesto, "Workers of the World Unite!" was the heart of his *Communist Manifesto* (1848) and one that he repeated during his "Inaugural Address of the Working Men's International Association" sixteen years later.

Marx's impact was significant because his agenda was persuasively argued, internally consistent, and logical. For example, he called for a universal right to free education but recognized that paying for it might be difficult. Thus, his belief in a "heavy progressive" income tax and the elimination of the right to inheritance not only fostered his ideal of greater income equality, but also, if implemented, would reap sufficient revenues to underwrite expensive social programs.

His appeal to workers in general was also attractive, in part because he looked at the entire environment, instead of piecemeal reforms. He argued for universal suffrage so that workers could help determine their own destinies, and he lauded the English "Ten Hours Bill," which lowered working hours. Health care for workers was another worry of his, as was the more reasonable eight-hour day, strict controls on child labor, and shopfloor safety.

Communism and Human Rights

The product of these beliefs, Communism, never worked in practice as Marx, Engels, and Lenin hoped that it would in theory, nor did it offer most of the now universally agreed-upon human rights. Communist theorists expected that after the revolution, rationality and good will would become the prime movers of society, once public ownership of the means of production had removed human greed. Instead, communist leaders merely installed new oligarchies that restricted human rights, rebuffed the popular will, prevented freely made associations from expressing themselves, and imprisoned, tortured, or killed those who protested too vigorously. This occurred despite Marxist-Leninist writings that vehemently denounced oppression. Communist regimes stemming from Marx's and Engel's theories also entered into wars, financed insurgencies, conducted reigns of terror, and financed international efforts to sabotage other governments in order to forcibly impose their will. The ultimate criterion was always success: indeed, Lenin baldly stated that, if necessary, two-thirds of mankind should be killed to ensure Communism's final triumph.

Nevertheless, socialist and communist theory was attractive because it addressed all the right questions, appealed to the masses' hopes as well as their miseries, and removed the onus for their condition (as well as the responsibility for its remedy) from the individual to the society as a whole. Interestingly enough, the socialists and Marxists did offer one salutary legacy not often ascribed to them: they helped establish, along with U. S. President Woodrow Wilson and his Fourteen Points (see Section 13), human rights as a legitimate international concern. Arbitrary rulers and individual states could no longer assume that their international neighbors would turn a blind eye toward oppression of their citizens, considering it purely an internal matter.

Rights in a Classless Society: Friedrich Engels

Marx's longtime collaborator, and co-author of *The Communist Manifesto*, Friedrich Engels (1820–1895) disagreed with the ahistorical and liberal notion of human rights argued by other German philosophers. In *The Anti-Duhring* he wrote, "The concept of truth has varied so much from nation to nation and from age to age that they have often been in direct contradiction to each other" (1878). Engels also argued that concepts of rights are unique to each society's economic epochs and to the leadership's conceptions. Consequently, he believed that a universal human morality and a common concept of right could only occur when class differences no longer existed. In that classless society an "eternal morality which is independent of time and changes in reality" would evolve. Until that happened, Engels expressed great disbelief in concepts of free will and freedom offered by other human rights theorists. Indeed, he argued that all methods of war were justified to seize political power, abolish capitalism, seize the reins of the world's economies, and establish the classless society. After the seizure of power, ten measures antithetical to early and modern notions of human rights were to be put into place, including forfeiture of landed property; destruction of all rights of inheritance; confiscation of all property belonging to "rebels"; nationalism of banks and transportation; state control of all means of production; enforced obligation of all citizens to work; and the establishment of "industrial armies." Only one element is now generally considered a human right: free education for all children in public schools.

13. Internationalism, Woodrow Wilson, and the League of Nations

"The War to End all Wars . . ."
—President Woodrow Wilson

As Western powers gradually became sovereign over much of the world through colonialism and trade, ideology and policy struggles that had been confined to Europe advanced to the international stage. Thus, the struggle between liberal and socialist concepts of politics and human rights that burgeoned in the early twentieth century spread far beyond Europe's borders. The international socialist movement reached new heights with the Bolshevik Revolution in Russia in 1917, while the League of Nations offered a universal template for the liberal human rights agenda after World War I.

The stakes were high, as four empires collapsed at the end of World War I. The czars in Russia were replaced by revolution in 1917. The Bolsheviks then replaced the provisional government, withdrew from the war, and proclaimed communist rule on the Marxist-Leninist model. The Ottoman Empire (Germany's ally) formally ended through the Treaty of Sevres (August 1920). Kaiser Wilhelm II's German Empire collapsed even before the Allies met in Versailles in 1919 for the Paris Peace Conference, wracked by four years of war with Britain, France, and their allies; and finally, the Austro-Hungarian Empire dissolved.

Self-Determination as a Human Rights Issue

The entangling European alliances that touched off World War I convinced many leaders that a more principled international arena and codes of conduct were needed. Moreover, claims of national self-determination (determination by the people of a territorial unit of their own future political status) increased during World War I and began to gain legitimacy as a human rights criterion. At Versailles, the "Big Four" (Italy, Britain, France, and the United States) could only agree on two things: that Germany was primarily responsible for the war and should pay the largest reparations to rebuild Europe (132 billion gold marks), and that Germany should also be forced to make significant territorial and suzerainty concessions. Beyond that, there was significant disagreement. The Treaty of Versailles ultimately created three new states in Central Europe: Czechoslovakia, Yugoslavia, and a renewed Poland, which ultimately ratified the national will of many of their peoples. Nevertheless, these reparations and the individual treaties signed after World War I between the Allies and Germany's partners left unsatisfied aspirations, bitter nationalist dissatisfaction, and hatred that ultimately led, at least in part, to the seeds of World War II.

Calls for self-determination provoked many and varied responses in a high-stakes political game. Socialists and liberals responded quite differently to these calls, given their dichotomous attitudes toward individual and group rights. Moreover, even avowed liberals like England's John Stuart Mill and American President Woodrow Wilson both agreed that political stability and a cohesive national body were essential precursors for national independence. However, Mill also argued that not all national bodies or territories were ready for independence, particularly those not yet at a self-sustaining level of social and economic development. His position ultimately justified the mandate system set up by the League of Nations to supervise and, theoretically, tutor such states to independence. By contrast, President Wilson argued for universal self-determination. Britain, the world's largest colonial power, not only refused self-determination as a concept but refused to accept Wilson's plan that the league or another body rule on the colonies. (Nevertheless, the war did alter Britain's relationship with its dominions, each of whom became signatories to the treaty after World War I, members of the league, and moved to commonwealth status in 1931.)

The Fourteen Points and the League of Nations

Earlier, President Wilson was reelected in 1916 on the slogan, "He kept us out of war." Not surprisingly, he justified the idealism of his "Fourteen Points" address to Congress in January 1918 by arguing that it would remove a major cause of future wars. The Fourteen Points included the right of national groups to self-determination, and it was, at base, an argument for rights for all. It stated that "it is the principle of justice to all peoples and nationalities, and their right to live on equal terms of liberty and safety with another, whether they be strong or weak." Wilson hoped to institutionalize these rights in a League of Nations, with borders established by homogenous ethnic and/or national groups. The league would be empowered to settle nationalistic conflicts as they occurred, with the United States assuming an international role as one of the five permanent members of the league's council. In effect, it would be the guarantor of peace through collective security. The package was so attractive that Germany's new chancellor, Prince Max von Baden (1867–1929), unsuccessfully asked Wilson for an end to the fighting based on his "peace without victory." The Austro-Hungarian Empire tried for an armistice, also, based on the Fourteen Points, before the Paris Peace Conference at Versailles actually began in 1919.

The opening session of the League of Nations, November 15, 1920 (UN/DPI Photo by Jullien).

Wilson's idealism contrasted with the rugged reality of positions taken by Britain's David Lloyd George and France's Georges Clemenceau. During the four months after Versailles, they gradually gained the upper hand, particularly with regard to harshness toward Germany, even though the Germans argued, with some justification, that their new democratic government was being punished for the Kaiser's imperialism. Wilson stood firm on the league's covenant, which showed concern for human rights, and he insisted that it be added to the treaty. His idealism also won out in some areas such as the concept of self-determination based on ethnic cohesiveness, re-creating, as it did, the state of Poland through the Polish Minority Treaty of 1919 and developing new states out of the Austro-Hungarian Empire.

Ironically, Wilson's stance on self-determination allowed Hitler less than twenty years later to swallow Austria (1936) and then occupy the Sudetenland of Czechoslovakia under the pretext of unifying the German people, and then annex it all in 1938 when France and Britain failed to oppose him. It also allowed Turkey to push nearly two million Armenians out of their Turkish homes (when they called for an independent state); more than a third died of thirst trekking to Syria.

The League of Nations was largely impotent by the late 1930s, and it was dissolved completely in 1946, when it was replaced by the United Nations.

The League's Legacy for Human Rights

The sheer horror of World War I cried out for changes that would protect the sanctity of human life. Some six thousand people were killed each day for four years (eight and a half million.) Sixty-five million men were soldiers, and of these about thirty-seven million were casualties, including perhaps seven million who were permanently disabled. About another 12.6 million died of war-related causes. Austria-Hungary suffered a 90 percent casualty rate, and Russia 76 percent, while the United States (entering the war late) only had an 8 percent rate.[21] With so many dead, Europe became a continent of widows and spinsters. National budgets were exhausted helping the survivors. Birthrates fell precipitously, national economies operated at a fraction of capacity, agriculture stagnated, and starvation and poverty loomed each winter.

In the face of all this, the Covenant of the League of Nations (1919) was designed to enhance security, peace, individual and group rights, and interstate cooperation. It proposed security guarantees as well as efforts to monitor and control disease (the worldwide outbreak of influenza that killed some twenty-seven million people was a horrible precedent), prohibit the exploitation of children and women, improve working conditions, and appropriately treat, educate, and eventually prepare colonial peoples for self-government through the mandates. (This system was to be racially, ethnically, and religiously blind in terms of administration.)

The covenant also showed concern for human rights in its mandate system for territories previously controlled by Germany, through Article 23 on labor conditions, and in the discussion of "the traffic in women and children." Moreover, the establishment of the International Labour Office (ILO) was an important step forward, although Japan tried—unsuccessfully—to introduce racial inequality into the covenant.

Although this period was a formative one, with a growing international acceptance of appropriate human rights norms, they still were piecemeal, restricted, and linked to particular issues rather than to a broad spectrum of rights worldwide. It wasn't until after World War II that the United States took the lead in codifying human rights on an international basis. Even now, more than fifty years later, the world still struggles with enforcing the implementation of human rights codes.

---

[21] See James L. Stokesbury, *A Short History of World War I* (New York: Quill, 1981), p. 310; and Merriman's discussion of the impact of World War I, especially pp. 1082-1083.

14. Totalitarianism, World War II, and the Holocaust

"One death is a tragedy, and a million is a statistic."
—Joseph Stalin

At the end of World War II, when the utter magnitude of the Nazi slaughter of Jews and others in the concentration camps was unambiguously known, the conscience of the world was mobilized, and human rights became an issue of legitimate, international debate. Other acts of sheer barbarism perpetrated by totalitarian regimes, from Europe to the Far East, only perpetuated the desire for a United Nations that would prevent the atrocities and international anarchy that had plagued the planet since 1918.[22]

Totalitarianism

Strikes, high unemployment, explosive inflation, and political instability spread turmoil through Europe after World War I and helped induce authoritarian and totalitarian governments[23] that roundly denied human rights and contributed to the antecedents of World War II. In Italy the rationality inherited from the Enlightenment was defeated by the irrationality of the Fascists, who came to power under Benito Mussolini in 1922.[24] Similarly, Adolf Hitler's National Socialist Party preyed upon the frustrations some Germans felt over the "unjust peace" of Versailles. In the Soviet Union, after Lenin's death in 1924, Joseph Stalin quickly assumed control of the Communist Party and eliminated his rivals. He also forced millions of relatively well-off peasants (kulaks) into collective farms and sent those who resisted to forced labor camps east of the Ural Mountains or simply killed them, while exiling their families.

The irrationality of Europe's authoritarian and totalitarian governments came to a head in World War II. Once it was over and the truth was known, the world reeled in horror. Out of that horror came a crusade against man's inhumanity.

---

[22] This section is informed by excellent historical discussions in the following volumes: T. C. Blanning, ed, *The Oxford Illustrated History of Modern Europe* (New York: Oxford University Press, 1996); John Merriman, *A Modern Europe: From Renaissance to the Present* (New York: W. W. Norton and Co., 1996); J. M. Roberts, *A History of Europe* (New York: Penguin Press, 1996); and Norman Stone, *Europe Transformed* (Cambridge, Mass: Harvard University Press, 1984).

[23] Authoritarian governments are those that favor absolute obedience to the government's authority, with very little individual freedom allowed. Totalitarian governments are mainly characterized by monolithic state unity that is upheld by authoritarian means.

[24] The key principles undergirding Fascism in the 1920s in Germany, Italy, and Spain included extreme nationalism, government by totalitarian or authoritarian regimes, racial politics, and an extreme emphasis on power.

The brutal legacy of the totalitarian states that precipitated World War II included seventeen million soldiers killed on all sides, with at least twenty to thirty five million civilians dead, ten to twenty five million of those in Russia alone (newly opened Soviet archives suggest the latter figure). Europe became a continent of "displaced persons," or DPs, many shell-shocked, orphaned, lost, or bereft of friends and family. Many never recovered from the psychic damage. With the advances in weaponry over World War I and the addition of Hitler's extermination policy, losses were four times as high as in World War I.

When initial reports of German atrocities began to leak out, the Allies began to emphasize human rights and plans for a new world order in their war aims. A turning point was President Franklin D. Roosevelt's "Four Freedoms" message to the U.S. Congress (January 1941). The Four Freedoms were freedom of speech, freedom of religion, freedom from want, and freedom from fear. President Roosevelt believed that these protections should prevail everywhere in the world. Other human rights documents from this period include the Atlantic Charter (August 1941), the Declaration of the United Nations (January 1, 1942), and the Declaration of Philadelphia (1944).[25] Finally, the preamble to the UN Charter (June 26, 1945) reaffirmed "faith in fundamental human rights, in the dignity and worth of the human person, in the equal rights of men and women, and of nations large and small"; this was one of the first times that human rights were explicitly mentioned in an international treaty.

The sheer audacity of Hitler's "final solution," the Bataan Death March, the brutal incarceration of Allied servicemen and civilians by Japan, and the starving of three million Russian prisoners held by Germany, among other atrocities, were all on a far grander scale in war than humankind had yet seen. These deliberate acts of inhumanity helped persuade the West in 1945 to hope for a true family of nations. "The United Nations has to work," it was argued. "One world or none" was the fear, given atomic energy.

The Holocaust

The irony of the Holocaust is that it led, finally, to a definitive repudiation of the belief in ultimate human progress that endured until the early twentieth century. Henceforth, philosophers, political theorists, theologians, the mass public and their leaders had to grapple with the reality of just how inhuman worldwide war could become. From that reckoning came the conclusion that such horror must not occur again, and a host of mechanisms were developed to prevent it. The sheer size, breadth, and audacity of

---

[25] Two famous passages of the Declaration of Philadelphia were included in the Constitution of the International Labour Organization (ILO) of the United Nations: "All human beings, irrespective of race, creed, or sex, have the right to pursue both their material well-being and their spiritual development in conditions of freedom and dignity, of economic security, and equal opportunity" and "Freedom of expression and association are essential to sustained progress."

the Holocaust tipped the balance toward serious Western concern for international human rights for the first time.

The Holocaust was multiethnic and widespread. Prior to World War II, Hitler's bizarre racial attitudes had become official dogma. The German Nazi party intended to create a "national community" within which there was no room for "outsiders," although an exception was made for non-German laborers vital to the war effort. However, Hitler deemed Poles and Russians racial inferiors and informed Heinrich Himmler (1900–1945), head of the elite *Schutzstaffel* or S.S. corps, in January 1941 that he needed at least thirty million Soviets killed because he needed their lands. This launched a killing spree by troops and the S.S. who slaughtered Soviet prisoners as well as civilians. They died by poison, gas, shooting, starvation, neglect, and exposure. At least 3.3 million Soviet prisoners of war (POWs) out of 5.7 million were killed or died in German prison camps. Likewise, once Warsaw was captured, Hitler sent troops to kill or incarcerate the entire Polish upper class. Similarly, five hundred thousand of Europe's Gypsies were killed because they were considered "not Aryan" and "asocial, biological outsiders."

Many other groups suffered human rights abuses at the hands of the Nazis, including "deficient" ethnic Germans. Starting in 1939 Hitler instructed his troops to kill some seventy thousand mentally retarded Germans (including children), until the public's objections grew passionate in 1941, when he ceased the practice. Other "asocial" individuals killed included recidivist criminals, socialists, and about 150,000 German Communists. German "outcasts" (homosexuals, alcoholics, those suffering from schizophrenia, depression, or other chronic mental diseases, and those considered "workshy") were sterilized, perhaps 320,000 to 350,000 of them between 1934 and 1945. Another 250,000 Germans were put in prison or ordered to emigrate because they opposed the regime, while at least fifteen thousand were given death sentences for "crimes against the state," including listening to the British Broadcasting Corporation (BBC).[26]

The largest group of nonsoldiers killed directly through Hitler's exclusionary policies were Jews, beginning in July of 1941. Jews were first murdered in mobile vans, but huge concentration camps with gas chambers and ovens were soon constructed. Those healthy enough were forced to work on short rations; if they fell ill or weak, they were gassed. Young children, the elderly, and pregnant women were generally gassed immediately, unless they had very special skills like forgery, printmaking, high degrees of musical skill, and so forth. Others were brutally tortured or maimed by "medical experiments." By the end of the war, some six million Jews were killed. Many of Germany's allies killed their own Jews, as in Romania and Croatia, or they shipped them off to concentration camps. Perhaps forty to fifty thousand European Jews survived the Holocaust.

---

[26] See Merriman's statistical analysis of World War II's impact, especially pp. 1259-1262.

Some of the most memorable and courageous acts of the war occurred when attempts were made to save local Jews. Denmark saved virtually its entire Jewish population by commandeering almost everything that could float to ferry them to neutral Sweden in October 1943. Elsewhere, isolated cases exhibited great bravery, such as the Christian family who sheltered Anne Frank's family in Amsterdam for much of the war.

The Nuremberg and Tokyo Trials

Illustrative of the conviction that mankind must cooperate was the success Americans and Soviets had in trying the war leaders of Japan and Germany before International Military Tribunals, established at American insistence. The most famous were the Nuremberg war criminal trials of twenty-two top Nazis. Eleven were convicted of waging aggressive warfare as well as "crimes against humanity" on September 30, 1946. Ten defendants were hanged; Hermann Goering committed suicide. Ultimately, 500,000 war criminals were found guilty in the American zone of occu-pied Germany; they received differentiated sentences. In Tokyo similar trials from June 1946 to May 1948 eventually hanged seven defendants, including former Premier Hideki Tojo. About four thousand other Japanese were charged with war crimes.

Although Nuremberg was criticized, the significance for the cause of human rights lay with the action taken in 1946 by the UN General Assembly to approve and ratify the Nuremberg Principles. These principles granted the right and authority to punish, even with death, violations of human rights. They also specified that soldiers may not be exonerated merely because of following the orders of superiors if they violate established rules of war.

In keeping with these steps, the UN General Assembly adopted the Universal Declaration of Human Rights in 1948, as well as the Convention on the Prevention and Punishment of the Crime of Genocide. Together with the Nuremberg Principles, they provided the context within which the West, and ultimately the world, came to agree on the formulation, protection, and promotion of international standards for securing human rights in wartime or peace.

—Carol Rae Hansen

PART TWO

The Universal Declaration
of Human Rights

Eleanor Roosevelt holds a poster of the Universal Declaration of Human Rights.
Lake Success, New York, November 1949 (UN Photo).

Chapter Two

An Overview of the Universal Declaration of Human Rights

Introduction

The creation of the Universal Declaration of Human Rights (UDHR) in 1948 marked the foundation of the modern human rights movement. It took the notion of rights and articulated it on the international level, as applicable to all. Fifty years later, the human rights movement is a truly global phenomenon, as individuals around the world cite the declaration and its rights as a way of describing their needs.

This chapter evaluates the declaration. It describes the historical context in which it was created, and then it examines the drafting process. Finally it examines the declaration itself—what it stands for, what its status is, how it works, how it views human rights promotion, and how it can claim to be universal. The following chapter evaluates each of the declaration's thirty articles in turn—what they mean, what the drafters' intentions were, how they have been elaborated on in subsequent instruments, and what issues they speak to today.

The Historical Background of the Declaration

In many ways the declaration and the human rights movement that followed from it came out of the worldwide revulsion at the atrocities that were committed during World War II. The declaration served as a direct rebuttal of the racist and fascist ideologies that had "disregard and contempt for human rights" at their root and led to "barbarous acts which have outraged the conscience of mankind" (UDHR preamble). The "Four Freedoms," as proclaimed by President Roosevelt in his State of the Union address to Congress on January 6, 1941, were repeated in the UDHR preamble: freedom of speech and belief and freedom from fear and want. These freedoms were seen as the "highest aspirations of the common people" (UDHR preamble), and when transformed into human rights provisions, became the basis for the new world order (the "social and international order" of Article 28) that the Allies hoped to create after the end of the war.

The United Nations (UN) was created by the Allies (who also called themselves the "United Nations" during the war) as the cornerstone of this new world order; the organization personified the "consciousness of mankind" that had been outraged during the war. In one of several references to human rights, the UN Charter begins by proclaiming a "faith in fundamental human rights, in the dignity and worth of the human person, in the equal rights of men and women and of nations large and small" (UN Charter preamble).

The charter then charges the organization with the task of achieving "international cooperation in promoting and encouraging respect for human rights and fundamental freedoms" (Article 1), and affirms members' obligations to respect human rights in general and to work jointly and severally for their protection. Both states and nongovernmental organizations (NGOs) pushed for the inclusion of a bill of rights in the charter. However, the charter did not end up containing specific provisions on the content of human rights. Instead it was decided that this would be articulated in one of the first legislative initiatives of the organization drafting an International Bill of Rights.[1]

---

[1] Strictly speaking, the declaration was not the first international human rights declaration. In late spring of 1948, the Organization of American States passed a resolution containing the American Declaration of the Rights and Duties of Man, a regional human rights instrument for the Americas.

Drafting the Declaration

The declaration was a product of the UN legislative process, involving various UN bodies. The Economic and Social Council (ECOSOC) mandated its subset, the eighteen-member Human Rights Commission (chaired by Eleanor Roosevelt), to draft the International Bill of Rights. Originally this was to take the form of a declaration (a statement of principles), a convention (containing the legal obligations of states), and measures of implementation (to enforce the obligations). The convention's name was changed to "covenant" and was then split into two covenants—the International Covenant on Civil and Political Rights (ICCPR) and the International Covenant on Economic, Social and Cultural Rights (ICESCR)—each incorporating elements of implementation within its structure.

The Human Rights Commission set up a drafting committee to formulate a draft of the declaration, based on an outline of proposals and supporting documents prepared by the Human Rights Division of the Secretariat, the permanent team of international civil servants at the UN. Input was given by the Commission on the Status of Women as well as the subcommissions (of the Human Rights Commission) on the Freedom of Information and the Press, and the Prevention of Discrimination and the Protection of Minorities. Some states also submitted suggested texts for the declaration.

The Human Rights Commission's draft was then considered by ECOSOC.

The text approved by ECOSOC was then proposed as a resolution before the General Assembly, the main legislative body in the UN where every member state has an equal vote.

As chair of the drafting committee, Eleanor Roosevelt had intended that it be composed of herself and three other members of the Human Rights Commission. Under pressure from other countries, however, she was forced to expand this to include more members. This varied in number throughout the committee's existence, and members included the distinguished French legal scholar René Cassin, as well as representatives from Australia, China, Chile, France, the Philippines, Lebanon, USSR, the Ukranian SSR, the United Kingdom, Uruguay, and Yugoslavia.

The original outline for the declaration was prepared largely by the Canadian international lawyer John Humphrey, who worked as head of the Human Rights Division throughout the drafting process. The drafting committee then asked René Cassin to draft a text, using Humphrey's outline. The contents of this draft formed the basis for the eventual wording of the declaration, and for this reason Cassin has been considered as the main "author" of it. However, Humphrey's memoirs and more recent research suggest that Cassin's draft relied heavily on Humphrey's proposal. It would seem that Humphrey deserves considerable credit for the drafting of the declaration, alongside Cassin.

Moreover, as Humphrey states: "The declaration . . . has no father in the sense that Jefferson was the father of the American Declaration of Independence. Very many people . . . contributed to the final result. It is indeed this very anonymity which gives the declaration some of its great prestige and authority."

At the time, Humphrey claimed that there was no particular philosophical basis for the outline, stating that it was a random synthesis of proposals sent to the Secretariat from all around the world. Humphrey subsequently acknowledged that this was not actually the case. He wrote, "With two exceptions all these texts came from English-speaking sources and all of them from the democratic West . . . . My draft attempted to combine humanitarian liberalism with social democracy . . . . I had myself decided what to put in and what to leave out."

Humphrey and other drafters were influenced by some of the foundational constitutional documents of the United States and Europe, such as the 1215 Magna Carta (England); the 1689 Bill of Rights (England); the 1789 Declaration of the Rights of Man (France); the 1787 United States Constitution and 1791 Bill of Rights. (These antecedents are discussed in detail in Part 1, Chapter 1.) These were complemented by specific proposals from national and international organizations and private individuals. Organizations included the United Nations Educational, Scientific, and Cultural Organization (UNESCO), the American Law Institute, the American Jewish Congress, the Women's Trade Union League, and the Inter-American Bar Association. Individuals included the author H. G. Wells, the distinguished international legal scholar Hersch Lauterpacht, and in UNESCO's report, the political scientists E. H. Carr and Harold Laski.

Although the Secretariat later cited extracts from the constitutions of a wide group of countries, this was done to foster an impression of a universal consensus in anticipation of the debates that would take place in ECOSOC and the General Assembly. Since the key decisions as to the content of the declaration were made at the drafting committee stage, inspiration for and conception of the rights in the declaration undoubtedly came primarily from the philosophical traditions and crucible of experience of the North American, European, and British Commonwealth members of the drafting committee and Secretariat.

The declaration was drafted during a window of opportunity after the end of World War II and before the tensions of the Cold War became so pronounced that international consensus was impossible. Even so, ideological conflict between the West and the Soviets figured in all of the debates up to and including the adoption of the declaration. Eleanor Roosevelt's shrewd tactic of making the declaration take the form of a nonbinding General Assembly resolution meant that it passed despite profound disagreements between states, since it was seen as not creating obligations for them in international law.

The covenants, on the other hand, were binding. They were not completed until 1966 and did not enter into force until 1976. Even now, many countries have not agreed to be fully bound by both the covenants, including, ironically, the United States. Similarly, the initiative for methods of implementation lost impetus because of states' reluctance to accept what they perceived as a violation of their sovereignty. Instead, elements of implementation became part of the covenants and have been introduced in a piecemeal fashion in other UN initiatives.

The effect of the Cold War on the drafting process was that two models of ideological models that followed from the Enlightenment competed to be reflected in the declaration. The Western capitalist model, with its emphasis on individualism, enterprise, and property rights, focused more on civil and political rights. The Soviet communist model, with its emphasis on group rights, individual duties, and the collective ownership of property, focused on economic, social, and cultural rights. The result was a declaration that accepted the importance of both individual liberty and the collective unit within which individuals live. Its seemingly unqualified formulation of free expression (Article 19) appealed to libertarians; the right to an adequate standard of living (Article 25) appealed to socialists.

The balance of the declaration as a whole, however, is unmistakably Western. As the driving force behind it, Eleanor Roosevelt frequently stamped down Soviet attempts to socialize it to a greater extent than was acceptable to her. (According to a *New York Times* reporter who covered the Human Rights Commission, "The

Russians seem to have met their match in Mrs. Roosevelt.") For example, economic and social rights were not articulated in terms of the state's obligations to make provisions for its people where necessary (even though this is clearly the implication). Similarly the limitations that were the logical corollary to many civil and political rights (an individual is limited in exercising his or her rights if they infringe the rights of another individual, for example) were dealt with in a separate article (29) rather than as part of each right. This lays greater emphasis on rights than on the duties to the state, which were of particular importance to socialist countries.

It is worth noting that concepts of economic, social, and cultural rights were not as antithetical to the West when the declaration was drafted as they would become in the later stages of the Cold War. The social agenda of postwar reconstruction in Europe and President Roosevelt's New Deal in the United States meant that, anticommunist sentiments notwithstanding, there was significant support in the West for the state's role in promoting the economic and social welfare of its people. The socialist aspects of the declaration were, therefore, those that the West could accommodate and ran alongside civil and political rights that were passionately supported. In contrast the Soviets felt that neither the economic nor the social rights went far enough and that many of the civil and political rights were phrased in unacceptably absolutist terms. While the declaration was a triumph for Eleanor Roosevelt, the Soviets and their allies (together with Saudi

Arabia and South Africa) ultimately abstained in the final vote.

Many of the declaration's articles were stated simply, in order to avoid taking a position on key aspects of the rights involved. To a certain degree, this was inevitable with such profound disagreements on much of the content. However, the drafters—notably Eleanor Roosevelt—sincerely believed that the purpose of the declaration was to state rights in a simple fashion. It would be for subsequent instruments like the covenants to elaborate on their meaning. For example, Eleanor Roosevelt objected to the proposal that Article 20, the right to assembly, should include examples of assemblies that are permitted. She felt that this was unnecessary, and the idea was dropped.

When the declaration proposal reached the General Assembly, the third committee of that body spent considerable time in debate before the vote in the full chamber. However, Humphrey reported that despite this the "final result was remarkably like the [Human Rights] Commission's text." The General Assembly passed the resolution (217[III]A) on December 10, 1948, eighteen months after the drafting process began. There were forty-eight votes in favor, eight abstentions, and two countries absent.

What Is the Universal Declaration of Human Rights?

The Foundation of Human Rights Law

International human rights law is a body of instruments and customary norms that, although existing between states, governs the relationship between states and their peoples rather than states and other states. As such, states have agreed on the international level how they will behave on the national level. How they treat their citizens becomes a matter of international, as well as national, law.

Although international law had made some progress in the formation of human rights norms, it was at a primitive stage at the time of the drafting of the UDHR. Customary norms covered only the most basic of human rights issues (such as the prohibition on slavery) and instruments were selective in both their subject matter (e.g., the Red Cross conventions on human rights during conflict) and the states that were covered by them (e.g., the Minorities Treaties imposed on some of the defeated powers of World War I).

The declaration built on these developments and created a fully formed charter, setting out the complete range of rights applicable to all people in the world. Rather like the creation of a bill of rights on a national level, the declaration was the first time that rights had been articulated in a comprehensive manner on the international level.

In doing so, it put the human being at the center of international law. The ultimate authority for the declaration is not states, but the qualities of humanity that all the people of the world share. This is because, as the preamble states, "recognition of the inherent dignity and of the equal and inalienable rights of all members of the human family is the foundation of freedom, justice and peace in the world." The focus away from the state to the individual is why the declaration is "universal" rather than "international."

Indeed, the declaration suggests that human rights observance is the prerequisite for state authority. The state is given respect by its citizens and by other states because it is the legitimate representative of the collective of individuals within its control. Human rights principles represent the contract between the individual and their state that is the basis for this legitimacy. Both agree to abide by rights and obligations that allow the state to protect the interests of all individuals without restricting the rights of any given individual any more than is necessary. For a state to be legitimate, therefore, it has to keep to the contract. If the state breaks it (when there is "tyranny and oppression"), it is no longer worthy of respect and has lost the authority to govern. Taking its cue from the philosopher Thomas Paine, the preamble states that "it is essential, if man is not to be compelled to have recourse, as a last resort, to rebellion against tyranny and oppression, that human rights should be protected by the rule of law." This qualified notion of legitimacy makes human rights scrutiny on the international level compatible with state sovereignty. Human rights are no longer only of concern nationally; they are a global issue.

The Nature of the Declaration

An international legal instrument often consists of a preamble, which contains statements of principle, and articles, which contain substantive provisions that, if part of a treaty, are binding on states that ratify it. The declaration is not as straightforward.

As has been stated, the declaration forms part of the International Bill of Rights, together with the International Covenant on Civil and Political Rights (ICCPR) and the International Covenant on Economic, Social, and Cultural Rights (ICESCR). It was intended as a preamble-style statement of principles, with the Covenants then containing substantive provisions. The declaration was passed as a nonbinding resolution of the UN General Assembly; the covenants are treaties that states ratify and are bound by. It is misleading, however, to see the declaration as merely a statement of principle. Both internally and externally, the declaration has enforceable elements to it.

Internally, the declaration makes a distinction between a preamble and articles. Many of the articles are clearly capable of being enforced, since they became the basis for the enforceable articles in the covenants and have been lifted into the text of many national constitutions. Other articles, on the other hand, are more preamble-style statements of principle that either stand alone (Article 1 on the philosophical basis of human rights; Article 28 on the conditions necessary for rights to be realized) or lead onto the more substantive rights (Article 2 on the equality that is the basis for nondiscrimination in Article 7; Article 22 on the economic, social, and cultural rights that are then set out in Articles 23–27).

Externally, the declaration has come to have considerable influence in international law, notwithstanding its status as a nonbinding General Assembly resolution that represents a "common standard of achievement" (preamble). It confirmed human rights as an integral component of international law. This in turn highlighted states' obligations in customary international law to refrain from certain practices that violated rights. In 1984 the UN Human Rights Committee stated that, according to customary international law,

> a State may not . . . engage in slavery, . . torture, . . subject persons to cruel, inhuman or degrading treatment or punishment, to arbitrarily deprive persons of their lives, to arbitrarily arrest and detain persons, to deny freedom of thought, conscience and religion, to presume a person guilty unless he proves his innocence, to execute pregnant women or children, to permit the advocacy of national, racial or religious hatred,

> to deny to persons of marriageable age the right to marry, or to deny to minorities the right to enjoy their culture, profess their religion, or use their own language . . . [and generally speaking deny] the right to a fair trial.

Therefore, although the declaration may itself fall short of being enforceable on states, many of its provisions are at the very least binding against them because of customary international law.

How the Concept of Human Rights Works

The declaration is concerned with the rights of individuals. Rights are what individuals are entitled to, by virtue of being human beings. This is therefore a focus on the most basic elements of being human. The drafters attempted to sum up the essential needs that they felt all individuals have, irrespective of differences between them, such as culture, religion, nationality, and gender.

The declaration splits these needs up into two categories—civil and political rights, on the one hand, and economic and social rights on the other. The categories are sometimes called "first" and "second" generation rights respectively.

Civil and political rights are those which, broadly, concern individuals enjoying control over their own lives. The declaration covers them in Articles 2–21, and they include the principles of equal treatment (Articles 2 and 7) and freedom of expression (Article 19). They often operate in a negative sense, in that they declare the right of an individual not to be prevented from doing something (e.g., joining an association, Article 20) or not to be treated in a certain way (e.g., being held in slavery, Article 4). In order to protect negative rights, the state must refrain from interfering in the individual's life.

Economic, social, and cultural rights are those which, broadly, concern the welfare of individuals in the sense of how they can support and sustain themselves. The declaration covers them in Articles 22-27, and they include the right to work (Article 23) and the right to education (Article 26). They often operate in a positive sense, in that they declare the right of an individual to have something (e.g., a humane standard of living, Article 25). In order to protect positive rights, the state must do or give something to improve the individual's life.

However, the distinction between positive and negative rights as between civil and political rights and economic and social rights is not straightforward. Although some civil and political rights require the state in effect to do nothing (e.g., not to torture individuals, Article 5), many actually require some form of positive action. This includes enforcing the negative obligations of individuals not to restrict the rights of others (e.g., preventing private individuals from torturing other individuals) and providing procedural guarantees that safeguard the protection of rights and the rule of law (e.g., the right to a remedy for violations, Article 8). Similarly, although many economic, social,

and cultural rights require the state to take positive action (e.g., providing social security, Article 22), some involve negative obligations, requiring the state not to interfere with individual choice (e.g., the right to free choice of employment, Article 23). Generally, human rights law scrutinizes a state's adherence to negative rights differently from its promotion of positive rights, since the former does not depend on the level of resources available to the state in the same way that the latter does.

In seeking to guarantee the realization of individuals' needs, human rights are necessarily concerned with regulating the relationship between individuals and those who affect this realization. Just as international law has traditionally concerned states, so international human rights law—although introducing the individual as a subject of international law—is conventionally seen as concerning the rights of individuals as against the state (the "public" actor), rather than as against other individuals or entities ("private" actors). Therefore, the right to education, for example, is about the state ensuring that individuals within its country are provided with education.

The enjoyment of some rights is influenced almost solely by the state, such as the right to a nationality (Article 15). However, the enjoyment of many rights is often influenced by both public and private actors. The right to education, for example, is affected by the state (e.g., in its operation of state-run schools) and by private actors (e.g., parents making choices for their children; the operation of privately run schools). Human rights law regulates both actors via the state: the public actor directly and the private actor indirectly. This is because the state, as the sovereign authority, can be construed as having ultimate responsibility not only for its own actions but also for the actions of those within its jurisdiction. For example, if a private school provides education in a discriminatory manner (contrary to Articles 7 and 26) and the state does nothing about it, then the state is arguably liable in international human rights law.

Recently this distinction between public and private has been criticized by those who argue that human rights law should be brought to bear on the behavior of private actors in a more imaginative way. Feminists argue, for example, that the starting point of public liability inevitably makes human rights focus more on those abuses perpetrated against men (e.g., when dealt with by the police, a public body) than those perpetrated against women (e.g., domestic violence, which takes place in a private place and involves a private actor). More generally, in a globalized and fragmented world, private actors—from multinational corporations to militias—are in many respects as determinative of individuals' rights as states. This shifts the balance away from the state's direct liability for its own actions to its indirect liability for the actions of those within its jurisdiction.

The drafters clearly had in mind the obligations of the state when they created the declaration. However, they drafted it in a way that deliberately left open the scope for conceiving ways of promoting rights and did not limit their focus to the behavior of states. Fifty years after the declaration, human rights scholars are beginning to suggest ways in which private actors can be brought within the purview of human rights law in a more meaningful way.

Human rights regulates relationships to enable individuals to realize their needs in different ways. Often such relationships involve rights and responsibilities (or duties) on both sides. For example, the right to freedom of religion (Article 18) concerns the individual's right to practice his or her religion but his or her duty not to force it on other people (which would violate other individuals' rights to practice their religions). This corresponds to the state's duty not to restrict the individual's practice of his or her religion in normal circumstances, but its right to do so when this involves forcing religious beliefs on other people. Sometimes, however, individual rights are absolute (such as the right not to be tortured in Article 5), in that the state has no right to restrict them in any circumstances.

The declaration articulates a model for regulating relationships which places an emphasis first and foremost on the individual's rights. In doing so it presumes that an individual is entitled to a right and requires a state to justify limiting the right if this is possible. In its practical application, therefore, human rights often amount to an evaluation of the legitimate boundaries of the state. The principles of Article 29, which test whether a state's limitation on rights is justified, are central to many human rights questions.

The declaration is a "common standard of achievement for all peoples and all nations" (preamble). It is a set of fundamental principles that applies to all people because it is rooted in the universal needs of the human condition. It tests particular situations to evaluate what an individual's entitlements are. In doing so, it takes into account the context in which the situation takes place. For example, with the right to education the amount of provision necessary depends on the resources of a state. A developed country would be expected to make more education available than a developing country. The "common standard" is whether both are making the best effort they can to direct all available resources to areas outlined in human rights law.

How the Declaration Envisions the Promotion of Human Rights

The declaration began what has become a worldwide movement to promote "universal respect for and observance of human rights" (preamble). This involves evaluating the human rights situation in countries to see whether it complies with international human rights law.

The drafters saw the promotion of human rights as important to develop "friendly relations between nations" (preamble). They had in mind the risk to peace posed by states who did not safeguard rights in their own territories and wished to enforce concepts that violated rights (e.g., the superiority of a certain race) on

other countries through violent means. The promotion of human rights in other states has now become a key part of the foreign policy of many countries, such as the United States. If respect for a state's sovereignty depends on the level of human rights protection in that country, then indirect and even direct interference from outside becomes justifiable. Thus human rights promotion by states can actually lead to hostile relations between nations— but from an attempt to promote rights, not destroy them.

The declaration envisions a broad range of enforcement mechanisms that reflect the diverse nature of human rights issues. It proclaims the necessity of "progressive measures, national and international" to ensure the "universal and effective recognition and observance" of rights (Preamble). The UN plays a key role in this process, by setting human rights standards and then monitoring states' compliance. States, NGOs, and international organizations have all been involved in implementing measures to promote human rights. These have ranged from coordinating development strategies (e.g., the activities of the UN Development Program) to sanctions (e.g., against apartheid-era South Africa).

The declaration insists, however, that this "recognition and observance" of human rights has to be "universal and effective" (preamble). It is not enough that states sign up to human rights treaties, if they continue to violate rights within their country. It is not enough for states to appraise other countries according to the standards of human rights, if they are not prepared to accept such standards themselves. It is not enough that some states observe human rights standards, if other states do not. It is not enough for human rights promotion mechanisms to deal with rights issues on a particular scale (e.g., individual violations) if they cannot deal effectively with those on another scale (e.g., mass violations of human rights like "disappearances").

Human rights promotion does not merely involve the creation of legal provisions on a national and international level. The principles that these laws uphold should become part of cultures and societies generally. People should be aware of their rights, and the language of rights should inform the way they relate to each other, their communities, and their country. The drafters had this in mind when they stated in the preamble that "every individual and every organ of society . . . shall strive by teaching and education to promote respect for these rights and freedoms." This in turn should lead states and other actors who play a decisive role in the lives of individuals to evaluate the boundaries of this role in terms of human rights principles. Therefore, it is important that the process of raising awareness is seen as a goal in its own right, rather than a spin-off of human rights law enforcement.

How the Declaration Can Claim to Be Universal

For an instrument that proclaims itself universal, the declaration came out of a process that was far from globally inclusive. It was based on the philosophical traditions of the West and drafted by a handful of individuals mostly from the West. It was passed in a General Assembly where many countries in the world were not represented because they were colonies (only one African country—Egypt—was a member), through a vote in which socialist countries abstained.

For this reason, the declaration and the human rights movement that it precipitated have been criticized as a neo-imperialist attempt by the West to "civilize" the majority of the world's peoples who do not share their cultural heritage. Indeed, the entire structure of international law is based on European notions of state sovereignty. The countries that emerged from colonialism or had been powerless during the so-called "Age of Empire" had little choice but to accept a system that they played no direct part in creating.

However, the power of the declaration is precisely that it has transcended the circumstances in which it was drafted. It has been able to do so because of two important features: its emphasis on the indivisibility of all rights and its simple enunciation of them.

First, the combined effect of Cold War compromise and New Deal social democracy created a declaration that forcefully underlined what has become a fundamental principle of human rights: the indivisibility of civil and political rights on the one hand, and economic and social rights on the other. The preamble reminds states that in the UN Charter they "reaffirmed their faith in fundamental human rights, in the dignity and worth of the human person and in the equal rights of men and women and have determined to promote social progress and better standards of life in larger freedom."

In articulating a model of interdependent civil, political, economic, social, and cultural rights, the declaration makes a bold attempt to incorporate all of the various needs that are emphasized differently around the world. Whereas some in the developed world view rights mainly in civil and political terms, this is a misrepresentation of the declaration. To object to a nation's emphasis on civil and political rights is not to object to the declaration itself, merely to a selective view of it.

Second, in phrasing rights in simple terms, the declaration managed, mostly, to sum up the basic human needs that prevail regardless of considerable changes in circumstances. The human rights instruments that came after it were necessary to flesh out the rights and explain how they could be realized in a practical manner. Inevitably, however, this makes them more contingent on the particular circumstances of the time when they were drafted and the views of those who drafted them. The European Commission on Human Rights, for example, included an exception to the right to life allowing judicial execution, a practice that was carried out in several European states at the time. Now it has been abolished in all the original states of the Council of Europe, and new member states are required to sign a protocol outlawing the death penalty.

The declaration, in contrast, has managed to retain meaningfulness despite the profound changes in history, politics, culture, and development since the time of its drafting. Peoples struggling for independence from colonial rule used it as the inspiration for their claim to self-determination. Groups in the West, such as the lesbian, gay, and bisexual community, invoke the principles of the declaration to support their rights in ways that would have been inconceivable when it was drafted but which are nevertheless consistent with its provisions. The nations of Africa, when drafting the African Charter on Human and People's Rights, emphasized individual duties as well as rights and so elaborated on the provisions of Article 29.

The declaration, therefore, stands as a beacon for the potential of the human rights movement, rather than a fixed code that has no relevance in these postmodern times. Despite the lack of progress in the international protection of human rights during the Cold War (the UDHR was the only global human rights instrument from 1948 to 1976) the declaration reemerged in the 1990s as the core of a new human rights movement. This movement is not about Western governments seeking to export their version of democracy, either as an alternative to Communism or to redeem the people of the developing world. It is not about "us" who have rights, and "them" who don't.

The contemporary human rights movement is a genuinely global phenomenon, as individuals around the world use the declaration as the starting point for articulating the needs that they have. A very different General Assembly from that which passed the declaration, this time made up of countries from all around the world, continues to elaborate many of the principles within the declaration. This has created a human rights agenda that is both rooted in the declaration and genuinely reflective of the diversity of needs around the world.

The language of human rights has been reclaimed from states and their leaders by the very people to whom the declaration originally spoke. States that have traditionally seen human rights as something to be exported, like the United States and United Kingdom, now find their own human rights records being criticized by the very movement they helped to create. Authoritarian leaders who claim that human rights are incompatible with their peoples' cultures find those very people using the language of rights against them.

In both cases, value is added to the validity of human rights as a genuinely universal phenomenon. It is "brought home" to those countries that are complacent; it is refashioned to reflect the human rights struggles of different cultures and regions.

Eleanor Roosevelt intended that the declaration be a "living instrument" so that it could precipitate the "common understanding" of rights and freedoms that the preamble states "is of the greatest importance." This approach can be credited for the continuing relevance and utility of the declaration to the human rights issues that people face. It is an inspiration for each individual's articulation of his or her particular needs; as Eleanor Roosevelt said, an "international magna carta for all men everywhere."

— Ralph Wilde

CHAPTER THREE

An Analysis of the Universal Declaration of Human Rights

PREAMBLE

Whereas recognition of the inherent dignity and of the equal and inalienable rights of all members of the human family is the foundation of freedom, justice and peace in the world,

Whereas disregard and contempt for human rights have resulted in barbarous acts which have outraged the conscience of mankind, and the advent of a world in which human beings shall enjoy freedom of speech and belief and freedom from fear and want has been proclaimed as the highest aspiration of the common people,

Whereas it is essential, if man is not to be compelled to have recourse, as a last resort, to rebellion against tyranny and oppression, that human rights should be protected by the rule of law,

Whereas it is essential to promote the development of friendly relations between nations,

Whereas the peoples of the United Nations have in the Charter reaffirmed their faith in fundamental human rights, in the dignity and worth of the human person and in the equal rights of men and women and have determined to promote social progress and better standards of life in larger freedom,

Whereas Member States have pledged themselves to achieve, in cooperation with the United Nations, the promotion of universal respect for and observance of human rights and fundamental freedoms,

Whereas a common understanding of these rights and freedoms is of the greatest importance for the full realization of this pledge,

Now, therefore, The General Assembly proclaims this Universal Declaration of Human Rights as a common standard of achievement for all peoples and all nations, to the end that every individual and every organ of society, keeping this Declaration constantly in mind, shall strive by teaching and education to promote respect for these rights and freedoms and by progressive measures, national and international, to secure their universal and effective recognition and observance, both among the peoples of Member States themselves and among the peoples of territories under their jurisdiction.

The preamble explains the motivations behind the declaration. The first three paragraphs outline the basis for the notion of human rights. The next four paragraphs declare a commitment to the promotion of human rights on the international level. The final paragraph explains what the declaration stands for, and how it should be implemented.

In the final paragraph, the preamble sets forth some goals for human rights promotion. Today it is widely understood that the promotion of human rights does not merely involve the creation of legal provisions on a national and international level. The principles that these laws uphold should become part of cultures and societies generally. People should be aware of their rights, and the language of rights should become part of the way they relate to each other, their communities, and their country. This in turn should lead states and other actors who play a decisive role in the lives of individuals to evaluate the boundaries of this role in terms of human rights principles. It is important that this process of awareness raising is seen as a goal in its own right, rather than a spin-off of the enforcement of human rights law. To this end, the United Nations General Assembly proclaimed 1995-2004 as the Decade of Human Rights Education.

ARTICLE 1

All human beings are born free and equal in dignity and rights. They are endowed with reason and conscience and should act towards one another in a spirit of brotherhood.

Article 1 is the cornerstone of the entire declaration. It echoes Western Enlightenment philosophy on the nature of rights and sets out the fundamental concept of humanity that is the basis for human rights. The notions of "reason and conscience" make women and men "human beings" [see Chapter 1, Section 6]. The concepts of liberty, equality, and fraternity (sic) are the basis for human relations between each other and with the state.

Even though Article 1 is a statement of principle, rather than a particular right, the drafters included it in the main body of the declaration to give the concept particular emphasis. It was felt that after the intolerance and brutality of World War II, the notion of humanity needed to be forcefully reasserted, rather than merely presumed. This is indeed why the United Nations engaged in drafting a set of principles to be "declared" that were at the same time considered by Western countries to be self-evident.

Article 1 acknowledges an origin of human rights in Western philosophical and religious traditions, notwithstanding the removal of references to "God" and "nature" that were proposed during drafting. Although "human beings" was adopted instead of the original proposal of "men," a suggestion to include "sisterhood" as well as "brotherhood" was rejected.

In declaring that "all human beings are born free and equal in dignity and rights," Article 1 underscores the Enlightenment idea that rights exist by virtue of the human condition. Individuals have rights because they are human beings, not because of their social status or because they have been given them by the state, rights are inalienable. Freedom and equality are the birthright of being human. Human rights law merely reflects this reality in a legal form, rather than bestowing rights upon people who would otherwise not have them. However, having a right is not the same as being able to exercise that right in a practical sense. Individuals whose rights are abused have not "lost" their rights—they are being prevented from exercising them. Human rights law is concerned with where the boundaries lie for the exercise of rights—not with the existence of the rights themselves.

The authority for the doctrine of human rights—why rights should be respected—is the "reason and conscience" of human beings. It is the ability to reason, to know the difference between right and wrong, and to be aware of other human beings and their needs, that distinguishes humans from animals. This is the part of Article 1 with the most overt philosophical or religious connotations, and during the drafting of the declaration, there was considerable debate as to whether reference should be made to the source of humanity's reason and conscience. It was originally articulated as "being endowed by nature with reason and conscience," with "nature" meaning either human nature (man's essential characteristics) or God. The drafters kept "nature" out, so that the declaration would not enshrine a particularly rigid definition of the basis for human rights.

Article 1 posits the basis for human relations when rights are protected: mutual tolerance, respect, and self-help (". . . should act towards one another in a spirit of brotherhood"). Individuals bind with one another in society as the best way of each attaining their individual potential: they achieve more together than they would separately. Society operates like a family (early drafts mentioned "family" instead of "brotherhood") where members are able to both follow their own paths and be part of something more than themselves. This leads on to Article 29, which sets out the duties of the individual which are the consequence of having rights.

The ideological basis for human rights is a constantly debated topic. Undoubtedly, the drafting of the declaration was rooted in the history and traditions of a particular group of countries. However, it was articulated in a way that is open and meaningful to the people with other histories and traditions who now make up the global human rights movement.

ARTICLE 2

Everyone is entitled to all the rights and freedoms set forth in this Declaration, without distinction of any kind, such as race, colour, sex, language, religion, political or other opinion, national or social origin, property, birth or other status.

Furthermore, no distinction shall be made on the basis of the political, jurisdictional or international status of the country or territory to which a person belongs, whether it be independent, trust, non-self-governing or under any other limitation of sovereignty.

Articles 2 and 7 both concern the concept of equality. Article 2 sets out the general principles; Article 7 sets out the practicalities of promoting equality in domestic law.

The main impetus for Articles 2 and 7 came from the horrible legacy of World War II, where people were sent to the gas chambers because of particular aspects of their identity: religion, culture, and ethnicity (the Jews and the Gypsies); nationality (the Poles); political opinion (Communists and other political opponents of the Nazis); physical ability (disabled people); and sexual orientation (homosexuals). Various "minorities treaties" after World War I had guaranteed equality and nondiscrimination for certain minorities, but were imposed selectively upon weak states in Europe. Following on from several references in the UN Charter, the drafters of the declaration wanted to emphasize the centrality of equality as the basis for all human rights, and applicable to all people (Article 2) as well as equal treatment as a particular right in and of itself (Article 7).

Equality in human rights law means the equal value of people who may be very different. A human rights-based society is one where the differences between people do not mean that they are entitled to different rights. No "distinction" should be made between people on the basis of arbitrary aspects of their identity. In other words, when decisions are made that affect people's rights, choices should not be made between certain groups in society, preventing some groups from the same opportunities as others. There should be "equal opportunity."

Societies are not homogenous. Various aspects of people's identities are determinative of how they regard themselves and are treated by others, from their gender to their religion. Each aspect may be derived from a particular group identity, such as a political movement or an ethnic tradition. In some cultures the notion of the group is extremely influential, and the 1986 African (Banjul) Charter on Human and People's Rights (ACHR) reflects the importance of this by declaring in Article 19 that "all peoples shall be equal. Nothing shall justify the domination of a people by another." In other cultures people may engage with many different groups and be affected by society differently between them. Human rights do not seek to erode the commonality between groups, nor prevent people from engaging with different groups, by seeking to homogenize people's identities. Instead it wants to promote tolerance and respect between different identities, allowing people to relate to the identities they prefer, without imposing those preferences on others.

Article 2 suggests that no distinction is justifiable. However, human rights law has come to focus on prohibiting distinctions based on certain grounds, rather than distinction in and of itself. For example, employers are allowed to choose between job applicants based on their merit but cannot normally choose employees because of their ethnicity. How are the prohibited grounds decided upon? One approach is to look at distinctions that do not have a "good reason" (i.e., one related to the subject matter of the distinction). For example, restricting the vote to people over a certain age has a good reason (voting requires adults who understand the political process), while restricting the vote to people of a certain ethnicity does not (it would be for another reason—racism—unrelated to the needs of voting). Another approach is to look at distinctions based on categories that have historically been denied equal rights, like women and members of minority groups.

The list of prohibited distinctions in Article 2 is not exhaustive (". . . any kind, such as . . ."). Other issues that have since been recognized as unjustified grounds for distinction include childcare status, ethnic descent, marital status, physical disability, sexual orientation and identity, and veteran status. During drafting, the Soviet Union wanted an exception to "political or other opinion" that would allow distinctions to prevent opinion which was itself discriminatory. This was blocked, since it was felt important that there be no hierarchy of ideas in terms of what can be expressed, even if the idea itself is condemned by the declaration. (The question of whether "hate speech" should be prohibited remains controversial.) The issues of gender and race were developed further in conventions of their own: the 1979 Convention on the Elimination of All Forms of Discrimination Against Women (CEDAW) and the 1969 Convention on the Elimination of All Forms of Racial Discrimination (CERD).

The second paragraph of Article 2 reflects the times during which the declaration was drafted. Some people in the world lived in territories which had been occupied by or were dominions of the defeated powers in the war and were being "protected" by the allied powers; others lived in colonies and did not enjoy the same rights as people in the colonizing country. These territories and colonies were often not sovereign states, and so not entitled to equal treatment with states in international law. Article 2 declares that, regardless of the status of their territory, the people within it are human beings and have rights equal to those of the people in sovereign states. This illustrates how human rights moved international law away from the idea that people have rights by virtue of where they live, and towards the idea that they have rights by virtue of being human.

ARTICLE 3

Everyone has the right to life, liberty and security of person.

Article 3 sets out the three main areas of rights in the sphere of personal integrity (the physical right over one's own body). This is the classic area where the state should ensure that it and other entities do not interfere with the individual, and it is the starting point for protecting individual dignity and rights in a practical sense.

The right to life is the right to be able to live, both in the sense of not being killed and being provided with the sustenance to stay alive (the right to health in Article 25). The right to liberty is the freedom to do whatever you want to do, from movement (Article 13) to expression (Article 19) to religious practice (Article 18). This is subject to the limitations outlined in Article 29, to protect the liberties of others. Particular limits on this right in the sphere of arrest, detention, and exile are dealt with in Article 9. The right to "security of person" is the right to be safe from physical interference, and it is further dealt with in Article 5 through the limitation on torture and cruel, inhuman, and degrading treatment or punishment. The right to life is covered below; the rights to liberty and security of the person are covered in the articles mentioned above.

The right to life is the most fundamental right of all. Although it was stated simply and bundled together with liberty and security of person in the declaration, subsequent treaties made it a freestanding article and attempted to develop those components that are implicit in it (e.g., the International Covenant on Civil and Political Rights, Article 6). However, attempts to define "life" and examine whether limitation of it is possible involve difficult ethical and religious questions, which are not susceptible to a clear-cut resolution.

How is "life" defined: where does it begin and end? The 1978 Inter-American Convention on Human Rights (IACHR), signed by the Organization of American States (OAS) states that life begins "generally at conception," but other instruments do not take a position on whether life begins at conception or birth. As with many human rights issues, pregnancy touches upon more than one right. Pro-life advocates cite their right to "manifest [their] religion" in Article 18 as well as Article 3 as a basis for seeking to prevent abortion. Pro-choice advocates cite the right of women not to be subjected to "interference with [their] privacy," insisting that Article 3 does not cover the fetus or at any rate should be balanced against the rights of the mother. As far as the end of life is concerned, human rights treaties often include a duty on the part of the state to protect life (e.g., ICCPR Article 6[1]). Could this ever be squared with euthanasia?

Can and should judicial execution (having the death penalty for certain crimes) be an exception to the right to life? All of the main human rights treaties clearly allow for judicial execution (e.g., ICCPR Article 6[2]). They only permit it in certain circumstances, however. It should be only for the most serious crimes and given after a court judgment; defendants should have the right to seek a pardon or commutation of the sentence; it should not be used on pregnant women, or people below eighteen or over seventy; and it should not be extended to new crimes or reestablished where it has been abolished. Furthermore, human rights campaigners have used the prohibition on cruel, inhuman, and degrading treatment from Article 5, arguing that if it is contrary to human rights to torture someone, it must be so to kill them, or at least to kill them in a particularly cruel or degrading manner.

Can the right of life be limited to protect other lives or society as a whole? Some human rights treaties, following on from the permissible limitations in Articles 29 and 30, do not prohibit the loss of life as a consequence of the necessary use of force (e.g., ECHR Article 2[2]). This can only be used to defend someone from violence, to effect an arrest, or to quell a riot. Furthermore, it must be used to protect or preserve another life, and it must be the only available option to achieve this.

ARTICLE 4

No one shall be held in slavery or servitude; slavery and the slave trade shall be prohibited in all their forms.

Article 4 seeks to outlaw situations where an individual's freedom is limited by being in some form of permanent subservience toward other individuals. Slavery is a situation where one individual is the property of another. Servitude is a wider notion, akin to slavery, where individuals are not owned by others, but have a considerable part of their freedom controlled by them.

Abhorrence of slavery was one of the earliest human rights concerns. Although slavery flourished in the nineteenth century, treaties were signed outlawing it as early as the Paris Peace Treaty of 1814. Along with measures against piracy, the prohibition on slavery was the precursor to the modern idea of universal jurisdiction for war crimes. These crimes give rise to universal jurisdiction because they are considered so shocking to humanity that any country in the world can try an individual suspected of committing them, even if the suspect is not their national, and the crime did not take place in that country or involve its citizens. From 1919 onwards several conventions focused exclusively on slavery and servitude (e.g., the 1927 Slavery Convention), and the League of Nations instituted a Slavery Commission to outlaw the practice. In prohibiting the slave trade as well as slavery, Article 4 acknowledges that those responsible for continuing slavery may be private actors, such as slave traders. Therefore, the state must take active measures, beyond simply outlawing slavery in law, in order to end the practice.

The notion of servitude has become gradually more important, since merely prohibiting relationships that conform to the formal notion of "property" did not prevent many of the most serious practices where people had their freedom limited. In many cultures "serfs" have been bound for centuries to live and labor on land owned by another person and are unable to change this status. The concept of servitude now also covers situations such as forced labor and debt bondage (also known as bonded labor), as well as treatment of women and children that is considered exploitative. This shift of emphasis was reflected in the creation in 1974 of the UN Working Group on Contemporary Forms of Slavery, which monitors the existence of slavery and slavery-type practices worldwide.

Forced labor is work that an individual is made to do against his or her will. Human rights treaties (e.g., ICCPR Article 8) accept that forced labor is permissible in certain circumstances, such as a criminal sentence, military or national service, service during times of danger or calamity which threaten the existence of the well-being of the community, and normal civic obligations. Such service must be rendered for the public good. Therefore it can only be conducted under the supervision and control of public authorities and should never be for the benefit of private individuals. Prisoners can only be made to work in a way that respects their dignity. Debt bondage is the pledge by a debtor of her or his personal services as security for a debt. This is permissible only if the value of the services is reasonably assessed, the services are applied to the liquidation of the debt, and the length and the nature of the services are limited and defined.

Human rights law also defines servitude as practices and customs that exploit women and children. In many cultures, the institution of marriage originated as the acquisition of the wife from her parents by her husband, akin to the acquisition of property. Conventions on women's rights, such as the 1979 Convention on the Elimination of All Forms of Discrimination Against Women (CEDAW), outlaw those aspects of marriage that perpetuate this servile status for the wife (CEDAW Article 16). These include arranged marriages that the woman does not have the right to refuse or in which she is inherited by another person upon her husband's death. The state is obliged to promote the removal of these practices through introducing a minimum age for and the civil registration of marriage so that the free consent of the parties can be established. Some instruments (e.g., the 1951 Convention for the Suppression of the Traffic in Persons and of the Exploitation of the Prostitution of Others) also view prostitution as akin to slavery and prohibit the keeping of brothels. Just as the abolition of slavery was originally not only a liberty issue but also a racial one, so the campaigns against current forms of slavery and servitude are as much about gender issues as they are about freedom.

Children's rights instruments (e.g., the 1989 Convention on the Rights of the Child [CRC]) focus on the relationship between the child and the parent as well as between the child and the state. This qualifies the notions that children are akin to the property of their parents and that parents have a free reign over their children until they reach the age of majority. They seek to outlaw child labor, as well as the more recent phenomena of child pornography and prostitution. In many "developing" nations, families cannot subsist without being able to involve all members in supporting the family unit. Child labor issues, therefore, cannot be addressed in isolation from the wider economic context involved.

ARTICLE 5

No one shall be subjected to torture or cruel, inhuman or degrading treatment or punishment.

Article 5 seeks to prohibit particularly appalling abuse perpetrated against individuals. The use of the word "inhuman" connects it to the concept of human dignity that is the basis for human rights, and subsequent human rights instruments state that it is incapable of being limited (e.g., ICCPR Article 4).

Article 5 covers both torture and treatment or punishment that does not amount to torture but which is cruel, inhuman, or degrading. It is one of the few declaration rights that is as important in times of war as it is in peacetime, because it is connected to the laws of war (also called humanitarian law) which govern the treatment of prisoners of war and civilians during conflict. Article 5 has led to specific UN and European conventions that deal with the right in more detail, and in the case of the 1989 European Torture Convention, include a monitoring body that has become in effect a regional prison inspection committee. The equivalent articles in regional treaties (ECHR Article 3 and IACHR Article 5) have led in Europe to many prisoners' rights cases, and in the Americas to investigatory visits by the Inter-American Commission.

The drafters of the declaration had in mind physical abuse of a horrific nature. The article was intended to prevent valid state activities, such as the investigation of crimes or the punishment of offenders, from going beyond what is humane. Examples of this might be criminal suspects being tortured in order to obtain a confession, or those found guilty of a criminal offense being publicly executed. It is the stereotypical human rights abuse and has traditionally been the subject of much human rights activism.

Article 5 has since come to be interpreted in a broader, more complex way. Feminist critiques have argued that being "subjected" to abuse should cover not only predominantly male victims of state violence, but also behavior between individuals, such as gender-related abuse like domestic violence. Furthermore, it now covers not only physical but also psychological abuse. For example, the European Court of Human Rights determined that the conditions on death row in the United States, with prolonged delays and frequent last-minute appeals, amount to cruel and inhuman treatment.

There is disagreement as to the scope of each aspect of Article 5. How far does punishment have to go before it becomes unacceptable? On the question of the death penalty, human rights tribunals have held that certain execution methods contravene the principles of Article 5, such as the use of gas, with its connection to the Holocaust, and the use of electric shocks, which echo torture methods.

ARTICLE 6

Everyone has the right to recognition everywhere as a person before the law.

Article 6 covers the right to have a legal personality. Individuals have obligations under the law and are entitled to use the law to protect their rights. The legal systems of most countries presume legal personality for all individuals.

The right to legal personality is the starting point for the application of human rights principles in a practical, legal sense. This is developed by the right to be treated equally by the law (Article 7) and the right to a remedy for human rights violations (Article 8). These articles are also part of the series of procedural guarantees ensuring that the machinery of law and order safeguards human rights. Other articles in this series are the right not to be arbitrarily arrested or detained (Article 9), the right to a fair trial (Article 10), and the right to be presumed innocent in criminal trials (Article 11). The drafters were responding to the fascism that had prevailed in parts of Europe, where those with power exercised control over individuals through oppressive force. Human rights seeks to regulate the use of power through the rule of law.

Law regulates the behavior of individuals and other actors, and their relations with each other, from enforceable agreements (contracts) to ownership of property, family law, torts and the prohibition of certain antisocial behavior (crime). It also describes the way the state is set up (constitutional law) and regulates how it operates (public or administrative law). In order to be a full part of all of the areas of human activity covered by law, an individual has to have legal personality. For example, contract law gives two individuals with legal personality the capacity to make an agreement which, if in conformity with the law, will bind both of them. If one violates the agreement, the other has the right to go to a court and have the court force the other person to honor it. Some people do not have the right to represent themselves—children, for example. However, they still have legal personality—it is just being exercised on their behalf.

Like Article 3 on the right to life, Article 6 avoids addressing the controversial issue of where legal personality begins and ends.

When does someone start to have legal personality, at conception or birth? In many legal systems abortion is prohibited apart from certain circumstances (e.g., when the life of the mother is threatened), and a fetus can be allowed to inherit in a will. In other countries abortion is prohibited entirely. This could be ascribing some form of partial legal personality to the fetus, or instead merely considering it an object protected by the law.

Another controversy surrounds the loss of legal personality. People who are "brain dead" can be kept alive artificially for many years, and at some point the life-support systems may be turned off. Missing persons are declared dead after a certain period of years. Can human rights law develop considerations to apply when such difficult decisions are made? At the very least it requires procedural guarantees so that the right to declare someone dead is not abused, such as when it is used to intentionally deprive someone known to be alive of their rights.

ARTICLE 7

All are equal before the law and are entitled without any discrimination to equal protection of the law. All are entitled to equal protection against any discrimination in violation of this Declaration and against any incitement to such discrimination.

Article 7 takes the principle of equality from Article 2 and suggests how it should be promoted on a legal level. Equality is put into practice through three approaches: equality before the law, equal protection under the law, and protection against discrimination.

Equality before the law means that the law should apply to all people equally. Nobody should be above the law by virtue of the particular status they have in society. The drafters considered highlighting certain groups who have sometimes escaped being fully subject to the law (such as judges and public officials) but decided that this was unnecessary. Equal protection of the law means that everyone should enjoy the same protection that the law can offer. This has in mind those countries where certain people were outside the full protection of the law (e.g., because they were not full citizens, like in apartheid-era South Africa).

Discrimination has been defined in CEDAW and CERD as any distinction, exclusion, restriction, or preference based on one of the prohibited categories (see Article 2), which has the purpose or effect of nullifying or impairing the recognition, enjoyment, or exercise, on an equal footing, of human rights. The test is whether the discrimination is reasonable and objective, and with the aim of achieving a legitimate purpose. Discrimination can be direct or indirect. Direct discrimination is when someone is prevented from doing something for a reason based on one of the prohibited categories, e.g., being denied the right to vote because of their religion. Indirect (or "disparate impact") discrimi-

nation is when a distinction is applied equally to all groups, but has a disparate impact on them. For example, after desegregation in the southern United States, applicants for some manual jobs were given educational tests that were irrelevant to the jobs in question. Because the effects of desegregation had left black applicants disproportionately lacking in education, they were at a disadvantage in completing the tests. Superficially neutral treatment was in substance discriminatory. Since the tests did not measure skills required for the jobs, they were ruled unlawful because they had a discriminatory effect which was not reasonable and did not achieve a legitimate purpose.

How far should the state go in combating discrimination? Many countries feel that it is not enough to have antidiscrimination laws on the statute books, but they should also play an active role in promoting tolerance and diversity and discouraging discriminatory practices. This has led, for example, to government commissions that help individuals who wish to bring discrimination cases in the courts. They support individual victims of discrimination and highlight problems generally.

Many countries have a history of discrimination in their societies, from slavery to the oppression of women. This can mean a background of injustice between groups, where the prosperity of one took place on the backs of the another (e.g., whites and blacks in the United States and South Africa). It can also mean gross inequalities between them (from levels of income to political representation), even when the discrimination that led to this has been outlawed. Antidiscrimination law cannot reverse overnight the legacy of discrimination in a particular society. This has led to "positive discrimination," where discrimination which would otherwise be prohibited is allowed or even mandated, so as to redress the balance. The consequence is that those groups who previously benefited from discrimination now suffer under it.

Positive discrimination perpetuates the idea of treating people differently according to the group they belong to. Critics argue that this risks promoting tensions between groups and thus the prejudice that leads to discrimination. They also point out that positive discrimination regards members of a group—such as racial minorities—as homogenous, even though each minority may have suffered differently in the past and so face a different legacy in the present.

Proponents of positive discrimination argue that it can be justified at least as a temporary measure to deal with a significant inequality in an especially important area of life. For example, it is important that the holders of public positions, such as judges and political representatives, are representative of the diversity in the society they have to judge or represent. Their positions are too important for them to be representative only of the stage that society has reached in having different backgrounds proportionally represented. Positive discrimination achieves diversity in these key positions at a quicker pace than would happen with standard discrimination law alone.

ARTICLE 8

Everyone has the right to an effective remedy by competent national tribunals for acts violating the fundamental rights granted him by the constitution or by law.

It is not enough to have rights on paper. Individuals need to be able to enforce them by having a remedy for violations. Article 8 declares that human rights remedies should ideally be provided on the national level, through individuals bringing complaints before national tribunals. Thus far, human rights law has developed a more sophisticated set of remedies in the civil and political sphere than it has in the economic, social, and cultural sphere.

Human rights law gives individuals legal rights on the international level. Therefore, international mechanisms have developed to monitor states' compliance with their human rights obligations, including tribunals where individuals can bring cases against their own states for violations of civil and political rights. Such tribunals include the UN Human Rights Committee, the European Court of Human Rights, and the Inter-American Commission and Court of Human Rights. Individuals of countries that allow their citizens access to human rights tribunals have international remedies for violations of international law.

However, state compliance with international human rights law means more than merely allowing individuals international remedies. States should incorporate their international obligations into national law, so that human rights questions can be determined by national courts. This allows a culture of human rights to develop, as a framework that applies to important everyday questions affecting individuals and their relationships with each other, the state, and other actors. Human rights are interpreted in tune with national traditions and cultures, and violations are remedied on a national level. Instead of having to take the costly and lengthy trip to an international tribunal, individuals can bring human rights cases to national courts as a matter of course. International tribunals remain a crucial remedy of last resort, when the national human rights system has failed to accord the full remedy appropriate for a particular violation. In the European Convention system, for example, there have been far more cases from countries that have not incorporated the provisions of the Convention into national law (such as, until very recently, the United Kingdom) than those who have incorporated it.

What amounts to an effective remedy by a competent national tribunal? Individuals are entitled to be able to go to a body, such as a court, have their human rights question decided, and obtain redress. The competent body need not necessarily be a court, but it must be able to adequately deal with the question before it and have the power to remedy the situation if necessary. Human rights questions to be decided in the civil and political sphere might include whether there is the threat of a rights violation in the future (e.g., a law which if enforced will violate rights), whether an individual has the right to do something (e.g., members of certain groups being denied the right to vote), and whether a particular action or situation violated human rights (e.g., the behavior of the police during a music festival). The redress should suit the issue at hand, which in the civil and political sphere range from compensation (e.g., for unlawful imprisonment) to a change of situation (e.g., allowing a newspaper to publish an article that had been censored) or law reform (e.g., amending discriminatory legislation).

ARTICLE 9

No one shall be subjected to arbitrary arrest, detention or exile.

Article 9 deals with three key limitations on the right to liberty in Article 3: arrest, detention, and exile. It concerns the boundaries for allowing such limitations.

An arrest takes place when an individual is prevented from moving freely by another individual. This takes place, for example, when a police officer reasonably suspects that someone may have committed a crime, and needs to command the suspect to accompany him or her to the police station for questioning. Detention is when an individual is confined within a certain area, usually a property or part of a property. This includes prison, a cell in a police station, "house arrest," or compulsory hospitalization. Exile is when an individual is banished from his or her country, either for a certain period of time or forever. Exile is now considered to be against customary international law, not least because it renders individuals stateless if they have no new country willing to grant them nationality (see Article 15).

These deprivations of liberty often take place in the context of criminal justice, both in the treatment of suspects and those convicted of an offense. They also occur in the context of medical health, education, immigration control, "vagrancy," and drug control.

Personal liberty is at the heart of human rights. Its importance has been stressed throughout Europe's history, from the Magna Carta of 1215 to the Declaration of Rights of 1789 during the French Revolution. Depriving individual liberty is not only serious in and of itself but also for the consequence it can have on other rights. It is an effective way of preventing the activities of political dissidents since it inhibits their freedom of movement (Article 13) and expression (Article 19), in turn undermining the democratic guarantees in Article 21. Moreover, other rights can be violated once an individual has been detained, such as torture and cruel, inhuman and degrading treatment and punishment (prohibited in Article 5).

Because of these concerns Article 9 states that deprivations of liberty can only take place when they are not arbitrary. The drafters, despite considering a more detailed explanation of what this basic concept meant, decided to leave it to subsequent instruments to elaborate a series of procedural guarantees (e.g., ICCPR Article 9 and ECHR Article 5), based on limitation principles in Article 29. These guarantees, described below, cover the basis for a justified deprivation of liberty, as well as safeguards to ensure that this standard is adhered to. They are reflected in many police rules and legal safeguards around the world. They are based on the premise that deprivation of liberty must be lawful, for a good reason, and proportionate to that reason.

The arrest or detention of an individual should be for the following reasons: first, to bring the individual before a competent legal authority when it is reasonably suspected that she or he has committed an offense; second, because the arresting officer reasonably considers it necessary to prevent the individual from committing another offense or fleeing after having done so; third, to ensure that a court order is enforced; fourth, to ensure that an individual does not enter the country without permission or to enforce a deportation or extradition order. In addition, detention is legitimate for the following reasons: first, when an individual has been convicted by a competent court; second, for the educational supervision of a minor; third, to prevent the spread of infectious diseases; and fourth, when an individual is of unsound mind, an alcoholic, a drug addict, or a vagrant.

People being arrested should be told the reason for the arrest, and the charges against them, at the time of the arrest and in a language that they understand. When an individual is arrested or detained, she or he is entitled to be taken promptly before a judge or other officer authorized by law (i.e., independent of the parties, especially public authorities like the prosecutor and the police) so that the lawfulness of his or her detention can be determined. When awaiting trial, individuals should not generally be held in custody, but their release can be subject to reappearing in court. If they are held in custody ("on remand"), this has to be justified (e.g., when there is a reasonable risk they will not return to court when requested, tamper with evidence or witnesses, or offend again). If any of these guarantees are not complied with, the individual is entitled to compensation.

ARTICLE 10

Everyone is entitled in full equality to a fair and public hearing by an independent and impartial tribunal, in the determination of his rights and obligations and of any criminal charge against him.

Article 10 declares the right to a fair trial (also called "due process"). Together with the provisions of other human rights instruments (e.g., ICCPR Article 14[1] and ECHR Article 6[1]), it sets out a series of guarantees which taken together make a trial fair. It is not enough that the law is just; the law must also be interpreted and applied in a just way. Moreover, justice must be subjective as well as objective: seen to be done as well as actually done. For example, a judge must not only prevent her political beliefs from influencing her judgments, but also not be a member of a political party.

Hearings should be fair to the parties involved. The drafters considered implicit in the phrase "in full equality" that for a trial to be fair, parties who cannot afford legal advice and representation should have it provided for them ("legal aid"). Human rights law has struggled in deciding how far this should go, since it involves questions of public resource allocation.

Should individuals be able to choose any lawyer they want, or have to accept the one appointed for them? Should legal aid cover all types of cases, or only "important" cases? Should legal aid be at a certain level so that the services provided are adequate for the case? If individuals are self-represented in court, they must have the procedure explained to them in a manner and language they understand. Individuals have the right to be physically present during the trial, at least when their presence is important to the case being determined. Justice delayed is justice denied, so trials must take place within a reasonable time. This is especially important when crucial issues are hanging in the balance, like child custody or criminal charges.

Hearings should be public so that the legal process is open to scrutiny. All of society has an interest in trials being fair, not just the parties who are having their legal issues determined. This is greater for some issues (e.g., criminal cases, where an individual is being prosecuted on behalf of society as a whole) than in others (e.g., family cases). Furthermore, this public interest has to be balanced against the rights of those involved in the trial. Therefore the press and public can be excluded from all or part of a trial if this is necessary to protect morals, public order, and national security; to safeguard the private lives of the parties; and to prevent prejudice to justice. Judgments should be made public except when doing so would threaten the interests of juveniles or when they concern the custody of children.

A tribunal should be "independent" (without any obligations to anything other than justice) and "impartial" (being neutral to the parties before it). The independence of the judiciary, from both other interests in society and other institutions of government (the executive and the legislature) is one of the cornerstones of a democratic constitution. As far as judges are concerned, this means that how they are chosen, how they do their job, and how they are discharged should ensure independence and impartiality. Judges themselves should be prevented from being part of any organizations that would compromise their integrity. They should also be protected from outside pressure, such as physical violence or bribes. Tribunals should be established by law: set up by the legislature rather than the executive. This implies that they be permanent rather than ad hoc, so that justice is uniformly rather than selectively applied.

Which legal issues are entitled to be tried in court in the first place? The declaration makes a distinction between two types of legal issue: that which determines rights and obligations and that which determines a criminal charge. Human rights law has developed a set of different fair trial standards for each category, reflecting the particular importance of ensuring fairness during criminal cases. Which category does any given issue fall under? The phrases have an autonomous meaning: if a situation seems like it falls into one of the categories, it does not matter whether the national law in question characterizes it as falling into the other one. Trials that determine rights and obligations are not limited to civil cases (private law like contract, tort, land, and trusts/equity) but any area where an individual's rights or duties are being determined by the court. Trials that determine a criminal charge concern offenses and penalties that would normally be associated with a crime, even if this word is not actually used.

ARTICLE 11

Everyone charged with a penal offence has the right to be presumed innocent until proved guilty according to law in a public trial at which he has had all the guarantees necessary for his defense.

No one shall be held guilty of any penal offence on account of any act or omission which did not constitute a penal offence, under national or international law, at the time when it was committed. Nor shall a heavier penalty be imposed than the one that was applicable at the time the penal offence was committed.

Article 11 elaborates the notion of fair trial as it is applied to criminal (penal) trials in four areas. It covers the presumption of innocence, the right to be tried in public, the right to mount a defense to the charges, and the prohibition of retroactive offenses or punishment. A criminal trial has to ensure the right of society to have a criminal brought to justice, without loopholes that allow those who are guilty to get off. But it also needs to protect the individual's right not to be branded a criminal if she or he is innocent. Conviction should not come at any cost; instead justice must be paramount.

The presumption of innocence is the hallmark of a criminal trial. In criminal trials people are judged according to the evidence. Only when the judgment is a finding of guilt is the person then convicted as a criminal. This means that, in legal systems like that of the United States, the burden of proving guilt is on the prosecution, who has to rebut a presumption that the person being tried is innocent. The accused has the benefit of the doubt and so guilt is found only if it is "beyond reasonable doubt." This principle leads to all kinds of rules about what evidence can be used to prove guilt.

Because of the particular importance of justice in criminal trials, human rights law has developed from Article 11 a considerably detailed series of procedural guarantees concerning the right to public trials and a defense. For example, the accused has to be able to mount an adequate defense, she cannot be compelled to testify against herself or to confess guilt, and if convicted she is entitled to have her conviction and sentence reviewed by a higher court.

At the same time, the notion of fairness means an emphasis on different aspects of criminal trials in different countries. For example, in some cultures the rights of victims are served by them being part of the process of prosecution, including in some cases having the right to exercise clemency in the case of a death sentence. The challenge for human rights law is to take the bedrock principles of Article 11 and elaborate them in a way that remains faithful to their meaning and reflects the traditions of different cultures.

The second paragraph of Article 11 reflects the principle of *nullum crimen, nulla poena sine lege*—there should be no crime or penalty without law. This means that if a person commits an act which was not criminal at the time but which the state later makes into a criminal offense, the person cannot then be tried for the criminal offense based on their earlier act. Similarly, when people are convicted of a crime, they cannot be given a greater sentence than that which existed for their crime at the time they committed it.

Some crimes are considered so shocking to the whole world that they are criminalized on the international level and characterized in a particular way. They form part of humanitarian law and include war crimes (atrocities that take place during conflict), genocide and crimes against humanity. However, not all states have made such crimes part of their national law. Article 11 therefore refers to both national and international law. This allows a country to introduce war crimes into national law after particular acts have been committed, and still be able to try individuals for those acts according to the new law without breaching the prohibition on retroactive criminality in Article 11.

ARTICLE 12

No one shall be subjected to arbitrary interference with his privacy, family, home or correspondence, nor to attacks upon his honor and reputation. Everyone has the right to the protection of the law against such interference or attacks.

Article 12 enshrines the right to privacy, that sphere of human life which is outside the scope of interference by other people and the state. It aims to preserve each human being's dignity by allowing him or her to develop a personal life that is respected. Although originally considered in the narrow sense of preserving secrecy about personal information, privacy has come to have a broader meaning, as the right of individuals to define and express their personalities and develop personal relations.

The most obvious form of interference with privacy is on the personal and physical level, both by the state and by other individuals whom the state does not effectively restrain. This supplements the human rights safeguards applicable to the criminal justice system in Articles 9-11. Procedures such as intimate body searches and opening prisoners' correspondence should be proportionate to the end they serve, and the information obtained should be used only for the particular purpose intended. Environmental abuses have also been characterized as a violation of the private life of individuals whose homes are blighted by noise or air pollution.

The rights in Article 12 now extend as far as the right of individuals to determine their identity and personality (such as name, physical appearance, sexual orientation, and gender) and develop relationships with other people. The right exists not just in a wholly private sense, but also in the way that the individual's choices are treated by society in public life. This includes how the state views such choices, whether it allows people with similar choices to associate with one another, and whether it protects them from interference by others. It is not enough for the state to permit homosexual acts in private, for example, if les-

bians, gay men, and bisexuals are denied the opportunity to develop their relationships and express their identities in public in the same way as heterosexuals.

The right to a family life has been interpreted in a similarly expansive manner. It has come to mean the right of members of a family unit, broadly defined, to enjoy each other's company and develop normally. At the same time, other important principles have been brought to bear on the operation of this family unit, requiring the state to "interfere" within families when necessary. The 1989 UN Convention on the Rights of the Child (CRC), for example, established that when issues of custody are to be decided within the family unit, the interests of the child, as opposed to the rights of each of the parents, should be paramount. Human rights tribunals have grappled with difficult questions in family matters, such as how much importance should be attached to the blood connection between family members. In one typical case where two rights were in conflict, the right of a pregnant woman to her physical privacy trumped the family-life right of the father of her unborn child to prevent her from having an abortion. Family life is also connected with the right to asylum in Article 14, in that it has sometimes been the basis for allowing the families of individuals granted asylum to reside in the country of asylum even though they themselves would not qualify for refugee status.

ARTICLE 13
Everyone has the right to freedom of movement and residence within the bor-

ders of each State. Everyone has the right to leave any country, including his own, and to return to his country.

Freedom of movement is the right to go around in a country without needing anyone's permission. Human rights treaties acknowledge that it is sometimes necessary to restrict freedom of movement and to permit restrictions that protect property rights, privacy, agriculture, security, and military installations, and ensure that borders are secure from illegal entrants and smuggling. Freedom of residence is the right to decide exactly where you want to live without needing permission, both in terms of what kind of area you choose (e.g., urban or rural) and which area in particular.

Article 13 enshrines a concept of free movement which is taken for granted in some countries in the world but remains an important human rights issue in other countries. During the drafting of the declaration, Soviet bloc states had strict movement restrictions, and the right to leave the country was forbidden. The concept of free movement was thus one of the aspects of the declaration that the Soviets found objectionable. During the Cold War, the language of human rights was used in ideological battles, as the West encouraged dissidents to defect from Soviet bloc countries through the "right to leave." Now the article is less meaningful in the context of repressive regimes, and more meaningful in connection with the sub-state conflicts that have characterized the post-Cold War era, with mass refugee flows and ethnic cleansing.

In the "developing" world, countries that host considerable refugee populations are wary of allowing refugees the unlimited right to move around their country and to reside where they choose. Such countries prefer to locate refugees close to the border of the state from whence they came. However, such areas may be difficult to live in, and can risk exposing the refugees to attacks from over the border by those who caused them to flee in the first place.

Freedom of movement and residence are rights that allow individuals to connect to the larger communities that they feel part of. They seek to prevent the state or other individuals from changing the ethnic, religious, or cultural characteristics of a particular area by forcing individuals to move in or out of it. As the breakup of the former Yugoslavia illustrated, such "cleansing" can take place both within and across state borders.

The rights to leave and return are aimed primarily at the asylum seeker, with regard to the country they are fleeing from rather than the country they take refuge in (the latter is covered by the right to protection in Article 14). This reflects a pragmatic desire to encourage states to allow individuals to flee persecution. Of course, once they have agreed to the rest of the declaration, such states are also obliged to prevent the human rights abuses that would lead someone to contemplate fleeing in the first place.

The right to leave is just that—whether the place an individual is going to will allow him or her to enter is a separate question. This is dealt with either through the right to asylum, or the right to return if she is entering her country of nationality. The right to emigrate to the country of her choice does not, therefore, exist in human rights law. The right to leave is taken for granted in many Western democracies, and few constitutions even mention it in their provisions. In countries where it is an issue, problems often center around actually being in a position to leave (such as being given a passport and not being detained) rather than the permission to leave itself.

ARTICLE 14

Everyone has the right to seek and to enjoy in other countries asylum from persecution.

This right may not be invoked in the case of prosecutions genuinely arising from nonpolitical crimes or from acts contrary to the purposes and principles of the United Nations.

Article 14 deals with the rights of refugees. Refugees are individuals who have had to flee a country because it cannot or will not protect their human rights. The country they go to (the "receiving state") has an obligation to offer them protection.

Article 14, therefore, is different from the other rights in the declaration, because it creates a human rights duty on the part of the receiving state which is itself based on another state failing to fulfill its human rights obligations. Like the laws of war, refugee law is now part of human rights law, but it actually pre-dates the declaration and retains a separate identity within human rights. Soon after the declaration, a Refugee Convention was signed in 1951

and a specific UN agency, the High Commissioner for Refugees, was set up to promote the rights of refugees.

Because of the implications of the notion of asylum—that a state has an obligation to a non-national, caused by something it has no control over—states have been reluctant to be fully bound to grant asylum. Article 14, therefore, refers to the right to seek and enjoy asylum rather than the right to be given it. Similarly, the Refugee Convention does not mention a right to asylum but instead amounts to a right not to be sent back to face persecution, also known as *non-refoulement*. This frames the state's obligation as negative—not to send back—rather than positive—to grant asylum.

The drafters had a particular type of refugee in mind with Article 14 and the 1951 Refugee Convention. World War II led to movements of refugees in Europe, such as the Jews, who were fleeing persecution because of their religion and culture. As the Cold War set in, Western states wanted to protect the rights of those individuals who were fleeing Communist countries because of political persecution. In both cases there was a strong connection between the receiving state and the refugee, whether because of the moral outrage of the Holocaust in the case of the Jews, or an ideological commitment to anti-Communism in the case of Cold War defections. Many receiving states saw refugee protection not as a temporary measure but as an entitlement for the individuals concerned to reside permanently as citizens. Refugee movements were primarily a European phenomenon, based on violations of core civil and political rights like freedom of expression. It is for these reasons that Article 14 refers to asylum from "persecution" and the 1951 Convention requires a "well-founded fear of being persecuted." Article 14 prevents individuals from claiming asylum "in the case of prosecutions . . . arising from non-political crimes" precisely because it had in mind prosecutions for political crimes, such as being imprisoned for speaking out against the government, as the basis for refugee status. In granting individuals the right to "seek and enjoy" asylum, Article 18 approaches the issue in terms of facilitating a state's desire to grant asylum, rather than imposing an obligation to do so whether it wants to or not.

The nature of refugee movements is very different now. They occur on a global scale and in much greater numbers. Refugees flee countries not just because of individual cases of political persecution but also for mass violations of human rights—in a civil war situation, for example. Frequently these problems are bound up in environmental and developmental issues, such as drought and famine, which connect up to economic and social rights (Articles 22–26). Most receiving states are in the "developing" world and do not have the economic resources to shoulder the burden of protecting those who are entitled to protection according to international law. Western countries no longer have the same moral or ideological commitment to offer protection yet retain the notion that it is akin to naturalization. Thus, refugees in such countries are often viewed with suspicion as "bogus," claiming asylum as a way of bypassing immigration requirements.

ARTICLE 15
Everyone has the right to a nationality. No one shall be arbitrarily deprived of his nationality nor denied the right to change his nationality.

Nationality is the legal status of being a member, or citizen, of a particular country. This status entails particular rights and duties on the part of both the citizen and his or her nation.

The connection between nationality and human rights is complicated. The Enlightenment philosophy that influenced the formation of human rights sought to transform the basis for nationalism from shared myths, culture, religion, and history to a reason-based contract between individuals, based on the mutual respect for rights. However, an uneasy confluence of both sentiments continues to characterize nationality within most countries.

Because of this, the legal consequences of possessing nationality are related to the protection offered by human rights law, but not synonymous with it. Human rights law governs the relationship between the individual (whether citizen or not) and the state within which he or she lives. The state is bound to respect the rights of all individuals within its jurisdiction, irrespective of their nationality. Therefore, since most people live in the state where they are citizens, human rights law is in many ways an explanation of how the state and its citizens should interact.

However, citizenship is more than merely having human rights protected—an entitlement that everyone has regardless of where they are in the world. It is the symbolic recognition by your country that you are a member of it. This is because of the abstract connection of "existence, interests and sentiments" (as the International Court of Justice termed it in 1955) that exists between people of the same nationality through their identity, culture, language, and tradition. International law is itself based on the concept of sovereignty: that states have authority to make agreements with each other because they are the representative (sovereign) of the individuals (citizens) that comprise them. A state acts as this representative because of the relationship of nationality that exists between it and its citizens.

The importance of nationality means that citizens are often entitled to additional rights from their state not accorded to noncitizens. For example, often only citizens are given the full right to take part in the government of the country (Article 21) or to be protected by the diplomatic mission of their country when abroad.

Throughout history individuals have been deprived of their nationality. In Europe, for example, German Jews were denationalized by the Nazi government because of their ethnicity, and after World War II Germans in other countries were denationalized because of their connection to Nazi Germany. Article 15 was drafted to deal with this problem by forbidding states from removing nationality unless the individual concerned has a new nationality to take up.

However, international law does not oblige other states to grant nationality to those who have had their nationality removed. Such people are therefore "stateless." Although they may have additional reasons that enable them to claim protection as refugees (e.g., if they left their former home country because of human rights abuse) or even to claim nationality (e.g., if they meet the state's immigration requirements, such as having particular skills), the mere fact of having been deprived of nationality is rarely a basis to make a successful claim for refugee protection or nationality.

This unfortunate gap underlines the uneasy relationship between human rights and nationality. Since states are obliged to respect the human rights of nationals and non-nationals alike, it is only the connection between them and certain individuals that gives rise to the particular privileges of nationality. Therefore, whereas the state with that particular connection cannot sever it, it does not follow that another state has the duty, above and beyond general human rights protection, to create a particular connection with a denationalized alien.

Yet the deprivation of nationality goes to the very core of an individual's need to belong. It is indeed for this reason that Article 15 was created and nationality declared a "right." Many nations are defined by the melange of different backgrounds from the immigrant groups that make up their population.

The tensions between the universal principles of human rights and the nation-centric legal order through which they are promoted mean that attempts to create obligations on the part of one state towards individuals from another state are particularly difficult.

ARTICLE 16

Men and women of full age, without any limitation due to race, nationality or religion, have the right to marry and to found a family. They are entitled to equal rights as to marriage, during marriage and at its dissolution.

Marriage shall be entered into only with the free and full consent of the intending spouses.

The family is the natural and fundamental group unit of society and is entitled to protection by society and the State.

Like the right to form associations in Article 20, Article 16 is concerned with a key relationship that individuals form between themselves: in this case marriage and the family.

Marriage is the state-approved agreement between two individuals to commit themselves personally to each other. Article 16 sets out the minimum conditions that should prevail, both in terms of who can marry and what marriage is. It also takes the principle of gender equality and applies it to the practicalities of marriage: the right to marry is given to both a man and a woman, and the decision to enter into marriage has to be with the consent of both of them. Marriage itself should also operate so that both partners have equal rights. This makes marriage an institution that involves both partners sharing

the rights and responsibilities of their joint life in a way that both agree upon.

For many individuals, marriage can have a particular basis and involve certain obligations, depending on their race, nationality, or religion. Whereas Article 16 clearly prohibits the state from forbidding people to marry because of their race, nationality, or religion, it is less clear is what its provisions mean when the traditions of race, nationality, or religion are in conflict with human rights as they apply to marriage, such as the concept of equal rights for both spouses. What happens when a woman consents freely to enter into a marriage where she will not enjoy the same rights as her husband? Human rights law is necessarily concerned with allowing individuals personal self-determination—the right to live their lives according to their own wishes. This may ironically include having the right to freely adopt an entire value system where their rights are compromised. However, human rights law is premised on the concept of human dignity, which is why agreements like debt bondage are outlawed even though there may have been people who would have freely entered into them. Do the provisions of Article 16 represent a similar move of bringing the concept of human dignity to override gender inequality in marriage irrespective of the wishes of the individuals concerned, or should people be allowed to do as they choose?

The family is mentioned as distinct from marriage ("to marry and to found a family"). So far, human rights law has only accepted this as meaning that marriage does not necessarily involve founding a family, rather than that founding a family does not necessarily occur through marriage. Founding a family includes all aspects of conceiving and raising children, from abortion to adoption, contraception, fertility treatment, fostering, and sterilization. The right impacts not only on the parents as individuals, but as members of racial, national, or religious groups. Procreation within communities is obviously fundamental to their continued existence. The prevention of this procreation, such as the Nazi eugenics policies, is one of the main ways that such groups can be attacked.

The final paragraph of Article 16 reflects the importance of marriage in most cultures. In many countries, "marriage" is of a certain character. First, it is exceptional, giving individuals who are married a preferential entitlement to many other rights. These might include income tax allowances and inheritance by one spouse of the other spouse's assets. These entitlements promote marriage as an institution, acting as an incentive for individuals to marry and a disincentive for individuals to remain single or to end their marriage. Second, marriage is exclusively heterosexual. It has traditionally been conceived in terms of different-gender couples—those involving a man and a woman. This excludes relationships between individuals of the same gender, not just from being able have their union blessed by society through marriage but also from all the rights and benefits that married couples often have.

However, the character of marriage as exceptional and exclusively heterosexual is being challenged. First, some countries are developing the notion of "registered partnerships," whereby individuals can enter into a marriage-like agreement. This involves rights and obligations between one another and between them and the state that usually fall short of what is involved in marriage but are more than would exist between two unmarried individuals who, for example, live together. Second, the rise of the lesbian, gay, and bisexual rights movement, particularly in "developed" countries, has led to calls for same-gender couples to have their relationships recognized by society and the law.

The challenge is for human rights law to be able to address society's need to protect and promote individual relationships without restricting the rights of individuals who wish this protection to take a different form from marriage or to cover different types of relationships than have traditionally been covered.

ARTICLE 17
Everyone has the right to own property alone as well as in association with others. No one shall be arbitrarily deprived of his property.

The right to property is the touchstone for many of the controversies concerning human rights as a universal concept. These have included ideological divisions, developmental claims, and environmental concerns.

When the declaration was drafted, the main ideological conflict was along the lines of the Cold War: the individual property rights of capitalism versus the collective property ownership of communism. Article 17, while making a nod to Soviet collectivism ("as well as in association with others"), essentially articulated the capitalist notion of individual property rights. The drafters did not attempt to include property rights in the ICCPR, and the 1950 European Convention on Human Rights only included it belatedly, as an optional protocol signed two years after the main convention.

Cold War differences were supplemented by other, equally profound disagreements in the years after the creation of the declaration, as new states of the "developing" world came into existence. Many of these countries saw the right to individual property as misplaced, since it focused on preserving the status quo, irrespective of how wealth had been obtained. During colonialism much of their wealth had been concentrated in the hands of a few people, and many of their national treasures had been plundered by colonial powers. They complained that respecting property rights not only rewarded this injustice but also prevented the citizens of their countries from being able to compete economically in such a way that they could develop too. These sentiments contributed to the New International Economic Order, a movement which sought to redistribute some of the resources of the "developed" world to the "developing" world (see Article 28).

Environmental concerns have also impacted the concept of property rights, since they challenge the notion that individuals have the right to do what they will with the property they own. It is relatively straightforward for human rights law to prohibit the use of property that affects the rights of others in an immediate sense—such as the burning of a forest which leads to smoke pollution in adjoining property—since the rights and interests of the two individuals concerned can, to a certain degree, be assessed and balanced against each other. However, both the burning and the removal of oxygenating foliage would also contribute to carbon dioxide levels and thus global warming, but this would not necessarily make a huge impact during the lifetime of the person who lit the match. It is much more difficult to think of the rights of future generations and attempt to take their interests into account.

The evolving nature of these controversies has meant that human rights law has developed the full meaning of Article 17 in a somewhat clumsy fashion. The 1948 American Declaration of Human Rights defined the kind of property that it was reasonable for each person to have as that which "meets the essential needs of decent living and maintains dignity of the individual and the home." The drafters of the Universal Declaration of Human Rights tried and failed to agree both on this and on the areas where the state would be entitled to deprive an individual of her property. Other human rights instruments state that property deprivation should take place only for reasons of public utility or social interest, and where just compensation is paid.

In the half century since the declaration, the spread of free market liberalism and privatization means that much of the world's resources and wealth are controlled by private actors. The challenge for human rights law is to see if it can play a meaningful role in reconciling the rights of those who own wealth with the wider, more long-term interests of the community around them.

ARTICLE 18

Everyone has the right to freedom of thought, conscience and religion; this right includes freedom to change his religion or belief, and freedom, either alone or in community with others and in public or private, to manifest his religion or belief in teaching, practice, worship and observance.

In many cultures, religion was the basis for the state itself, and religious law governed the relationship between individuals and their state. Democracy secularizes the state, with the social contract and individual rights displacing religion as the governing doctrine. Therefore, it is in Article 18 that the only reference to religion is found in the declaration.

The concept of religious toleration, now subsumed within human rights, began in ancient times and influenced the development of human rights in the modern age. In Europe the Judeo-Christian message that human beings are blessed by God was a precursor to the natural law concept of the inherent dignity of human beings as the basis for their rights (see Part 1, Chapter 1, Section 4). At the drafting stage, a suggestion to refer to God as having bestowed this human dignity was rejected. Instead, the declaration proclaimed human rights as a wholly secular concept. Religion was mentioned merely in terms of religious toleration as one of a series of rights. This echoed the minorities treaties signed after the World War I in Europe (see Article 2), which included religious groups as protected minorities.

As a result, Article 18 established matters of individual conscience as a private issue. Moreover, it undermined the notion of religious faith as exceptional, by including "thought," "conscience," and "belief" alongside it. The importance of established religion to the majority of the world's peoples, however, required more elaboration. In particular, the scope of the right to change religion and to manifest it in worship led to profound disagreements during drafting, resulting in a compromise that deliberately left many questions unresolved.

The right to change or abandon a religion (apostasy) is the predicate to the notion of secular democracy. It is, however, incompatible with those interpretations of faiths that forbid apostasy (e.g., in Islam) or do not allow people not born into the faith to convert to it (e.g., in Hinduism). Moreover, many of the drafters felt that including the right to change religion would further encourage the public manifestation of proselytizing religions that sought to convert nonbelievers through missionary activities. In the final vote its inclusion was supported by just over half of the drafters. Later human rights treaties (e.g., ICCPR Article 18.2) attempted to resolve this problem, restricting those manifestations of religion which attempted to convert by declaring the right of individuals not to be coerced into having or adopting a religion.

Compared with some articles in the declaration, Article 18 is quite detailed, and it was not elaborated to the same degree in subsequent treaties. Much of this detail comes in the section on public manifestation, which spells out essential elements in terms of who is involved, where it takes place, and what particular activities are conducted. However, the key question is how far this manifestation can go before it goes against the beliefs or manifestation of other religions or the rights of nonbelievers and public morality. The drafters saw the answer to this in different ways, from restricting certain extreme practices such as self-mutilation, to a more widespread state involvement in organized religion. They were unable to agree how Article 29, which outlines acceptable limitations on human rights, could be applied to reconcile these issues. Instead they formulated Article 18 so that, in conjunction with Article 29, it merely set the parameters within which subsequent treaties and their tribunals could see how concerns would be resolved in practice.

This is a difficult task, since human rights must balance the need to promote diversity and individual freedom without denying the importance of religion and conscience in shaping and defining many countries. Many laws, for example, have a religious origin, such as the restrictions on abortion and divorce in Catholic Ireland. Sometimes government decisions—such as going to war—may be undertaken with the support of the majority of the country who view it as promoting their common interests. The state takes a position on a difficult moral issue, which is then binding on its citizens (who have to comply with abortion laws, for example, or be conscripted to support the war effort). Should individuals be allowed to conscientiously object to being bound?

This dilemma illustrates the tension that can exist between popular majority rule—that the state does what is in the interests of the majority of its citizens—and the human rights notion that there are certain things that the state cannot do to individuals, even if they are popular in society as a whole. Human rights can, therefore, be seen as antidemocratic, insofar as they seek to prevent the "tyranny of the majority." Human rights tribunals have trodden carefully in response to this dilemma. In religious issues, they have tended to give states considerable scope to decide what is appropriate for their particular societies. In matters of conscientious objection, they have stated that individuals have the right not to serve in the armed forces if doing so would go against their conscience. However, they can be obliged to perform some alternative form of national service.

ARTICLE 19

Everyone has the right to freedom of opinion and expression; this right includes freedom to hold opinions without interference and to seek, receive and impart information and ideas through any media and regardless of frontiers.

Article 19 articulates one of the most important aspects of democracy: the ability of individuals to engage in a free exchange of information and ideas. It covers the holding of opinions, and both the expressing and the receiving of information and ideas, through any media and across national boundaries.

In the period between the two World Wars, international treaties typically restricted that expression which was seen as potentially harmful to good relations between states (e.g., the 1924 USSR/UK General Treaty). However, during World War II the Allies came to believe that threats to international peace came precisely from those states in which freedom of expression was restricted, leading President Roosevelt to include free expression as one of his Four Freedoms. In the short period after the war and before the declaration, many international agreements, including the Paris Peace Treaties, included free expression provisions.

Freedom of expression was identified as a key component of human rights from the very first discussions about the content of the declaration. When the Human Rights Commission was originally mandated to draft the declaration, free expression was included as one of only three examples of its content. The ambassador from the Philippines, who was himself the head of a chain of newspapers, set up a conference to discuss freedom of expression with a resolution declaring that the right was the "touchstone of all the freedoms to which the UN is consecrated." Cold War battles over the nature of free expression dominated negotiations on the content of Article 19. Soviet proposals argued for censorship and a state-run media on the grounds that unlimited free expression risked allowing the incitement of war and fascism and that the state was the only means, through the equal provision of resources, for expression to be genuinely free. Through the forceful interventions of Eleanor Roosevelt, the unqualified notion of free expression prevailed as Article 19 of the declaration.

Subsequent human rights treaties elaborated the meaning of Article 19 and incorporated the limitations from Article 29 in their free expression articles (e.g., ICCPR Articles 19.3 and 20). In an example of somewhat unnecessary extra detail, these treaties explain that media includes oral, writing, print, art, or any other (e.g., ICCPR Article 19.2), which in the age of cyberspace seems dated compared with the simplicity of Article 19. Limitations are permitted to protect the rights of others; to license broadcasting, cinema, and television; to prevent disclosure of information held in confidence; to maintain the authority and impartiality of the judiciary; to protect children and adolescents; and in an echo of the interwar precursors to Article 19, to prevent propaganda for war. In cases before international human rights tribunals, states must justify restricting speech on the above grounds; in the area of political speech, countries have rarely succeeded in justifying restrictions.

ARTICLE 20
Everyone has the right to freedom of peaceful assembly and association.

No one may be compelled to belong to an association.

Freedom of association and assembly is integral to the notion of civil society in a democracy. It allows individuals a sense of belonging to something bigger than themselves, but different from the country they are a national of. It facilitates the process of civil society by developing ideas and interacting with other ideas and processes.

Freedom of association is the right of individuals to form a body corporate. An association often promotes the interests of a particular issue or identity, whether ethnic, ideological, religious, political, economic, labor, social, cultural, or sporting.

Freedom of assembly is the right of individuals to come together, whether on the basis of a particular association or not. Assemblies can take many forms, from political demonstrations and rallies to meetings, marches, picketing, carnivals, and festivals. They play an important role in shaping the society within which they take place, both politically (such as campaign rallies) and culturally (such as dance clubs and raves). Some can take place in more than one country and promote solidarity amongst those with a common agenda, like the student protests in North America and Europe in the late 1960s and early 1970s. In an information age, virtual assemblies—through television (such as the worldwide viewing of a football match), radio, or on-line—have in many ways displaced assemblies where the participants are physically present. However, physical assemblies are still instrumental in allowing groups who are not well-established to express themselves in a manner which may, through virtual means, seize the attention of a wider audience, like the protests in China's Tiananmen Square in 1989.

The rights in Article 20 impact not only on the individuals who are members of a particular association or attend a particular assembly but also the association and assembly itself, other associations and assemblies, and other individuals and bodies, both state and nonstate.

Associations can represent the primary focus of allegiance and identity for the individuals concerned. Such an enterprise can therefore challenge the state, whether it be on a supranational level, such as the European Union integration process, or a subnational level, such as minority groups like the Basque separatists in Spain. The drafters of the declaration were reluctant to encourage this and so shied away from declaring rights for groups, such as minorities, rather than individual members of such groups. However, despite Soviet amendments that sought to ban fascist and similar associations, the drafters did not go as far as to prohibit certain groups that posed a threat to the state.

Assemblies similarly affect other actors. What starts as a march or a strike may end up precipitating a revolution, and even when this is unlikely assemblies may nevertheless threaten the rights of others. The state has a duty not just to allow assemblies to take place, but also to restrict them if this is necessary to preserve other rights (if they are not "peaceful"). However, to what degree should an assembly threaten other rights before restrictions are justified? The racist marches that have taken place in Europe in recent years, for example, not only risk violence (if the marchers attack hostels of asylum seekers, for example) but also risk increasing racial tension because of what they stand for. Should human rights law require that not only the method of demonstration be "peaceful," but also the message that is being demonstrated?

The declaration was drafted at a time when the spaces where assemblies might take place in "developed" countries, such as public highways or town squares, were public and under the control of the state. However, in "developing" countries this may not be the case; and in "developed" countries, private properties, such as shopping malls, have in many instances displaced municipal spaces as the important public areas in towns and cities. Should private owners have some kind of duty to allow peaceful assemblies on their property? Can human rights law conceive a way of acknowledging the public role of such spaces, while recognizing that they are also private property?

ARTICLE 21

Everyone has the right to take part in the government of his country, directly or through freely chosen representatives.

Everyone has the right to equal access to public service in his country.

The will of the people shall be the basis of the authority of government; this will shall be expressed in periodic and genuine elections which shall be by universal and equal suffrage and shall be held by secret vote or by equivalent free voting procedures.

Article 21 addresses one of democracy's key elements: that the state should be run by the people on whose behalf it acts. It is therefore concerned with the constitution of government itself, rather than how government relates to its citizens once constituted.

The first paragraph suggests the two ways in which government by the people can be effected. Direct democracy means that all the individuals in a country are the government, in that they personally make decisions as to how it is run. This was first practiced during a period in ancient Greece, where citizens would cast lots to decide issues of the day (of course, not every individual was a citizen; see Part One). Now, much bigger countries are based on representative democracy, where the people choose a limited number of individuals to govern on their behalf. However, direct governance still takes place, for example, when a particular issue is decided through a referendum, a vote of the people rather than a decision by their government representatives.

The third paragraph explains how representative democracy works: the government's right to run the country depends on the will of the people. No government is legitimate unless this is the case. Governing as a result of the will of the people suggests a wide process of connectivity between the people and their government, where all groups in society have a fair, meaningful, and ongoing influence on how government operates. One of the key elements of this connectivity is then outlined: that a government should be elected. Elections are the process whereby governmental representatives are selected by a vote of the people. To be periodic, they should take place on a regular basis. To be genuine, they must be true to the spirit of their meaning, involving real choices between alternatives rather than the mere fact of having chosen between candidates.

Universal and equal suffrage means that all individuals in society are entitled to vote in elections and that each one of their votes has an equal value. This reflects the fact that in many cultures groups of people, from women to ethnic groups, have been denied the right to vote. Voting procedures should be free in the sense that people should be freely able to exercise their entitlement to vote and to freely choose whom or what to vote for.

In recent years the guarantees in Article 21 have become the focus of much human rights activity, with international agencies working around the world to promote free and fair elections. It has also been suggested that there is an emerging right to democratic governance in international law. Democracy, however, is more than periodic elections and a free press. Indeed, the declaration can be seen as a charter for democracy, setting out the relationships between the individual and the state, and individuals and other individuals, so as to achieve a fair society. To evaluate this complex process is perhaps to evaluate democracy itself.

In Bosnia-Herzegovina, for example, the international community is engaged in a process of constructing a democratic civil society in a country emerging from both communism and the tragic violence of recent years. Human rights is at the center of this process, which involves everything from rebuilding housing and allowing refugees to return to their homes (Articles 25 and 13) to creating democratic structures and monitoring elections (Articles 13, 19 and 21).

The complexity of this enterprise illustrates how democracy is an ongoing process that impacts all areas of human life, not merely a settled set of constitutional rules and procedures which once followed make a state democratic. Human rights law offers a methodology to constantly evaluate the nature of democracy and to inspire an ever-greater realization of its goals.

ARTICLE 22

Everyone, as a member of society, has the right to social security and is entitled to realization, through national effort and international co-operation and in accordance with the organization and resources of each State, of the economic, social and cultural rights indispensable for his dignity and the free development of his personality.

Article 22 is an introduction to economic, social, and cultural rights. These rights are then elaborated in the rest of the declaration: in Article 22 itself (social security), Article 23 (work), Article 24 (rest and leisure), Article 25 (adequate standard of living), Article 26 (education), and Article 27 (cultural life).

No equivalent introductory article prefaces the civil and political rights in the declaration. Some of the drafters argued that this would give economic, social, and cultural rights prominence over civil and political rights. However, the majority felt that an introductory article was necessary to highlight the equivalence to civil and political rights of what was, at the time, seen as a relatively new category of rights.

Economic, social, and cultural rights are different in character from civil and political rights. The latter often concern activities which individuals conduct without help from the state, e.g., the right to hold an opinion. They seek to prevent the state from restricting these activities any more than is necessary. The former, however, often focus more on what individuals are entitled to be provided with. As such they are inextricably linked with the capacity of the state to make such provisions, which in turn depends on how developed the state is and on the particular economic conditions at the time.

The implementation of economic, social, and cultural rights is, therefore, different from and more complex than that of civil and political rights. Fundamentally, it is based on the idea of social justice, both on national and international levels. This is to occur progressively through cooperation, rather than immediately through enforcement like civil and political rights. Standards are set, which social and economic policies should aspire to rather than immediately facilitate. States are obliged to make the best national effort they can, depending on their organization and resources. All states are not expected to have the same amount of resources to use in public assistance, but each is expected to use what they are capable of in a responsible manner. Furthermore, there should be international cooperation in the provision of economic, social, and cultural rights,

which again depends on the organization and resources of states. Taken to its logical conclusion, this involves the redistribution of wealth from rich countries to poor ones, to enable those poor countries to provide basic economic, social, and cultural rights when they cannot do so on their own.

The inclusion of economic, social, and cultural rights in the declaration did not simply come out of a compromise between the capitalist West and the communist Soviet bloc. Some of the strongest advocates of Articles 22 through 28, like Eleanor Roosevelt, were actually from Western countries where the welfare state was expanding after the austerity of the war years. However, such advocates did insist that economic, social, and cultural rights were articulated in terms of the individual's rights rather than also setting out the state's corresponding duties (e.g., the right of the individual to free education, meaning the duty of the state to provide free education).

The declaration proclaims that civil and political rights on the one hand are indivisible from economic, social, and cultural rights on the other. Since then, however, many states have emphasized one set of rights over the other. Some in the "developing" world have focused on economic, social, and cultural rights to highlight the need of their peoples for basic support in order to survive. This led the "developing" nation-dominated General Assembly to proclaim a "Right to Development" in 1986: the right of "developing" countries to be given assistance by "developed" countries. Others in the "developed" world focused much more on civil and political rights, and their legal systems developed sophisticated provisions for safeguarding such rights, from national bills of rights to the European Convention system. The declaration, in including both sets of rights, underlines the principle that one cannot exist without the other. Being able to vote is not sufficient if you do not have enough food, but just because you do not have enough food does not mean you do not also need to be able to vote. Fifty years later, the prescience of the declaration is demonstrated by the widespread acknowledgment of the interdependence of the two categories of rights.

ARTICLE 23

Everyone has the right to work, to free choice of employment, to just and favorable conditions of work and to protection against unemployment.

Everyone, without any discrimination, has the right to equal pay for equal work.

Everyone who works has the right to just and favorable remuneration ensuring for himself and his family an existence worthy of human dignity, and supplemented, if necessary, by other means of social protection.

Everyone has the right to form and to join trade unions for the protection of his interests.

Article 23 contains quite detailed provisions concerning employment rights. They cluster around four areas: work, equal treatment, fair pay, and trade unions. They attempt to bring certain minimum standards, through state regulation, to an area that is in many cases wholly private: economic activity.

The drafters saw the "right to work" of the first paragraph in a free market sense—the individual's right to be allowed by the state to go to work if she or he wants to. Subsequent instruments suggest a more socialist concept of the duty of the state to create jobs for individuals. ICESCR Article 6(2) reflects the tensions between these economic theories, mentioning the importance both of measures to promote full employment and of conditions that safeguard fundamental political and economic freedoms for the individual.

In the second paragraph, Article 23 brings the discrimination provisions of Article 7 to bear on the workplace. Employers can pay people differently because of differences relating to work (e.g., the degree of skills or experience needed for the job) but not because of differences unrelated to work (e.g., the gender of the person concerned). ICESCR phrases it as "equal pay for work of equal value" because the value attached to particular work may be based on the fact that it is performed predominantly by people from certain groups (e.g., women and nursing). It is not enough that a female nurse is paid equally to a male nurse if nurses generally are paid less than other professions (performed predominantly by men) that are of "equal value" to nursing.

The third paragraph declares that pay should be fair ("just"), reflecting an adequate compensation for the work that has been performed ("favorable"). It should enable people to be able to have an "existence worthy of human dignity," that is, to maintain the standard of living that is set out in Article 25. If this is not possible on its own, then the state should step in to provide social protection.

The idea that pay is for "himself and his family" reflects the traditional conception of work as something performed by men in order to provide for their wives and children. The principle of gender equality from Article 2 and (in marriage) Article 16 demands that gender biases like these are removed from all areas of life. However, this means much more than equal pay for equal work. It requires a reconception of the workplace so that it is no longer necessarily designed to provide pay for individuals who have to support the entire family.

The final paragraph highlights the importance of another civil and political right, freedom of association, in the context of employment issues. Trade unions are associations in which workers join together to safeguard their interests as they are outlined in the other paragraphs of Article 23. The promotion of the right to organize became one of the hallmarks of the International Labour Organization (ILO), as enshrined in its Constitution of 1919. The ILO has also elaborated the character of the right through its conventions. Trade unions do not have to be approved by public authorities to be legitimate associations, and they have rights as between each other and different organizations. Human rights law also now protects the right of the individual to choose not to join a trade union without being fired.

ARTICLE 24

Everyone has the right to rest and leisure, including reasonable limitation of working hours and periodic holidays with pay.

The corollary to the right to work is the right to have time off from work. Whereas Article 23 looks at having a job and how the job works, Article 24 looks at having time away from the job and what happens then ("rest and leisure").

The right to have regular periods away from work is perhaps the most fundamental aspect of labor rights, apart from having work itself. Rest allows individuals to recover from the physical and mental exertions of work, promoting their personal welfare and capacity to work effectively. It also allows them to exercise their minds and bodies outside the work environment ("leisure"), whether through sports, the arts, travel, developing personal relationships, or engaging in public life where they live.

In many cultures a publicly enforced weekly day of rest has been a long tradition, often of religious origin. The European Social Charter reflects this by declaring that it should "coincide with the day recognized by tradition or custom in the country or region concerned as a day of rest." Here secular human rights attempts to accommodate notions of rights based on particular traditions. But different religions, for example, have different notions of holy periods and observe them during different periods of the week (e.g., Judaism from sundown Friday to sundown Saturday; Islam on Saturday; Christianity on Sunday). Rest and leisure are not to be understood in a vacuum, therefore, but with reference to the other concepts that they are connected to, from freedom of religion to cultural rights, minority rights, gender issues, and antidiscrimination.

Article 24 outlines the basic aspects of the right to rest. First, working hours should be limited to a reasonable period. This concerns the same issues surrounding the right to work in Article 23—attempting to set minimum standards in the realm of economic activity. It is different from a day of rest, which is applicable in the same way to all jobs. Instead the standard is what is reasonable, which suggests not only objectively reasonable (i.e., what every worker should be entitled to) but also subjectively reasonable (i.e., reasonable according to the particular job and individual concerned). Second, holidays should be periodic and with pay.

These two aspects have been developed in many ILO conventions, which attempt to set an hourly maximum for the working week and minimum yearly holiday entitlement. Such conventions stress the importance of taking into account the effect on productivity, competitiveness, inflation, technology, and the views of workers' and employers' organizations when such decisions are made.

ARTICLE 25

Everyone has the right to a standard of living adequate for the health and well-being of himself and of his family, including food, clothing, housing and medical care and necessary social services, and the right to security in the event of unemployment, sickness, disability, widowhood, old age or other lack of livelihood in circumstances beyond his control.

Motherhood and childhood are entitled to special care and assistance. All children, whether born in or out of wedlock, shall enjoy the same social protection.

Article 25 declares the basic social right to a humane standard of living. This covers both essential aspects of life generally, and safety-net guarantees when individuals have no means of supporting themselves. It is based on the idea that a civilized society does not allow people to go without when it has the capacity, through redistributing some resources, to help them.

An individual's standard of living is the degree to which she can meet her basic survival needs: sustenance, shelter, and health. These should be "adequate for... health and well-being." They should include food, clothing, housing, medical care, and necessary social services. Other instruments add recreation to this list.

The degree to which individuals can sustain their own lives and to which society can help them when they cannot depends on the level of development in their country. Therefore, Article 25 suggests where available resources should be targeted to, rather than prescribing a particular level of provision. These considerations should be borne in mind not as discrete objectives but as part of an integrated process of development within a country.

Individuals are in no position to be able to exercise any of their rights if they cannot maintain their health. Particularly crucial health needs include the prevention of stillbirths and infant mortality; the improvement of environmental and industrial hygiene; the prevention, treatment, and control of diseases; and the provision of medical care to the sick. Declarations on the rights of people with mental and physical disabilities (of 1971 and 1975) highlight the specific health needs of such people, from particular treatment to education and training.

How is the right to health reconciled with other rights? Individuals around the world engage in practices (such as cosmetic surgery, dieting, drug use, female genital mutilation, sadomasochistic activities, son preference, and traditional childbirth procedures), which involve varying degrees of risk to the health of themselves and others. Should the objective health risk justify preventing individuals from engaging in such practices? Or should individuals be allowed to do whatever they want to their own bodies? Furthermore, should the parents of children who are subjected to such practices have the power to consent to something that is so invasive to the child concerned?

The second half of the first paragraph discusses social security, a set of basic provisions for individuals who, through no fault of their own, are unable to support themselves. It is intended to tide them over if they have lost their job, so that they can remain healthy until another job opportunity comes along. It supports those people who cannot fully support themselves, whether because of illness or disability. Historically, people have been entitled to assistance when they reach a certain age, to reflect the contribution they have made to their families and to society. In some countries this usually amounts to a pension—a payment of money enabling them to get by. The principles of equality in Article 2

require, however, that people should not be presumed incapable of work by virtue of being a certain age. All people should be assessed for employment according to merit criteria that are age-blind.

ARTICLE 26

Everyone has the right to education. Education shall be free, at least in the elementary and fundamental stages. Elementary education shall be compulsory. Technical and professional education shall be made generally available and higher education shall be equally accessible to all on the basis of merit.

Education shall be directed to the full development of the human personality and to the strengthening of respect for human rights and fundamental freedoms. It shall promote understanding, tolerance and friendship among all nations, racial or religious groups, and shall further the activities of the United Nations for the maintenance of peace.

Parents have a prior right to choose the kind of education that shall be given to their children.

Article 26 sets out the right to education. In detail that is unusual for the declaration, Article 26 defines education in general terms and then makes suggestions as to what should be provided, the role the state should play, and the wider goals that education should serve.

Education is defined in the second paragraph. Subsequent declarations have elaborated on this, such as the 1974 United Nations Educational, Scientific, and Cultural Organization (UNESCO)

Recommendation that education is "the entire process of social life by means of which individuals and social groups learn to develop consciously within, and for the benefit of, the national and international communities their personal capacities, attitudes, aptitudes and knowledge. This process is not limited to any specific activities."

As far as the individual is concerned, education is thus conceived in the broadest terms possible. It develops the human personality—physical, emotional, intellectual, spiritual, psychological, and social—in a way that leads to personal self-determination and fulfillment and to rewarding engagement with other human beings and society as a whole. This covers both the conventional schooling system in most countries (elaborated in paragraph 1) and the ongoing process of personal development, through activities as diverse as reading and learning new languages, which take place throughout life. Schooling can be described either in terms of the type of learning which takes place (e.g., "fundamental" to cover basic literacy, arithmetic, and orientation in society; "technical" to cover particular skills; and "professional," which is aimed at a particular job) or in terms of stages through which students pass (primary/elementary school; secondary/middle/high school; further education such as university and polytechnic).

Playing a central role in the provision of education has traditionally been seen as one of the most basic state responsibilities, in terms of both funding and regulating access. In funding, Article 26 declares as an ideal that education shall be free, but by suggesting where priorities should lie acknowledges that in many countries universally free education at all levels is not economically viable. In regulating access Article 26 declares that entry to higher education should not be based on any factors other than ability (see Article 2).

As far as the wider goals of education are concerned, Article 26 underlines the importance of fostering the civic virtues, such as respect for the human person, human dignity, coexistence, peace, and justice, that are the basis for human rights. This echoes the 1924 Declaration of Geneva which stated that a child should be "brought up in the consciousness that its talents must be devoted to the service of its fellow men (sic.)." The drafters were particularly mindful of the need to prevent through education the hatred that led to the Holocaust, choosing positive language and discussing what education should inspire, rather than a negatively phrased Soviet proposal that education should "combat the spirit of intolerance and hatred."

Subsequent human instruments suggest further essential components of the right to education, which link it up to other human rights issues such as gender, health, the right to life, and freedom of religion. The gender discrimination convention (CEDAW), for example, articulates in Article 10(h) a right to access "specific educational information to help ensure the health and well-being of families, including information and advice on family planning." However, the more specific provisions become, the greater the opportunity for conflict between different ideas of rights. Whereas CEDAW Article 10(c) prescribes that education should involve the "elimination of any stereotyped concept of the roles of men and women . . . by encouraging coeducation . . . by the revision of textbooks and school programs and the adaption of teaching methods," the 1960 UNESCO Convention Against Discrimination in Education allows education segregated by gender as long as there is equal provision of education for both genders and at the same level.

The UN has declared 1995–2004 the Decade of Human Rights Education, reflecting the reality that human rights promotion not only involves making states accountable for the way they treat individuals, but also fostering a culture of rights within societies by making individuals aware of their rights and responsibilities.

ARTICLE 27

Everyone has the right freely to participate in the cultural life of the community, to enjoy the arts and to share in scientific advancement and its benefits.

Everyone has the right to the protection of the moral and material interests resulting from any scientific, literary or artistic production of which he is the author.

This article concerns the right to culture, which, like ethnicity and religion, can be as influential over individuals' lives as the legal regime within which they live. Involvement in the culture of one's group, whether through speaking a particular language or wearing certain dress, is impor-tant for an individual's sense of belonging and identity.

Article 27 is an uneasy attempt to reconcile individualism and communitarianism. In declaring cultural life to be "of the community," it acknowledges that human life is more than just the sum of a series of individual choices. However, it focuses on cultural life solely in terms of the individuals who engage in it, either as participants who are entitled to enjoy it and share its benefits or as producers who are entitled to the rights over their "product." It does not ascribe rights to the culture, or community, itself. Since the declaration, debate has raged about group rights: ascribing human rights to particular groups, such as religious or cultural minorities and indigenous people, rather than merely looking at the right of individuals within such groups to live out the identities that they derive from their group. At the root of many conflicts is the inability of particular groups, based on some combination of culture, religion, nationality, ethnicity, language, and history, to coexist. It was for this reason that the drafters of the declaration were reluctant to ascribe rights to minorities, fearing that this would lead to claims of statehood by many groups within states. However, the other side of that fear is that groups can also be the majority, imposing their particular culture on different minorities. The community should therefore be one where different groups coexist, rather than where one particular group becomes synonymous with the community as a whole.

Human rights law is based not on promoting or discouraging a particular culture, but rather on allowing cultural traditions to exist and coexist with other traditions. The key component is freedom—that individuals should never be pressured into, or prevented from, becoming involved in cultural life. However, how does one measure freedom from, say, a coercive imposition of particular cultural values? It is comparatively straightforward when someone declares that they are being forced to do what they do not want to do. How meaningful is consent when social and cultural pressures have a less direct, but equally powerful, effect on an individual's decisions?

Paragraph two of this article raises the question of how human rights law should safeguard cultural and scientific rights. Confiscation or eradication of cultural heritage has occurred throughout history, from Lord Elgin removing the Parthenon Marbles from Athens to London, to the destruction of Tibetan monasteries by China. It can occur for cultural or scientific reasons, such as a sense of obligation to preserve what would otherwise be spoiled, or attacking what binds a particular group of people together by destroying the material manifestations of their commonality. It can also occur for entirely unrelated reasons, such as the acquisition of wealth. It can be perpetrated by and against both states and individuals. International law approaches this matrix of interests in two ways. First, the concept of intellectual property or copyright/patent, articulated in the second paragraph, allows individuals rights over their own products. Second, various UNESCO conventions have set up regimes for the restitution of cultural property taken from states illegally or dur-

ing conflict. These have been supplemented by private initiatives, such as individuals bringing cases in the U.S. courts to claim back art confiscated by the Nazis from those it was sold to.

This is a process that is far from straightforward, however. Cultural or scientific property often has significance both to the individual who created it and the community of which it is a part. A particular scientific breakthrough may have a huge impact on humanity, like the discovery of penicillin; a work of art may come to represent the very nation itself, like the Statue of Liberty. The challenge for the law is to be able to protect the rights of all people for whom cultural and scientific property is important.

ARTICLE 28

Everyone is entitled to a social and international order in which the rights and freedoms set forth in this Declaration can be fully realized.

After the preceding articles enumerate the various rights of the declaration, Article 28 declares the importance of nurturing an environment which allows rights to flourish. It is a statement of principle rather than a particular individual right, looking at rights in a holistic way: in terms of the general circumstances in which they can be best attained.

At the time of drafting, Article 28, like the declaration as a whole, reflected the ideals of the postwar era and the emerging tensions of the Cold War. The United Nations, like the League of Nations before it, was founded on a desire to prevent the horrors of war and social deprivation that had come before it. It was to be the start of a new order, where human relations on a national and international level would promote the ideals of human rights that would be enshrined in the declaration. However, states disagreed as to the extent of the state's role in creating the new order. This resulted in a declaration which sets out various individual rights, but does not elaborate directly on the role of the state in ensuring the realization of these rights. Instead of adopting an article setting out these state obligations, as was proposed, the drafters instead adopted Article 28, which makes a much broader statement about the conditions that are necessary for the declaration to realize its potential.

With the decolonization that came after the declaration, newly independent states used the principles of Article 28 to argue that they were entitled to assistance from "developed" countries. They did not have the means to provide anything close to the economic, social, and cultural rights of the declaration, and they conceived a New International Economic Order where wealth would be redistributed more evenly across the globe through aid and nationalization. This led the General Assembly to declare a "Right to Development" in a resolution of 1986.

Fifty years after the declaration was drafted, the generality of Article 28 is actually much more appropriate than more specific proposals on state obligations would have been. A matrix of different actors and situations determines the human rights situation in any given case. For example, the right to education is dependent on a multiplicity of factors, including how the state runs its own education service, how it regulates private education providers, how parents make decisions about the education of their children (e.g., on religious grounds), how individuals can reach the stage where they can access what education is available (e.g., resources, nondiscrimination), and how everything in that particular country operates (e.g., its stage of development and therefore level of public resources; the level of insecurity from human or natural threats like war or environmental problems). As one moves further away from the state's own actions and toward the actions of others or external phenomena, it becomes less helpful to focus on the state's direct role in promoting the right concerned and more helpful to look at the indirect role it (and other actors and states) play in effecting an entire situation where that right can be enjoyed.

ARTICLE 29

Everyone has duties to the community in which alone the free and full development of his personality is possible.

In the exercise of his rights and freedoms, everyone shall be subject only to such limitations as are determined by law solely for the purpose of securing due recognition and respect for the rights and freedoms of others and of meeting the just requirements of morality, public order and the general welfare in a democratic society.

These rights and freedoms may in no case be exercised contrary to the purposes and principles of the United Nations.

Article 29 concerns the corollary to individual rights—that individuals have duties, both in terms of other individuals and the state. These duties form the basis for permissible limitations by the state on individual rights. They provide means for reconciling conflicts between different rights and between the exercise of individual rights and the maintenance of the community in which such rights are exercised.

Human rights law is concerned with the relationship of rights and responsibilities between the individual and the state. It sets out individuals' rights (e.g., the right to marry and the right to education), which correspond to the state's responsibilities or duties to allow individuals to exercise their rights (e.g., the duty not to interfere with individuals' wishes to marry; the duty to provide education). The state represents the common interests of all of the individuals within its jurisdiction—the community. This common interest sometimes requires a choice between the competing rights of individuals (e.g., one person's right to freedom of information and another person's right to privacy), or the preservation of society itself (e.g., insisting that everyone take certain immunizations). Both these actions necessarily involve state limitations on the rights of individuals, which correspond to individuals' responsibilities or duties to the common good. Limitations on rights are the necessary corollary to living in a community where human rights can be protected, and as such are actually promoting rights.

In many civil and political rights situations, the key question is not whether a particular right exists, but whether a particular limitation is justified. Human rights legal instruments have developed a set of considerations, following on from Article 29, that should be borne in mind when determining where the boundaries of rights and responsibilities should be. The ACHR contains an entirely separate section (Chapter 2) which sets out individuals' duties to the community. These include caring for parents in times of need and paying taxes. The ECHR, ICCPR, and ACHR incorporate limitations within the provisions of each article (where they are permissible), to suggest what boundaries are appropriate for each right. The following paragraphs explain how these boundaries normally work.

First, the limitation must be for a legitimate purpose (a good reason). This can be the protection of the rights of others (e.g., making actions that cause harm to others criminal offenses), or the preservation of society itself ("morality, public order and the general welfare"). This prevents the state from limiting rights for reasons other than the public good (e.g., restricting freedom of movement to prevent the activities of political opponents) or for no reason at all.

Second, the limitation must be determined by law. To be lawful, a limitation must be something that the state has the authority to do by virtue of the law, rather than solely because it has the power to do so. Furthermore, the law must be open, accessible, and foreseeable, so that individuals are aware of what powers the state has to limit their rights and can make sure that it does not exceed those powers.

Third, the limitation must be only that which is necessary to achieve the legitimate purpose ("securing due recognition for . . . meeting the just requirements of . . ."). In other words, the action by the state must be proportionate to the goal being pursued. It is not enough that there is a particular interest that needs protecting by the state, and the state has the right to protect it. The protection must go only as far as is required; otherwise, some rights would be restricted unnecessarily. The degree to which limitations are deemed necessary depends on the importance of the particular right involved. Some human rights are considered absolute (incapable of limitation), such as the prohibition on slavery (Article 4). Other rights are seen as very important and it is difficult to justify restricting them, such as freedom of expression (Article 19), which is considered one of the vital features of a democratic society.

Only when each element of the limitation test has been passed is a particular restriction justified. For example, political groups may wish to hold marches in town centers, exercising their rights to freedom of expression (Article 19) and movement (Article 13). This risks threatening other people's rights, from those who may have their right of way blocked (freedom of movement) to those who might have their property damaged (right to property, Article 17). It also risks threatening public order generally if the march gets out of control. Limitations would therefore be for legitimate purposes. In deciding what powers the police should have in law with respect to marches and rallies, the govern-

ment should consider what is necessary for them to serve all the above legitimate purposes adequately. The police should then look at any given situation and assess which of their powers it is necessary to exercise in those particular circumstances. They may have been given wide powers to impose considerable restrictions on where people can march (for example, if two rival marches are to take place and there is a serious risk of violence). However, if the march in question does not warrant these restrictions (e.g., no risk of violence) then to use the full powers available would be disproportionate to the interest being protected, and thus unlawful. It is not enough, therefore, to ask whether the means will achieve the end; the means must be only those which are strictly necessary to achieve the end. The police should be able to do all that is necessary to protect the public, but no more.

ARTICLE 30

Nothing in this Declaration may be interpreted as implying for any State, group or person any right to engage in any activity or to perform any act aimed at the destruction of any of the rights and freedoms set forth herein.

Article 30 is the companion to Article 29 in that it declares the basis for certain limitations on rights: that no one should be allowed to use his or her rights to compromise the rights of others. For example, an individual from a political party does not have the right to own all the news media in a country (exercising the right to own property in Article 17) so as to control what is written about contrasting political ideas (restricting freedom of expression and information [Article 19] and threatening the democratic nature of the political process [Article 21]).

Sometimes individuals or groups attempt to challenge the security of the state. Terrorism, for example, is the threat and use of violence within a country, aimed at changing the way the country is organized. Human rights law is based on the idea of a democratic society where such change is effected peacefully through the political process outlined in Article 21. Individuals require such a democratic state to protect their rights. When challenged, therefore, the democratic state needs to be able to take extraordinary measures, even limiting rights, to ensure the continued existence of the very entity that can protect rights in the first place. These measures take place in what is sometimes called a state of emergency and might involve curfews (restricting freedom of movement [Article 13]) and the closure of regular public services (restricting the right to education [Article 26]), for example. The balance of rights and duties between the individual and the state shifts much more toward the state, since the ordinary limitation possibilities in Article 29 are insufficient to address the situation properly.

It is exactly in such emergency situations that human rights are most at risk. Therefore, human rights law has developed a set of principles against which extraordinary measures can be tested so as to ensure that they do not shift the balance toward the state any more than is necessary. The test to decide when a state can derogate, or detract, from its human rights responsibilities is akin to the test for justifying a limitation, but it is formulated in a different way to respond to the different issues involved.

First, the state has to be faced with a situation that justifies a derogation. It must be an actual or imminent emergency, involving the whole nation, threatening the continuance of the organized life of the community, and the normal limitations are inadequate. This means it has to be something more than an everyday public order threat, such as a war or a public emergency. A regular parade would not usually justify a derogation; a series of violent terrorist incidents might.

Second, the rights that are to be derogated from must be capable of derogation. Certain rights have to be maintained even in the gravest emergency: the right to life (Article 3), the prohibition on slavery (Article 4), the prohibition on torture and inhuman or degrading treatment (Article 5), the right of habeas corpus (to go before a judge when you have been detained, from Article 9), and the prohibition on retroactive criminal offenses (Article 11). Furthermore, states have obligations in humanitarian law (the laws of war) which prevent them from violating certain rights even during war (e.g., attacks on civilian targets). If a right is in one of these nonderogable categories, it cannot be restricted.

Third, even if the situation requires a derogation and the right is capable of derogation, the derogation itself must be strictly required by the needs of the situation. This is similar to the proportionality/necessity test for limitations in Article

29: rights must only be derogated from to the extent necessary to deal with the threats from the emergency situation. If a natural disaster threatens the food supply to a country, for example, this does not in and of itself justify limiting freedom of expression.

The application of the derogations test involves a difficult balance between grave threats to society on the one hand and draconian restrictions on individual rights on the other. It concerns not only the rights of individuals generally but also the rights of those suspected or found to be behind the threat itself. It is sometimes argued that those who seek to destroy others' rights forfeit their own rights in the process. As such, the state should not have to follow the derogation test when dealing with them; for example, it can torture terrorist suspects and deny them due process to obtain vital information about possible future terrorist acts. However, human rights law is based on the concept of human dignity: that individuals possess rights simply because they are human, not because of anything they have or have not done. A state which treated certain individuals as outside human rights law would be endorsing a compromise to the value of human dignity, therefore threatening its own authority to protect such values, just as the terrorist suspect was doing.

— Ralph Wilde

PART THREE

The Contemporary
Human Rights Movement

The International Court of Justice at the Peace Palace, The Hague (UN Photo).

CHAPTER FOUR

An Overview of the Human Rights Movement

The modern human rights movement is a "child" of the twentieth century, and more specifically, a legacy of the horrific crimes committed against humanity in World War II. It is, in part, as much the story of the international governmental bodies working in the field (see Chapter 5) as it is of the formal nongovernmental organizations, informal groups, and individuals dedicated to promoting human rights concerns (see Chapter 6). What links the two is the strength of the Western tradition of concern for human welfare—a focus since at least the days of the Greeks and Romans, but refined, forged, and tested in the crucible of human want, war, and wealth over the last three thousand years. These roots generated sturdy trunks born of the English, American, and French revolutions, which blossomed throughout the West into rights not even dreamed of in the seventeenth and eighteenth centuries.

Historical Overview

Until the atrocities committed by the Axis states (Germany, Italy, and Japan) in World War II fundamentally altered the climate of interstate discourse, virtually all states were unwilling to allow outsiders to critique the treatment of their citizens. Leaders of most states considered the handling of rebels, prisoners, the destitute, the handicapped, women, and children purely an internal matter—governed by history, religion, and tradition. The legacy of that parochialism allowed totalitarian states to abridge the human rights of their and other states' citizens on an enormous scale. Few totalitarian dictators ever believed that they would receive their comeuppance, for as Stalin scoffed, "How many [military] divisions does the Pope have?"

Changed attitudes concerning human rights following World War II suddenly allowed international public scrutiny of virtually all countries, coupled with virtually instantaneous sharing of rights data via radio, wire services, and then television. The result was an explosion of information on human rights violations, which ignited interest on the part of ordinary citizens who could now unite together to effect change. The human rights movement was, thus, born.

In this climate the United Nations was created. Its charter included requirements that conventions and declarations to protect human rights be enacted, which led to the establishment of the United Nations Commission on Human Rights, chaired by Eleanor Roosevelt. Two years later, after considerable negotiation and compromise, the Universal Declaration of Human Rights (UDHR) was approved by the General Assembly on December 10, 1948 (see Chapter 2) with a vote of forty-eight in favor, zero against, and eight abstentions, including South Africa, Saudi Arabia,[1] and the Soviet Union.[2] (The other abstainers were subservient to Moscow.)

The promise—and the deficiencies—of the Universal Declaration were the additional impetus needed to help build a movement. Because the declaration was not a legally binding international document, it could only cajole and inspire states, rather than command their obedience, even to "universal" standards. The effort to implement the declaration took some twenty years and tens of thousands of individuals; finally the draft texts of two key treaties were accepted by the General Assembly. Another ten years passed before the International Covenant on Civil and Political Rights and the International Covenant on Economic, Social, and Cultural Rights[3] became operational in 1976. During that process, ordinary citizens learned that states move slowly, but worldwide bodies can inch forward at a glacial pace. Into that near vacuum of policy enforcement, groups of citizens organized to expose abuses, shame perpetrators, and educate the public. Some of the most successful groups, as well as their antecedents or descendants, are highlighted in Chapter 6. They are known collectively as nongovernmental organizations or NGOs.

Some of these NGOs worked hard to influence the United Nations, glacial though its progress was. Several other important international documents were shepherded

---

[1] Interestingly, the Saudi delegates objected not because the declaration recommended individual freedoms with which they were familiar in the Koran (rights of men concerning culture, education and work as religious commandments legally guaranteed), but because it lacked a unifying framework—for them, a belief in God. They viewed the declaration as competing with the Koran in its claim of universality, and judged it, instead, as purely applying Western practice and philosophy onto a world far different. Further, the Saudis feared Western secularism would undermine their own state and feared the declaration because it "lacked a scientific basis."

[2] The Soviets argued that they already had a Declaration of Rights of the People of Russia, dating from November 15, 1917, and a 1936 constitution that enumerated and protected those rights.

[3] These are known together as the International Bill of Rights.

through the UN system between 1948 and 1976, notably declarations that further refined the Universal Declaration. Although most consider declarations in the UN context vital in clearly understanding treaty documents (or conventions), their lack of enforcement mechanisms often limits their usefulness until, or if, a companion treaty follows. In one example to the contrary, the 1975 Declaration on the Protection of All Persons from Being Subjected to Torture and Other Cruel, Inhuman, or Degrading Treatment or Punishment, was a success largely due to the work of one NGO, Amnesty International. Because the twelve articles in the torture declaration offered practical and clear-cut advice for states in evaluating their employees, they also aided aggrieved citizens and human rights movements in proving their cases.

Perhaps the most successful human rights efforts occurred in the wake of the 1975 Helsinki Accords (see below), when Amnesty International's antitorture efforts, including the torture declaration and convention and worldwide letter-writing campaigns by legal, religious, medical, and psychiatric bodies, dramatically influenced the lives of persons incarcerated for their beliefs. Well-organized and funded NGOs can move proverbial mountains. The efforts of Amnesty International were instrumental in the passage of the follow-on 1984 UN convention on torture, which reinforced the declaration and was an important enforcement step. Amnesty International also directly influenced the passage of other subsequent declarations and led to other treaties affecting the treatment of incarcerated persons worldwide. These efforts radically changed the environment for persons accused of crimes and even helped facilitate the campaigns of the 1980s and 1990s that liberated many celebrated prisoners. Other NGOs followed, such as Doctors Without Borders, Human Rights Watch, and many others—so much so that some of the most influential constituents in the movement are NGOs working alongside international and individual government organs.

The Cold War in the History of the Human Rights Movement

In the 1950s and 1960s the Soviets repeatedly called for a European security conference, hoping to legitimate its control over the states of East and Central Europe, now firmly lodged behind the Soviet's "Iron Curtain." When the West finally agreed to such a conference, which opened in 1972, it did so only if human and economic rights were added to the discussions and only if the United States and Canada were full participants also. The result of this conference, the Helsinki Accords (officially the Final Act of the Helsinki Meeting of the Conference on Security and Cooperation in Europe, or CSCE), was signed in 1975 by all European and North American states (except Albania). It added dramatic impetus to the successes of NGO efforts on behalf of human rights.

When the Helsinki Accords were published and disseminated behind the Iron Curtain, Helsinki monitoring groups (see

Chapter 6) sprang up, arguing that their governments must implement the Accords. These groups were brutally attacked in the Soviet Union and in Czechoslovakia especially, although they also received adverse notice elsewhere in the rest of the bloc. This negative response only heightened Western concerns, and in a series of review conferences between East and West, the East was ultimately so embarrassed and harassed that substantial change began to occur.

After 1985, with the rise of Mikhail Gorbachev in the Soviet Union, the USSR increasingly accepted the humanitarian and human rights principles articulated in Basket Three[4] of the Helsinki Accords. Once the East and Central European revolutions of 1989 occurred, Basket Three offered a standard of behavior for the reform regimes that followed. At the 1990 Helsinki follow-up meeting in Copenhagen, all of the newly established European states unanimously endorsed multiparty democracy, political pluralism, independent judiciaries, special protection for minority groups, and the separation of the state from free political parties.

This all occurred as an exercise in diplomacy. Not only did the accords lack any "divisions," as Stalin put it, but they had no charter, no budget, and no secretariat. They operated with ad hoc support from the foreign ministries of member states, augmented by a huge NGO community and the world's press. At a time when progress on destabilizing arms control issues loomed large, the success that this diplomatic instrument offered in East-West relations was impressive. Without the accords, the transformation of East and Central Europe, as well as the USSR, would likely not have come so soon or so peacefully.

A Case Study in Human Rights Policy: The Carter Administration

Ever since the founding of America its political elite has grappled with the classic debate over isolation versus engagement in great power politics. Coupled with that debate in the twentieth century has come the struggle over to what degree morality must dictate foreign policy. Few contemporary statesmen, or indeed politicians, adhere to pure idealism, which focuses on morality as the only or primary calculations of the national interest. Similarly, few are whole-hearted supporters of realism, which flouts morality in favor of a pure pursuit of realpolitik, or national interest. Nevertheless, less principled leaders and states use realism as their prime paradigm in directing their nation's conduct, and to engage and defeat them states espousing higher principles must also then pursue realism in foreign affairs.

At the center of the United States' first human-rights-oriented foreign policy effort since World War II—after its relative disengagement during the 1950s and part of the 1960s—the Carter administration grappled with the trade-off between geopolitics and human rights. Although the

---

[4] The Helsinki Accords were thematically organized into topics or "baskets."

Carter administration used virtually all means at its disposal to influence states accused of human rights violations, it was caught up in the reality of state politics, even within its own administration, by practitioners of subtly different persuasions. The superpower rivalry, arms control issues, the grain trade, regional conflagrations, the Soviet invasion of Afghanistan, global energy policies, conflicts with traditional allies, the hostage crisis in Iran,[5] and immigration policy all deeply affected President Jimmy Carter's hopes for human rights influence. Nevertheless, because Carter's political emphasis struck a chord with deep-seated American values, it helped heal the bitterness left over from the Vietnam War in the American body politic, just as it added immeasurably to the lives of millions worldwide.

Critics, however, accused the Carter administration of inconsistency, particularly with regard to the implementation, or lack thereof, of stiff responses to human rights violations in states of importance to the United States that were dictated by realism. Similarly, President Carter's policies toward right-wing dictatorships were sometimes criticized for being too harsh, just as he was maligned by many human rights bodies for being too lenient with China and the Shah's regime in Iran.[6] (Ironically, others argued that Carter's

human rights preoccupation actually alienated the Shah, directly or indirectly leading to his overthrow in 1979 and helping usher in the hostage crisis.) Those who did not understand America's twin poles of isolationism and engagement and those who scoffed at the policy trade-off between idealism and realism in foreign policy saw these apparent zigzags in policy as ripe for criticism.

The high profile of President Carter's efforts internationally occasioned skepticism and active resistance. When the United States sponsored a resolution "calling on the United Nations to appoint a High Commissioner for Human Rights," it was defeated sixty-two to forty-nine, with twenty-one abstentions. The swing votes leading to its defeat came from the developing world and Communist states.[7]

Nevertheless, in the light of intervening years, it seems clear that President Carter's emphasis on human rights as a key priority in geopolitics has reverberated in a salutary fashion around the world. The key issue for him and for subsequent presidents and world leaders is always the question of political will. For as Felie Gaer, executive director of the International League for Human Rights, said in testimony before the House Committee on Foreign Affairs in February 1986: "The

---

[5] The U.S. Embassy was overrun during the Iranian revolution, and fifty-two U.S. citizens were captured. Subsequently, an abortive military effort was launched to rescue them.

[6] Former U.S. UN representative Jeane J. Kirkpatrick's article in *Commentary* in November 1979, entitled "Dictatorships and Double Standards," highlighted aspects of the new human rights policy that would be undertaken by the Reagan administration. Politically, and from the standpoint of foreign policy, it was highly damaging because it implied that the United States condoned abuses if they were undertaken by authoritarian governments friendly to the United States.

[7] *The New York Times*, December 6, 1977.

Two Concepts of Foreign Policy

In the international human rights context, President Carter is the best example of an idealist in American foreign policy. Idealists argue that the pursuit of morality in foreign policy is compatible with national security concerns. They also argue that America's leadership role in the world is so vital that it must set the very highest standards so that America and its allies can help influence a more peaceful and just world.

On the other end of the spectrum is Hans J. Morgenthau, author of *Politics Among Nations* and founder of the realist school. He argued that the choice for leaders is not between the national interest and moral principles, but rather between moral principles divorced from political reality and moral principles derived from political reality. America's senior foreign policy elites have tended to be most sympathetic to the realist school of foreign policy. In recent years, President Richard M. Nixon and his Secretary of State Henry Kissinger have evidenced it, as has President Carter's National Security Adviser Zbigniew Brzezinski, President George Bush, and Secretary of State George Shultz.

United States needs to do more than make declarations and to provide free transport for fleeing dictators .... The U.S. government has leverage to use—if it chooses to use it. *It has the power to persuade governments*" [emphasis added].

Ongoing Controversies in the Human Rights Movement

Although international consensus on the importance of human rights has increased in the last fifty years, the questions raised during the formation of the movement are far from answered.

Human Rights as Western Imperial Legacy

In the contest for rights the West was dealt a strong hand. Not only was there a firm belief in the value and efficacy of inherited institutions, but the West supported a substantial and growing population, it maintained fleets of trading and warships, and it possessed the world's most powerful weapons and largest armies, along with the most efficient network of transport and communications. By the end of the nineteenth century, Western political and economic clout extended far beyond European settlement. By 1914 almost all of Africa, Latin America, south and southeast Asia, and Oceania had come under European or American political control. Farms, mines, and plantations were opened in many largely virgin areas, often at places remote from Western or any other sort of civilization. New products like tea, rubber, nickel, and oil mingled together with old ones like gold and diamonds; new two-way commercial ventures were established (like cotton and cloth in India and Egypt); and traders, missionaries, and settlers moved into every area previously considered inaccessible.[8]

These efforts by colonial powers—and the peoples and commodities who moved under their imprimatur, whether loose or deliberate—fundamentally altered the older distributions of populations, cultures, and orientations in the world. Mountain barriers, oceans, and even parched and windswept plains were no longer sufficient to halt the Western advance, and few militaries were able but to stall the march of Westerners and their ideals, religion, trade, and technology.

As such, human rights philosophy and the subsequent movement in support of it flowered in the West and dispersed along old lines of influence around the globe. Nevertheless, only in Western democratic societies, with their shared philosophies and historical and economic development, does the support for human rights run as deeply in philosophy, society, and law. The Western emphasis is centered on the liberty of the person. Not only does he or she have the right to hold and express individual intellectual and religious beliefs, but he or she also possesses the right to physical security. By contrast, other traditions—Asian, African, Islamic, and to a lesser extent Latin—lack the same emphasis on individual political rights. Illustrative of these differences is the actual language of the Universal Declaration, which devotes only three of its thirty articles to economic rights,[9] the emphasis of which is more common in more traditional, communal societies. Similarly, socialist states, irrespective of the region, also lack an emphasis on civil rights, emphasizing group and economic rights instead.

Cultural Differences and Human Rights

"The debate on human rights assumes that in spite of the differences that characterize the spectrum of world cultures, political conduct can be conceptualized by certain common norms and attitudes. In the modern global system, Westerners have concentrated on discovering common denominators rooted in Judeo-Christian traditions and from which a calculus of human rights would emerge. This emphasis on Western common denominators projects a

---

[8] McNeill, William. *The Rise of the West: A History of the Human Community*. Chicago and London: The University of Chicago Press, 1963. p. 731.

[9] Articles 17, 23, and 24 are primarily economic. Article 17 focuses on property rights, while Article 23 deals with appropriate wages, the right to work, and equal pay for equal work. Article 24 focuses on the right to leisure.

Latin America

The Central and South American countries that compose Latin America were settled in the modern age primarily by the Spanish and Portuguese. Over the intervening centuries these Europeans blended with indigenous Indian tribes to produce an ethno-racial group that was augmented by the arrival of African slaves, other Europeans, Asians, and North Americans. As such, the peoples are a polyglot, but the dominant political culture is still Western, albeit with a Latin flavor.

In the period after World War II, an aversion to political rights and free and fair elections was justified (by some governments) by the threat of Communism. The argument that human rights should be held in abeyance until after development also continued to apply. Many assessments suggest that both justifications were convenient excuses needed to justify a military junta or a coup.

Indeed, the legitimacy of a regime is a question that has plagued many Latin American countries for some time. This problem is particularly acute when otherwise apolitical militaries cannot meet their oaths to preserve, protect, and support a civilian regime that has ceased to exist through turmoil, anarchy, or disputed elections. The Latin political culture in the post-World War II period became so chaotic at times that military intervention became legitimate, because the military was popularly viewed by the citizenry as their final guardian of popular sovereignty.

However, with the worldwide growth in pluralism in the 1980s and 1990s, much of Latin America also enjoyed a return to civilian rule—as well as greater popular sovereignty and strengthened commitment to human rights issues.

parochial view of human rights that excludes the cultural realities and present existential conditions of Third World societies. What has occurred is the reshaping of politics to accommodate various theories of political behavior gleaned from Western traditions."

—Abdul Aziz Said[10]

At the root of the cultural differences concerning rights was the fundamental dichotomy that existed between Western and non-Western societies. Western industrial states have traditionally placed a substantial emphasis on individual rights, with government initially only grudgingly guaranteeing some basic economic support for the least fortunate. By contrast, non-Western traditional societies have tended to meet their needs more communally, stressing reliance on

[10] Abdul Aziz Said, "Human Rights in Islamic Perspectives," in *Human Rights: Cultural and Ideological Perspectives*, edited by Adamantia Pollis and Peter Schwab (New York: Praeger, 1979). See also selected works of the same era by Seyyed Hossein Nasr, founder of the Imperial Academy of Philosophy of Iran, Ali Mohammadi of Farabi University, and Hadi Sharifi of the Imperial Academy.

the family and the group. Not yet heavily industrialized, with a majority of the population in agriculture, and with a limited educational base, a marginal climate and/or limited resources, these societies are centered around the clan, the tribe, extended families, and/or local, isolated communities. The group, thus, becomes the defining element of society, not the individual, particularly if the society is on the margin, with scant hope of survival without the entire populace tightly organized.

When Western views on rights met Eastern, African, and to a lesser extent Latin views, further distinctions emerged. Westerners tend to emphasize individual responsibility for economic and social progress within a broader state economic structure, while many non-Western states find these to be key duties of the state. In the latter, individual political or human rights are clearly communal if considered at all, and of lesser importance.

When these largely African and Asian states became independent of colonial powers in the wake of World War II, little changed for the individual, although as groups the populace became sovereign states. What had traditionally been a set of obligatory responsibilities toward the group now became responsibilities due the state; what rights had been bestowed by the group now became the purview of the state to bestow (or withdraw) as it so wished. As Indira Gandhi of India told *The New York Times* in 1975, "It is not individuals who have rights but states."

Decolonization, Development, and Human Rights

Decolonization and subsequent efforts toward economic development of newly independent nations offer ongoing and fundamental challenges to the human rights movement. In Africa and Asia the British Westminster model employed during colonial rule, which emphasized individual rights, was incorporated into virtually all constitutions during decolonization and has survived largely intact over the decades. Departures from the model tended to be in states with civil upheavals, where authoritarian and/or military leaders scrapped the inherited constitutions of civilian rule. In those states either a one-party state was imposed or a military junta ruled. In both cases, political liberties withered on the vine, usually covered by transparent appeals to communal and economic rights that would be respected. Typically, "preventive" detention laws were put in place, freedom of speech, press, and association was restricted, most if not all political parties were outlawed, the judiciary and legislative functions were subsumed under the authoritarian or military rulers, and normally nonpolitical groups such as aid societies, religious bodies, and educational institutions were allowed to exist only if they subsumed themselves under the rulers' control. Soon the promised economic rights disappeared under nationalizations of key industries, with political leaders and their cronies siphoning off the lion's share of the proceeds. The Philippines' Ferdinand Marcos and Zaire's Mobutu Sese Seko were particularly adept at such schemes.

Many authoritarian and military-led states argued that democratic ideals and human rights should be sacrificed in the present and pursued in the future in order to concentrate on economic development. It was argued by many that development would bring economic rights, which in turn would meet the needs for human dignity by emancipating the masses from colonial exploitation and dependence. Julius Nyerere in Tanzania, Sékou Touré in Guinea, and Kwame Nkrumah in Ghana all prominently espoused this argument, winning converts at home and abroad. In like manner, the explosion of Latin military dictatorships of the 1950s through 1980s or the Greek military coup of 1967 justified the removal of personal freedoms in the name of preserving order. When trials of torturers were held following Greece's liberation from the military in 1974, the torturers were not tried for gross abrogation of human rights but merely "misuse of authority," since no law made torture illegal in Greece![11]

Rights in the postcolonial era tended to be defined with regard to colonialism. Most postcolonial states achieved independence at an early stage of economic development, with low gross domestic products (GDPs), low levels of literacy and savings, little indigenous capital generation, and a population still primarily in agriculture or pastoral pursuits. If the colonial legacy in a state was relatively benign, then the transition to a Western-style concept of rights was generally not seriously challenged. Where the colonial administration was rapacious and the economic impact exploitative, then postcolonial rights tended to be viewed against that prism, with economic concerns paramount, rather than civil concerns celebrating the rights of the individual. In states where the per capita income was exceedingly low, rights came to be assessed as freedom from want and the money needed to educate and clothe children, with something left over for feeble, later years. Medical access, educational access, and free or low-cost land were all far more important than somewhat abstract concepts of political rights.

Indeed, until mass secondary education has become standard and a rising middle class has succeeded sufficiently well that it has something to lose (as began to occur in the West in the eighteenth and nineteenth centuries), most developing societies do not naturally and intimately focus themselves on individual rights. The educated few, government elites, and sometimes the church, as well as the expatriate community, tend to be those most intimately involved in helping protect individual rights until the rising tide of development makes the concept real and vital to the masses.

In that vein it is worth stating something widely observed about developing states in the post-World War II period: support for democratic development is

---

[11] Amnesty International evaluates Greece's failure to enact laws forbidding torture in *Torture in Greece: The First Torturers' Trial 1975* (London: Amnesty International Publications, 1977).

rarely more than skin-deep. Because Western political democracy is not only based upon deep levels of educated participation but upon legal guarantees, it is often dispensed with by authoritarian or military regimes in the developing world. The decades of the 1960s and 1970s were especially worrisome to those who feared sweeping tides of authoritarianism and misery wiping out fledgling democratic governments. One-party states became common in Africa, as charismatic leaders like Sékou Touré, Nyerere, and Nkrumah stamped out political dissent. Nkrumah argued that "the Convention People's Party (CPP) is Ghana and Ghana is the CPP."[12]

Throughout the 1980s and 1990s, participatory democracy—or polyarchy, as Robert Dahl coined it to avoid anti-U.S. or anti-Western bias—began to sweep the globe, first in Latin America and later in key states in Africa and Asia. As these more pluralistic states came to power, so did greater willingness to reinstitute Western notions of rights. The press became freer, dissent opened up, parties blossomed, and conditions for women and children improved.

The Problem of Enforceability

The problems of enforcing human rights arise from the multiplicity of instruments, entities, and individual interests at play in the human rights movement. There is no single ideology that defines what human rights are and no monolithic structure that has the jurisdiction to supervise their enforcement.

Although Eleanor Roosevelt, as chair of the Human Rights Commission, stated in 1948 that the Universal Declaration of Human Rights "is not a treaty; it is not an international agreement, it is not and does not purport to be a statement of law or legal obligation,"[13] many who worked on the issue clearly hoped that it would go beyond the recommendation format and become the new international norm. They recognized that the declaration format was the best they could hope to achieve in 1948.

Over time the Universal Declaration has come to be regarded as binding upon the signatory states, with many citing Article 6 of the Convention on the Elimination on All Forms of Racial Discrimination, adopted by the General Assembly and put into force in 1969, and the Preamble of the International Covenant on Economic, Social, and Cultural Rights of 1966 as having made the declaration binding by reaffirming the declaration's principles. Custom has also reaffirmed the declaration's principles as binding in international law.[14]

Since the Universal Declaration a rapidly growing number of states have incorporated explicit support for human

---

[12] Kwame Nkrumah, *I Speak of Freedom* (New York: Praeger, 1961).

[13] United Nations General Assembly, Official Records: Third Session, First Part, Plenary, 180th meeting (New York), 860.

[14] See, for example, the Statute of the International Court of Justice, which specifies in Article 38, that customary law can be considered binding when custom shows "evidence of a general practice accepted as law."

Islam: A Rival Cultural Tradition

The role of government, the state, religion, and the rights of the individual are fundamentally different under Islam from what exists in the West. An Islamic government exists to ensure that the *Shariah* (laws stemming from the Koran, the Sunnah,[15] the Ijma,[16] and the Ijtihad[17]) is enforced. In these states God is viewed as the ultimate arbiter and legislator. It is assumed that all, rulers and ruled, are jointly entwined in an enterprise that will promote God's glory. As such, human legislation is far less important than it is in the West, since it is believed that God's wishes are clear and that only relatively minor matters need go before the judges.

According to scholar Abdul Aziz Said, Islamic legal theory "provides no adequate machinery to safeguard individual rights against the state."[18] As a result, various Islamic states, or states with a significant proportion of their populace who are Muslim, have designed a variety of coping strategies. On one end of the spectrum Saudi Arabia applied the *Shariah* fully and literally. By contrast Pakistan has provided for individual rights through a liberal analysis of the oldest sources of Islamic law. Turkey took another tack: since modern Turkey's founding by Kemal Ataturk (1881-1938), Turkey has guaranteed individual rights in a secular state. Similarly, Egypt has attempted to accommodate both Islam and Christianity in a constitution-based state on the British model. All three of these latter states, along with others, have found the struggle to protect individual liberties along Western lines difficult, given the recent growth of Islamic fundamentalism.

The record of human rights protection in Islamic states is varied. With traditional Islamic codes viewed as losing their utility as safeguards for rights within Islam, and with modern philosophical and state constructs not yet fully accepted, individual rights and their protectors are in turmoil. With divisions in Islam serious enough to fight major conflicts over (such as in Afghanistan and in Iraq) and with continuing hostility and rivalry among sunni, shia, and rival sects (such as the Wahhabis who rule Saudi Arabia), a common agenda for individual rights in Islamic states is not assured.

Like the Judeo-Christian tradition, there is much in Islam that would seem to augur well for the protection of individual dignity. The concept of *dhimmis* promises Christians, Jews, and other groups that an Islamic country is committed to protecting the possibility of existing within an Islamic state. Moreover, the Koran encourages moderate life, without inordinate emphasis on wealth-building: "And thus we have made you a people with moderate virtues in order that you may be a witness to men" (2:143). Islam

---

[15] These are the Hadith and the decisions of Muhammad.
[16] These are the consensus of opinion of the Ulama (judges).
[17] These are the counsel of judges on a specific case.
[18] Said, 88.

also fears poverty, for it can lead the poor away from God. Thus, a Muslim expects his or her state to help meet the basics of housing, food, and clothing for all.

Humans are viewed as being created in the image of God and are considered God's representatives (*khalifah*) on earth. Humans are expected to receive certain rights from their God, with individual freedom achieved in perfect subservience to God. Because this type of freedom is individual, and eternal, Muslims don't look for it through public legislation. Rather, an individual is free in Islam until his freedom hinders the community; at that point, the state intervenes. Similarly, the *Shariah* describes rights and freedoms, but they come with obligations towards God and others. The *Shariah* states that unless obligations are accepted and fulfilled, individuals are not allowed rights. Similarly, without fulfillment of obligations, any claims of freedom from the state are not acceptable.

The twentieth century and its emphasis on human rights has spawned a debate in the Islamic theological and philosophical world concerning rights. One branch of theology, which includes the Asharites, does not weigh human freedom as legitimate. They believe that God's grace determines all. Most Muslim philosophers, however, grant that human freedom exists, all the way back to Avicenna, Averroes, and Farabi, who knew the works of Aristotle, Plato, and the Stoics. However, they did not accept the Greek notion of human freedom but argued instead for freedom for the individual within Islam. This group-based freedom "denies some of the essential Western liberal conceptions of freedom. From the Islamic perspective, the anarchy of liberal individualism cannot be a creative seedbed of culture."[19]

Political freedom, thus, is offered far less latitude than spiritual freedom. Indeed, a constant rivalry exists in Islamic states between temporal rulers and spiritual. In the past the conflict between free will and God's determinism have "produced periods of submission characterized by anarchy and assassination."[20] Political leaders at times are zealous in their support of religious doctrine, while other leaders at other times refuse to do so. As such, religious-based zealotry then induces periods of great conflict between Islamic states and within them, as well as between Islamic countries and their neighbors. The violence that results clearly betrays any latent efforts to protect the sanctity and dignity of the person.

In sum, Islam is at a stage in human history wherein international modes of human rights behavior are challenging it to change faster than it can without a bitter, internecine struggle for secular, political, and religious power. Islam has yet to accommodate the nation-state within its traditional culture and religion. In order to meet prevailing international norms of human rights, a fundamental social revolution would be required in most Islamic states.

[19] Ibid., p. 93.
[20] Ibid, p. 94.

rights, and often guarantees of proper treatment, in their constitutions as well as in the treaties establishing regional bodies. The charters of the Organization of American States (OAS), the Council of Europe, and the Organization of African Unity (OAU) are such examples. This growing organizational entrenchment of liberties gives further support for binding the declaration's principles in international law. These instruments amount to a legal patchwork that lawyers and activists in the international arena must struggle to negotiate.

An enforcement issue indigenous to Western states deals with who holds the upper hand—the individual or the state. This rivalry is a two-hundred-year-old issue, but it now has taken on a new dimension with the rise of "welfare states," especially in Western Europe. Starting with the English Petition of Rights and the American and French declarations, more was given to the individual and less was expected of the individual from the state. Over the past two centuries, individual responsibilities and obligations decreased, while individual freedoms grew. By contrast, however, greater rights, prerogatives, and freedoms presumed greater state efforts to protect them. The poor, the landless, children, women, and laborers all needed help in bad times and protection from their rapacious fellows. As such, the state was required to expand its capacity to meet these new needs. Today the state is caught between two poles of human rights advocates. Whenever it intercedes on behalf of one individual or group, it can be accused of denying or neglecting others.[21]

— Carol Rae Hansen

[21] In addition to sources cited in other footnotes, additional sources for this chapter include: Jan Austin, *Congressional Quarterly Almanac, 1995* (Washington, D.C.: Congressional Quarterly, Inc., 1995), pp. 2-93-2-94; Alexander DeConde, ed., *The Encyclopedia of American Foreign Policy: Studies of the Principal Movements and Ideas*, Volume I (New York: Charles Scribner's Sons, 1984), pp. 122-123, 606-609, 649-650, 821-823, 865-866; Liz Heffernan, ed. *Human Rights: A European Perspective* (Dublin: The Round Hall Press, 1994), especially pp. 1-65; Joel Krieger, ed., *The Oxford Companion to Politics of the World* (New York and Oxford: Oxford University Press, 1993), pp. 225, 272-273, 386-387, 401-403, 792-793, 852-853; Frank N. Magil, *Great Events from History II: Human Rights Series*, Volumes 2,3,4,5 (Pasadena, Calif.: Salem Press, 1992), pp. 590-593, 808-811, 843-847, 849-853, 855, 879-882, 902, 1032-1035, 1038-1042, 1137-1141, 1391-1395, 1644, 1841, 1847-1851, 1903-1907, 1909, 2057-2061, 2174-2175, 2204-2207; Admantia Pollis and Peter Schwab, eds., *Human Rights: Cultural and Ideological Perspectives* (New York: Praeger Publishers, 1979), especially pp. 1-18 and 32-43; John T. Rourke, ed., *Taking Sides: Clashing Views on Controversial Trends in World Politics* (Guilford, CN: The Dushkin Publishing Group, Inc., 1995), pp. 272-287, 350-369; William Safire, *Safire's New Political Dictionary* (New York: Random House, 1993), pp. 341-343, 413-414, 464, 634-635, 685-686.

CHAPTER FIVE

Governmental Organizations

Despite the diversity of the globe's cultures and appropriate reservations made in international documents to preserve sovereignty, international standards for the promotion and protection of human rights have been established and accepted—at least nominally—by sovereign states worldwide. Of course, these supranational standards are not always met, because regimes will still rebuff international standards they see as inconvenient or illegitimate; insurgencies rarely meet these standards either, because most see all means as legitimate to their ends. Nevertheless, legitimate governments[1] have acquiesced to these universal standards, even if they do not fully meet them.

This chapter examines the efforts of the international community to expand and enforce human rights protections at the governmental level.

United Nations

Department of Public Information
United Nations
New York, NY 10017
PH: (212) 963-4475
FX: (212) 963-0071
WWW: http://www.un.org

The basis of the UN's support for human rights lies with three documents: the Universal Declaration of Human Rights (UDHR, 1948), which is nonbinding, the International Covenant on Civil and Political Rights (ICCPR, 1966), and the International Covenant on Economic, Social, and Cultural Rights (ICESCR, 1966). (Both the ICCPR and the ICESCR are legally binding, entering into force in 1976.) Together, these are informally called the International Bill of Rights. This "bill" is reinforced by a provision allowing individuals to protest against their own

---

[1] Legitimate governments are those accepted by a majority of their populace as having the appropriate authority to govern, whether or not they are ratified by Western beliefs in due process, organized elections, and popular sovereignty.

governments. An optional protocol (operable in March 1979) to the ICCPR created a method for dealing with people who attest that they are victims of violations of the covenant by their home state.

The ICCPR imposed on the roughly 130 states that have signed it an immediate obligation to guarantee the civil and political rights that it enumerates. By contrast, the ICESCR requires its party member states to take progressive steps to safeguard the economic and social rights listed in its articles. The latter will tend to differ, depending upon the stage of development that has been achieved by various states.

Around this core a variety of more specific agreements have grown up. The most important of these include the Genocide Convention (1948), the Convention on the Elimination of All Forms of Racial Discrimination (1969), the Convention on the Elimination of All Forms of Discrimination Against Women (1979), the Convention Against Torture (1984), and the Convention on the Rights of the Child (1989). A variety of UN commissions and sub-bodies in Geneva and New York now work year-round to monitor compliance with the above.

Office of the High Commissioner for Human Rights

Palais de Nations
CH-1211
Geneva 10
Switzerland

PH: 41 22 9173156
FX: 41 22 9170213
WWW: http://www.unhchr.ch
E-Mail: secrt.hchr@unog.ch

The UN's Office of the High Commissioner for Human Rights (OHCHR) was established by the UN General Assembly in 1993 to oversee all UN activities relating to the promotion of human rights. The office is headed by the High Commissioner, whose rank is that of an Under-Secretary-General reportable directly to the Secretary General of the UN. The OHCHR operates several organizational units and branches, including a Staff Office and Administrative Unit, the Research and Right to Development Branch, the Support Services Branch, and the Activities and Programmes Branch.

The OHCHR also oversees the activities of the Commission on Human Rights (see below), which has been operating since the founding of the United Nations and has been the organ primarily responsible for developing the Universal Declaration of Human Rights and the subsequent body of human rights law that followed from it.

With the appointment of Mary Robinson, former president of Ireland, as High Commissioner for Human Rights at the UN, the OHCHR has both elevated its profile and enhanced early warning activities. The Center for Human Rights has also been consolidated into the Office of the High Commissioner, and the High Commissioner has been made a member of the Secretary General's executive committee.

Commission on Human Rights

Palais de Nations
CH-1211
Geneva 10
Switzerland
PH: 41 22 9173156
FX: 41 22 9170213
WWW: http://www.unhcr.ch/html/menu2/2/chr.htm

Now operating under the auspices of the Office of the High Commissioner for Human Rights (OHCHR), the Commission on Human Rights has been the central body responsible for developing human rights policy since 1947, although the UN General Assembly and various other UN bodies deal with human rights concerns at times. The Commission on Human Rights develops human rights laws and standards and promotes human rights by undertaking studies and developing recommendations and international documents that focus on human rights. The commission is composed of representatives from fifty-three member states elected for three-year terms.

The UN Commission on Human Rights also supervises the human rights records of member states through public forums and regular reviews, and it appoints special *rapporteurs* to monitor specific human rights problems in particular countries and regions.

It has established a number of other groups to promote its efforts, such as the Working Group on Enforced or Involuntary Disappearances and the Sub-Committee on the Prevention of Discrimination and Protection of Minorities. These groups meet with offending governments to discuss alleged violations of human rights. If the findings are sufficiently serious, the commission may investigate further in order to remedy the situation.

In addition, the OHCHR offers advisory services and technical assistance, supervises educational courses, and offers an annual program of fellowships for officials who deal with human rights. A number of subsidiary bodies assist with this work, such as the Sub-Commission on the Prevention of Discrimination and Protection of Minorities and special officials who are given fact-finding assignments, in countries such as Iran, Chile, Afghanistan, El Salvador, Bosnia, and Guatemala. The commission also asks working groups to evaluate concerns that might become the impetus for new declarations or conventions. Topics studied in the past include disappearances, executions, torture, and self-determination.

United Nations High Commissioner for Refugees

UNHCR Public Information
P.O. Box 2500
1211 Geneva 2
Switzerland
PH: 41 22 739 8502
FX: 41 22 739 7314/15/16
WWW: http://www.unhcr.ch
E-Mail: hqpi00@unhcr.ch

The United Nations High Commissioner for Refugees (UNHCR) is the most prominent of a number of institutions addressing refugee problems. The UNHCR now works in roughly one hundred countries worldwide. Given a worldwide population approaching five billion, it may seem that the twenty-two million people served by UNHCR in 1997 was small. Due to limited resources and the fact that many cannot reach UNHCR stations, the number that could be served is far grander. Consider the fact that in 1998, in addition to formal refugees (outside their country of origin), some forty-two million people worldwide were termed temporary migrants, another six million immigrants, and between four and fifty million internally displaced (within their country of origin).

Despite the de facto universality of the Geneva Convention, refugee and asylum status are limited. For example, there is no individual right to asylum; rather, each state holds the right to grant or deny the right to asylum (protection) for individuals fleeing persecution in their own country. Indeed, Article 14 of the Universal Declaration states that refugees have the right to "seek" asylum and to "enjoy" such asylum if it is granted. While there is an obligation in international law to determine refugee status, there is not an international right to asylum (see Part 4, "Refugees"). In recent years, new types of protections, including "humanitarian refugee status" or "B refugee status," attempt to help people who cannot prove individual persecution, but who have otherwise compelling reasons to flee.

A series of institutions addressing refugee problems, including the UNHCR, have attempted to tone down political aspects of refugee affairs and focus instead on humanitarian relief and moral dilemmas. Some of the adjustments they have made include changes to the policies of asylum, the addition of extended voluntary departure (protection in a second state short of asylum for a period of time until conditions at home improve), settlement in a third state, or even eventual voluntary repatriation to the nation of origin. Since the mid-1990s the UNHCR and the UNHCHR have worked together to meet desperate needs in Bosnia, Rwanda, Burundi, Georgia, Cambodia, Colombia, Haiti, Guatemala, and Vietnam, among other states.

Other Bodies at the UN

A variety of entities have been created by the various human rights conventions to consider and evaluate implementation efforts. In 1970, for example, a Committee on the Elimination of Racial Discrimination was created through Article 8 of the Convention on the Elimination of All Forms of Racial Discrimination. It is composed of eighteen experts elected by the states to serve four-year terms. They evaluate reports on the measures that states have taken to implement the convention. The committee is allowed to set up ad hoc conciliation commissions to mediate between states parties in disputes about the convention's application.

Other committees include the Committee on Economic, Social, and Cultural Rights that was created by the Economic and Social Council in 1985; the Committee on the Elimination of All Forms of Discrimination Against Women that was

Human Rights Awareness

One of the most vital aspects of the UN's commitment to human rights lies with its public education campaign. In essence, it has attempted to "cultivate an environment in which rights consciousness will become part of the culture in which people live and are educated."[2]

Many believe that the Convention on the Rights of the Child, adopted by the General Assembly in November 1989, is illustrative of the best the UN can do in terms of public education. Designed in the short term to protect children in all the theatres within which they can be abused, it is also intended to "create an entirely new world environment for the protection of human rights." Recognizing that raising the next generation with an appreciation of human rights is the best chance of institutionalizing the gains made before the end of the twentieth century, the convention is a bold one: "If all the children of the world, or a substantial number of them, are brought up in a society in which they see their own rights honored and in which they are taught to respect the rights of others, the world can only be a better place as a result."[3]

---

created in 1982 as a product of the Convention on the Elimination of All Forms of Discrimination Against Women (Article 17); and the Committee Against Torture, which was created in 1987 as a result of Article 17 of the Convention Against Torture.

Council of Europe

Point I
F67075 Strasbourg Cedex
France
PH: 33 3 88 41 20 00
FX: 33 3 88 41 27 81
WWW: http://www.coe.fr/
E-Mail: point_i@coe.fr

The Council of Europe is an international organization that strives, according to their public information materials, "to strengthen democracy, human rights and the rule of law throughout its member states." It currently has forty members and focuses much of its activity on emerging democracies in Central and Eastern Europe. It complements, whenever possible and appropriate, the official activities of the European Union.

At the end of World War II great concern existed regarding Europe's political future. Winston Churchill described Europe's plight and his hopes for unification based on democratic pluralism this way:

What is the plight to which Europe has been reduced? . . . Over wide areas a vast quivering mass of tormented, hungry, careworn and bewildered human beings gape at the ruins

---

[2] Tom O'Malley, "A Look to the Future," in *Human Rights: A European Perspective*, edited by Liz Heffernan (Dublin, Ireland and Portland, Oregon: The Round Hall Press, 1994).
[3] Ibid.

of their cities and homes and scan the dark horizons for the approach of some new peril, tyranny or terror . . . . [The] remedy . . . is to recreate a European family . . . . We must create a United States of Europe.[4]

Churchill's hopes were held by sufficient others, such that by August 3, 1949, the Council of Europe was founded, committed to, in the words of its statute, "spiritual and moral values which are the common heritage of their peoples and the true source of individual freedom, political liberty and the rule of law, principles which form the basis of all genuine democracy."

Two underlying factors motivated Europeans to institutionalize support for human rights: Hitler's legacy and the specter of Communism. Hitler's legacy was fresh in the minds of war-weary Europeans, who knew that totalitarianism does not begin overnight, but grows gradually through the continual suppression of liberties. Girdled with the knowledge that they would have to police their own societies, Europeans also feared the emerging "Soviet menace." During the short year between the Hague Congress, wherein the Statute of the Council was drawn up, and its signature by the Europeans, Berlin was blockaded by the Soviets and resupplied by America's airlift, the Greeks fought a civil war deeply influenced by Communism, and the Communists took over the pluralistic government of Czechoslovakia in a coup.

The Council of Europe was designed with two entities at its base: The Consultative Assembly and the Committee of Ministers. As such, it bridged the drive for unification with the recognition that the state was sovereign in the twentieth century. The Committee of Ministers included the foreign ministers of the member states, in which each state had one representative. The Consultative Assembly was designed as a body of parliamentarians from the various European states, representing not their countries but their parties within those states.

The Consultative Assembly began the process of establishing a European Convention on Human Rights in 1949. The drafting of that convention was influenced by the Universal Declaration and by Europe's rich history in identifying rights worthy of protection, as well as the means by which to do so. Eleven rights were eventually drawn up in the convention: the right to life; freedom from torture and inhuman or degrading treatment; freedom from slavery or servitude; the right to individual liberty; the right to a fair trial; prohibition of *ex post facto* [after the fact] criminal legislation; freedom of expression; freedom of peaceful assembly and association; and the right to marry and found a family.[5]

Other rights concerned with education, elections, and the right to private property were included in the First Additional Protocol to the convention. The convention was ultimately ratified by the nineteen European states not behind the Iron Curtain. (East and Central Europe had been prevented at that time by

---

[4] *The New York Times*, September 20, 1946.
[5] The Council of Europe, *Collected Texts, European Convention on Human Rights* (Strasbourg, 1977).

the Soviet and/or their own Communist regimes from joining the European Convention and NATO.)

The European Convention on Human Rights, which became operative on September 3, 1953, "is the one truly functional, readily accessible, and effective system for the protection of human rights established on a supranational level."[6] It guaranteed in Article 1 rights to all persons within the jurisdiction of its signing states, with individuals given "an effective remedy before a national authority" in Article 13 (effectively, this was a right of redress).

Generally, human rights in Europe have been most enthusiastically promoted by the European Court of Justice (ECJ) and by the European Parliament (both organs of the European Union, formerly known as the European Community or European Economic Community), more than by the Council of Ministers or by the Commission.[7] Ironically, although the ECJ was not initially inclined to protect individual rights (as seen by early cases such as *Stork v. High Authority* [1959], *Geitling v. High Authority* [1960], and *Sgarlata v. Commission* [1965]), by *Stauder v. City of Ulm* in 1979 it acknowledged that "human rights [are] enshrined in the general principles of Community law and protected by the Court."[8] Subsequent rulings reinforced this principle, and recent actions by the ECJ dealing with human rights have expanded the ECJ's jurisdiction.

The European Commission on Human Rights

Conseil de l'Europe
F-67075 Strasbourg Cedex
France
PH: 33 88 412018
FX: 33 88 412792
WWW: http://www.dhcommhr.coe.fr

Under the auspices of the Council of Europe, the European Commission on Human Rights (ECHR)—also known as the *Commission Européenne des Droits de l'Homme* [CEDH]—was founded in 1953 and currently has thirty-three members, with a staff of one hundred. Committee work is conducted in French and English. Members are elected by the Committee of Ministers of the Council of Europe. The ECHR evaluates petitions made by individuals and individual states concerning human rights violations of the European Convention on Human Rights and renders a judgment on the admissibility of such petitions. The ECHR also acts as an intermediary between conflicting parties and helps secure a negotiated settlement. When a settlement cannot be reached, the ECHR provides an assessment of whether or not the convention has been breached. It may also send a case or cases to the Court of Human Rights.

Although less effective perhaps than the European Court of Justice or the

---

[6] John T. Wright, "Human Rights in the West," in *Human Rights: Cultural and Ideological Perspectives*, edited by Adamantia Pollis and Peter Schwab (New York: Praeger, 1979).

[7] R. M. Dallen, "An Overview of the European Community Protection of Human Rights with Some Special References to the U.K." in *The Common Market Law Review*, 1990.

[8] See case 11/70 [1979] *European Court Reports* 419.

European Parliament (both organs of the European Union), the commission, too, has been active with a variety of rights measures such as Directive 75/117/EEC on equal pay or Directive 76/2070/EEC on equal treatment, as well as its recommendation to the European Community (now called the European Union or EU) to join in the European Convention on Human Rights on April 4, 1979. The commission showed itself to be an aggressive promoter of rights with regard to South Africa and began to tie European Community foreign assistance to issues of human rights following the lead set by the Carter administration.

The European Council of Ministers, the decision-making body of the European Union, has not been mute either, although its role has been less extensive. It did adopt a Declaration on Democracy in April 1978, as well as offer forceful statements on human rights issues relating to South Africa, the USSR, Sri Lanka, and the breakaway provinces of the former Yugoslavia. The council also joined with the parliament and the commission to issue a Joint Declaration on Human Rights stressing the "prime importance" they place on the "protection of fundamental rights."

The Organization of African Unity

P.O. Box 3243
Addis Ababa
Ethiopia
PH: 251 1 51 77 00
FX: 251 1 51 26 22
WWW: http://www.undp.org/popin/oau/oauhome.htm
E-Mail: pdsoau@padis.gn.apc.org

The OAU was founded in May 1963 by a group of diplomats representing thirty-two African states who met in Addis Ababa, intending to dedicate the OAU to eliminating colonialism on the continent. It was somewhat active in the decolonization process, through its work with the United Nations Special Committee, but became much less active in that area over the years. One area that it has focused considerable attention on is refugee affairs, with a number of conferences held and declarations issued over the years.[9]

Its seminal effort on behalf of human rights was the passage of the African Charter on Human and People's Rights in 1981. Consistent with the OAU's charter, it recognizes in Article 2 that everyone is entitled to all the rights and freedoms recognized and guaranteed therein, without distinction of any kind such as race, ethnic

---

[9] These include the Pan-African Conference on the Situation of Refugees in Africa (Arusha, Tanzania, May 1979); The Second International Conference on Assistance to Refugees in Africa ("ICARA II," 1984); the Oslo Declaration and Plan of Action on the Plight of Refugees, Returnees and Displaced Persons in Southern Africa ("SARRED," August 1988); the Khartoum Declaration on Africa's Refugee Crisis Adopted by the Seventeenth Extra-Ordinary Session of the OAU Commission of Fifteen on Refugees (Khartoum, Sudan, September 1990); the Addis Ababa PARINAC Conclusions and Recommendations (March 1994); the Oslo PARINAC Declaration and Plan of Action (Oslo, June 1994); and the Tunis Declaration on the 1969 OAU Convention Governing the Specific Aspects of Refugee Problems in Africa (Tunis, June 1994).

group, color, sex, language, religion, political or any other opinion, national and social origin, fortune, birth, or other status.[10]

The OAU established a commission supporting human rights to implement the African Charter. Its primary role is to interpret all the provisions of the charter at the request of a state party, an institution of the OAU, or an African organization recognized by the OAU. The commission is also empowered to investigate cases through mechanisms protecting the sovereignty of individual states while ensuring timely judgement and reporting procedures. Final reports summarizing investigations can include recommendations for change, although Article 55 of the OAU's charter offers a number of loopholes by which states can declare the commission's intervention invalid.

The commission is instructed in Article 60 to "draw inspiration from international law on human and peoples' rights . . . the Charter of the United Nations, the Charter of the Organization of African Unity, the Universal Declaration of Human Rights, [and] other instruments adopted by the United Nations and by African countries...." Article 60 is somewhat circumscribed by Article 61, which states that the commission "shall also take into consideration, as subsidiary measures to determine the principles of law . . . African practices consistent with international norms on human and peoples' rights, customs generally accepted as law, general principles of law recognized by African states as well as legal precedents and doctrine." The latter caveat has allowed some states to flout the OAU's authority as well as the commission's.

Other human rights procedures and instruments are also in place. Article 62 of the charter also indicates that each member state must submit a report every two years describing its progress in meeting human rights goals, although fully comprehensive reporting has not yet been achieved. In 1996 the OAU met to consider the formation of an African Court of Human and People's Rights to complement the work of the commission. While agreement has been reached concerning the need for such a court, plans for it have not been finalized.

The OAU represents states, not peoples, and attempts to become a construct that will bridge the divide between ideologically and geographically diverse states. As such, it often papers over differences and its resolutions are not implemented uniformly, or at all in some cases. Virtually all major controversies have been postponed at least once for fear of division. In so doing, the OAU has often abdicated moral leadership for the continent, sometimes paving the way for one-party states run amuck and charismatic leaders who did little more than enrich themselves while their territories were bled dry of resources (see Chapter 4). Due to its consensual nature, the OAU has been unable to intervene effectively in many states, despite considerable public knowledge of the human rights violations of Haile Mariam Mengistu of Ethiopia, Idi Amin of Uganda, and Siad

---

[10] The African [Banjul] Charter on Human and People's Rights was adopted June 27, 1981 (see the OAU Doc. CAB/LEG/67/3 rev. 5, 21 I.L.M. 58 [1982], which entered into force on October 21, 1986).

Barre of Somalia, for example. Atrocities committed during civil wars, insurgencies, and regional conflagrations have also gone largely unchecked by OAU efforts.

In summary, when faced with differences among members and with more sophisticated diplomatic challenges in far more complex intrastate and interstate conflict, the OAU has not always been able to meet the task. Given its financially weak status, with members unable to be compelled to pay their dues, the OAU is hamstrung on many fronts. In addition, it lacks enforcement machinery. Still, there is a persistent effort on the continent to strive to meet international standards. With the resolution of conflict in southern Africa, efforts for reconciliation, and hopes for sustainable development, the South African model may be one that can inspire progress elsewhere in Africa.

The Organization of American States

19th Street and Constitution Avenue, NW
Washington, D.C. 20006
WWW: http://www.oas.org/homepag.htm
E-Mail: pi@oas.org

The Organization of American States (OAS) is the main body in the Americas focusing on multipurpose cooperation. These efforts at cooperation began in 1889 and today encompass the OAS itself, the Inter-American Treaty of Reciprocal Assistance (Rio Treaty), and the Inter-

American Development Bank. The Charter of the OAS was written in 1948 as the basis for constitutional cooperation for the region and has been amended twice, via the Protocol in 1970 and again in 1985. By 1991 all thirty-five sovereign states of the Americas had become members. The OAS is organized around issues of mutual security (Rio Treaty), nonintervention and sovereign equality, peaceful settlement of disputes, economic cooperation and development (IADB), and representative democracy and human rights.

The primary means by which the latter are secured are the activities of the Inter-American Institute of Human Rights (IIHR) or *Instituto Interamericano de Direitos Humanos*, which is based in San Jose, Costa Rica.[11] This group was founded in 1980 and is staffed with approximately seventy-five professionals. Work is conducted in English and Spanish. The IIHR was established by an agreement between the Inter-American Court of Human Rights and the Republic of Costa Rica. This group is designed to encourage and strengthen democratic governments and the provision of human rights throughout the region by research, specialized training, educational policies, technical assistance, and political mediation for and with governments, civil bodies, and international organizations. IIHR provides an interdisciplinary course on human rights concerns each year, as well as programs on security forces, the role and value of ombudsmen, and the administration of justice. The IIHR provides an annual report, a quarterly bulletin, a semiannual study, a magazine, research and

[11] Its location is the Apartado Postal 10081, San Jose 1000, Costa Rica. PH: 506 2340404, FX: 506 2340955, E-Mail: instituto@iidh.ed.cr

project reports, articles, monographs, books, and press documents.

From the mid-1960s through 1979 the United States focused on human rights within the OAS context in a heightened fashion. However, the region's concerns about U.S. dominance in the area—and its anti-Communist focus and trade restrictions based upon it—tended to undercut coordinated OAS activities on behalf of human rights. The most positive area of cooperation that occurred in the 1970s, and continued into the 1980s was the support for human rights within the OAS bureaucracy. The American Convention on Human Rights, agreed to in 1969, was fully operational in 1978 for those states that had ratified it. It augmented the strength of the Inter-American Commission on Human Rights and created the Inter-American Court of Human Rights.

World Health Organization

Headquarters Office in Geneva (HQ)
Avenue Appia 20
1211 Geneva 27
Switzerland
PH: 41 22 791 21 11
FX: 41 22 791 0746
WWW: http://www.who.org
E-Mail: info@who.ch

The World Health Organization (WHO), established in 1948, subsumed the efforts of the *Office International d'Hygiène Publique* (dating from 1907), and the Health Organization of the League of Nations (dating from 1919). WHO's focus is fundamentally oriented toward protecting the human rights of all, in that it intends to help all peoples achieve the highest possible level of health. WHO hopes to do this through environmental hygiene, disease eradication, improved nutrition, reporting and sharing of data, and advice and counseling. Most of the world's states belong to WHO. It is supported by annual assessment of UN members, but it also enjoys income from trust funds established to treat AIDS, tropical diseases, river blindness, and other diseases.

Beginning with the leadership of Halfdan Mahler, a Dane, WHO began to address human rights concerns politically, with a special focus on the world's poorest and sickest. It had tremendous success in these efforts. Not only did WHO help to eradicate the scourge of centuries—smallpox—but it gave developing states the standing to negotiate with multinational corporations and ample assistance in budgeting, planning, and forecasting. Simple steps dramatically affected the health of the poor, including WHO's successful challenge to the infant formula industry by advertising the value of breastfeeding and oral hydration to control death by diarrhea in infants and small children. It also challenged the pharmaceutical giants by arguing for a list of two hundred key drugs that should be sold in the developing world, instead of the three to five thousand drugs marketed there previously.

In 1978 WHO also began to plan for "Health for All by the Year 2000," in conjunction with UNICEF. It argued for primary health care, with a focus on preventive and curative health, to be delivered by non-physician personnel. Donor dollars were focused directly on rural areas, and were not channeled through middlemen or government officials.

Despite its best efforts WHO has not been able to alleviate the root causes of poor health: poverty, pollution, urban blight, dirty water, and a general lack of medical services. However, continued action on building latrines, improving water supplies, vaccinations, improved nutrition, and maternal and infant health efforts all increase the capacity of developing world citizens.

The Courts

International human rights law is still in an early stage of development. When we consider the centuries invested in English common law from which much of the English-speaking world derives its own legal procedures, international human rights law was clearly born complex but largely untested.[12]

European Court of Human Rights

Along with the European Commission on Human Rights and the Committee of Ministers, the Council of Europe's European Convention on Human Rights created a European Court of Human Rights.[13] All of the states that signed the convention agreed to accept the compulsory jurisdiction of the European Court as well as the right of an individual to petition that court, a factor viewed at the time as a major departure in international law.

The complaint procedure that is intended to mediate between states is seldom used, and it is unlikely that it will be a frequently utilized strategy in the foreseeable future, given politics in Europe. However, the individual right to petition has generated enough cases to keep the European Court perpetually occupied. Although considerable time passed before the court established its legitimacy (twenty-six years passed before one hundred cases were tried), use of it eventually began to snowball (only four years later another one hundred cases were tried).

Cases submitted to the court began to grow dramatically, beginning in the 1980s. In 1980 the commission accepted 396 applications, a figure that grew to 596 in 1985 and 1,657 in 1990. With these grew the number of cases referred to the court: eight were sent in 1980, twelve in 1985, sixty-one in 1990.[14]

Indeed, some feel that the procedures envisaged in 1950 cannot today meet current concerns. For example, because the court cannot easily cope with the demand for adjudication, the delays of over five years to receive a decision from the European Court of Human Rights or the Committee of Ministers[15] mean that the court cannot meet

---

[12] See the following for a discussion of possible global legal standards: Jonathan I. Charney, "Universal International Law," *American Journal of International Law* (October 1993) or Dipak K. Gupta et al., "Creating a Composite Index for Assessing Country Performance in the Field of Human Rights," *Human Rights Quarterly* (April 1993).

[13] On the World Wide Web at http://www.dhcour.coe.fr/.

[14] M. O'Boyle, "The Reconstruction of the Strasbourg Human Rights System," *Dublin University Law Journal 14* (1992).

[15] A. Drzemczewski, "The Need for a Radical Overhaul," *New Law Journal* (January 1993).

the guarantee of Article 6(1) for a "fair and public hearing within a reasonable time by an independent and impartial tribunal established by law," especially since the domestic court proceedings that occur before a petition is submitted cause even further delays. Moreover, now that the Maastricht Treaty, the international legal instrument governing the European Union, has given the European Court of Justice (ECJ) the right to choose for itself the human rights that are to be protected, there are times that the ECJ's interpretation will be different from that of the European Court of Human Rights with regard to an assessment of certain aspects of positions held by the European Court. As such, international disputes within Europe can, and have, arisen.

International War Crimes Tribunal for Rwanda and the Balkans

In 1993 the UN Security Council, acting under Chapter VII of the charter, established an ad hoc war crimes tribunal for the former Yugoslavia,[16] for crimes committed in the territory of the former Yugoslavia since 1991, and on November 8, 1994, the Security Council established a similar tribunal on crimes against humanity and genocide in Rwanda and against Rwandan citizens in neighboring states between January 1, 1994, and December 31, 1994, by resolution 955.[17] The UN Security Council approved the rules of procedure and the statutes under which they are governed, it elected judges and appointed registrars as well as prosecutors, and it initiated the investigations.

Many have said that the tragedy of the Balkans, Bosnia, Kosovo, et al, is that it has happened on Europe's doorstep—a continent that should not allow such tragedies to occur again, given the lessons of World War II. Despite the best efforts of seasoned diplomats like Britain's former Foreign Minister David Owen, America's former Secretary of State Cyrus Vance, the threat of NATO airstrikes, American and allied military buffers and monitoring efforts, the humanitarian assistance of hundreds of organizations, the mediation of the Council of Europe and the European Community, tragedy has replayed itself—albeit to a lesser degree than World War I and World War II's epic conflagrations. Hundreds of thousands at the very least have been stripped of their most basic civil rights, deprived of their homes and villages, and subjected to unspeakable tortures, rapes, beatings, shootings, and starvation.

Under the terms of the International Tribunal for the former Yugoslavia, the tribunal has "the power to prosecute persons committing or ordering to be committed grave breaches of the Geneva Conventions

---

[16] The full name is the International Tribunal for the Prosecution of Persons Responsible for Serious Violations of International Humanitarian Law Committed in the Territory of the Former Yugoslavia Since 1991. See UN Doc. S/25704 at 36, annex (1993) and S/25704/Add.1 (1993), adopted by the Security Council on May 25, 1993, UN Doc. S/RES/827 (1993).

[17] The International Criminal Tribunal for Rwanda, Rules of Procedure and Evidence, can be found in UN Doc. ITR/3/REV.1 (1995).

of August 12, 1949. Bosnia remains an intractable problem, with slow implementation of the Dayton Accords. Some successes have been registered, including municipal elections and the indictment of war criminals. In July 1997 the first war criminal was arrested and another was killed in self defense. With a now stronger role for the Human Rights Commission called for in the Dayton Accords and the International Commission on Missing Persons helping families find their lost members, conditions are beginning to improve slowly. The UN's International Police Task Force is working to evaluate and train candidates for multiethnic police bodies in the federation, and to a much smaller extent in Republika Srpska, where locals are proving intransigent. President Plavsic's continued inability to overpower indicted war criminal Radovan Karadzic poses problems with resolving the future of Bosnia and the leadership of the Serbs. Similarly, refugees are slow to return, given continued security issues in minority areas. In general, greater protection needs to be guaranteed via the Dayton Accords in terms of freedom of movement, freedom of the media, and joint institutions. The most serious problem remaining, which is linked to further progress in all other areas cited above, is the fact that the majority of indicted war criminals are still free in Bosnia. More importantly, some, like Karadzic, are still influencing politics in Srpska.[18]

The record in Croatia is mixed. After considerable pressure by the international community, on October 10, 1997, Croatia surrendered ten indicted Croat war criminals to the International Criminal Tribunal for the former Yugoslavia; the larger part of Croat war criminals are now incarcerated. All has, unfortunately, not been well in Croatia; authoritarian leader Franjo Tudjman has dominated the media and controlled the judiciary and the election process to derail and harass his democratic opposition, despite monitoring of elections.

Securing long-term peace clearly requires the ultimate imposition of justice, and herein the UN War Crimes Tribunals for the former Yugoslavia and Rwanda are vital forces of justice, healing, and ultimately peace. Since the international community has agreed that those guilty of crimes against humanity must be exposed and/or punished, the lumbering progress of the tribunals must continue. With some fifty indicted criminals, including Ratko Mladic and Radovan Karadzic, still at large, huge efforts must still be made to bring the rest to justice.

The Rwanda Tribunal has had greater success in obtaining custody of indicted criminals, as well as in improving staffing and administrative and morale difficulties. Overcoming substantial societal barriers, the Rwanda Tribunal made international history in 1997 by indicting criminals for sexual abuse and the rape of women.

Nevertheless, the conditions inciting the atrocities and criminal conduct have not been wiped out. The U.S. State Department's report on human rights for

---

[18] See U.S. Department of State's "Overview to Country Reports on Human Rights Practices for 1997," as well as individual country reports, Washington, D.C.: Bureau of Democracy, Human Rights and Labor (January 30, 1998).

1997 showed an increasing threat to civilians, citing the Great Lakes area of Africa, where Hutu insurgents in Rwanda, Burundi, and the eastern Democratic Republic of the Congo (DROC) have allied themselves with the "openly genocidal ex-FAR and Interahamwe, and the Burundian Palipehutu."[19] The State Department characterized the situation as exhibiting "serious abuses on all sides." Even though former President Mobutu has left, the DROC human rights situation is still extremely dangerous, with many allegations of civilian massacres occurring during President Kabila's efforts to take power.[20]

In sum, although the process and the outcome are not perfect, the tribunals are "unique in trying to bring justice to ongoing conflicts as a way of seeking to end them, something that no other international institution of justice has ever attempted."[21]

International Criminal Court

The tribunals (see above) themselves have helped pave the way for progress in 1997 and 1998 in establishing a permanent International Criminal Court (ICC). President Bill Clinton of the United States has called for the court to be created before the year 2000. Efforts to create such a court have a long history. After World War I there was an unsuccessful effort, but the military war crime tribunals at Nuremberg and Tokyo helped provide additional impetus for a permanent court. The 1948 Genocide Convention (not ratified by all key states until more than forty years later) specified such a court, and the International Law Commission (ILC) of the UN General Assembly was mandated in the 1950s to codify the Nuremberg principles and prepare a draft statute. The Cold War, however, and a general refusal by many states to accept compulsory international legal jurisdiction, prevented an early resolution of the issue.

However, in 1989 Trinidad and Tobago, tiny entities on the world stage, reintroduced the idea at a more fruitful time, with the collapse of the Warsaw Pact and the ending of the Cold War, along with growing violence in the former Yugoslavia. In November 1994 the ILC presented its final version of the draft statute and recommended that a conference of Plenipotentiaries be called to draw up a treaty to enact the statute. The UN General Assembly then established an ad hoc committee to review the draft, which was done in 1995. A Preparatory Committee of the General Assembly met twice in 1996 and three times in 1997 to draft a text that would accommodate the several major states that still remained opposed or undecided on the issue. In June 1998 an International Treaty Conference was held in Rome. The final Rome statute establishing the court, dating July 17, 1998, includes independent prosecutors, investigators, and judges. The court's focus

[19] Ibid., p. 3.
[20] Ibid.
[21] Ibid., p. 7.

will be crimes against humanity broadly, with specific investigations against genocide and war crimes. Sexual violence against women will also be investigated, if nation of origin courts do not do so.[22]

Some key bodies in various regions have also joined the call for the International Criminal Court. In part due to South Africa's generally successful efforts at reconciliation, the Southern African Development Community (SADC) has proven to be supportive of the International Criminal Court. South African President Nelson Mandela summed up the views of many when he argued, in addressing the SADC meetings, that respect for state sovereignty should not outweigh support for democracy and human rights.[23]

—Carol Rae Hansen

---

[22] The draft statute used as a basis for negotiations in Rome can be found, along with the final Rome Statute, at the United Nations website: http://www.un.org/icc and the Coalition for an International Criminal Court's website at http://www.igc.org/icc.

[23] In addition to sources cited in other footnotes, additional sources for this chapter include: U.S. Department of State, "Preface to Country Reports on Human Rights Practices for 1997, " (Washington, D.C.: Bureau of Democracy, Human Rights and Labor, U. S. Department of State, January 30, 1998), pp. 1-2; U. S. Department of State, "Introduction to 1997 Human Rights Report," (Washington, D.C.: Bureau of Democracy, Human Rights and Labor, U. S. Department of State, January 30, 1998), pp. 1-10; John T. Wright, "Human Rights in the West: Political Liberties and the Rule of Law" in Adamantia Pollis and Peter Schwab, eds., *Human Rights: Cultural and Ideological Perspectives* (New York: Praeger Publishers, 1979), pp. 19-31.

CHAPTER SIX

Nongovernmental Organizations

Profound organizational change in the world has occurred in the wake of the Universal Declaration of Human Rights, signed on December 10, 1948. In but fifty years, an astonishing group of private, voluntary, nongovernmental organizations have grown up to promote international responsibility and accountability for protecting human rights. These bodies, mostly springing from monitoring groups, have promoted additional covenants and laws, sponsored popular movements, and championed thousands of intercessions on behalf of prisoners of conscience. Many of them link with each other to expose states that exploit their citizens; others embolden local citizens to organize and launch themselves into political movements capable of redressing wrong. At the very least, they mobilize public opinion worldwide on behalf of the victimized. Their impact is remarkable, given often brutal interference with their activities by the governments that they expose.

The organizations listed below are illustrative of the thousands of human rights bodies that have sprung up in the wake of the Universal Declaration of Human Rights. Most are located in North America or have major branch offices here, and their activities, publications, and staff are located at the addresses listed below; others are international, with a specific regional or thematic focus. In general, most of these groups are fairly large in terms of budget and staff. This selected list includes a potpourri of issues, themes, and organizational types that highlight the rich panoply of human rights protection organizations. Wherever possible, data has been included on the founding of the body, its membership, main languages in which it operates, and the scope of its activities, national or international.[1] Contact information can include e-mail and World Wide Web addresses. This list is not meant to be exhaustive, and contact data and organizational titles can change over time. Unless otherwise listed, data is from 1998.

— Carol Rae Hansen

---

[1] Sources include brochures, submissions for nonprofit status and other materials produced by these bodies, other public domain materials, Internet literature and website materials, as well as information from the following: Lucille Whalen, *Contemporary World Issues: Human Rights, A Reference Handbook* (Santa Barbara, Calif., and Oxford, England: ABC-CLIO, 1989); Liz Heffernan, ed., *Human Rights: A European Perspective* (Dublin, Ireland, and Portland, Ore.: The Round Hall Press, 1994); *Encyclopedia of Associations* (Detroit: Gale Research, 1998), Vol. 1-4.

The Africa Fund

50 Broad Street, Suite 711
New York, NY 10004
PH: (212) 785-1024
FX: (212) 785-1078
WWW: http://www.prairienet.org/acas/afund.html
E-Mail: africafund@igc.org
Founded: 1966

Mission: Established in 1966 by the American Committee on Africa, The Africa Fund (AF) states that it supports democracy-building and economic justice efforts, defends human rights concerns, with a special focus on African problems, and attempts to release political prisoners jailed in Africa.

Current Activities: The Africa Fund was active in the postcolonial independence struggles of many African states and worked with special attention to problems in Southern Africa, especially those of South Africa, Rhodesia/Zimbabwe, Mozambique, and Angola. AF provides direct and indirect assistance to Africans (including legal assistance), helps educate American citizens on African issues through its publications, press releases, and lectures, and encourages the United States government to invest in Africa's economic development and in democracy-building. Formerly: (1969) Africa Legal Defense and Aid Fund.

Publications: Newsletters, books, literature lists, computer mailing lists, and annual reports.

American Civil Liberties Union

125 Broad Street
New York, NY 10004-2400
PH: (212) 549-2500
Publications Ordering:
1-800-775-ACLU (2258)
WWW: http://www.aclu.org
E-Mail: aclu@aclu.org
Founded: 1920
Scope: National

Mission: Public information materials produced by the American Civil Liberties Union (ACLU) state that it is primarily focused on civil rights in the United States, but on selected projects the ACLU also works for the protection of human rights for all peoples worldwide, including prisoners, mental patients, welfare recipients, soldiers, children, and women.

Current Activities: The national office's efforts are enhanced by a large number of local and affiliated chapters, with the New York office providing guidance, administrative support, speakers, and some funding. The New York office is also directly involved in lobbying legislatures countrywide from the local to the national level. Past activities have included speech-making, public education, publications, and press conferences.

Publications: The ACLU supports an extensive publications program, including handbooks, public policy reports, press releases, newsletters, and books.

American Friends Service Committee

1501 Cherry Street
Philadelphia, PA 19102
PH: (215) 241-7000
FX: (215) 241-7275
WWW: http://www.afsc.org
E-Mail: afscinfo@afsc.org
Founded: 1917
Scope: International

Mission: The American Friends Service Committee (AFSC) was founded by American Quakers as a means of providing a constructive alternative to military service in World War I. Today the AFSC develops programs to enhance the work of its specialists in the fields of justice, peace, service, and development. These programs are directed by a Quaker Board and Corporation that represents a wide spectrum of Quakers in America.

Current Activities: The AFSC's international missions are headquartered in Philadelphia. They are supported by ten regional offices in the United States and carried out through a variety of program operations abroad. In all of its efforts the AFSC works for the abolition of war and the fulfillment of human rights. The Quaker Board and Corporation consider these two vital goals as the means by which humans can cooperatively create a nonviolent world in which all peoples may live together in peace. In the United States the AFSC focuses on a variety of program priorities, including exclusion and unequal opportunities in education (especially for women and minorities), fair employment,

the administration of land rights (particularly with regard to indigenous peoples), justice in the broadest terms, welfare reforms, and food programs, especially access for children.

Publications: The AFSC has an extensive program and produces press releases, leaflets, newsletters, books, and pamphlets on a regular basis.

Amnesty International

International Secretariat, London
Amnesty International of the U.S.A.
322 8th Avenue
New York, NY 10001
PH: (212) 807-8400
TF: (800) AMNESTY
FX: (212) 627-1451
WWW [International Secretariat]:
http://www.amnesty.org
WWW [AIUSA]: http://www.amnesty-usa.org
E-Mail: admin-us@aiusa.org
Founded: 1961
Members: 1,000,000 worldwide; 290,000 AIUSA
Local Groups: 4,300 worldwide; 400 USA
Scope: International, with supporters in 162 countries and territories

Mission: Amnesty International (AI) states that it is the largest human rights organization in the world and works to promote all the human rights enshrined in the Universal Declaration of Human Rights. It was launched in 1961 by British lawyer Peter Benenson. AI works impartially to release from prison, house arrest, or detention individuals detained anywhere in the world because of their conscientiously held beliefs, their sex, religion, language, ethnic origin, and/or color—provided that they haven't used or advocated violence. AI states that it opposes executions without reservation, torture, and "disappearances," and it always advocates fair, impartial, and prompt trials for all prisoners, political or not. Its international focus also includes "abolishing the death penalty and other cruel, inhuman, or degrading treatment of prisoners."

Current Activities: With a million members, subscribers, and regular donors in more than one hundred countries and territories, AI is nationally organized into sections in fifty-five countries. It works toward its goals through nationwide "adoption groups" that attempt to release prisoners of conscience through an "Urgent Action Network," which uses letter-writing campaigns on behalf of persons in immediate danger. AI's public service materials indicate that it is also active in public demonstrations, human rights education projects, fundraising concerts, individual appeals in particular cases, and global campaigns on broader issues. More than one hundred delegations are sent annually to dozens of countries to highlight AI's concerns.

AI has consultative status with the United Nations and the Council of Europe and has cooperative relations with the Organization for African Unity. AI was the recipient of the 1977 Nobel Prize for Peace. Volunteers are active in AIUSA and the International Networks, which are organized into educators; legal professionals; religion; company approaches; health

professionals; freedom writers; urgent action; women; trade unionists; writers and journalists; youth and student groups; children; lesbian and gay concerns; military, security, and police.

Publications: AI issues more than one hundred major external documents on violations a year. *Amnesty Action*, a newsletter published three times a year, has a circulation of 308,000; *Amnesty International Report*, an annual, covers human rights conditions in 151 countries. AIUSA also produces mission reports, country briefing papers, press briefings, and other special reports on an ad hoc basis.

Anti-Defamation League

823 United Nations Plaza
New York, NY 10017
PH: (212) 490-2525
WWW: http://www.adl.org/
E-Mail: webmaster@adl.org
Founded: 1913

Mission: Inspired by the 1913 murder of Leo Frank by an anti-Semitic mob, the Anti-Defamation League (ADL) was founded by Chicago lawyer Sigmund Livingston. Public affairs materials indicate that the ADL attempts to promote understanding among peoples of different creeds, races, and ethnic backgrounds. The ADL has also established relations with Christian institutions to promote sensitivity in Jewish-Christian contacts. It works closely with governments and their embassies abroad in order to lessen tensions and enhance ties between disparate peoples. The ADL's leadership indicates that it is firmly committed to fighting discrimination, bigotry, and anti-Semitism in all forms; it also attempts to protect the human rights of Jews throughout the world through a variety of projects. The ADL is actively working with the FBI and police departments in the United States to develop and distribute film and print materials intended to sensitize law enforcement officers to circumstances involving hate crimes.

Current Activities: The ADL utilizes a broadly gauged program of films, speakers, press releases, public exhibits, and written materials to make its case. As part of a multigenerational educational effort, it also teaches historical perspective, factors leading to conflict, and means to avoid violence. Active in advocacy and lobbying campaigns, the ADL raises funds to further its aims and acts in a liaison capacity with like-minded groups. The ADL is now working with software manufacturers to create filters for home computers to screen out materials directed toward children that could be considered an incitement toward hate. The ADL attempts to intercede with legislative and judicial bodies on behalf of its projects and regularly strives to meet with executive department officials.

Publications: The ADL supports a major publications program, which includes films, books, monographs, press releases, reports on specific topics, and periodicals on a variety of subjects, including discrimination and intergroup relations, social and political issues, prejudice, multicultural education, and the Holocaust.

Arab Organization for Human Rights
al-MunZZamah al-`Arabiyyah li-Huquq al-Insan
17 Midan Aswan
Mohandseen, Giza, Egypt
or
P.O. Box 82
1211 Geneva 28, Switzerland
PH: 20 3466582
FX: 20 3448166
WWW: http://haynese.winthrop.edu/mlas/aohr.htm
Founded: 1983
Scope: International

Mission: The Web site and public domain informational materials of the Arab Organization for Human Rights (AOHR) state that it works to promote and protect human rights in Arab countries "in accordance with international standards" (specifically, the International Bill of Rights). It also attempts to link individuals and organizations that have an interest in improving human rights compliance in ten Middle Eastern countries.

Current Activities: The AOHR's current program emphasizes five areas of special concern: amnesty for those sentenced for political reasons; the release of anyone detained or imprisoned for their conscientiously held beliefs or for reasons of race, sex, color, or language; improvements in conditions for those imprisoned for reasons of conscience; the institution of free and fair trials for all; and legal assistance "where necessary and possible." To this end, AOHR helps to coordinate the efforts of various human rights bodies and individuals that ask it for assistance in the Middle East. It acts as a liaison body to the press. The AOHR also shares data on human rights abuses and efforts to meet international guidelines, it undertakes its own research, and it offers educational programs for professionals and laypersons interested in the field. The AOHR is organized into subcommittees dealing with women, legal issues, and freedom of expression.

Coordinates with: The Arab Lawyer's Union.

Publications: Publishes an annual report on the region, periodicals, a monthly newsletter, and an annual report.

Bread for the World

c/o Librarian
1100 Wayne Avenue, Suite 1000
Silver Spring, MD 20910
PH: (301) 608-2400
FX: (301) 608-2401
WWW: http://www.bread.org
Founded: 1973
Members: 44,000
Scope: International

Mission: Bread for the World (BW)'s Web site indicates that it is a group of Christians united in working against poverty and hunger worldwide. BW also hosts and supports the Bread for the World Institute, which produces educational products and other research on policies related to food policy, economic development, hunger, the status of women and children in developing countries, and agricultural and conservation issues, among many others.

Current Activities: Individual members of BW take active roles, including routine contact with their churches and other civic groups, as well as with their members of Congress and other government officials in order to influence American policy toward world hunger. BW also focuses on conditions that affect hunger internationally, such as insufficient financial aid to developing countries, natural disasters, debt burdens and moratoria, military spending, agricultural policies and land reform, trade in primary products and insufficient international investment, structural unemployment, and so forth. BW maintains a speakers bureau as well as reference libraries. BW works with the aid of PeaceNet and HandsNet. BW's staff, volunteers, and members are organized into the following divisions: government relations, grassroots organizing, media, and network development.

Publications: BW produces background papers (five per year), circulation 40,000+; a hymnal; newsletters on hunger-related legislation and member activities; an annual report; an annual report on the state of world hunger; and an annual guide to assist churches in hunger education.

Cambodian Human Rights and Development Association

1 St. 158, Beng Raing
Daun Penh
Phnom Penh, Cambodia

PH: 855 23 428653; 855 23 482407
FX: 855 23 427229
E-Mail: adhoccambodia@
pactok.peg.apc.org
Founded: 1991
Members: 50,000
Scope: National

Mission: The Cambodian Human Rights and Development Association (CHRDA) works to protect human rights and the primacy of the justice system in Cambodia.

Current Activities: CHRDA offers legal advice and assistance to Cambodians, and it collects and shares data on violations with interested citizens, the press, and other groups working in the field. CHRDA also has specific interests in economic development, women's literacy, and health and welfare issues. To these ends, CHRDA lobbies political leaders, the press, and the public. It also maintains contacts with regional and international human rights organizations.

Publications: Press releases.

The Carter Center

One Copenhill
453 Freedom Parkway
Atlanta, GA 30307
PH: (404) 331-3900
WWW: http://www.emory.edu/CARTER_
CENTER/homepage.htm
E-Mail: carterweb@emory.edu
Founded: 1982
Scope: International

Mission: Founded in 1982 by former United States President Jimmy Carter and Mrs. Rosalynn Carter, the Carter Center is a nonprofit public policy institute based in Georgia. The center states that it is "dedicated to fighting disease, hunger, poverty, conflict, and oppression through collaborative initiatives in the areas of democratization and development, global health, and urban revitalization." Active in sixty-five countries, the center is a separately chartered and independently governed member of the Emory University community, and human rights are a constituent part of its concerns.

Current Activities: The center sponsors conferences, shares archival materials, conducts research, provides speakers, and produces occasional publications on a variety of topics.

Center for the Study of Human Rights

Columbia University
1108 International Affairs Building
New York, NY 10027
PH: (212) 854-2479
FX: (212) 316-4578
WWW: http://www.columbia.edu/
cu/humanrights
E-Mail: cshr@columbia.edu
Founded: 1977

Mission: University publications indicate that this group of twenty-three academic advisers and ten directors encourages the teaching of human rights issues and promotes research in the field. The Center for the Study of Human Rights (CSHR) conducts meetings, symposia, and an annual conference in June.

Current Activities: CSHR's printed materials indicate that it provides teaching fellowships at Columbia University, a number of research internships, and extensive academic training in the field, as well as advice to students considering such a focus. CSHR also develops curriculum and offers consultation services on human rights research, resources, and on education and training programs elsewhere in academia.

Publications: CSHR produces a quarterly newsletter, bibliographies on key issues, periodic calendars of events, Columbia and Barnard's course listings, and data on internships, scholarships, and other aid. CSHR also publishes the proceedings of its conferences, as well as a topical bibliography and human rights syllabi. An annual report is produced, along with occasional papers and human rights documents of a vital nature.

Children's Watch International

22 Trowbridge Street
Cambridge, MA 02139
PH: (617) 492-4890
FX: (617) 492-4890
Founded: 1994
Scope: International

Mission: Children's Watch International (CWI)'s annual report and public affairs materials state that it attempts to improve the quality of life for children around the world, including their legal status, care, physical conditions, and environment. CWI says that it "represents and publicizes the needs and human rights of children who are victims of violence, in both domestic situations, such as child prostitution or child labor in hazardous industry, and in armed conflicts in national, international, civil, and ethnic conflicts."

Current Activities: CWI conducts research, undertakes studies, and evaluates information on the human rights violations of children throughout the world, including data assembled by UNICEF, WHO, other United Nations bodies, various NGOs, and key donor states. CWI utilizes a small but active group of students and volunteer monitors to augment more permanent staff. Recent activities include celebrations for children and individual national compliance monitoring concerning the UN Convention on the Rights of the Child. CWI also maintains a reference library and awards the Child Advocate of the Year annually.

Publications: Annual report.

Chinese Association for Human Rights

102 Kuang Fu S. Rd., 8th Floor
Taipei 10553, Taiwan
Founded: 1979
Members: 663
Scope: National

Mission: The Chinese Association for Human Rights (CAHR) monitors human rights issues in the People's Republic of China. CAHR utilizes international sources of information, as well as its own monitoring, in following issues of concern in China.

Current Activities: The CAHR provides legal help to citizens and foreigners when there are bona fide cases of human rights violations, as well as when cases of police interrogations occur, in order to ensure that detainees receive all possible protections allowed by law. The CAHR also undertakes its own research in the field, provides an annual human rights seminar on human rights issues in Asia and the Pacific, and archives a limited number of materials in the field.

Publications: CAHR produces a quarterly newsletter in the field (in English), a quarterly report (in Mandarin), an annual directory, and a human rights index.

Committee for Children

2203 Airport Way South, Suite 500
Seattle, WA 98134-2035
PH: (206) 343-1223
FX: (206) 343-1445
WWW: http://www.cfchildren.org
E-Mail: info@cfchildren.org
Founded: 1981
Scope: International

Mission: The Committee for Children (CFC)'s public information materials indicate that it creates curricula for preschool through senior high, with a focus on helping prevent sexual and physical abuse, as well as youthful violence, though public information campaigns, curriculum development, and professional training. CFC develops training programs for instructors that highlight child abuse and help school systems create prevention programs. CFC also conducts research in the field.

Current Activities: See above. CFC also holds an annual conference in the summer.

CFC works actively with like-minded NGOs, school systems, archivists, publishing concerns, attorneys, educators, the law enforcement community, and the interested public in providing speakers and resource materials.

Formerly: Children's Rights, Inc.

Publications: CFC publishes books, curricula, and curriculum guides. It also produces catalogs of resources (semiannual), free, circulation of 200,000; a newsletter with book reviews and research reports; a free training calendar, circulation 10,000; and videos.

Committee of Concerned Scientists

53-34 208th Street
Bayside, NY 11364
PH: (718) 229-2813
FX: (718) 229-7540
WWW: http://www.libertynet.org/ccs/
E-Mail: ccs@math1.cims.nyu.edu
Founded: 1972
Members: 5,000

Mission: The Committee of Concerned Scientists (CCS)' public affairs materials state that it unites scholars and scientists around the world for "the protection and advancement of the scientific and human rights of scientists throughout the world." CCS members are divided into the following divisions: Astronomy, Biology, Chemistry, Computer Science, Dental Sciences, Engineering, Industrial Labs, Mathematics, Medical Sciences, Physics, Psychology and Psychiatry, and Social Sciences.

Committee on Human Rights of the U.S. National Academy of Sciences, National Academy of Engineering and Institute of Medicine

2101 Constitution Avenue, NW
Washington, D.C. 20418
PH: (202) 334-3043
FX: (202) 334-2225
WWW: http://www.2.nas.edu/oia/2146.html
E-Mail: chr@nas.edu
Founded: 1976

Mission: The National Academy's public affairs office indicates that the Committee on Human Rights of the U.S. National Academy of Sciences (CHRNAS) is composed of members elected to the Institute of Medicine, the National Academy of Engineering, or the National Academy of Sciences. CHRNAS attempts to encourage foreign governments to release scientists, engineers, and health care professionals who have been imprisoned abroad for their conscientiously held beliefs (not violently expressed), which may be religious, moral, and/or political.

Current Activities: CHRNAS's professional staff monitors conditions around the world, collects data produced by governments and other NGOs, and recommends plans of action to the members. CHRNAS sends delegations to countries where prisoners of conscience are held and reports on their findings. These reports are disseminated widely and are often used for lobbying with the U.S. Department of State, the U.S. Congress, and foreign governments. Formerly: the Committee on Human Rights of the U.S. National Academy of Sciences.

Publications: Various documents and studies.

Committee to Protect Journalists

330 Seventh Avenue, 12th Floor
New York, NY 10001
PH: (212) 465-1004
FX: (212) 465-9568
WWW: http://www.cpj.org
E-Mail: info@cpj.org or media@cpj.org
Founded: 1981
Members: 468
Staff: 18
Scope: International

Mission: The Committee to Protect Journalists' (CPJ) Web site states that it is a nonpartisan and nonprofit body founded by U.S. journalists in 1981 to monitor abuses against the press and to promote press freedom worldwide. The CPJ indicates that it helps journalists who have been subjected to human rights violations, and works to limit and/or remove restrictions placed on foreign correspondents and local journalists by governments. Full-time staff includes area specialists for Africa, the Americas, Asia, East and Central Europe, the former Soviet Union's successor states, the Middle East, and North Africa.

Current Activities: CPJ keeps U.S. and foreign journalists alerted to abuses, especially where attacks on the press are most likely to occur, and protests aggressively on behalf of these human rights violations. It researches and publishes information on violations, brings exiled foreign journalists to America for press conferences designed to highlight their cases, sponsors delegations of journalists to locations where such human rights abuses are prevalent, and works with press groups abroad to develop campaigns on behalf of harassed journalists, as well as to share information. The CPJ also organizes letters of protest to foreign leaders and writes urgent action appeals designed to free journalists unjustly imprisoned or to improve their conditions. As part of this effort the CPJ gives several annual Press Freedom Awards to journalists for their courage in reporting, as well as the Burton Benjamin Award for "distinguished achievement in the cause of press freedom." CPJ maintains a library and speakers bureau, and it conducts research programs. CPJ offers luncheons and seminars and maintains a press freedom database with several thousand documented case histories of attacks against journalists. It utilizes the International Freedom of Expression Exchange (IFEX), a global e-mail coordinating body, to work cooperatively on an international basis.

Publications: CPJ produces an annual survey of press freedom around the world in roughly 120 countries; a "Dangerous Assignments" listing; newsletters; articles; and a quarterly journal.

Doctors Without Borders

(Médecins Sans Frontières)

[U.S. Office] 6 East 39th Street, 8th Fl.
New York, NY 10016
PH: (212) 679-6800
FX: (212) 679-7016
WWW [International organization]:
http://www.msf.org
WWW [U.S. chapter]:
http://www.dwb.org/index.htm
E-Mail: dwb@newyork.msf.org
Founded: 1971
Scope: International

Mission: Doctors Without Borders (DWB), also known by its French name, *Médecins sans Frontières*, was founded by French medical professionals in 1971. It provides assistance to victims of natural disasters, insurrections, and war. DWB is nonpolitical in orientation and international in staff: more than two thousand volunteers provide assistance in roughly eighty countries every year.

Current Activities: DWB has developed an enviable reputation in a short time for courageous, aggressive, and highly effective interventions into some of the most dangerous conflict areas around the world. When other NGOs leave, many DWB teams are willing to stay, although their targeting by some insurgent groups and the heightened level of physical violence against NGOs worldwide have somewhat curtailed the groups efforts. DWB can offer virtually a full spectrum of medical support, but each mission is dictated by local conditions, accessibility, and indigenous support. DWB acts in a liaison capacity with like-minded NGOs for follow-on care.

Publications: DWB publishes a newsletter and a thrice-yearly "Alert," as well as some books.

Franklin and Eleanor Roosevelt Institute

511 Albany Post Road
Hyde Park, NY 11238
WWW: http://newdeal.feri.org/feri/ and http://www.udhr50.org/
E-Mail: jhamrah@idsi.net
Scope: International

Mission: The Roosevelt Institute's Web site indicates that it hopes to "inform new generations of the ideals and achievements of Franklin and Eleanor Roosevelt and to inspire the application of their spirit of optimism and innovation to the solution of current problems." Franklin, the thirty-second president of the United States, and his distant cousin and wife Eleanor (the niece of President Theodore Roosevelt), were both formidable individuals who made significant contributions. Eleanor's efforts on behalf of social betterment, her six years as America's delegate to the UN, and her leadership of the Commission on Human Rights are all worthy of study. Similarly, the institute believes that Franklin Roosevelt's "Four Freedoms" are "essential to a flourishing democracy," and they have established programs to promote those freedoms in the United States and abroad. In the United States the institute works with educators to improve the teaching of the major events of the Roosevelt years in America's schools.

Current Activities: The Roosevelt Institute supports an extensive agenda, most notably its commitment to the UN. A major achievement has been its leadership of a fiftieth anniversary celebration of the Universal Declaration of Human Rights in the United States in 1998, which involved more than sixty other NGOs and a focus on inspiring youth to promote human rights worldwide, along with a Web site to celebrate "Human Rights Year" (http://www.udhr50.org).

The institute's many programs utilize the FDR Library in Hyde Park and the Roosevelt Study Center in the Netherlands for research and teaching. The institute also established an International Center at Moscow State University (focusing on studies of the 1930s and 1940s), and three additional centers are planned for Asia, Africa, and South America. Integral to these programs are FDR Library Summer Intern Program and the Franklin and Eleanor Roosevelt Distinguished Lecture Series. An awards program has also been created to recognize excellence and achievement in issues of significance to the Roosevelts, including the Roosevelt International Disability Award and the Four Freedom Awards. The institute has also created the New Deal Network, an Internet teaching resource designed to explain the significance of President Roosevelt's legislative reform program, known as the New Deal.

Federation Internationale des Ligues des Droits de L'Homme

SEE INTERNATIONAL FEDERATION OF HUMAN RIGHTS LEAGUES

Gesellschaft Für Bedrohte Völker

SEE SOCIETY FOR THREATENED PEOPLES

Human Rights in China

485 Fifth Avenue, 3rd Floor
New York, NY 10017
PH: (212) 661-2909
FX: (212) 972-0905
WWW: http://www.hrichina.org
E-Mail: hrichina@igc.org
Founded: 1989
Scope: National

Mission: Human Rights in China (HRC)'s Web site indicates that it is "an independent, international organization founded by Chinese scientists and scholars in March 1989." HRC indicates that it monitors human rights conditions in the People's Republic of China; documents and publicizes abuses; promotes human rights "advocacy and education among Chinese people inside and outside the country;" and works to create a grassroots human rights movement in China while also encouraging "international scrutiny of China's human rights situation." Inside China, HRC attempts to alert the Chinese people to international human rights standards and the means of enforcement, as well as help those harassed or imprisoned in China (who protested nonviolently) in exercising their rights through the Chinese legal system.

Human Rights Information and Documentation Systems International Secretariat

48, chemin de Grand-Montfleury
CH-1290 Versoix, Switzerland
PH: 41 22 7555252
FX: 41 22 7555260
WWW: http://homepage.iprolink.ch/~huridocs
E-Mail: huridocs@oln.comlink.apc.org
Founded: 1982
Scope: International

Mission: Human Rights Information and Documentation Systems International (HURIDOCS)'s brochure indicates that it hopes to promote access to and dissemination of data on human rights through "more effective, appropriate, and compatible methods and techniques of information handling." HURIDOCS links human rights groups in 156 countries.

Current Activities: HURIDOCS does not collect information; it works with other groups to coordinate the development of documentation processes, and it encourages the use of standard formats. Other bodies in the field can then utilize and exchange that information according to their own needs. HURIDOCS also evaluates difficulties other bodies are having in storing and utilizing their information, especially with regard to "the capabilities and needs of NGOs." Where appropriate and when requested, it shares advice with those groups. HURIDOCS also creates and shares techniques for information handling, such as variable formats, matrices, and software for use in documenting human rights issues and violations. HURIDOCS provides educational and training courses, workshops, and materials.

Publications: HURIDOCS produces a directory of NGOs; news brochures, two to three times a year (in English, French, and Spanish); a newsletter, circulation 2,700; a standard format book for bio materials; and other reference books.

Human Rights Internet

8 York Street, Suite 302
Ottawa, Ontario, Canada K1N 5S6
PH: (613) 789-7407
FX: (613) 789-7414
WWW: http://www.hri.ca
E-Mail: hri@hri.ca
Founded: 1976

Mission: Human Rights Internet (HRI) was launched in the United States in 1976 to support the work of NGOs through the sharing of information. Headquartered in Canada, HRI focuses on protecting internationally recognized standards of human rights through research, education, and the sharing of information between various individuals and groups in the field.

Current Activities: HRI strives to serve as a clearinghouse for data, linking itself to a variety of NGOs, government archives, and libraries interested in expanding their holdings and research capacity in the field. HRI responds to inquiries about publications, research, instructional resources, and the products and activities of various human rights bodies. With a relatively long history, its resource collection has longitudinal scope, with many cross-references, allowing in-depth researches in historical cases not available elsewhere. According to their Web site, HRI databases "include information on thousands of human rights organizations, bibliographic abstracts of the literature, bodies which fund human rights work, human rights awards, education programs on human rights, and children's rights information." Information can be requested from the Information Documentation Centre. Affiliated with: The International Studies Association; the United Nations. Formerly: Internet: International Human Rights Documentation Network.

Publications: HRI produces a quarterly magazine, *Human Rights Tribune*; an annual publication, *Human Rights Internet Reporter*, which indexes thousands of publications received by HRI; and other specialized directories and publications.

Human Rights Watch

350 Fifth Avenue, 34th Floor
New York, NY 10118-3299
PH: (212) 290-4700
FX: (212) 736-1300
WWW: http://www.hrw.org
E-Mail: hrwnyc@hrw.org
Founded: 1978 as Helsinki Watch (now Human Rights Watch/Helsinki)
Scope: International

Mission: Human Rights Watch (HRW)'s Web site and other public domain materials indicate that it was established by the Fund for Free Expression (organized in 1975) as an organization that linked the Watch Committees—Helsinki Watch, Americas Watch, and Asia Watch. HRW indicates that it is dedicated to protecting the human rights of people around the world. HRW states that it stands with victims and activists to prevent discrimination, uphold political freedom, protect people from inhumane conduct in wartime, and bring offenders to justice. HRW investigates and exposes human rights violations and attempts to hold abusers accountable. HRW challenges governments and those who hold power to end abusive practices and respect international human rights law. HRW also enlists the public and international community to support the cause of human rights for all.

Current Activities: HRW is a "parent" organization with several divisions: Africa (Sub-Saharan), Americas (Latin America and the Caribbean), Arms, Asia, Children's Rights, Europe and Central Asia, Middle East (Middle East and North Africa), and Women's Rights. HRW supports special initiatives in the following areas: Academic Freedom, Corporations and Human Rights, Drugs and Human Rights, Free Expression, Prison Conditions, and the United States. HRW has organized Congressional Friends of Human Rights Monitors (a separate organization) and is affiliated with the Free Expression Project. HRW links its monitors and its offices through PeaceNet and e-mail. HRW sends missions to investigate abuses and it publicizes those abuses worldwide. Moreover, HRW observes court proceed-

ings, investigates election preparations and evaluates the performance of states in upholding human rights standards, including the actions of the U.S. government. HRW utilizes letter-writing campaigns to influence policy in abusive states as well as to improve conditions for prisoners. It also testifies before the U.S. government on abuses worldwide, and works with the UN, the OAS, European bodies, and various NGOs to facilitate joint goals.

Publications: HRW has released an annual survey of human rights practices worldwide since 1990; it generates numerous press releases and special investigative studies. HRW also offers a semiannual catalog of human rights publications; a quarterly newsletter, circulation 15,000; brochures; and an annual report.

Other Offices: Washington, D.C.; Los Angeles, CA; London, UK; Brussels, Belgium.

Institute for Global Communications
producer of PEACENET

[Visitors] Presidio Building 1012, 1st Floor
Torney Avenue
[Write to] P.O. Box 29904
San Francisco, CA 94129-0904
PH: (415) 561-6100
FX: (415) 561-6101
WWW: http://www.igc.org/igc/
E-Mail: igcdc@ugc.org
PeaceNet: peacenet@igc.org
Founded: 1986
Membership: 12,000+
Scope: International

IGC's Mission: With the slogan, "Connecting People Who Are Changing the World," the Institute for Global Communications (IGC) is a nonprofit group providing information and Internet services for organizations and individuals. PeaceNet, IGC's first network, was founded in Palo Alto, California, in 1986. Since then IGC has expanded to provide Internet tools and on-line services for those working on conflict issues (ConflictNet, 1989), the environment (EcoNet, 1987), women's issues (WomensNet, 1995), and labor issues (LaborNet, 1992). It also offers e-mail and international collaboration with similar bodies abroad. According to its Web site, in 1990 IGC co-created the Association for Progressive Communications (APC), which includes twenty-five affiliated members and forty partners promoting social change in 130 countries. Since 1992 IGC has been "the primary information and communications service provider at UN world conferences."

PeaceNet's Mission: PeaceNet's public affairs materials indicate that it is a communications network that offers software for electronic mail, conferencing, access to specialized databases, and a variety of other activities. Some human rights groups use PeaceNet to communicate with their members in the field, to advertise their activities, to inform interested supporters regarding legislation or events, or to seek assistance on a variety of issues. Amnesty International uses PeaceNet for its Urgent Action Alerts, which notify supporters of prisoners of conscience who are under threat of torture or death, in order to generate a large number of letters to govern-

ment authorities so as to mitigate the sentence imposed against the prisoner.

Current Activities: PeaceNet's subscribers and members change routinely, so it does not offer the continuity of other bodies, but its volume and access to major organizations give it legitimacy and weight in the field. PeaceNet is especially helpful to single-issue bodies that need rapid communication chains engaged on behalf of life-threatening situations. It is also useful to small NGOs without sufficient funds to launch major telecommunications projects themselves.

Institute for the Study of Genocide

John Jay College of Criminal Justice
899 Tenth Avenue, Room 325
New York, NY 10019
PH: (212) 582-2537
FX: (212) 582-9127
Founded: 1982
Scope: International

Mission: The Institute for the Study of Genocide (ISG)'s public domain information indicates that it is composed of scholars, professors, students, and the interested public concerned with past, present, and future cases of genocide. ISG members pursue research and publication on the causes, prevention, and consequences of genocide worldwide.

Current Activities: Specifically, the ISG encourages its members and others to pursue historical, contemporary, and predictive research on the causes of genocide, mass political killings, ethnic "cleansings," and other mass violence toward humans and to share that information with those who can make a difference, including governmental bodies and academic institutions. The ISG also researches and evaluates actual cases of genocide; it focuses on human rights abuses that might be considered genocide; and it publicizes deterrents to genocide and strategies to help victims. The ISG also attempts to link with other groups internationally as well as with bodies that hold historical, personal, and/or archival materials dealing with the subject.

Publications: ISG periodically reports on its work and offers educational materials, lectures, symposia, and discussion groups. It offers a semiannual newsletter.

Inter-American Commission on Human Rights

1889 F Street, NW, 8th Floor, Room 820E
Washington, D.C. 20006
PH: (202) 458-6002
FX: (202) 458-3992
WWW: http://www.cidh.org
Founded: 1948
Scope: Regional

Mission: The Inter-American Commission on Human Rights (IACHR)'s public domain materials indicate that IACHR is a private voluntary body composed of citizens of member states that belong to the Organization of American States. This body is organized to encourage and protect human rights in North America, Central America, and South Africa, as well

as in the Caribbean. The IACHR maintains a five thousand-volume library that specializes in human rights law. It holds three meetings a year, focusing on specific difficulties in regional human rights practices, the sharing of data, and NGO and individual networking.

Publications: IACHR issues reports annually on countries in the regions, as well as an annual report.

International Centre for Human Rights and Democratic Development

63, rue de Bresoles,
Montreal, Quebec,
Canada, H2Y 1V7
PH: (514) 283-6073
FX: (514) 283-3792
WWW: http://www.ichridd.ca/
E-Mail: ichrdd@ichrdd.ca
Founded: 1988
Scope: International

Mission: The International Centre for Human Rights and Democratic Development (ICHRDD), according to its public domain informational materials, is a Canadian institution with an international mandate. ICHRDD was established by an Act of the Parliament of Canada in 1988 and officially inaugurated in 1990. The Centre characterizes itself as independent and nonpartisan. It states that it initiates, encourages, and supports the promotion, development, and strengthening of democratic and human rights institutions and programs as defined in the International Bill of Rights.

Current Activities: ICHRDD has a mandate from the Canadian government to work closely with citizens' groups, international organizations, and governments around the world. Its prime focus is to encourage democratic development, reduce human rights abuses wherever possible, and avoid their recurrence. The Centre supports a variety of efforts to stimulate cooperation between NGOs and governments in order to promote respect for human rights and democratic development. The Centre funds research and political analysis, monitors events in key areas, intervenes where its actions might be fruitful, and offers financial assistance in some instances. ICHRDD excels in its public education and advocacy mandate in Canada and abroad.

Areas of special interest include women and indigenous peoples, NGO access to multilateral institutions, North-South and regional networking, and support for democratic movements. ICHRDD utilizes research, seminars, conferences, study missions, public events, and publications. Its primary regional foci are the Americas, Africa, and Asia on four thematic priorities: globalization and human rights, justice and the rule of law, women's rights, and indigenous peoples' rights. The Centre has NGO consultative status (Category II) with the Economic and Social Council of the United Nations and is on the International Labour Organization's Special List of NGOs.

Publications: ICHRDD produces a newsletter; democratic development studies; a human rights essay series; occasional papers; and the "Women's Human Rights in Conflict Situations" newsletter.

International Federation of Human Rights Leagues
(Federation Internationale des Ligues des Droits de l'Homme)

International Headquarters
17 Passage de la Main d'Or
75011 Paris, France
PH: 33 1 43 55 25 18
FX: 33 1 43 55 18 80
WWW: http://www.fidh.imaginet.fr/uindex.htm
E-Mail: fidh@hol.fr
Founded: 1922
Scope: International

Mission: Traditionally referred to by its French acronym, the FIDH is the oldest international human rights organization in the world. It was founded in 1922 to encourage liberty, justice, peace, and equality—all principles subsequently enumerated in the Universal Declaration of Human Rights. The FIDH has either consultative or observer status with the UN, UNESCO, the Council of Europe, and the African Commission for the Rights of Individuals and Peoples.

Current Activities: The FIDH monitors human rights violations around the world and sends observers to trials where the issue of human rights violations is paramount. It develops plans for public protests and mounts judicial inquiry missions abroad where the declaration's standards are not met. It conducts its own research as well as commissions research by others; the FIDH also links its efforts with those of the UN, various human rights bodies, and its own constituents, and it sponsors an annual congress.

Publications: The FIDH produces a weekly letter (in French); a newsletter, monthly (in Arabic, English, and Spanish); biweekly mission reports; and books.

International Human Rights Law Group

1200 18th Street, NW, Suite 602
Washington, D.C. 20036
PH: (202) 232-8500
FX: (202) 232-6731
E-Mail: ihrig@aol.com
Founded: 1978
Members: 200
Scope: International

Mission: The International Human Rights Law Group (IHRLG) states that it is a membership body composed of government officials, attorneys, law students, educators, and the concerned public who seek to protect and enhance human rights around the world.

Current Activities: IHRLG relies on a highly trained and motivated group of staff and volunteer legal professionals to meet an ambitious annual agenda. IHRLG's rich panoply of tools include: limited and comprehensive litigation activities, filing complaints before international human rights bodies (as well as regional bodies), preparing Congressional testimony and legal briefs on international human rights norms, organizing and staffing election-observing

trips abroad, and information exchanges on election observing. IHRLG's institutional memory and archival capacity make it a rich source of context on international cases for governments and NGOs alike.

Publications: IHRLG publishes guidelines for election observing, legislation digests, chronicles of international treaties, and reports on human rights violations and elections.

International PEN
PEN American Center

568 Broadway
New York, NY 10012
PH: (212) 334-1660
FX: (212) 334-2181
WWW: http://www.pen.org/
E-Mail: PEN@pen.org
Founded: 1921

Mission: Established to protect the principles of free transmission of thought and to preserve the free press, PEN was founded in London by John Galsworthy in 1921. PEN is an international organization whose members include historians, journalists, translators, critics, playwrights, essayists, editors, and novelists. In the early years its activities were more philosophical than activist; today the opposite is true.

Current Activities: PEN members agree to oppose any suppression of freedom of thought and expression in their home state. PEN has active chapters starting with the high school level and has expanded widely in colleges and universities, writing and journalistic centers, and major metropolitan areas. Through its strong university bases worldwide, PEN is a able to mobilize articulate and erudite writers on behalf of harassed and imprisoned writers worldwide. Its many appeals on behalf of imprisoned writers were especially effective during the Helsinki process criticism of Warsaw Pact states, and it continues to effectively lobby members of legislatures worldwide.

Publications: PEN produces press releases and action alerts, among other documents.

International Religious Liberty Association

c/o Dr. John Graz
12501 Old Columbia Pike
Silver Spring, MD 20904-6600
PH: (301) 680-6680
FX: (301) 680-6695
WWW: http://www.irla.org
E-Mail: 74532.1055@compuserve.com
Founded: 1893
Members: 70,000
Scope: International

Mission: Officials at the International Religious Liberty Association (IRLA) say that they seek to publish and proclaim the principles of and the universal right to religious liberty, that they help to promote respect for religious rights and freedoms of all human minorities as well as majorities, and that they seek to secure worldwide recognition of and respect for the basic human right to freedom of conscience and belief. Formerly: (1946) National Religious Liberty Association.

Publications: IRLA publishes a semiannual journal in French and German and a bimonthly newsletter.

International Society for Human Rights
(Internationale Gesellschaft für Menschenrechte)

Borsigallee 16
D-60388 Frankfurt am Main, Germany
PH: 49 69 4201080
FX: 49 69 4201083
E-Mail: 101533.2364@compuserve.com
Founded: 1972
Members: 4,000

Mission: The International Society for Human Rights (ISHR)'s public information materials indicate that its membership base is comprised of educators, students, medical professionals, lawyers, and other interested citizens from forty-two countries, largely in Europe. ISHR indicates that these members encourage human rights awareness and advocacy as well as provide physical and professional assistance to individuals and organizations in totalitarian countries. ISHR also attempts to foster international tolerance and understanding, collaborating with other international bodies, especially European, in the field.

Current Activities: ISHR concentrates on encouraging those fundamental human rights enumerated in the Universal Declaration of Human Rights. To this end, ISHR works with journalists to generate publicity in human rights cases; it helps politicians and governments working to protect rights by offering investigative resources, data-sharing, and publicity; it organizes advocacy bodies that intervene in specific cases; and it drafts and disseminates appeals, provides press releases, and organizes public demonstrations highlighting such cases. ISHR also shares information with other groups and individuals, including archival and database materials. Individual working groups focus on China, the former Yugoslavia's derivative states, Korea, Latin America, Poland's minorities, Romania and ethnic minorities in Romania, Russia and the former Soviet Union's derivative states, South Africa, Vietnam, Laos, Cambodia, West Africa. ISHR now incorporates the former Permanent Committee for the Defense of Human Rights.

Formerly: (1981) *Gesellschaft für Menschenrechte.*

Publications: ISHR produces a bimonthly newsletter (in German); a bimonthly magazine (in English); press releases (German, Russian, English, Spanish); a bimonthly German journal; a quarterly Spanish newsletter; and pamphlets in various languages.

International Women's Rights Action Watch

University of Minnesota
Humphrey Institute of Public Affairs
301 19th Avenue, S.
Minneapolis, MN 55455
PH: (612) 625-5093
FX: (612) 624-0068
WWW: http://www.hhh.umn.edu/
bulletin/centers/iwraw.html
E-Mail: iwraw@hhh.umn.edu
Scope: International

Mission: The Humphrey Institute's public information materials indicate that the International Women's Rights Action Watch (IWRAW) is a communication and resource body for an international network of over four thousand groups and individuals focused on implementing the Convention on the Elimination of Discrimination Against Women (CEDAW).

Current Activities: IWRAW could not function without its elaborate network of cooperative relations with other NGOs in the developing world, as well as with the CEDAW secretariat and the members of the CEDAW committee. IWRAW routinely monitors CEDAW meetings and reports on the committee's efforts. Through an elaborate information-gathering process, it considers the status of women in the various countries considered each session and offers its findings to the committee in advance of its session. It communicates with virtually every type of NGO concerned with women's status around the world and also shares its findings with the press and the interested public. IWRAW offers an annual conference and seminar in New York City, held in cooperation with the Committee to Eliminate Discrimination Against Women.

Publication: IWRAW produces books in various languages, a quarterly journal, a newsletter, videos, and bulletins about women's rights.

Latin America Human Rights Association
(Association Latinoamericana para los Derechos Humanos)
Rumipamba 862 y Av. republica
Apartado 17-07-9296
Quito, Ecuador

PH: 593 9 738225
FX: 593 9 445974
Founded: 1980
Scope: Regional

Mission: The Organization of American States (OAS) lists the Latin America Human Rights Association (LAHRA) as one of several large human rights bodies in the region concerned with human rights violations in the Caribbean and Latin America.

Current Activities: With a limited staff and a large region, as well as a concern not to unnecessarily duplicate OAS activities, LAHRA has chosen to focus on only a few areas of concern: democracy-building, women, children, the work of NGOs, specific country analyses, the Indians of the Amazon, the environment, and legal studies. LAHRA attempts to build an awareness of the need to protect human rights, a constituency for those rights, as well as governmental support for rights protections in all three branches of government.

Lawyers Committee for Human Rights

330 Seventh Avenue, 10th Floor
New York, NY 10001
PH: (212) 629-6170
FX: (212) 967-0916
WWW: http://www.lchr.org
E-Mail: lchrbin@lchr.org
Founded: 1978
Members: 800

Mission: The Lawyers Committee for Human Rights (LCHR)'s public affairs materials indicate that it is a public interest law institute that promotes international human rights and refugee law as well as proper legal procedures. It specializes in cases where volunteer lawyers and other legal professionals can help enhance international human rights standards. LCHR is deeply involved in promoting the pro bono representation of indigent political asylum appeals in the United States, and the organization encourages the use of the pro bono model worldwide. LCHR also investigates alleged human rights abuses in justice systems for subsequent follow-up by local attorneys. LCHR has developed training materials and conferences as well as educational workshops for attorneys on a wide variety of human rights problems as well as on refugee and asylum law. LCHR grants the Roger Baldwin Medal of Liberty every two years to organizations or individuals who have made a significant contribution to human rights anywhere in the world. Formerly: Lawyers Committee for International Human Rights.

Current Activities: Through its International Human Rights Program, it has investigated patterns of abuse in the Middle East, Africa, Eastern Europe and the Soviet Union, Asia, Latin America, and the Caribbean. LCHR has sufficient staff to do some firsthand investigative reporting, but it relies primarily on press reports and data shared with other NGOs in the field. Its forte is the development of formats and plans of action that similar organizations can follow elsewhere.

Publications: LCHR publishes quarterly newsbriefs and an annual critique of the U.S. Department of State's *Country Reports on Human Rights*. It also reports on developments in asylum laws and on committee projects. The LCHR some-times publishes (in cooperation with the Human Rights Watch Committees) the results of investigations in detailed and carefully researched reports.

Médecins Sans Frontières

SEE DOCTORS WITHOUT BORDERS

National Association of Human Rights Workers

c/o Florida Commission on Human Relations
Building F, Suite 240
325 John Knox Road
Tallahassee, FL 32303
WWW: http://www.fairhousing.com/nahrw/
Founded: 1947
Scope: National

Mission: This membership organization's public affairs materials indicate that it is composed of professionals in the governmental and public interest fields dealing with a broad range of human rights issues, with a special focus on civil rights and civil liberties, religious understanding, and interracial and inter-ethnic relations.

Current Activities: Traditionally, the National Association of Human Rights Workers has utilized a speakers' bureau, research activities, and statistical analyses to support its efforts. Its long-term nature has given it substantial institutional memory,

and volunteer support over the years has been a mainstay. One of its standing committees focuses specifically on international human rights. It has always primarily been a support group for professionals in the field.

Formerly: National Association of Intergroup Relations Officials (NAIRO).

Publications: Quarterly journal, bimonthly newsletter.

Organization Mondiale Contre la Torture

SEE WORLD ORGANIZATION AGAINST TORTURE

Physicians for Human Rights

100 Boylston Street, Suite 702
Boston, MA 02116
PH: (617) 695-0041
FX: (617) 695-0307
WWW: http://www.phrusa.org
E-Mail: phrusa@phrusa.org
Founded: 1986
Members: 5,000
Scope: International

Mission: Physicians for Human Rights (PHR)'s public affairs materials indicate that it is a body of scientists, concerned citizens, and health professionals. PHR brings the skills of the medical profession to the human rights arena. PHR attempts to defend imprisoned health professionals, works to prevent the participation of doctors and other medical personnel in torture, and strives to prevent physical and psychological abuse of citizens by their governments.

Current Activities: Among the most effective bodies in its field, PHR rigorously plans and mounts missions to more than thirty-five countries to investigate and protest human rights abuses. Relying on the extensive and highly educated Boston-area medical community, it draws upon its large membership to support its efforts. PHR maintains a speakers' bureau and conducts a variety of educational programs, both locally as well as around the United States, with some abroad. Its library focuses on reference materials, and its holdings include some two thousand books, periodicals, clippings, audiovisual materials, monographs, and archival materials. The library's focus includes torture, medicine and human rights, land mines, and torture treatment. PHR has also developed effective letter-writing campaigns on behalf of imprisoned health care professionals, and it provides humanitarian assistance to victims. PHR was a co-recipient of the 1997 Nobel Peace Prize for its work to ban landmines. Formerly: (1987) American Committee for Human Rights.

Publications: PHR's extensive publications include reports on mission findings and monthly medical action alerts. It also publishes journal articles, medical testimony on victims of torture, physicians' guides to political asylum cases, and other reports.

Project Diana: Online Human Rights Archive

Maintained by the Orville H. Schell, Jr.
Center for International Human Rights
Yale Law School
P.O. Box 208215
New Haven, CT 06520-8215
PH: (203) 432-7480
FX: (203) 432-1040
WWW: http://diana.law.yale.edu/
E-Mail: schell@diana.law.yale.edu

Mission: The Diana Database consists of linked Web sites that provide human rights documents (with a focus on law and litigation) on the World Wide Web. Named in honor of Yale University law librarian Diana Vincent-Daviss, there are four Diana sites in all, each with different documents. (The other sites are the University of Cincinnati College of Law [http://taft.law.uc.edu:81/Diana/], the University of Minnesota Human Rights Library [http://www1.umn.edu/humanrts/], and the Bora Laskin Library at the University of Toronto [http://www.law-lib.utoronto.ca/Diana/].) Sites must be searched separately.

Current Activities: One of Project Diana's major contributions is the collection of large bodies of consistent documents in archival format, a rare product even today. These collections include: documents from the United Nations, including copies of documents in the United Nations Human Rights Center in Russian; documents from the Organization for African Unity; documents from HURIDOCS (see separate entry), which are standard formats for documenting human rights violations;

bibliographies on international terrorism, and public international law. Every effort is made to distribute information on these resources, as well as access to the databases, broadly. International NGOs with dissemination capacity have joined with Project Diana to expand its reach.

Research Center for Religion and Human Rights in Closed Societies

475 Riverside Drive, Suite 828
New York, NY 10115-0448
PH: (212) 870-2481
Founded: 1962

Mission: The Research Center for Religion and Human Rights in Closed Societies offers a unique and unrivaled archive of documents vital to understanding human (and especially religious) rights violations that have occurred, or are occurring, in the states of East/Central Europe and the former Soviet Union. Many records, or fragments of records, date to before World War II.

Current Activities: Scholars, writers, government officials, the press, clergy, business specialists, students, and archivists utilize the products of this center. It translates and evaluates underground and official documents and articles concerned with religious life in "communist, former communist, and other totalitarian societies, focusing particular attention on the violation of religious freedom and human rights." Relying heavily on a network of volunteers and board

members, the center sponsors press conferences, provides press releases, and provides Congressional testimony on key issues. Formerly: (1971) International Council of Churches in the United States of America. Also cited as: Religion in Communist Dominated Areas (RCDA).

Publications: The center produces a quarterly journal, which includes case histories, book reviews, translated documents, research reports, and cartoons; circulation 3,500.

Robert F. Kennedy Center for Human Rights

1367 Connecticut Avenue, NW, Suite 200
Washington, D.C. 20036
PH: (202) 463-7575
FX: (202) 463-6606
WWW: http://www.rfkmemorial.org/center_for_human_rights.htm
E-Mail: hrcenter@rfkmemorial.org

Mission: The stated mission of the Robert F. Kennedy (RFK) Center for Human Rights is to encourage and support the work of the RFK Human Rights Awards Laureates, twenty-three of whom have been honored. The center's projects are intended to "enhance and complement the work of the laureates and promote respect for human rights in their countries."

Current Activities: The RFK Center evaluates cases of alleged human rights abuses and publishes the results of its investigations; it lobbies to alert the public to these abuses and attempts to free prisoners of conscience. The RFK Center also uses its excellent political ties in the United States to pressure governments abroad, businesses, and international groups to adhere to previously agreed upon international standards of human conduct. The RFK Center tries to enable its laureates to expand their efforts with professional guidance and technical support on fundraising, publicity, and influence-building. The center also takes the products of the laureates' work and disseminates them in the United States, thereby expanding their contact base, linking them informally, and giving them technologically advanced access to a wide range of resources that they are unlikely to achieve at home. The RFK Center holds consultative status with the UN.

Society for Threatened Peoples

(Gesellschaft für bedrohte Völker)
Postfach 20 24
D-37010 Goettingen, Germany
PH: 49 551 49906-0
FX: 49 551 58028
WWW: http://www.gfbv.de/fr_gfbve.htm
E-Mail: info@gfbv.de
Founded: 1970
Members: 7,300
Scope: International

Mission: The Society for Threatened People (usually known by its German acronym, GfbV) states that it is composed of supporters in more than twenty nations who attempt to protect religious and ethnic groups around the world that are the victims of human rights violations.

Current Activities: GfbV exhaustively catalogs violations of human rights that occur among threatened peoples and publicizes them in Germany and abroad; its target audience tends to be primarily European. GfbV focuses on ethnic, national, and religious groups, especially those in minority status in individual states. It has taken a special interest in violations in closer proximity, such as the Balkans, but also has a substantial capacity to investigate violations in Spanish-speaking areas around the world. GfbV holds conventions and meetings; it has sponsored public education efforts and encourages other similar groups to do the same. Also known as: Society for Endangered Peoples.

Publications: GfbV publishes a journal, *Pogrom*, and a leaflet, *Bedrohte Völker Aktuell* (News about Threatened Peoples).

Third World Foundation of North America

3250 Prospect Street
Washington, D.C. 20007
PH: (202) 625-2750
FX: (202) 625-7401
WWW: http://www.ThirdWorld.org
E-Mail: webmaster@thirdworld.org
Founded: 1989

Mission: The Third World Foundations' Web site and staff indicate that it was founded by professor Cyril Ponnamperuma to "bring together scientists and government officials from the developing and developed nations to promote sustainable resource renewal, management and use." His plan derived from his work with the Third World Network of Scientific Organizations and the Third World Academy of Sciences.

Current Activities: The foundation assembles geographically based databases that can be used for a variety of purposes: health, agriculture, environmental impact, food security, economic forecasting, women's education, and population control. The foundation's main focus is to provide the data necessary for indigenous scientists and policymakers to solve their own problems. Recently, the foundation contracted with NASA to train developing world scientists in these techniques (especially remote sensing), with a specific focus on health care (eliminating vector-born diseases such as river blindness and malaria) and rural telemedicine. The Third World Foundation also uses its databases to promote resource renewal projects in Somalia, Bangladesh, and Jordan. The foundation is linked to the Third World Academy of Science (based in Italy), which is funded by UNESCO, as its North American branch. Its collections feature a library of technical papers (including annotated bibliographies), a news section, and an electronic forum. The Third World Foundation also develops conferences, exhibits, symposia, and workshops exhibiting its projects and promoting its ideas.

UNICEF International Child Development Centre

Piazza SS. Annunziata, 12
50122 Florence, Italy

PH: 39 055 2345258
FX: 39 055 244817
WWW: http://www.unicef-icdc.org
E-Mail: florence@unicef-icdc.it
Founded: 1988

Mission: Public information materials of the UNICEF International Child Development Centre (ICDC) indicate that it was founded as an international training center and data collection body that focuses on the rights of children worldwide. It was developed to support the capacity of UNICEF and its parent and companion bodies in order to encourage a new global ethic for the proper treatment of children.

Current Activities: ICDC's primary goal is the implementation of the United Nations Convention on the Rights of the Child. It works closely with NGOs in Europe, with various European UN-affiliated groups, and with private foundations and individuals that have a special interest in children. As such, it gathers information from governments and NGOs to augment its database, sponsors forums, and publishes a variety of documents.

United States Committee for Refugees

1717 Massachusetts Avenue, NW, Suite 701
Washington, D.C. 20036
PH: (202) 347-3507
FX: (202) 347-3418
WWW: http://www.refugees.org.
E-Mail: uscr@irsa-uscr.org
Founded: 1958
Members: 13,000
Scope: International

Mission: The United States Committee for Refugees (USCR) was founded in 1958 to coordinate U.S. participation in the United Nations International Year of the Refugee. USCR's public affairs materials and Web site indicate that it is an information and advocacy body, showcasing the millions of refugees in the world to the American public. USCR states that it "defends the rights of all uprooted people regardless of their nationality, race, religion, ideology, or social group." The basic rights outlined by USCR are the right to not be forcibly returned to one's homeland if there is a "well-founded fear of persecution," the right to a fair hearing to determine an individual's status, and the right to humane treatment.

Current Activities: USCR performs a variety of monitoring and advocacy functions, both in regions from which refugees are fleeing and in regions where they have arrived. Public relations materials indicate that USCR's agenda includes interviews with refugees; the recording of any abuses they have suffered; the provision of supplies to meet immediate health and safety needs; a basic appeal to journalists, other aid agencies, and concerned governments, as well as the interested public; and follow-on care to help refugees support themselves and eventually return to their area of origin if conditions improve.

Beyond crisis situations, USCR meets routinely with foreign and U.S. leaders; it encourages UN agencies that attempt to cope with refugee needs; it communicates with voluntary bodies in the field; it monitors legislation and hearings of the U.S. Congress and U.S. government policy on refugee issues; it undertakes its own research and develops statistics. It also maintains libraries that are open to the public and offers online services of various sorts, including research. Affiliated with: The Immigration and Refugee Services of America.

Publications: USCR publishes the *World Refugee Survey* (annual), magazines, reports (monthly), and papers on specific refugee problems.

Witness

c/o Lawyers Committee for Human Rights
333 Seventh Avenue, 13th Floor
New York, NY 10001
PH: (212) 845-5242
FX: (212) 845-5299
WWW: http://www.witness.org
E-Mail: witness@lchr.org
Founded: 1992

Mission: Conceived in 1992 in partnership with the Lawyers Committee for Human Rights, Peter Gabriel, and the Reebok Foundation, Witness gives human rights advocates the tools to document human rights abuses. According to Witness materials, their work "advances human rights through the use of video and related communications technologies . . . . Witness is a public resource that promotes the innovative use of video technology and materials to strengthen the fight for human rights."

Current Activities: Witness says that it gives the tools of modern technology directly to NGOs in order to document human rights abuses as they occur in cities, towns, and villages worldwide. It provides human rights activists with camcorders, microphones, cassettes, and batteries; its Web site offers tips and advice on using the equipment. The footage is used by international media and in courts and tribunals to provide documentary evidence of human rights abuses. In conjunction with the U.K.-based International Television Trust, Witness has produced films about human rights struggles. Witness is also in the process of constructing a multimedia archive of evidence that will serve the human rights community.

Publications: Brochures and videos about Witness can be borrowed from the Lawyers Committee for Human Rights.

World Organization Against Torture

(Organization Mondiale Contre La Torture)

International Secretariat
PO Box 35-37 Rue de Varembé
CH-1211 Geneva CIC 20
Switzerland
PH: Tel: 41 22 733 31 40
FX: Fax: 41 22 733 10 51
E-Mail: omct@omct.org
Or
OMCT USA
1015-18th Street N.W.
Washington, D.C. 20038
PH: (202) 861-5494
FX: (202) 659-2724
WWW: http://www.omct.org
E-Mail: msklar@igc.apc.org
Founded: 1985
Scope: International

Mission: Usually known by its French acronym, OMCT's public information materials indicate that it is the main international coalition of NGOs fighting against torture and other forms of inhuman treatment. It has a network of almost two hundred full-time member organizations and supports NGOs in roughly one hundred states.

Current Activities: OMCT says that it has working relationships with several thousand local and regional NGOs and regularly sends urgent appeals and cases of serious human rights violations to more than one thousand institutions. Its activities include the circulating communications concerning cases of torture, summary execution, and forced disappearance; assisting victims of torture requiring medical, social, or legal support; and defending the fundamental rights of children particularly those in conflict with the law, in armed conflict, in the street and those who are victims of violence because of discrimination. OMCT also helps other interstate institutions in the human rights field through data-sharing, encouragement, joint publicity, and some financial collaboration; it organizes international and regional conferences dealing with promoting and protecting human rights; it organizes or participates in investigative missions to states actively engaged in torture; and it engages in public education campaigns. OMCT holds consultative status with the Economic and Social Council and the International Labour Organization, and the African Commission for Human and People's Rights. Meetings and symposia are offered three to four times a year.

Publications: OMCT publishes books in English, Spanish, and French; handbooks; a quarterly journal (in English); and bulletins.

CHAPTER SEVEN

Human Rights Activists

Introduction

"The prudent see only the difficulties, the bold only the advantages, of a great enterprise; the hero sees both; diminishes the former and makes the latter preponderate, and so conquers."
—Johann Lavater

A hero can live in any age—but he or she must inspire the imagination, excite the spirit, prick the conscience, and show the way. Just as their forerunners did, today the true heroes of the human rights movement are those who took the theory of the Universal Declaration and its antecedents and made it into a buckler and shield, a sword and a promise, for the downtrodden, the poor, the bereft, and the needy.

A hero gives unselfishly for a noble cause. Surely those profiled below, along with many others this one volume lacks the space to describe, were and are heroes to many who have never met them. Many, indeed, have won the Nobel Peace Prize, awarded annually by the Nobel Foundation for outstanding achievement in the promotion of world peace. It is no accident that so many of those profiled below have received such an accolade.

The orientation and occupations of human rights activists have been many and varied. They are statesmen and scholars, diplomats and lawyers, judges and military officers, mothers, educators, and the religiously inspired. Many had no formal training in "human rights," for indeed there was not such a field when they began their work. Many, moreover, work for nothing in this world, looking only to a higher authority for the justification of their struggles and ambitions.

Although Western philosophy undergirds the twentieth century's human rights movement, post-World War II heroes have been citizens of many states. Their generosity makes them citizens of the world. The litany below includes Irish and Polish Catholics, a Polish Jew, Chinese and Burmese, Costa Ricans and British, Tibetan and American,

French and Czech, Pakistani and Guatemalan, Norwegian and Latin, Russian and Argentine, Egyptian and South African. They come in all hues, of both sexes, and every conceivable background. What unites them is a vision of a better world.

Some have been famous, taking their previously achieved stature and turning it to the cause of humanity. Former U.S. President Jimmy Carter, who launched a global reawakening of rights in power politics, now in his later years directly influences the lives of other individuals through his work with Habitat for Humanity. Then, too, some have been elevated for their compassion and devotion, such as Vaclav Havel, a playwright who so inspired his countrymen and women before the fall of the Iron Curtain that he was a natural focus around which the new government of Czechoslovakia was built.

Many have lived their belief in God daily just as intensively as Mother Teresa, but few with such capacity to influence the entire world. A holy man of another tradition, Tenzin Gyatso, the fourteenth Dalai Lama, helped ensure that the world would never forget the plight of the Tibetan people in the wake of Tibet's annexation by China. Father Oscar Romero, a Salvadoran priest, made an impact at a vital time in his country's life, as did Bishop Desmond Tutu, who won the Nobel Peace Prize in 1984 and chaired the Peace and Reconciliation Commission in South Africa from 1996-98, helping to heal the wounds of apartheid.

Some have used their professional training to great effect, as Bernard Kouchner did when he founded *Médecins sans Frontières* (Doctors Without Borders), giving the world a potent new weapon against innocent suffering during insurrections and war. Some are noteworthy for their focus on issues meriting worldwide attention, such as Raphael Lemkin, the Polish lawyer who first coined the term "genocide" in 1944 to describe Nazi atrocities. Writers like the Argentine journalist Jacobo Timerman and Egyptian author Nawal El Saadawi have championed the human rights cause. Like the suffragists of old, the late twentieth century witnessed labor organizers' tremendous impact on some societies. Lech Walesa, the Polish union organizer who later turned politician, led his country after Communism and won the Nobel Prize.

Some have themselves suffered great persecution and forged their inspiration and strength in great travail. Elie Wiesel is one such example, a Nobel laureate for his writings on the Holocaust. Fang Lizhi, a Chinese astrophysicist, is another, as is Wang Dan, a Chinese activist jailed for his leadership in the Tiananmen Square uprising. And Nelson Mandela's dignity and strength throughout his twenty-seven years in prison both galvanized the antiapartheid movement and shamed the South African government.

Others, such as Amnesty International founder Peter Benenson, formed great organizations, multiplying a thousandfold or even a millionfold their voices on the world stage. On a smaller scale, but especially important in Latin America, Argentine protesters Hebe de Bonafini and Maria Adela de Antokoletz courageously let their nation, their region, and the world know the plight of the "disappeared." Most recently, Jody Williams served as the American co-coordinator of the International Campaign to Ban Landmines, which captured worldwide attention and the Nobel Prize in 1997.

Some human rights activists worked "within the system," using the best of the world's governmental machinery to render aid to the helpless, protection for the powerless, and inspiration to the hopeless. Fridtjof Nansen, a Norwegian statesman and scientist who became the first UN High Commissioner on Refugees, was one of these. Mary Robinson, Irish lawyer and former president of Ireland, has earned high praise for her principled and articulate leadership of the UN High Commission on Human Rights.

Others have focused their life energies on nationalistic concerns that many in the world would never know about were it not for their efforts. Faraway places, unfamiliar names, and a culture of poverty tend to blind many in the West to the travails that many in the world face. Aung San Suu Kyi opened eyes to atrocities committed in Burma, as did Bishop Carlos Filipe Ximenes Belo and Jose Ramos-Horta for East Timor. The plight of children in poverty was highlighted by Iqbal Masih's efforts in Pakistan, while Rigoberta Menchu's efforts on behalf of Guatemala's Quiche Indians emphasized the difficulties of indigenous peoples far beyond her borders, and won her the Nobel Peace Prize in 1992. Similarly, Ken Saro-Wiwa, a Nigerian activist, helped his Ogoni people to resist pollution and the despoiling of their homeland.

Just as the heroes of old did wonders, there can always be heroes today and tomorrow. The life work of the individuals profiled below gives all of us great hope that the world will be a better place.

— Carol Rae Hansen

Aung San Suu Kyi

Leader of National League for Democracy
(1945 to)

For the strength of her convictions in demanding justice for the Burmese people, Aung San Suu Kyi has attracted worldwide admiration. In a country considered one of the world's most censored nations, she is fearless in her nonviolent quest for peace and human rights.

Suu Kyi's birth marked her life. She was born June 19, 1945, in Burma, the daughter of the revered leader, Aung San, who negotiated Burmese independence from British rule. On the eve of independence in 1947, he was assassinated.

Aung San Suu Kyi and her two brothers were raised in the Buddhist faith. At fifteen

Aung San Suu Kyi (CORBIS/Alison Wright).

she continued her education in India, where she learned of Gandhi's principles of nonviolence and civil disobedience. In 1967 she received a degree from St. Hugh's College, Oxford, England. She went to work at the United Nations Secretariat in New York in 1969. While away from home for most of twenty years, she maintained a closeness to Burma through her studies—she wrote a biography of her legendary father and studied modern Burmese literature. Suu Kyi married Tibetan scholar Michael Aris in 1972 and they had two sons, Alexander and Kim.

News that her mother was dying brought her back to Burma in 1988. That spring a student uprising in Rangoon, Burma's capital, stirred dissent against the twenty-six-year military rule. Mass demonstrations demanded an interim civilian government, fair elections, and restoration of civil liberties. On August 8, demonstrators were met with brute military force and thousands were killed.

Suu Kyi announced on August 26, 1988, that she was joining the struggle, forming the National League for Democracy. In 1989 she was given the choice to leave the country or stay under house arrest. She stayed, and despite her arrest the National League for Democracy won the 1990 election by a landslide. However the new military council, the State Law and Order Restoration Committee (SLORC), refused to transfer power to the democratically elected civilian government.

Although she was out of touch with her family for years at a time, they were a source of strength; her husband edited her book *Freedom from Fear* and, with their sons,

accepted prizes on her behalf. Suu Kyi was awarded the Sakharov Prize for Freedom of Thought from the European Parliament and the Norwegian Thorolf Rafto Prize for Human Rights in 1990. In 1991 she won the Nobel Peace Prize in honor of her struggle for democracy, human rights, and ethnic reconciliation for Burma.

In July 1995 her house arrest was lifted. Her release has been conditional—she is denied freedom of movement and association—and her supporters face interrogation and arrest. Nonetheless she continues to speak and act defiantly against SLORC. A symbol of hope for Burma, Aung San Suu Kyi combines the moral, spiritual, and political strength to weaken the grip of tyranny.

For further information
Aung San Suu Kyi. *The Voice of Hope.* London: Penguin Books, 1997.
Aung San Suu Kyi with Alan Clements. *Freedom from Fear and Other Writings.* New York: Viking Penguin, 1991.

—Carol Devine

Belo, Bishop Carlos Filipe Ximenes

Apostolic Administrator for East Timor
(1948 to)

The first Catholic bishop to win the Nobel Peace Prize, Carlos Filipe Ximenes Belo has dedicated his life to human rights of the East Timorese against Indonesian military, economic, and cultural domination.

Belo was born on February 3, 1948, in Baucau, East Timor. He went to missionary schools and in 1973 began philosophical and ecclesiastical studies in Portugal and Rome. In 1975 East Timor was invaded by Indonesia; despite international condemnation, East Timor has remained under Indonesian control since that time.

Belo was ordained a Salesian priest in 1980. In 1981 he returned to East Timor as director of Fatumaca College, where he earned the respect of young East Timorese and with them experienced the intimidation of the Indonesian military. He was hired in 1983 as the Apostolic Administrator of the Dili diocese after his outspoken predecessor, Mgr. Martinho do Costa Lopes, was pressured to resign. Both Indonesian authorities and the Vatican thought Belo would be a quiet replacement.

Eighty percent of East Timor is Catholic, and Belo was well aware that he led the only body in East Timor independent of the Indonesian government. Unable to ignore the potential role of the church in protecting East Timorese national identity and human rights, Father Belo quickly displayed his moral authority. He began to make bold statements against Indonesian military rule, advocating for a political and diplomatic end to the occupation. In 1985 he signed a statement by the East Timor Council of Priests to the Indonesian junta warning that occupation threatened the survival of East Timorese peoples. He was later forced to remove his signature, but he refused to be silenced: in a December 1987 pastoral letter, Belo accused the Indonesian military of regularly practicing torture.

Belo was ordained as bishop in 1988. The following year he sent a private letter to United Nations Secretary General Javier Perez de Cuellar pleading for help. His outraged public condemnation of the 1991 massacre of East Timorese natives by the Indonesian military in Santa Cruz increased global attention. In February 1993 he called for special status for East Timor, cultural and religious autonomy within Indonesia, and a United Nations-supervised referendum.

Bishop Belo continues to make declarations against the Indonesian regime despite death threats and two assassination attempts in 1989 and 1991. The Indonesian government accuses him of obstructing efforts to reach a settlement. But the outside world hears his message. South African Archbishop Desmond Tutu nominated him for the Nobel Peace Prize in 1995. That same year he received the John Humphrey Freedom Award. In 1996 he was jointly awarded the Nobel Peace Prize with pro-independence East Timorese spokesperson Jose Ramos-Horta for their sustained efforts to open negotiations with Jakarta to bring peace and freedom to their country.

A foundation of hope within East Timor, Bishop Belo works to move the country towards peace and reconciliation. Through the leadership of the church, he improves social and community services for those suffering under the occupation and he makes daring calls seeking to protect the culture, dignity, and security of the East Timorese people.

For further information
Cox, Steve, and Peter Carey. *Generations of Resistance: East Timor.* New York: Cassell, 1995.
Pilger, John. *Distant Voices.* London: Vintage, 1994.

—Carol Devine

Benenson, Peter

Founder of Amnesty International
(1921 to)

Outraged by a 1960 newspaper account of the imprisonment of two Portuguese students who raised a toast to liberty in a public cafe, British lawyer Peter Benenson began a crusade to mobilize public opinion in support of political prisoners around the world. This "Appeal for Amnesty 1961" became Amnesty International, one of the largest and most active human rights organizations in the world.

Peter Benenson was born in London on July 31, 1921, to British army officer Harold Solomon and his wife, the daughter of Russian-Jewish millionaire Grigori Benenson. Flora Benenson raised Peter alone following her husband's death in 1930, and Peter later took the Benenson surname to honor his grandfather. In 1937, while still a student, Peter organized a school group to raise money for children left orphaned by the Spanish Civil War. He threw himself into further humanitarian work, leaving school to help resettle thousands of Jewish children fleeing Nazi-occupied Europe. He joined Britain's war effort in 1940 as part of a military intelligence unit working to crack German communication codes.

After the war Benenson studied law, joined the British Labour party, and developed an interest in international civil liberties. He served as an observer at politically motivated trials in fascist Spain and Soviet-controlled Hungary, and organized a group of British lawyers to act as independent observers at other questionable trials in several different nations. The group later became the British section of the International Commission of Jurists, an organization that works for the legal protection of human rights around the world.

By 1959 Benenson's interest in human rights left him increasingly frustrated by the limitations of his legal career. In late 1960 the story of the imprisoned Portuguese students inspired him to devise a new approach to human rights advocacy. He gathered a group of lawyers, journalists, and activists for a yearlong campaign on behalf of what his colleague Eric Baker described as "prisoners of conscience"— people imprisoned for the peaceful expression of their beliefs. On May 28, 1961, Benenson published an article in the *London Observer*, appealing to readers to join "Appeal for Amnesty 1961," a letter-writing campaign demanding the release of political prisoners in six different nations. The British response to his editorial was overwhelming, and the editorial was picked up by newspapers in New York, Paris, and Zurich. By the following year Benenson's plans for a limited campaign were discarded, and the growing numbers of letter-writing volunteers were reorganized as Amnesty International.

Though a key player in Amnesty International's beginning successes, Benenson was forced to withdraw from day-to-day management of the organization in 1967 because of health problems. In the mid 1980s, he cofounded the World Organization Against Torture, a non-governmental organization headquartered in Switzerland. He lives outside of Oxford, England, where he continues to be active with local Amnesty International groups. Amnesty International is now the world's largest human rights organization, and its strategy of organizing public opinion against oppressive governments has succeeded in freeing tens of thousands of political prisoners throughout the world.

For further information
Power, Jonathan. *Amnesty International: The Human Rights Story*. New York: McGraw Hill, 1981.
Amnesty International. *The Amnesty International Handbook*. Claremont, Calif.: Hunter House, 1991.

—Rebecca Sherman

Bonner, Elena

Physician
(1923 to)

The wife of one of the Soviet Union's most famous dissidents, Elena Bonner has suffered extraordinary persecution at the hands of the Soviet government. Bonner and her husband, Andrey Sakharov, worked together to advocate for democracy and human rights throughout Russia, work that Bonner has continued alone since Sakharov's death in 1989.

Born in Merv, Tajikistan, on February 15, 1923, to an Armenian father and a Jewish mother, Elena Bonner was raised in comfort in Moscow, where her stepfather held a prominent position in the Communist Party. In May 1937 her stepfather was arrested. He was later executed during the purges, Stalin's campaign to rid himself of political opposition. Her mother, Ruth Bonner, was arrested later that year, leaving Elena and her brother in the care of their grandmother. When the Soviet Union entered World War II in 1941, Bonner volunteered as a nurse and was sent to the front, where she was seriously wounded.

The war injury caused severe and permanent damage to her vision. Following two years of treatment for her injuries, she went to medical school and worked for the next several years as a doctor.

In 1970, while attending a trial of human rights activists, she met Andrey Sakharov, a prominent nuclear physicist turned dissident. The two were married in 1972. Bonner plunged into activism along with her husband; when in 1975 Sakharov was denied permission to leave the country in order to accept his Nobel Peace Prize, Bonner went to Norway to accept it on his behalf.

With the increasing international prominence of Sakharov and Bonner came increased harassment from the Soviet government. Their situation deteriorated further when they were banished to the remote city of Gorky in 1980. During their exile Bonner's health deteriorated and she was denied adequate medical care. Sakharov went on three hunger strikes, during which he was forcibly hospitalized and tortured, before Bonner was allowed to travel to the United States for open-heart surgery. After recuperating from a sextuple bypass operation, she returned to the Soviet Union in June 1986 to resume her life of exile with Sakharov. Six months later, as part of the political reforms that became known as perestroika, they were invited back to Moscow by Soviet leader Mikhail Gorbachev.

Since Sakharov's death in 1989, Elena Bonner has worked for peace, democracy, and human rights throughout the territories of the former Soviet Union. She serves as chairperson of the Andrey Sakharov Foundation, an international organization for the promotion of human rights.

For further information

Bonner, Elena. *Alone Together*. Translated by Alexander Cook. New York: Alfred A. Knopf, 1986.

Bonner, Elena. *Mothers and Daughters*. Translated by Antonina W. Bouis. New York: Alfred A. Knopf, 1991.

—Rebecca Sherman

Carter, Jimmy

Thirty-ninth president of the
United States

(1924 to)

U.S. President Jimmy Carter (CORBIS/Leif Skoogfors).

As president of the United States from 1977 to 1981, Jimmy Carter declared that human rights would be the cornerstone of U.S. foreign policy. Though the Carter administration frequently failed to live up to his idealistic rhetoric, Carter managed to effectively communicate his humanitarian concerns to several oppressive regimes by linking U.S. aid to their record on human rights. Since returning to private life in 1981, Carter has shown a tenacious commitment to peace and social justice, working around the world to promote health, sustainable agriculture, human rights, and democracy.

James Earl Carter, Jr. was born on October 1, 1924, in the small town of Plains, Georgia. His father, James Earl Carter, Sr., was a successful farmer and businessman. His mother, Lillian Gordy Carter, defied convention by continuing to work as a nurse after her marriage, providing free nursing care to poor black families in the fiercely segregated South. A driven student and a devout Baptist, Carter graduated from the U.S. Naval Academy in 1946, married Rosalynn Smith, and embarked on a naval career, working on the development of nuclear submarines. Following his father's death in 1953, Carter resigned from the navy and returned to Plains to take over the family farms. His involvement in local affairs led to an interest in politics: he was elected to the Georgia senate in 1962 and became governor of Georgia in 1970. As a political newcomer and Washington outsider, he won a surprising victory in the 1976 presidential elections, narrowly edging out incumbent Gerald Ford.

As president, Jimmy Carter attempted a major shift in American foreign policy, creating a new role for the United States as a defender of human rights abroad. Drawing on his deeply felt Christian morality, he declared, "Our commitment to human rights must be absolute." Perhaps inevitably, political realities ensured that Carter fell short of his absolute ideal. Though he had notable successes exerting pressure on some human rights violators, like Argentina's military dictatorship, he was accused of failing to act against abuses in strategic countries like Iran, Indonesia, and El Salvador.

Though Carter was politically compromised in some areas of foreign policy, his personal commitment to peace exhibited itself dramatically when he brought perennial enemies Anwar Sadat of Egypt and Menachem Begin of Israel to the negotiating table at the presidential retreat at Camp David. Carter personally engineered the historic peace accord between the two nations, bringing an end to thirty years of hostility and war. It was the most triumphant achievement of his presidency.

Since losing his reelection bid in 1980 to Ronald Reagan, Carter and his wife Rosalynn have founded the Carter Center in Atlanta, an advocacy center for international social issues ranging from peaceful conflict resolution to improved farm yields and the eradication of Guinea worm disease across Africa and Asia. As a private citizen, he has used his negotiating skills to defuse tense conflicts in Korea, Haiti, and Bosnia. He has led international teams of observers to monitor elections in Latin America, Africa, and the Middle East. A regular volunteer with the international housing organization, Habitat for Humanity, Carter recently launched a domestic antipoverty initiative, and he is an outspoken advocate of a more equitable distribution of wealth and resources. He has been nominated for the Nobel Peace Prize seven times, and has been called "America's finest ex-president."

For further information
Bourne, Peter G. *Jimmy Carter: A Comprehensive Biography from Plains to Postpresidency*. New York: Simon & Schuster (Scribner), 1997.

Smith, Gary. "What Makes Jimmy Run?" *Life Magazine*, November 1995.

—Rebecca Sherman

Cassin, René

Jurist and statesman
(1887 to 1976)

A legal scholar and internationalist, René Samuel Cassin was the principal author of the Universal Declaration of Human Rights, issued by the United Nations in 1948. In 1968, on the twentieth anniversary of the declaration, Cassin was awarded the Nobel Peace Prize for creating what has become the legal cornerstone for the defense of human rights around the world.

The son of Jewish merchant Henri Cassin and his wife Gabrielle Dreyfus, René Cassin was born on October 5, 1887, in Bayonne, in southern France. He studied law, economics, political science, and literature in Aix-en-Provence and Paris, receiving his doctorate in 1914. The outbreak of World War I interrupted his plans to begin practicing law in Paris. Instead he was drafted into the French infantry, serving until 1916, when he was severely wounded by shrapnel and discharged from the army.

After the war Cassin resumed his legal career, becoming a professsor of law at the University of Paris in 1929 and serving as a French delegate to the League of Nations from 1924 until 1938. The lingering effects of his war wound plagued him for the rest of his life, but his own physical suffering inspired him to begin humanitarian work, organizing aid and rehabilitation efforts for his fellow war veterans. He helped to create the International Confederation of Disabled

Soldiers, an organization that tried to encourage a lasting peace by bringing together veterans and former enemies from all over Europe. He later described his humanitarian work between the wars as an attempt to honor "the supreme commitment" of millions of World War I veterans "who sacrificed themselves that this war might be the last."

When France fell to the invading German army at the start of World War II, Cassin was one of the first civilians to follow General Charles de Gaulle to London, where he became a member of de Gaulle's Free France government in exile. After Germany's defeat Cassin returned to France and was appointed president of France's highest administrative court. He also devoted himself to international humanitarian work. A founder of the United Nations Educational, Scientific, and Cultural Organization (UNESCO) in 1944, he served as the French delegate to UNESCO until 1954. He was a French representative to the United Nations from 1946 until 1968, working on the UN Commission for Human Rights.

On this committee he made his most profound and lasting contribution to human rights. Working under committee chair Eleanor Roosevelt, Cassin crafted the Universal Declaration of Human Rights, thirty articles which first establish that "All human beings are born free and equal." Though the Universal Declaration of Human Rights was officially adopted by the United Nations General Assembly on December 10, 1948, Cassin spent the next eighteen years lobbying to make the declaration legally binding through effective implementation and enforcement provisions, a quest in which he ultimately felt himself unsuccessful.

In 1968 Cassin received the Nobel Peace Prize after devoting more than fifty years of his life to peace, justice, and human rights. In his acceptance speech, he described the declaration as "the first document of an ethical sort ever produced by organized humanity." The Nobel committee called it a first step toward a world society in which the rights of the individual are accorded the same respect as the rights of nations. Cassin died in Paris on February 20, 1976.

For further information

Haberman, Frederick, ed. *Nobel Lectures: Peace.* New York: Elsevier Publishing Company, 1972.
Obituary, *New York Times*, February 21, 1976.

—Rebecca Sherman

Fang Lizhi

Physicist and political dissident
(1936 to)

Nuclear physicist Fang Lizhi has challenged Communist orthodoxy and advocated greater intellectual and political freedom in China for more than forty years. He was a hero and inspiring example for the student movement against the Chinese government, crushed by tanks at Tiananmen Square in June 1989.

Sometimes called "China's Andrey Sakharov," Fang was born in Beijing in 1936, the son of a postal clerk. He entered Beijing University in 1952 as a student of theoretical and nuclear physics. It was there he met his future wife, Li Shuxian, a fellow physics student. In 1955 he began a career of public dissent when he seized control of a university stage during a meeting of the Communist Youth League to speak out for independent thinking.

Fang graduated from Beijing University in 1956 and was assigned to work at the Chinese Academy of Sciences' Institute of Modern Physics Research. He was expelled from the Communist Party for advocating educational reform during the "Let a Hundred Flowers Bloom" relaxation of 1956. Fang's science credentials helped him keep his post at the Institute, where he prospered until 1966, when the cultural revolution erupted. Political power was seized by a radical Communist faction that targeted intellectuals, among others, as the enemy. Fang was imprisoned in solitary confinement for a year and then "sent down" to the countryside to work with peasants. He was considered sufficiently "rehabilitated" in 1978, following the death of Mao Zedong and the rise of Deng Xiaoping.

Deng's "open door" modernization policies helped Fang step into the spotlight. In 1978 he left China for the first time on conference trips and teaching assignments that took him to Munich, the Vatican, Colombia, England, Japan, and the United States. Overseas travel broadened his outlook and left him even more willing to speak his mind. Interviewed by the Chinese journalist Dai Quing in December 1986, Fang paraphrased Albert Einstein to proclaim, "Scientists must express their feelings about all aspects of society, especially when unreasonable, wrong, or evil things emerge."

From 1986 to 1989 Fang emerged as an outspoken domestic and international critic of the limits Deng Xiaoping placed on Chinese political freedoms. Hard-liners saw the internationally known scientist as an instigator of student unrest—a threat to the order needed to modernize China and open it to the outside world. China's student activists saw Fang as a hero willing to champion intellectual dissent.

After the Tiananmen crackdown, Fang took refuge in the American Embassy in Beijing for a year before he was allowed to leave for the United States. In 1992 he joined the faculty of the University of Arizona as professor of physics and astronomy. He has since served in many human rights organizations, including Human Rights in China, Human Rights Watch, International League for Human Rights, and the Committee of Concerned Scientists. In addition to activity in many scientific organizations, Fang Lizhi has published more than 230 papers and has authored, coauthored, or edited some twenty books.

In 1996 Fang received the Nicholson Medal for Humanitarian Service "for his courageous struggle for democracy and human rights in China over the past four decades; for his continued commitment to teaching and his outstanding leadership in physics research despite difficult circumstances; and his continued dedication to students, colleagues, and those fighting for human rights."

For further information
Gargan, Edward A. *China's Fate: A People's Turbulent Struggle with Reform and Repression, 1980-1990.* New York: Doubleday, 1990.
Schell, Orville. "China's Andrey Sakharov." *The Atlantic Monthly*, May 1998.

— Frederic A. Moritz

Goldstone, Richard J.

Judge and prosecutor
(1938 to)

Justice Richard Goldstone is a member of the South African Constitutional Court and the former chief prosecutor for the United Nations International Tribunals on Crimes Against Humanity in Rwanda and in Bosnia and Croatia. Throughout his career he has used both national and international law as a force for societal change.

Richard Goldstone was born in 1938 in Boksberg, near Johannesburg. A third-generation South African, Goldstone was encouraged by his grandfather, who had taught him to read and play chess, to pursue the study of law. It was while attending university that Goldstone made his first friendships across color lines and was introduced to the realities of apartheid. His privileged life contrasted sharply with that of his black peers, who lived in poverty in legally segregated areas and were required to carry a government ID at all times.

After graduation from the University of the Witwatersrand in 1962, Goldstone practiced corporate and intellectual property law in Johannesburg. In 1980 he became a judge of the Transvaal Supreme Court. Goldstone employed the visibility of the bench as a means for making ordinary South Africans aware of the injustices of apartheid. In one of his most famous rulings, Judge Goldstone significantly weakened the Group Areas Act, which established different areas of the country for different racial groups. Typically, people violated the act simply because there was no housing in their legal area. When found guilty they were often evicted immediately, even if there was nowhere else for them to go. Goldstone found that an eviction was not automatically required by the Group Areas Act and that a separate hearing on the question of eviction had to be held. The court also decreed that the availability of alternate housing was to be an important consideration in the eviction hearing. After this ruling, evictions under the act virtually ceased. Goldstone went on to become a judge of the Supreme Court in 1989 and currently serves as a justice of the South African Constitutional Court.

From 1991 to 1994 South Africa was undergoing a political transformation from a system of apartheid to a democracy. To aid in this transition, the Commission of Inquiry into Public Violence and Intimidation was established in October 1991 to investigate human rights abuses committed by the various political factions in South Africa. Goldstone was asked by Nelson Mandela to serve as chair of the commission; his leadership resulted in the inquiry being dubbed the Goldstone Commission. Known as a committed and compassionate jurist within South Africa, as well as a proponent of international human rights, his presence signaled South Africa's commitment to justice and its intention to rejoin the world community.

Turning his attention from national to international human rights, Goldstone became chief prosecutor for the International Tribunals on Crimes Against Humanity in Rwanda and the former Yugoslavia in 1994. In this position Goldstone crafted indictments that led to the creation of new human rights laws, as well as procedural laws. He served as prosecutor for three years, then returned to the South African Constitutional Court, which he continues to serve.

The work of the Goldstone Commission in upholding human rights set a high standard for justice in the new, post-apartheid South Africa. As prosecutor of the International Tribunals, Justice Goldstone and his colleagues began paving the way for a permanent International Criminal Court charged with investigating crimes such as those committed in Bosnia and Rwanda. The United Nations is currently drafting a treaty that would establish such a court.

For further information
"Will Justice Be Done?" *U.S. News and World Report*, December 25, 1995.
"Answering for War Crimes: Lessons from the Balkans," *Foreign Affairs* 76, 1 (February 1997).

—Jo Lynn Southard

Tenzin Gyatso, His Holiness the Fourteenth Dalai Lama

Spiritual and temporal leader of Tibet
(1935 to)

The fourteenth Dalai Lama leads the Tibetan people's struggle to peacefully free Tibet from over thirty years of Chinese oppression. While serving as the spokesperson for Tibetans, he also shares a global message of universal responsibility, compassion, and the necessity of dialogue for solving conflicts without violence.

Lhamo Dhondrub, his name at birth, was born on July 6, 1935, to a peasant family in the Amdo province of eastern Tibet. At the age of two he was discovered to be the reincarnation of the Buddha of Compassion and leader of Tibet. In 1939, he traveled with his family to Lhasa, the capital of Tibet, and was enthroned in 1940. At six he began Tibetan Buddhist education and in 1959, at age twenty-four, received the Geshe degree, the equivalent of a doctorate.

In 1950 China began the invasion into the isolated, independent country of Tibet and started suppressing Tibetan religion, culture, and rule. The Dalai Lama asked for help from the United States, India, and Britain to stop China's annexation. Once in exile, he also pleaded with the United Nations to halt the illegal occupation. Despite the United Nations' condemnation of China, no action was taken. Finally in 1959 the Dalai Lama went to India to establish the Tibetan government in exile.

More than one hundred thousand Tibetans have followed him into exile and continue to escape from brutal persecution. He helps the refugees and tries to preserve Tibetan religion and culture by creating schools, monasteries, and a library of historical works. He has also transformed the absolute monarchy of Tibet into an elected democracy.

Since the 1970s the Dalai Lama has traveled extensively to meet political and religious leaders to defend Tibet's integrity and to speak on his people's nonviolent attempts to end merciless repression. He also translates his Buddhist training of compassion, logic, and wisdom into modern and impassioned messages on the interconnectedness of all people and actions. He has met with Pope John Paul II, led interfaith ceremonies, and addressed the UN Conference on Human Rights in Vienna in 1993.

At the 1987 Congressional Human Rights Caucus in Washington, D.C., he proposed a Five Point Peace Plan, a pragmatic attempt to negotiate a settlement for Tibet. The plan, which laid out his vision of a free Tibet as a demilitarized democratic state and a zone of peace, was rejected by China.

The Dalai Lama has won numerous peace and human rights awards and honorary degrees, testimonies to his tremendous contribution to the world community. In 1989 he was awarded the Nobel Peace Prize for leading the struggle for Tibet while opposing violence, and for developing a philosophy of peaceful solutions to international conflicts, human rights, and environmental problems.

While seeking self-determination for Tibet, he urges nonviolence for conflicts on both moral and practical grounds. The Dalai Lama is a living "God-King," but he is also a warm and humble individual who makes ancient principles of compassion relevant today. Respect for human rights must not be an abstract ideal, he says, but a foundation of society.

For further information

Hicks, Roger, and Ngakpa Chogyam. *Great Ocean: An Authorized Biography of the Buddhist Monk Tenzin Gyatso, His Holiness the XIVth Dalai Lama.* Dorset: Element Books, 1984.

Piburn, Sidney, ed. *The Dalai Lama and a Policy of Kindness: An Anthology of Writings by and about the Dalai Lama/Winner of the Nobel Peace Prize.* Ithaca, NY: Snow Lion Publications, 1993.

—Carol Devine

Havel, Vaclav

President of the Czech Republic

(1936 to)

Playwright Vaclav Havel, human rights advocate and outspoken critic of the

Vaclav Havel (CORBIS/Miroslav Zajíc).

Czechoslovakian Communist government, was elected president of Czechoslovakia in 1989. Upon the country's division in 1993, Havel became president of the Czech Republic.

Vaclav Havel was born into a bourgeois family in Prague, Czechoslovakia, on October 5, 1936. In 1957, after studying economics for two years at the Czech Technical University, Havel was drafted and served in the army. It was here that he wrote his first plays. After his discharge in 1959, Havel began working as a stagehand, eventually working his way up to assistant director and playwright at the Theater on the Balustrade in Prague. In 1963 his play *The Garden Party* became an international success. A satire of the government, *The Garden Party* was the first Czech absurdist drama.

As chair of the Club of Independent Writers, Havel was a highly visible participant in the Prague Spring of 1968, a time of democratization and liberal reforms.

Prague Spring ended when the Soviet Union invaded on August 20, 1968. Havel was an outspoken critic of the invasion of his homeland; in retaliation his work was banned and he was dismissed from his theater position. Nonetheless, he continued to write plays and to work against the Communist government. In 1975 Havel wrote a letter to President Gustav Husak, outlining the suffering of Czechoslovakians under Communist rule; the letter was widely, though clandestinely, circulated. The following year, the members of the Plastic People of the Universe, an underground rock band, were arrested for anti-state activity. Havel used his contacts in the arts, both inside and outside of Czechoslovakia, to publicize and protest the arrests. These activities led to the 1977 creation of Charter 77, a human rights initiative signed by hundreds of intellectuals and artists.

Havel emerged as one of three representatives of the Charter 77, which called on the government of Czechoslovakia to honor its commitments as a signatory to both the International Covenant on Civil and Political Rights (ICCPR) and the International Covenant on Economic, Social and Cultural Rights (ICESCR). Along with others associated with Charter 77, Havel was arrested and imprisoned. It was the first of his many incarcerations for antigovernment activities, the longest being from 1979 to 1983, and the most recent ending in May 1989.

In November 1989 Havel became a leader of the Civic Forum, the opposition movement that led to the end of Communist rule. On December 29 of that year Vaclav Havel was elected president of newly demo-

cratic Czechoslovakia. The elections of July 1992 disclosed a huge divergence between Czechs and Slovaks as to how the country should be run; the two halves became separate Czech and Slovak Republics. On January 26, 1993, Havel was elected the first president of the Czech Republic and was reelected on January 20, 1998.

Vaclav Havel is unique in being both a political artist and an artistic politician. He is widely respected for his political leadership in securing human rights inside the Czech Republic, as well as for his intellectual contributions to the human rights movement on a global scale. The recipient of numerous awards and honorary degrees, Havel speaks in forums around the world on a variety of human rights issues, including the importance of language, culture, and the arts.

For further information
Havel, Vaclav. *Disturbing the Peace: A Conversation with Karel Hvizdala*. Translated by Paul Wilson. New York: Alfred A. Knopf, 1990.
Symynkywicz, Jeffrey. *Vaclav Havel and the Velvet Revolution*. Minneapolis: Dillon Press, 1995.

—Jo Lynn Southard

Kouchner, Bernard

Cofounder and president of Médecins sans Frontières
(1939 to)

Adynamic spokesperson for victims of war and disasters, Bernard Kouchner is an outspoken founder of the humanitarian organization *Médecins sans Frontières* (Doctors Without Borders). Kouchner helped establish the legitimacy of "the right to intervene," to provide assistance to the suffering, even if it is against the will of their government.

Bernard Kouchner was born on November 1, 1939, in Avignon, France. He studied medicine in Paris, specializing in endoscopy of the digestive system. At school he was an active member of the Communist students' union, but while students were demonstrating in Paris in the spring of 1968, Kouchner was volunteering with the French Red Cross in Biafra, the eastern part of Nigeria. There he was influenced by the French doctor, Max Recamier, who believed the importance of saving an individual's life transcended politics. As a witness to the slaughter of the Ibo ethnic group by the Nigerian military, Kouchner was outraged and unable to keep the Red Cross oath of silence. He returned to Paris in 1969 and denounced the Nigerian government to the international media.

With a group of French doctors, Kouchner cofounded *Médecins sans Frontières* (MSF) in 1971. Based on the belief that human suffering is the responsibility of everyone, not just governments, MSF sends medical volunteers into trouble zones around the world. Kouchner split with MSF in 1979 and in 1988 formed *Médecins du Monde* (MDM), also a nongovernmental agency dedicated to providing an independent voluntary medical corps in disaster and war zones. He served as president of MDM until 1988.

Admired for his media savvy by some and considered a media opportunist by others, Kouchner brought attention to the plight of the Vietnamese boat people by taking the hospital-ship *"L'Ile de Lumiere"* on the South China Sea. Indignant at the lack of international concern for the famine and war-stricken Somalia, he had TV cameras follow him in 1992 when he collected rice bags from children in France and carried them into Mogadishu.

His political career began in 1988 as minister of social affairs and employment with responsibility for social integration. During his posting from 1989 to 1993 as secretary of state for humanitarian action, he helped translate the concept of humanitarian intervention into two United Nations resolutions. He proposed to the United Nations General Assembly on December 8, 1988, a resolution on the right of access to victims of natural disasters and emergency situations. In 1991 the United Nations intervened in the affairs of a sovereign nation for the first time when it sent advisors to assist the Kurds in northern Iraq.

Kouchner has been a member of the European Parliament, chairman of the development and cooperation committee since July 1994, and presently serves as secretary of state, ministry of employment, with responsibility for health. For his contribution to humanitarianism he received numerous prizes, including the 1979 Dag Hamarskjold Prize for human rights and the Louise Weiss European Parliament Prize for his book, *L'Ile de Lumiere*.

Bernard Kouchner's concept of the right to intervene has provoked dialogue among intellectuals, aid workers, politicians, and jurists on the application of humanitarian intervention. His efforts have also led to lasting organizations that save lives and promote peace.

For further information
Who's Who in France, 1992-1993.
Leyton, Elliott. *Touched By Fire: Doctors Without Borders in a Third World Crisis*. Plattsburgh, NY: McClelland & Stewart/Tundra Books, 1998.

—Carol Devine

Lemkin, Raphael

Author of the Genocide Convention
(1901 to 1959)

A Jewish legal scholar who lost forty-nine members of his family to the Holocaust, Raphael Lemkin invented the word "genocide" to describe the systematic destruction of a nation or ethnic group. He devoted the later years of his life to the creation and ratification of an international treaty outlawing genocide.

Born on June 24, 1901, on a farm near Bezwodene in eastern Poland, Lemkin studied philosophy and law at universities in Poland, Germany, Italy, and France. He returned to Warsaw to practice law as a public prosecutor, but as conditions worsened for Jews in Eastern Europe, he became interested in developing international legal safeguards to protect ethnic minorities. His work on this issue, as well as on the anti-Semitic policies of the Polish government, led to his dismissal from public office in 1933. Wounded while fighting with the Polish resistance during the 1939 German invasion, Lemkin survived six months hiding in forests before he escaped to Lithuania and then to safety in Sweden. His family remained behind in Warsaw, where they were murdered by the Nazis.

While in Sweden Lemkin began work on a monumental collection and analysis of the laws the Germans and their allies imposed upon conquered territories. He continued work on the book while at Duke University in North Carolina and completed it in Washington, D.C. In *Axis Rule in Occupied Europe* (1944), he introduced the term "genocide," which he derived from the Greek word *genos,* meaning race or tribe, and the Latin *cide,* or killing. The book established him as a leading expert on German war crimes, and he served as a member of the United States' legal counsel at the Nuremberg trials after the war.

Though Lemkin joined the law faculty at Yale University in 1948, the real work of his postwar life took place at United Nations headquarters in New York. He became a daily visitor to the United Nations, slowly gathering support for his proposal to create an international treaty making genocide a crime. He convinced the UN General Assembly to place the issue on their agenda in 1946, and he drafted the text of the convention. On December 9, 1949, the UN General Assembly adopted the Convention on the Prevention and Punishment of the Crime of Genocide.

Lemkin spent the remaining ten years of his life lobbying for ratification of the treaty by national governments. He died in New York on August 28, 1959. The convention outlawing genocide, which he worked so hard to create, came into force under international law in 1961 and has been a tool for pursuing justice following genocide in Bosnia-Herzegovina and Rwanda. His most lasting legacy is the word "genocide" itself, one of the terms that defines the history of the twentieth century.

For further information
Rosenthal, A. M. "A Man Called Lemkin." *The New York Times*, October 18, 1988.
Rothe, Anna, ed. *Current Biography 1950*. New York: H. W. Wilson Company, 1951.

—Rebecca Sherman

MacBride, Sean

First chairperson of Amnesty International

(1904 to 1988)

An ardent Irish nationalist who began his career in the Irish Republican Army, Sean MacBride became a leading advocate for human rights, nuclear disarmament, and media accountability. A foreign minister of Ireland and the first chairperson of Amnesty International, MacBride shared the 1974 Nobel Peace Prize for his committed work for peace both within government bodies and through nongovernmental organizations.

MacBride was born to Irish exiles in Paris on January 26, 1904. His mother, Maud Gonne, was a nationalist and philanthropist, and a close friend of the poet William Butler Yeats. His father, Major John MacBride, was executed by the British in 1916 for his leadership role in the Easter Rising, an unsuccessful armed rebellion against British rule in Ireland. Raised in Paris, London, and Dublin, MacBride joined the fight for Irish independence at an early age, becoming the leader of a military unit of the Irish Republican Army (IRA) at age sixteen. Though he fought with a militant IRA faction during the Irish civil war, he eventually came to renounce violence. He worked as a journalist for several years before pursuing a legal career specializing in constitutional and criminal law.

After World War II, MacBride formed a radical political party and launched a career in politics, serving as a member of the Irish parliament for eleven years. From 1948 until 1951 he was Ireland's minister for external affairs, playing a key role in shaping the European Convention on Human Rights. He was a founding member and the first chairperson of Amnesty International, leading the organization from 1961 until 1974. Not content to be just the chief administrator, he also conducted extensive field research for Amnesty International on human rights abuses in Asia, Africa, and America.

From 1968 to 1974 MacBride chaired the Special Committee of the International NonGovernmental Organizations on Human Rights. For seventeen years he lobbied for nuclear disarmament and an end to the arms race as chairperson and president of the International Peace Bureau, an international network of pacifist groups. From 1963 until 1970 he was also secretary-general for the International Commission of Jurists, working for the legal protection of

Sean MacBride *(CORBIS/Hulton-Deutsch Collection).*

human rights around the world. In 1973 the United Nations General Assembly appointed him high commissioner for Namibia, a country then illegally occupied by South Africa. In recognition of his tireless efforts on behalf of human rights, he shared the 1974 Nobel Peace Prize with Eisaku Sato of Japan. In 1977 the Soviet government awarded him the Lenin International Prize for Peace for his work in Namibia.

In 1980 MacBride authored a controversial report for the UN Educational, Scientific, and Cultural Organization (UNESCO) on the cultural, political, and socioeconomic implications of the unequal access to and control of means of communication. This groundbreaking work established a new set of principles to guide the creation of a more equitable and responsible media.

After MacBride's death in Dublin on January 15, 1988, an annual symposium called the MacBride Round Table was established to continue his work on communications issues. His support for Irish nationalist causes lives on through the MacBride Principles, a set of antidiscrimination guidelines that he wrote in 1984 for foreign companies doing business in Northern Ireland. The Sean MacBride Peace Prize is awarded annually by the International Peace Bureau to the individual or organization that best exemplifies MacBride's lifelong commitment to peace and justice around the world.

For further information

Larsen, Egon. *A Flame in Barbed Wire: The Story of Amnesty International.* New York: W.W. Norton & Co, 1979.
Laszlo, Ervin, Linus Pauling, and Jong Youl Yoo, eds. *World Encyclopedia of Peace.* Vol. 3. New York: Pergamon Press, 1986.

—Rebecca Sherman

Machel, Graca

Chairperson of the United Nations Study on the Impact of Armed Conflict on Children
(1945 to)

Graca Machel served as the first minister of education in Mozambique after its independence from Portugal. As a UNICEF ambassador and a United Nations chairperson, she has been a tireless advocate for the rights of children and refugees.

Machel was born in Gaza province in the south of Mozambique in 1945. An excellent student, Machel attended Lisbon University, where she studied Germanic languages. At the same time she joined the Front for the Liberation of Mozambique (FRELIMO), the armed struggle that led to Mozambique's independence from Portugal in 1974. When FRELIMO formed a government in 1975, Machel was named minister of education and culture, the only woman in the cabinet. Later that year she married Samora Machel, the first president of Mozambique. Under her leadership at the Ministry of Education, enrollment in primary and secondary schools increased dramatically. When Machel became minister, 40 percent of Mozambique's children attended school; by the end of her tenure, 75 percent of girls and 90 percent of boys were enrolled.

Soon after Mozambique's independence, the governments of Rhodesia (now Zimbabwe) and South Africa financed the Mozambique National Resistance (RENAMO), which made war against the FRELIMO government. The devastating conflict raged on until 1992, leaving 2.5 million refugees and more than 250,000 orphaned children. It also resulted in the destruction of most of Mozambique's schools and health clinics; the state of education was once again as desolate as when Machel first became minister.

In 1986 Samora Machel died in a mysterious airplane accident. Since that time Graca Machel has focused her energy on development in Mozambique and children's human rights throughout the world. In 1994 she was named to chair the United Nations Study on the Impact of Armed Conflict on Children. The subsequent report, in addition to giving a voice to children victims of violence, highlighted a disturbing new trend in warfare—the systematic targeting of children in military attacks. Machel was awarded the Nansen Medal in 1995 to acknowledge her work on behalf of refugee children.

Machel was married to South African President Nelson Mandela in 1998. She has remained active in Mozambique and internationally, serving as a UNICEF goodwill ambassador, president of the National Commission of UNESCO in Mozambique, president of the Foundation for Communal Work, and chairperson of the National Organization of Children of Mozambique.

For further information
Christie, Iain. *Samora Machel.* New York: Saint Martin's Press, 1989.
Newitt, Malyn. *A History of Mozambique.* Bloomington: Indiana University Press, 1995.

—Jo Lynn Southard

Mandela, Nelson

President of South Africa
(1918 to)

Nelson Mandela was awarded, with F. W. de Klerk, the 1993 Nobel Peace Prize for a lifetime of effort to bring the oppressive South African system of apartheid to an end. In 1994 Mandela was elected as South African president by a multiracial electorate in the country's first democratic election.

Mandela was born near the capital of the Transkei, South Africa, on July 18, 1918. His father, a chief of the Thembu tribe of the Xhosa nation, prophetically named him Rolihlahla, which means "troublemaker" in the vernacular. When he was nine years old, his father died and Chief Jongintaba Dalindyebo of the Xhosa nation became his guardian. Mandela credits the chief with teaching him how to be a leader.

Mandela was the first person in his family to attend school; there he was given, as was the custom, the English name Nelson. He continued to attend missionary schools through college. In 1941 Mandela left the University College at Fort Hare, a prestigious black African University. That year he also declined an arranged marriage, and in doing so, left the protection of his guardian. He completed his B.A. by correspondence while clerking at a white law firm in Johannesburg. Mandela attended law school at the University of Witwatersrand, where he was the only black law student. In 1952 Mandela and Oliver Tambo opened the sole black law firm in the country.

In 1942 Mandela joined the African National Congress (ANC) and in 1944, he was one of the organizers of the Youth League of the ANC, the ANCYL. The ANCYL transformed the organization from one trying to work within the system to a mass movement, employing civil disobedience tactics in its quest for full citizenship and suffrage for all South Africans. For the next two decades Mandela held a variety of positions as administrator, organizer, and policymaker in the ANCYL and the ANC, although the organizations were banned by the government in 1960. In 1962 Mandela was arrested and charged with unlawfully leaving South Africa and incitement to strike. He was convicted and sentenced to five years. While serving this sentence he was convicted of sabotage and sentenced to life in prison.

Nelson Mandela's incarceration brought international attention to the apartheid system. In 1962 the United Nations voted in favor of sanctions against South Africa for the first time; the International Convention on the Suppression and Punishment of the Crime of Apartheid entered into force in 1976 with signatures from over ninety countries.

After thirty years of often violent struggle, the South African government was forced in 1990 to acknowledge that apartheid was no longer viable. President F. W. de Klerk released Mandela from prison on February 11, 1990. His release produced banner headlines throughout the world.

In 1991 Mandela was elected president of the ANC. In this role he participated in multiparty talks with the government of South Africa aimed at ending apartheid. Two years later the talks produced an interim constitution and a date for the first democratic elections in South Africa. The 1993 Nobel Peace Prize was awarded jointly to Mandela and de Klerk for their extraordinary work in ending apartheid in South Africa. In April 1994, the ANC won the elections and Mandela became president of South Africa. He married human rights activist Graca Machel in 1998.

Eradicating the effects of apartheid in South Africa has barely begun. But under Mandela's leadership, the country has made great strides. The nonviolent transition from apartheid to democracy is in itself a remarkable achievement, and a new constitution will take effect in 1999. As he enters his eighth decade, Nelson Mandela's political life may be winding down, but his impact in South Africa and around the world will be felt for generations.

For further information
Mandela, Nelson. *Long Walk to Freedom: The Autobiography of Nelson Mandela.* Boston: Little, Brown and Company, 1994.
Waldmeir, Patti. *Anatomy of a Miracle: The End of Apartheid and the Birth of the New South Africa.* New York: W. W. Norton & Company, 1997.

—Jo Lynn Southard

Masih, Iqbal

Child labor activist
(1982 to 1995)

Iqbal Masih spent half his short life as a bonded laborer in a carpet factory in his native Pakistan. After escaping at the age of ten, he began a phenomenally successful career as an activist, campaigning against child labor both in his home country and abroad.

Born to impoverished laborers in rural Pakistan, Masih was bound out to a local carpet maker at the age of four in order to work off his father's debt of 600 rupiah (about $12). For the next six years, he worked twelve-hour days tying knots on a carpet loom, frequently chained to the loom as he worked. As a result of the inadequate food and strenuous working conditions, Masih was left severely underdeveloped for his age.

At age ten, Masih escaped from his employer and attended a meeting organized by the Bonded Labour Liberation Front (BLLF), a human rights organization founded in 1988 to pressure the government of Pakistan to enforce laws prohibiting child and bonded labor. Armed with a new knowledge of his legal rights, Masih refused to return to the carpet mill. He enrolled in a primary school run by the BLLF and became an active participant in the organization's campaign to free child workers. Over the next two years he helped to liberate some three thousand children from bonded labor.

His precocious activism attracted international attention. He was honored by the International Labour Organization in Sweden and awarded the 1994 Human Rights Youth in Action Award by the Reebok Foundation. While in the United States to accept the Reebok award, he was named "Person of the Week" by ABC News.

On April 16, 1995, a few months after his return to Pakistan, Masih was gunned down in front of his grandmother's house in the village of Muridke. The BLLF asserts that the murder was engineered by the carpet industry, but the Pakistani government claims that there is no evidence to support such charges. The government has harassed and jailed people calling for an investigation into his death.

Masih's murder triggered an international outcry against the use of child labor in the carpet industry. The publicity his murder generated sparked a growing movement by consumers in Europe and North America to hold industries accountable for their use of child laborers.

For further information
Parker, David L., LeeAnne Engfer, and Robert Conrow. *Stolen Dreams: Portraits of Working Children.* Minneapolis: Lerner Publications Co., 1988.
Silvers, Jonathan. "Child Labor in Pakistan." *The Atlantic Monthly* 277, no. 2 (1996).

—Rebecca Sherman

Menchú, Rigoberta
Chair of the Indigenous Initiative for Peace
(1959 to)

Rigoberta Menchú was awarded the Nobel Peace Prize in 1992 for her work on behalf of indigenous peoples in Guatemala. Menchú has traveled throughout the world advocating for indigenous peoples, women, and other victims of government oppression.

Born in 1959 in Chimel, a village in the northern highlands of Guatemala, Rigoberta Menchú was the sixth of nine children in a poor Quiché Indian family. In addition to cultivating their small plot of land, the Menchús spent several months a year working and living on the larger coffee and cotton plantations. According to her autobiography, Menchú began working on the plantations at the age of eight and never attended school. In 1977 her father joined the Committee for Peasant Unity, an organization devoted to land protection, higher wages, and other basic survival issues of indigenous peoples. The entire Menchú family became active in the committee.

In 1979 Menchú's sixteen-year-old brother was kidnapped by soldiers, tortured, and burned alive in a public execution witnessed by the Menchú family. In 1980 Rigoberta's father was one of several peasants who occupied the Spanish embassy in Guatemala City, in an effort to draw attention to the plight of indigenous people. Tragically, the government ordered the embassy burned, killing Menchú's father and his comrades, as well as Spanish officials. Later that year her mother, Jauna Menchú Tum, was kidnapped, raped, tortured, and killed by the army. Leadership of the Committee for Peasant Unity fell to Menchú. At the age of twenty-one, she organized a strike by eighty thousand Guatemalan peasants, virtually paralyzing the country for several days in 1980. Fearing for her life, she fled to Mexico, where she remained in self-imposed exile for twelve years.

As an adult, Menchú taught herself Spanish so that she might speak more effectively on behalf of her people. Throughout the 1980s Menchú continued her activism, while developing her leadership and political skills. During this period Menchú traveled around the world, speaking on behalf of indigenous peoples. Her memoir, *I, Rigoberta Menchú, An Indian Woman in Guatemala*, was published in 1983. Despite subsequent questions about the accuracy of parts of the book, the memoir's success brought international attention to the treatment of indigenous people by the government of Guatemala.

In 1992 the Nobel Peace Prize was awarded to Rigoberta Menchú. This announcement was not without controversy. Critics maintained that Menchú had participated in violent guerrilla actions against the Guatemalan government, while the tradition of the prize is to honor those who espouse nonviolence. However, the committee noted it was only the Guatemalan government that labeled Menchú a guerrilla; she has focused her energies on reconciliation and peace. Despite suffering horrendous violence at the hands of the government, Menchú believes in nonviolent revolution as a means for transforming Guatemala. She was the youngest and first indigenous person to receive the Nobel Peace Prize; she used the prize money to establish the Rigoberta Menchú Tum Foundation, dedicated to promoting the human rights of indigenous people.

It was largely due to Menchú's efforts that the United Nations declared 1993 the International Year for Indigenous Populations and named her goodwill ambassador. In 1995 she became the personal advisor to the general director of the United Nations Educational, Scientific, and Cultural Organization (UNESCO) and the promoter of the United Nations Decade of Indigenous Peoples. She also is head of the Indigenous Initiative for Peace.

Rigoberta Menchú has been instrumental in publicizing the trials of indigenous peoples throughout the world, as well as all victims of poverty, racism, and government oppression. Her work and her many honors, particularly the Nobel Peace Prize, pay special tribute to the lives and struggles of indigenous women.

For further information

Menchú, Rigoberta. *I, Rigoberta Menchú, An Indian Woman in Guatemala*. Edited by Elisabeth Burgos-Debray. Translated by Ann Wright. London: Verso Editions, 1984.
Ashby, Ruth, and Deborah Gore Ohrn, ed. *Herstory. Women Who Changed the World*. New York: Viking, 1995.

—Jo Lynn Southard

Mendes, Chico

Union leader
(1944 to 1988)

Chico Mendes struggled for social justice and human rights for his fellow rubber-tappers in the Amazonian rainforest of Brazil. His life's work and his death ultimately affirmed the interconnectedness of human and environmental rights; the enjoyment of basic rights depends upon protection of the environment.

Francis "Chico" Mendes Filho was born in 1944 in Acre, in the Amazonian interior. For decades, his family made their living by tapping giant rubber trees for their sap, the basic ingredient of natural rubber. The harvesting could continue indefinitely as long as the trees were in good health. By the age of eleven, Mendes was a full-time tapper. In the forest he met Euclides Fernandez Tavora, a tapper who taught him to read and write and about the race and class struggle in Brazil.

Mendes once said that he was an environmentalist without knowing it at first. He began advocating for schools for children and better conditions for tappers. Then Mendes and other tappers organized the Rural Workers Union of Brazil to help improve the lot of tappers and ranch hands and to resist the clearing of forests and roads for large cattle ranchers. Mendes became president of the union, gaining notoriety for his courage, integrity, and commitment to nonviolent civil disobedience. In 1987 he went to Miami to address directors of the Inter-American Development Bank to ask them to stop funding a highway being cut through the rainforest. Mendes argued that an intact rainforest ecosystem could sustain a substantial population of productive rubber tappers, but that the destruction of the natural landscape would lead to the destruction of a way of life.

Mendes was well aware of the punishment meted out to environmental activists by individuals or companies who wished to make a profit despite the environmental and human cost. In the previous decade, up to a thousand activists including indigenous laborers, politicians, and priests who opposed development of the Amazon had been beaten or killed in Brazil. On December 22, 1988, Mendes was murdered in Acre. Rancher Darly Alves da Silva and his son Darci Alves Pereira were convicted of the killing and sentenced to ten years in jail. They escaped from Rio Brancho prison during a riot in 1993; da Silva was recaptured in 1996 but Pereira remains free.

In Brazil today the invasion of indigenous land continues, and the rainforest burns despite greater protections afforded by the Brazilian government. But Mendes' advocacy resulted in the creation of the Chico Mendes Extractive Reserve, a tract of nearly one million acres of protected rainforest for tapping and gathering nuts. His ideas about sustainable extraction have guided international conservationists.

Mendes' work was recognized in 1987 with the award of the Global 500 Roll of Honor Award from the United Nations Environmental Program. He won the 1988 National Wildlife Federation's National Conservation Achievement Award and the Environmental Award from the Better World Society. Chico Mendes' experience as a rubber tapper and his struggle to save this way of life exemplified how the environmental and human rights movements are inseparable.

For further information
Revkin, Andrew. *The Burning Season: The Murder of Chico Mendes and the Fight for the Amazon Rainforest.* Boston: Houghton Mifflin Company, 1990.
Mendes, Chico, with Tony Gross. *Fight for the Forest: Chico Mendes in His Own Words.* London: Latin America Bureau, 1989.

—Carol Devine

Mothers of Plaza de Mayo (Mothers of the Disappeared)

Grassroots protest group

The Mothers of Plaza de Mayo (Mothers of the Disappeared) is a collective of Argentine women who protest regularly at a Buenos Aires plaza, demanding information about their children who have "disappeared." Their defiance of the military junta focused world attention on the "dirty war" waged in Argentina between 1976 and 1983.

In the early 1970s Argentina experienced an extreme form of civil war. The military regime that assumed power in 1976 made use of horrendous violence: thousands of people vanished without a trace and in many cases they were executed. These came to be known as disappearances because the government refused to acknowledge that they had taken the victims, much less murdered them. Reliable estimates place the number of those who disappeared at between ten thousand and fifteen thousand.

Parents and friends reported the disappearances to the Ministry of the Interior, but found it impossible to get any information. Mothers visited the ministry—as well as police stations and jails—over and over again in search of their children. Gradually, an informal network of grieving parents developed, hoping to share information or at least comfort one another. The women soon realized they were wasting their time at the ministry and formulated an alternate plan.

On Saturday, April 30, 1976, a small group of women gathered around a statue in the middle of the plaza for a public protest. They returned the next week, and the next, in ever-increasing numbers. As the group expanded, police harassment began—the mothers suffered verbal abuse, beatings, and frequent arrests. The treatment only increased the mothers' commitment: before long there were several hundred women marching in the plaza every week.

A mother with photograph of her missing son (CORBIS/Owen Franken).

Among them were María Adela de Antokoletz, who was seeking information about her son, Daniel Victor, and Hebe de Bonafini, who had lost two sons, Jorge Omar and Raúl Alfredo. Bonafini and Antokoletz assumed leadership of the loose-knit organization in 1977, after founding mother Azucena Villaflor de Vicenti was kidnapped while picking up her mail.

International renown came to the mothers in 1978, when Argentina hosted the World Cup. Hoping to put a pleasant face on Argentina, the military stepped up harassment in the plaza, resorting to tear gas and attack dogs to drive the women away. The mothers continued their protest, and they caught the eye of the foreign media. Encouraged by the attention, representatives of the mothers began traveling the world, visiting political and religious leaders to plead their cause. They exposed the Argentine military to intense international criticism.

Military rule ended in 1983, after Argentina's defeat by Britain in the Falklands War. This opened the way for public airing of the human rights abuses. In 1984 the National Commission on Disappeared Persons (CONADEP) issued a report with 8,961 names of the disappeared, based on testimony from friends, relatives, and other witnesses. In the wake of the report, the mothers split into two factions. The more mainstream Linea Fundadora essentially supports CONADEP and works with other human rights, church, and labor groups to identify victims and provide support to grieving relatives. Meanwhile de Bonafini continues to lead the more radical Mothers of the Plaza de Mayo; she has repeatedly criticized the CONADEP report and called for repeal of the laws granting amnesty to the military, saying, "We don't want their confessions, we want them in jail forever." The protests at the plaza continue.

The Mothers of the Plaza de Mayo became a leading example of nonviolent political struggle in Latin America, and their success has served as an inspiration to grassroots organizations everywhere. Indeed, new protest groups have recently sprung up in Argentina: Los Hijos de Plaza de Mayo ("The Children of the Plaza") and Los Abuelas de Plaza de Mayo ("The Grandmothers of the Plaza").

For further information
Simpson, John, and Jana Bennett. *The Disappeared and the Mothers of the Plaza: The Story of the 11,000 Argentinians Who Vanished.* New York: St. Martin's Press, 1985.
Mellibovsky, Matilde. *Circle of Love Over Death: Testimonies of the Mothers of Plaza de Mayo.* Translated by Matthew Proser. Willimantic, Conn.: Curbstone Press, 1997.

—Frederick A. Moritz
and Hilary Poole

Nansen, Fridtjof
Scientist, explorer, and diplomat
(1861 to 1930)

Using the same talents for innovation and organization that marked his career as a pioneering Arctic explorer, Norwegian scientist and statesman Fridtjof Nansen worked tirelessly on behalf of millions of refugees and prisoners of war.

Born on October 10, 1861, near Oslo, Norway, Nansen spent his childhood immersed in outdoor sports and activities. As a student of zoology at the University of

Christiania, he took his first voyage to the Arctic in 1882. Fascinated with the Arctic, he organized and led scientific research expeditions to the region, winning a reputation for heroism as a polar explorer.

In 1905 Nansen was pressed into diplomatic service during the collapse of Norway's political union with Sweden. After helping Norway achieve independence, he spent two years as the new country's minister to Great Britain before resuming his scientific studies. But the start of World War I in 1914 compelled his return to politics as a diplomat. After the war he was appointed as a Norwegian delegate to the newly formed League of Nations, the precursor to the United Nations.

One of the League's first concerns was the repatriation of prisoners of war trapped in Russia, Siberia, and southeastern Europe. Given the responsibility to get the prisoners home, Nansen arranged transport for 450,000 former prisoners from twenty-six countries. The International Red Cross then asked him to take on an even larger problem: a famine threatening more than thirty million Russians with starvation. His attempts to organize a relief campaign were hobbled by international opposition to the new Communist government of the Soviet Union. Although his unstinting personal efforts were credited with saving some seven million people, the political obstacles that prevented him from saving all of the famine victims came as a severe blow to his faith in the League's—and the world's—commitment to humanitarianism.

Still, his work for the League was not over. Charged with the difficult task of finding homes and employment for over a million war refugees, Nansen created his own brand of identity papers, issued to displaced persons. Called the "Nansen passport," it was accepted by more than fifty countries, allowing thousands of refugees to travel and resettle under the protection of the League of Nations. He also single-handedly brokered a mass evacuation of refugees in the aftermath of war between Greece and Turkey, arranging the exchange of half a million ethnic Turks living in Greece for hundreds of thousands of Greeks living in Turkey. For his efforts on behalf of refugees and famine victims, Nansen was awarded the 1922 Nobel Peace Prize.

In the last years of his life, Nansen's work increasingly involved the plight of Armenian refugees. He devoted his energies to the creation of an Armenian homeland but was again thwarted by international opposition. On May 13, 1930, he died at his home near Oslo, worn out by a decade of feverish work for humanitarian causes. His work was carried on, first by the Nansen International Office for Refugees, established by the League of Nations in the fall of 1930, and later by the United Nations High Commissioner for Refugees (UNHCR). The UNHCR honors Nansen's standard for humanitarian involvement through the United Nations' Nansen Medal, given annually for exceptional service to refugees.

For further information

Christensen, Christian A. R. *Fridtjof Nansen: A Life in the Service of Science and Humanity*. Geneva: United Nations High Commissioner for Refugees, 1961.

Sörensen, Jon. *The Saga of Fridtjof Nansen*. Translated by J. B. C. Watkins. New York: Norton, 1932.

—Rebecca Sherman

Perez Esquivel, Adolfo

Sculptor, leader of nonviolent resistance
(1931 to)

Adolfo Perez Esquivel, the Argentine sculptor and Catholic lay leader, won the 1980 Nobel Peace Prize for years of activism challenging the kidnappings, executions, and "disappearances" carried out by his country's military government. He helped found an ecumenical movement to resist both leftist terrorism and government repression throughout Latin America.

Born in Buenos Aires in 1931, Perez Esquivel completed his university education at the National School of Fine Arts and at the National University of La Plata. He taught for twenty-five years in primary, secondary, and university schools; his sculpture has been exhibited internationally. He was known as a soft-spoken father, married to a musician and composer.

In the 1960s Perez Esquivel began working with popular organizations involved in the Christian nonviolence movement in Latin America. In 1973 he founded the Ecumenical Movement of Peace and Justice, made up of Catholics, Protestants, and others who sought a nonviolent solution to the collision between the militant left and the militant right. In 1974 he became secretary general of the Peace and Justice Service, a Buenos Aires-based human rights network with activists throughout Latin America.

Perez Esquivel was arrested—but not charged—when he approached Argentine authorities for a passport to attend a human rights conference in Europe in April 1977. His imprisonment drew protests from Amnesty International and others both in Argentina and abroad, and it focused international attention on Argentine human rights abuses. Perez Esquivel won release in June 1978 after spending most of his imprisonment in solitary confinement.

The end of military rule in 1983, after Argentina's defeat by Britain in the Falklands War, opened the way for public airing of the human rights abuses. In 1984 the National Commission on Disappeared Persons (CONADEP) issued a report based on public testimony from friends, relatives, and other witnesses. It listed the names of 8,961 people who "disappeared" at the hands of the dictatorship. Reliable estimates place the number of those who disappeared even higher—between ten and fifteen thousand. Argentine law provides that victims and their families may submit claims for compensation until the year 2000; by early 1998 Argentina's human rights secretariat had received more than ninety-six hundred claims from former prisoners of the military regime and seven thousand claims from the families of persons who died or disappeared.

Perez Esquivel has continued his human rights work as president of the Honorary Council of the Latin American Servicio Paz y Justicia and of the International League for the Rights and Liberation of Peoples (Milan, Italy). His published works include *The Poncho Christ* and *Walking Together with the People*. He has also been active in the Committee of 100 for Tibet, formed in 1992 to spotlight human rights abuses in Tibet.

Perez Esquivel based his activism on his own Roman Catholicism and on Indian leader Mahatma Gandhi's philosophy of nonviolence. He told an interviewer, "We do not respond to violence with more violence, but rather we seek to change the mechanisms by which society is governed."

For further information
Rock, David. *Argentina, 1516-1987: From Spanish Colonization to Alfonsin.* Berkeley: University of California Press, 1987.
Rosenberg, Tina. *Children of Cain: Violence and the Violent in Latin America.* New York: William Morrow, 1991.

—Frederic A. Moritz

Ramos-Horta, Jose

Spokesperson for the East Timorese
(1949 to)

Jose Ramos-Horta has struggled for twenty-three years against the brutal occupation of his country, East Timor, by Indonesia. In 1996 the Nobel Peace Prize committee commended him, along with Bishop Belo, head of the Timorese Catholic Church, for their painstaking efforts to seek a diplomatic and peaceful solution in East Timor.

Ramos-Horta was born in Dili, East Timor, on December 26, 1949, to a Timorese mother and Portuguese father. Both his father and grandfather had been exiled from Portugal to East Timor, which was a Portuguese colony for more than 250 years. Ramos-Horta trained and worked as a journalist from 1969 to 1974. He helped establish the Revolutionary Front for an Independent East Timor (FRETILIN), and when FRETILIN declared independence from Portugal, Ramos-Horta was appointed foreign minister. On December 7, 1975, just days after he left East Timor

to seek international standing, Indonesian armed forces invaded. He pleaded with the United Nations Security Council to stop the annexation. They condemned the military invasion but took no action. Between the years of 1976 and 1981, approximately 200,000 East Timorese were killed as a direct result of occupation. Four of Ramos-Horta's eleven brothers and sisters were killed by the Indonesian army.

Ramos-Horta stayed in the United States from 1975 to 1989, earning a Masters of Peace Studies at Antioch University. In 1983 he studied international law and human rights in the Hague, Netherlands, and Strasbourg, France. During this time he served as permanent representative of FRETILIN to the United Nations and wrote of his experiences in the diplomatic world in *Funu: The Unfinished Saga of East Timor.*

The continuing oppression in East Timor before the indifferent eyes of the international community did not demoralize him. To share his knowledge of the United Nations system with other human rights activists, Ramos-Horta founded the Diplomacy Training Program at the University of New South Wales, Australia, in 1989. He teaches as a visiting professor in Australia when he is not in Portugal or speaking internationally in his capacity as special representative of the National Council of Maubere Resistance (CNRM), an alliance of East Timorese pro-independence groups, or as personal representative of Xanana Gusmo, the leader of the resistance, who has been in prison since 1992. In April 1992 Ramos-Horta presented CNRM's detailed peace plan to the European

Parliament Human Rights Subcommittee; the plan aims to achieve a referendum in East Timor on self-determination.

In recognition of his lasting contribution to the rights and freedoms of oppressed peoples, Ramos-Horta received the 1993 Professor Thorolf Rafto Human Rights Prize and in 1996 was awarded both the Nobel Peace Prize and the first United Nations People's Organization Prize. A powerful speaker, Ramos-Horta inspires people worldwide with his optimism for East Timor. Determined to share what he has learned in exile and in the complex arena of international politics, he advocates for greater enforcement of human rights instruments and the rule of law.

For further information
Carey, Peter, et al. *East Timor at the Crossroads.* Honolulu: University of Hawaii Press, 1995.
Ramos-Horta, Jose. *Funu: The Unfinished Saga of East Timor.* Trenton, N.J.: Red Sea Press, 1987.

—Carol Devine

Robinson, Mary
United Nations High Commissioner of Human Rights
(1944 to)

The first woman to be elected president of Ireland, Mary Robinson gave up her office to accept an appointment as the United Nations High Commissioner of Human Rights. A lawyer with a long-standing interest in civil liberties and women's rights, Robinson used her position as the Irish head of state to compel the attention of Ireland—and the world—to human rights issues ranging from civil strife in Northern Ireland to genocide in Rwanda.

Mary Robinson (UN/DPI Photo by James Bu).

Born on May 21, 1944, in the town of Ballina, County Mayo, young Mary Bourke was an outstanding academic achiever. At the age of twenty-five, armed with law degrees from both Dublin and Harvard, she became the youngest-ever professor of law at Trinity College Dublin and went on to win a seat in the Irish Parliament as a member of the Labour Party. The following year she married lawyer Nicholas Robinson.

During twenty years as a senator in the Irish Parliament, Robinson was a strong advocate for a host of controversial issues relating to the rights of women, supporting contraception, divorce, and abortion. She also became a noted expert on European human rights law, served on several international commissions on civil liberties during the 1980s, and founded the Irish Centre for European Law in 1988.

Robinson's avowed support of unpopular liberal and feminist causes made her an unlikely choice as the Labour Party's candidate for president in 1990. She described her surprise victory as proof that the women of Ireland "instead of rocking the cradle had rocked the system." Robinson turned her office into a powerful vehicle for dialogue and social change. During her seven years in office, she engaged the Irish people on issues as diverse as the effect of the Irish diaspora on the identity of modern Ireland, and the need for humanitarian intervention in famine-ravaged Somalia. Her integrity won the admiration of even her political opponents and made her one of the most popular public figures in recent Irish history.

Robinson's appointment as head of the UN Office of the High Commissioner of Human Rights in September 1997 was hailed by human rights groups, who believe that she will be able to transform the high commissioner's office into a vital force for the protection of human rights worldwide.

For further information

Horgan, John. *Mary Robinson: A Woman of Ireland and the World.* Niwot, Colo.: Roberts Rinehart, 1997.
Robinson, Mary. *A Voice for Somalia.* Dublin: O'Brien Press, 1992.

—Rebecca Sherman

Romero, Oscar

Archbishop
(1917 to 1980)

Archbishop Oscar Romero was a voice for justice and peace during El Salvador's civil war. Speaking out from his pulpit on behalf of the poor and oppressed, he demanded peace and became a source of truth about the activities of the Salvadoran death squads.

Oscar Arnulfo Romero was born on August 14, 1917, in Cuidad Barrios in El Salvador. He became a carpenter's apprentice at age thirteen. Romero visited the town church every day after work, and when he was fourteen years old, he entered the Minor Seminary in San Miguel against his father's wishes. In 1937 Romero went to the National Seminary in San Salvador. After seven months the bishop sent Romero to Rome to complete his studies under Pope Pius XI.

On April 4, 1942, Romero was ordained. The war disrupted his studies in Rome and he returned to El Salvador. He served as a parish priest in Anamoros and Santa Domingo and became famous for his preaching; at one time the town's five radio stations broadcast his mass simultaneously. Father Romero visited the jails and the countryside, and he organized the distribution of food and nutritional education to the poor.

Romero was appointed archbishop of San Salvador in February 1977. Like Bishop Ximenes Belo of East Timor, Romero was at first believed to be a moderate. Soon after becoming archbishop, his friend Father Rutillo Grande was assassinated by a paramilitary death squad. Taking his cue from the outspoken Grande, Romero refused to appear in public ceremonies with the army and government until the truth of Grande's murder was uncovered.

Grande's assassination propelled Romero to reshape the role of the church as a defender of the poor as well as a conciliator for peace. In his sermons he denounced "structural sin"—social, economic, and cultural sins that create poverty.

In February 1980 Archbishop Romero wrote a letter to U.S. President Jimmy Carter, pleading that the United States stop sending weapons to the Salvadoran government, saying "they will be used for more repression against my people." Archbishop Romero became the voice and conscience of El Salvador to the world. He received a nomination for the Nobel Peace Prize.

On March 23, 1980, Archbishop Romero made a plea on a Catholic radio station that the Salvadoran army stop killing its own people. He was denounced as a traitor and a servant of international communism; the following day he was shot dead while officiating a mass.

Peace finally came to El Salvador in 1992, but not before more than seventy-five thousand Salvadorans had been killed. Romero said he had no appetite for martyrdom, that a life of love lives beyond death. For the people of his country, Romero orchestrated a spiritual revival and built the path for peace.

For further information
Brockman, James. *Romero: A Life*. Maryknoll, N.Y.: Orbis Books, 1990.
Romero, Oscar. *The Violence of Peace: The Pastoral Wisdom of Oscar Romero*. Translated by James Brockman. North Farmington, Pa.: Plough Publishing House, 1988.

—Carol Devine

Saadawi, Nawal El

Physician and author
(1931 to)

A doctor and psychiatrist, feminist and political activist, author of historical and political studies as well as novels and short stories, the Egyptian activist Nawal El Saadawi is one of the most versatile and prolific critics of Arab societies.

Saadawi was born on October 27, 1931, in a small Egyptian village, the daughter of a provincial official and a spirited mother who, in Nawal's words, "hated marriage even though my father was, in her view, an ideal husband." While a secondary school student, she led nationalistic demonstrations against British rule and the Egyptian king. She studied medicine and psychiatry at Cairo University and later at Columbia University in the United States. For some fifteen years she worked as a physician and a director of health education at the Ministry of Health in Cairo. After two brief marriages she married writer and doctor Sherif Hetata in 1964. Hetata, "a truly liberated man" as Saadawi has called him, has greatly supported her work.

Her first book, *Women and Sex*, discussed the inferior position of women under Islam. When it was published in 1971 it brought her international renown but also led to her dismissal from the Ministry of Health. She joined the Cairo Literature Institute as a writer and teacher.

In her most famous book, *The Hidden Face of Eve: Women in the Arab World* (1977), she gives a moving account of her circumcision—amputation of the clitoris, performed without anesthetic—when she was six years old. In her medical studies she found a great deal of material about the traumatizing effect of this operation on millions of women in the Arab world. The book deals with the many ways in which the female identity has been suppressed, but also gives examples of women who have managed to play crucial roles in various stages of the social and religious development of Islam. *The Hidden Face of Eve* has been translated into twenty languages.

On September 6, 1981, Saadawi was arrested in Egypt under the "law for the protection of values from shame." She herself was relatively well treated, but she observed the arbitrary administration of justice and the harsh fates of her fellow inmates. Supporters staged a worldwide campaign for her release, and she was freed in late November of the same year. She published testimony on her ordeal in *Memoirs from the Women's Prison* (1983).

Saadawi has been attacked by an overwhelming number of Arab critics for her political ideas, feminism, radicalism, sexually explicit language, writing style, breach with Islamic traditions, and more. Despite this, her books have sold in great numbers in the Arab world and she is a coveted speaker in countries where a level of liberalism is tolerated. "I sometimes feel exhausted and discouraged," Saadawi says. "Yet I have never felt that what I am doing is futile, for in moments of regret I am always rescued by a young man or woman who has read my books and informs me of the influence they have had on his or her life."

For further information

Saadawi, Nawal El. *The Nawal El Saadawi Reader.* London: Zed Books, 1997.
Saadawi, Nawal El. *Memoirs from the Women's Prison.* Translated by Marilyn Booth. Berkeley: University of California Press, 1994.

—Daan Bronkhorst

Sakharov, Andrey

Scientist and peace activist
(1921 to 1989)

One of the creators of his country's hydrogen bomb, Russian physicist Andrey Dmitriyevich Sakharov abruptly ended his involvement in the Soviet nuclear weapons program in the middle of his career, driven by concern over the effect of nuclear weapons testing on human health. Persecuted by the Soviet government for his call to abolish nuclear weapons, Sakharov won the Nobel Peace Prize for his work as a leader in the Soviet human rights movement.

Born in Moscow on May 21, 1921, to a liberal, well-educated family, Sakharov gained a reputation as one of his country's most brilliant students while studying physics at Moscow University. After World War II, he was assigned to a top-secret team of scientists working on the development of nuclear weapons, where he became one of the principal architects of the Soviet hydrogen bomb.

Andrey Sakharov (CORBIS/Owen Franken).

Following successful tests of the bombs in the early 1950s, Sakharov began to worry about biological damage caused by the atmospheric radiation released by those tests. In 1958 he published a paper calculating the numbers of people who would become ill or die as a result of their exposure to nuclear weapons testing. When the tests did not end despite this evidence of the harm they caused, Sakharov grew uneasy with the Soviet government that had until then honored and indulged him as one of its top nuclear physicists.

His fall from grace with Soviet authorities was sealed in 1968, when he wrote a manifesto against nuclear weapons and political repression. His essay was smuggled abroad and published, attracting immense international attention because of Sakharov's stature as one of the world's preeminent physicists. Sakharov was immediately removed from his position in the Soviet nuclear program, and he and his wife Elena Bonner became targets of constant harassment by the KGB, the Soviet secret police. In 1970 he formed the Committee for Human Rights, an organization dedicated to the defense of prisoners of conscience and the struggle for political reforms in the Soviet Union.

For his courage in speaking out for human rights despite threats against himself and his family, Sakharov was awarded the Nobel Peace Prize in 1975. He was not allowed to leave the country to receive it, so Bonner, a human rights activist in her own right, traveled to Norway to accept the award in his place. Sakharov continued his work as an outspoken critic of his country's repressive policies until 1980, when, incensed by his denunciation of the Soviet invasion of neighboring Afghanistan, the authorities banished him and his wife to internal exile in the remote city of Gorky, 250 miles east of Moscow. In Gorky he struggled to continue as before but was hampered by his enforced isolation, poor health, and unrelenting harassment by the KGB.

In 1986 Soviet President Mikhail Gorbachev called Sakharov out of exile to assist him with perestroika, a radical attempt at restructuring Soviet society and the political system. Sakharov embraced the reforms with a vengeance, often criticizing Gorbachev when changes were not made fast enough.

At the time of his death in 1989, Andrey Sakharov was a member of the Soviet Congress of People's Deputies and one of the most widely revered public figures of his nation. Called a "saint" and "the conscience of his country," his moral integrity in the face of oppression had an enormous impact both in his own country and abroad.

For further information
Lozansky, Edward, ed. *Andrey Sakharov and Peace.* New York: Avon Books, 1985.
Sakharov, Andrey. *Memoirs.* Translated by Richard Lourie. New York: Alfred A. Knopf, 1990.

—Rebecca Sherman

Saro-Wiwa, Ken
Playwright and environmentalist
(1941 to 1995)

Ken Saro-Wiwa fought until death for the rights of the indigenous poor in Nigeria. As he said himself, he used his skill as a writer to help the Ogoni people to stand up to the Nigerian regime and to protest the devastation of their land by the Shell Oil Corporation and its subsidiaries.

Kennule Beeson Saro-Wiwa was born on October 10, 1941, in Bori, southeastern Nigeria, into a large Ogoni family. The Ogonis are a small ethnic group among the 250 tribes comprising Nigeria's ninety million people. Saro-Wiwa studied at the University of Ibadan and taught at his own high school and at universities in Lagos and eastern Nigeria. He wrote plays, children's books, novels, and penned a very popular television series. A prominent satirist, Saro-Wiwa laughed at the ridiculous and was admired for his charismatic wit.

Royal Dutch Shell arrived in Nigeria in the 1960s and, in a joint venture with the Nigerian state, the oil company reaped multimillion dollar per day revenues from oil extraction in the Niger Delta. In 1990 Saro-Wiwa helped found the Movement for the Survival of the Ogoni People (MOSOP), which protested the ruin of Ogoniland without any of the revenue going to the impoverished Ogonis. Royal Dutch Shell polluted the air, fouled the land, and killed the fish, said Saro-Wiwa in 1992 to a Geneva Conference on Indigenous Populations.

In May 1994 four Ogoni chiefs were murdered at a meeting attended by some of Saro-Wiwa's opponents. Saro-Wiwa was charged with complicity in their death and was imprisoned. Nigeria branded him a militant leader and claimed his arrest and trial were not punishment for his environmental crusade but for his involvement in premeditated murder. International observers disagreed, arguing that this was clearly a politically motivated case.

From prison Saro-Wiwa continued the struggle. The Ogoni movement eventually forced Shell to say they would cease drilling unless the inhabitants would reap economic benefits from it. The campaign also led Shell to do the first environmental study of the Niger Delta. Saro-Wiwa was recognized for his defense of the environment and human security for indigenous groups in Nigeria; he was nominated for the 1996 Nobel Peace Prize, and he won the Goldman Environmental Prize in 1994.

Saro-Wiwa and eight other Ogonis were hanged on November 10, 1995, despite international pleas for clemency and intense criticism of a flawed trial. After his death many countries adopted political sanctions against Nigeria. His son Ken carries on the fight for the Ogonis.

Ken Saro-Wiwa's dedicated battle against injustice in Nigeria fused the link between indigenous human rights and environmental rights. Not only did he put a necessary spotlight on the ecological and social responsibilities of multinational companies, but he exposed a despotic military regime's human rights violations to the world.

For further information
Saro-Wiwa, Ken. *A Month and a Day—A Detention Diary*. New York: Penguin, 1996.
Saro-Wiwa, Ken. *Sozaboy*. San Francisco: Addison Wesley, 1995.

—Carol Devine

Soyinka, Wole
Author
(1934 to)

Nobel Prize-winning author Wole Soyinka has played the role of academic, artist, and activist. He has campaigned, both at home and in exile, for human rights and the restoration of democracy in Nigeria.

Born on July 13, 1934, in Isara, Nigeria, Soyinka showed remarkable intellectual and creative talents from an early age. He first studied literature at the University of Ibadan, then at the University of Leeds, England, where he graduated with honors. Activism ran in Soyinka's family: his autobiography, *Aké: The Years of Childhood* (1981) describes his gradually growing awareness of politics and concludes with the description of a tax revolt in the late 1950s, organized by his mother.

Soyinka became a professor of literature and drama, teaching at universities in Nigeria, at Cambridge and Sheffield in England, and at Cornell University in the United States. His first play was produced in London in 1955, and in the early sixties he founded his own theater groups in Nigeria. He has since written some thirty plays, including pieces for opera and television, plus five books of poetry.

Nigeria became independent from Great Britain in 1960, and the new government began constructing the Nigerian legal system. Soyinka has stated that as soon as he heard about the new laws, he realized that "the first enemy was within." For example, Nigerian law gives authorities ample room to stifle opposition and free speech. When his novel *The Interpreters* was published in 1965, he was arrested for allegedly having forced a radio announcer at gunpoint to broadcast distorted election results. The charge was clearly fictitious, yet he was detained for three months.

Two years later when a civil war broke out in Biafra, a region in the south of Nigeria, Soyinka got involved in peace work and was again arrested. Though there was never a formal indictment, he was held for two years. Many of his colleagues from the international writers' organization PEN campaigned on his behalf. The detention, combined with the success of his plays, made him the best known African writer of the time. In prison he kept a diary and wrote poems on toilet paper and cigarette wrappings, which friends managed to smuggle out. His work was later published in *The Man Died: Prison Notes of Wole Soyinka* (1972).

In 1993 the results of a democratic presidential election were annulled, and power was assumed by a military regime headed by General Sani Abacha. Soyinka went into exile in November 1994; while abroad he has been accused of treason and received numerous death threats. He has since lived mainly in the United States but traveled extensively in Europe and Africa. At one time he secretly reentered Nigeria to get his children out of the country.

In *The Open Sore of a Continent* (1996) he wrote that the Nigerian regime was guilty of "the most treasonable act of all time" when it robbed the population of its democratic rights. His critique of the Nigerian military has become sharper over the years, in particular after the execution of Ken Saro-Wiwa and other activists in November 1995.

After the death of General Abacha in June 1998, Soyinka expressed guarded optimism about the opportunity for positive change in Nigeria, but he also warned the international community not to be lulled into complacency by the potentially empty promises of the new regime. Now as ever, Soyinka is a forceful and articulate spokesperson for democracy and human rights in his homeland and Africa at large.

For further information

Soyinka, Wole. *The Man Died: The Prison Notes of Wole Soyinka*. New York: Farrar, Straus, and Giroux, 1988.

Soyinka, Wole. *The Open Sore of a Continent*. Oxford: Oxford University Press, 1996.

—Daan Bronkhorst

Mother Teresa

Roman Catholic missionary

(1910 to 1997)

Saying that she saw Jesus in the faces of the poor, Catholic missionary Mother Teresa founded homes around the world where volunteers from the order that she founded, the Missionaries of Charity, could care for the dying and the destitute, as well as lepers, AIDS victims, and abandoned children.

Mother Teresa was born Agnes Bojaxhiu on August 26, 1910, in the Yugoslavian city of Skopje, now part of Macedonia. Nicknamed Gonxha ("flowerbud" in Albanian), she was the youngest child of a prosperous Catholic Albanian family. Her father, Nikola, died suddenly after World War I, leaving Agnes to be raised by her mother, a deeply religious woman known for her generosity to the poor. Agnes' adolescence was marked by academic success and an increasing devotion to the Catholic Church. At age eighteen she left home to become a nun and a missionary with the Sisters of Loreto, an Irish order with a presence in India.

She made her final vows in 1937, taking the name Teresa to honor Saint Thérése of Liseux. For the next seventeen years she was a teacher, and later headmistress, at Saint Mary's School, an exclusive girls' school in Calcutta. While traveling on September 10, 1946, she heard what she described as the voice of God, telling her to leave the convent to serve the poor. After two years of waiting for the Catholic Church to grant her permission, she left Saint Mary's in 1948 to teach children from the streets of Calcutta. In 1950 she founded the Missionaries of Charity, a new order with a special mission to serve the poor.

From its early beginnings, the Missionaries of Charity quickly expanded. After a devastating encounter with a dying woman left abandoned on the street, Mother Teresa founded a home where sick indigents could die with dignity. To this home for the dying in Calcutta she soon added a home for children and a leprosy clinic. The extreme selflessness of her work first attracted attention and support from local leaders in India and then from international Catholic groups. In 1960 she began to travel abroad for speaking engagements, raising tremendous amounts of money in donations and becoming an unlikely media celebrity. Her fame grew almost as fast as her order, which expanded from its original base in Calcutta to reach across India and then around the world. She became known as a "living saint," winning numerous religious and secular awards, including the 1979 Nobel Peace Prize.

By the time of her death on September 5, 1997, Mother Teresa had become one of the most widely revered people of the twentieth century. Nevertheless, her charity work has been criticized by activists who fault her for actively discouraging any examination of the socioeconomic conditions that create poverty. Her homes have been criticized for lacking rudimentary medical care, while she herself has been denounced for her strident opposition to family planning and for her willingness to accept money and praise from dictators like Jean-Claude Duvalier of Haiti, and corporate criminals like American swindler Charles Keating. She answered all of her critics by insisting that she was neither a human rights activist nor a social worker, but only a servant of Jesus, a "pencil in the hand of God."

For further information

Muggeridge, Malcolm. *Something Beautiful for God: Mother Teresa of Calcutta*. New York: Harper & Row, 1971.
Sebba, Anne. *Mother Teresa: Beyond the Image*. New York: Doubleday, 1997.

—Rebecca Sherman

Timerman, Jacobo

Journalist

(1923 to)

As the head of a prominent Buenos Aires newspaper, Jacobo Timerman defied terror and intimidation to publicize ongoing massive human rights violations perpetrated by the government during Argentina's "dirty war."

Born in the Ukrainian town of Bar in 1923, Timerman and his family immigrated to Argentina in 1928. An adolescent during World War II, he worked with Zionist youth groups towards the creation of a Jewish state in Palestine. After the war he began a career as a reporter and commentator in magazines, newspapers, television, and radio. During the next thirty years he developed a style of tough investigative journalism that sought not just to report the news but to shape the course of events. Drawing on his natural instinct for what readers wanted, he exerted considerable influence on Argentine public opinion.

In 1971 he founded a newspaper, *La Opinión*, which was frequently critical of violence and terrorism sponsored by Argentina's leftist guerrilla groups. He was especially critical of the democratically elected government of Isabel Perón for its failure to rein in the violence. When Perón's government was overthrown in March 1976, Timerman supported the new military regime led by General Jorge Rafael Videla, hoping that the military would bring security to the battered nation.

Timerman's hopes proved short-lived. Videla's government launched an all-out campaign against "subversion" in Argentina. Known as the "dirty war" for its systematic abuse of human rights, this campaign eventually claimed thousands of victims who were kidnapped, tortured, and, in most cases, secretly murdered. Because the government refused to release any information about the fate of kidnap victims, they collectively became known as *los desaparecidos*, the disappeared. Journalists were among the military's first victims. Despite death threats and intimidation from the government, Timerman publicized the daily disappearances and murders in *La Opinión*.

He was to pay a heavy price for exercising freedom of the press. On April 15, 1977, he was seized from his home by a gang of armed men. Bound and blindfolded, he was taken to a secret location, imprisoned, tortured with electrical shocks, and subjected to anti-Semitic abuse. His disappearance became a cause célèbre among the international human rights community and drew the attention of members of the U.S. government. Bowing to the international pressure, Videla's government was forced to admit that it was holding Timerman and went through a show of allowing him due judicial process. In September 1979, after a struggle between the Argentine Supreme Court, which wanted him released, and the military, which wanted him dead, Timerman was stripped of his citizenship and expelled from Argentina.

In exile Timerman wrote *Prisoner Without a Name, Cell Without a Number,* a grisly account of the torture and abuse he suffered during his thirty months as a prisoner. This book, which appeared while the regime was still in power, has become one of the classic indictments of the "dirty war" in Argentina. In its graphic descriptions of Jewish prisoners singled out for torture and abuse, it was the first work to expose the Argentine military's ties to Nazi ideology.

Timerman returned to Argentina in 1984, after the military government was replaced with civilian rule. Now living in retirement in Uruguay, he has written extensively about human rights abuses both in Argentina and abroad, particularly in Israel and Chile; he has also been active in organizing Argentine journalists to protest continued abuses against freedom of the press.

For further information

Timerman, Jacobo. *Chile: A Death in the South.* Translated by Robert Cox. New York: Alfred A. Knopf, 1987.

Timerman, Jacobo. *Prisoner Without a Name, Cell Without a Number.* Translated by Toby Talbot. New York: Alfred A. Knopf, 1981.

—Rebecca Sherman

Tutu, Desmond

Anglican archbishop and chair of Truth and Reconciliation Commission

(1931 to)

While most of the South African antiapartheid leadership was either in prison or in exile, Desmond Tutu became the international face of the antiapartheid movement. As prelate of the Anglican Church in South Africa, Tutu was a highly visible and outspoken opponent of the South African government.

Tutu was born in Klerksdorp, in the western Transvaal, on October 7, 1931. He attended Johannesburg Bantu High School and Pretoria Bantu Normal College; he received his bachelor's degree from the University of South Africa. Tutu followed in his father's footsteps and became a teacher. He taught for three years, until 1958 when the government took control of the schools. Tutu left teaching and began to study theology.

Bishop Desmond Tutu (David Turnley/©CORBIS).

Tutu studied at Saint Peters Theological College in Johannesburg and was ordained in 1961. The next year he traveled to England where he undertook further study, receiving his master of theology in 1966. He combined his love of teaching with his new training and taught theology in South Africa until 1972. He returned to England and spent three years as the associate director of the Theological Education Fund of the World Council of Churches.

In 1975 Tutu became the first black dean of Saint Mary's Cathedral in Johannesburg; in 1976 he was appointed the first black bishop of Lesotho, a tiny country in the middle of South Africa. Tutu became the general secretary of the South African Council of Churches (SACC) in 1978, again the first black person to serve in that capacity. The council received funding from outside South Africa that allowed it to provide assistance to the families of political prisoners and those killed or wounded in demonstrations. Tutu's position afforded him great visibility as a critic of apartheid, a systematic program of discrimination and racism. By this time the majority of antiapartheid movement leaders had been effectively silenced; they were imprisoned, in exile, in hiding, or dead. As the head of SACC, Tutu was not so easily muzzled.

Tutu remained general secretary of SACC for nine years. He received numerous honorary degrees and human rights awards during this time, culminating in the Nobel Peace Prize in 1984. In 1985 Tutu left SACC and became the first black Anglican bishop of Johannesburg. In 1986 he became head of the South African Anglican Church with his appointment as archbishop of Cape Town. Archbishop Tutu remained a highly visible force in the antiapartheid movement until the fall of the apartheid government in South Africa.

Tutu retired as archbishop in 1996. President Nelson Mandela named him head of the Truth and Reconciliation Commission, which was charged with investigating political violence committed under apartheid.

For years Desmond Tutu was the most visible antiapartheid spokesperson in the world. He helped expose the evil of apartheid to the world. A believer in nonviolence, Archbishop Tutu was quick to remind the world that apartheid was the greatest violence of all.

For further information
Tutu, Desmond. *The Rainbow People of God: The Making of a Peaceful Revolution*. New York: Doubleday, 1994.
Waldmeir, Patti. *Anatomy of a Miracle: The End of Apartheid and the Birth of the New South Africa*. New York: W.W. Norton & Company, 1997.

—Jo Lynn Southard

Walesa, Lech

First president of Poland
(1943 to)

Speaking on behalf of exploited Polish workers, Lech Walesa harnessed the spirit and determination of a previously unconnected group of activists and ignited the human rights struggle in Poland.

Walesa was born in 1943 in Popowo hamlet, Poland. His father was sent to a concentration camp by the Germans during World War II and died only months after his release. In 1961, at age eighteen, Walesa began working as an electrician at a state agricultural machinery center. At age

Lech Walesa (CORBIS/Steve Raymer).

twenty-four he moved to the Baltic port of Gdansk and became a ship electrician. In 1970 Walesa witnessed a series of brutal events that fed his interest in the welfare of fellow workers: twenty-two workers were burned alive while welding a ship whose fuel tanks had been filled early to save time; and later that year police shot and killed forty-five shipyard workers who were striking against price increases.

Walesa became increasingly active in the union movement, and on August 14, 1980, he led the infamous Lenin Shipyard strike in Gdansk. Incensed by an increase in prices set by the Communist government, strikers made twenty-one demands, including the right to organize free and independent trade unions. Walesa became the chairman of the Inter-Enterprise Strike Committee (MKS). The strikes spread to factories across the nation.

In November 1980 Walesa became head of Solidarity (*Solidarnösc*), the first legal independent trade union in a Soviet-controlled country. Unions around the world welcomed Walesa's visits in 1981. In June he joined a delegation to represent Solidarity and other trade unions at the International Labour Organization (ILO).

After five hundred days of Solidarity, martial law was imposed in December 1981 and thousands of Solidarity members, intellectuals, and opposition leaders were arrested, including Walesa. From within and outside prison, members continued to strike and ran an underground movement. Walesa was released from prison in 1982. In 1983 he won the Nobel Peace Prize for his work, which the committee considered symbolic of hope and freedom.

On December 9, 1990, Walesa became Poland's first democratically elected president, winning more than 74 percent of the vote. During Walesa's five years as president, Poland became a model of political reform for Eastern Europe. He led the country through a painful transition to democracy and free markets, instituting unpopular financial shock therapy. Currently retired from politics, he now leads the Lech Walesa Institute, whose aim is to advance the ideals of democracy and free-market reform throughout Eastern Europe and globally.

Walesa embodies the potential power of one civilian standing against tyranny. He is a people's leader with natural skill for negotiation, whose remarkable struggle for human rights in Poland had lasting repercussions across Europe.

For further information
Rybicki, Arkadiusz and Lech Walesa. *The Struggle and the Triumph: An Autobiography*. New York: Arcade Publishers, 1994.
Walesa, Lech. *A Path of Hope*. London: Pan Books, 1987.

—Carol Devine

Wang Dan

Student activist

(1969 to)

Wang Dan, Chinese activist and a leader of student protest during the 1989 Tiananmen Square democracy movement, has become a symbol of an entire generation of idealistic university students who challenged China's authorities by demanding democratic reforms.

Born on February 26, 1969, to Beijing University-educated parents, Wang Dan as a young boy dreamt of a career as an astronaut. His interests switched to literature and history, and then quickly to politics. As a history student at his parents' alma mater, Wang cofounded a discussion group called the Democracy Salon.

On June 4, 1989, Tiananmen Square was the site of a dramatic student protest, which was brutally suppressed by the Chinese army. Wang Dan served four years in prison for his part in the protests. In 1989 he won the Reebok Human Rights Award for his leadership role in the prodemocracy student movement.

Wang was released from prison in February 1993 but lived under police surveillance and harassment. In early 1994, during an upsurge of dissident activity, Wang outlined his ideas in an essay entitled "The Democracy Movement in Post-Deng China." He argued that the student leadership at Tiananmen Square was inadequately prepared and "made immature assessments of the actual situation." In May 1995 Wang was arrested again and held without charge for seventeen months at an undisclosed location outside of Beijing. In October 1996 he was sentenced for subversion to eleven years in a northeast China prison. Wang was accused of "disturbing the social order" for having coauthored and signed various petitions to the government as the sixth anniversary of the Tiananmen Square crackdown approached. He was also accused of publishing articles in the overseas press and receiving donations from abroad for the provision of humanitarian aid to imprisoned and released dissidents. Wang's mother, father, and sister personally pleaded Wang's innocence in a trial and sentencing which took only four hours. The conviction placed Wang once again in the spotlight as a symbol of Chinese repression of prodemocracy dissidents.

On April 19, 1998, the Chinese government released Wang Dan and placed him on a plane for the United States. The release was widely received as a goodwill gesture to the United States in preparation for President Bill Clinton's planned visit to Beijing in June. Wang declared his first goal in America would be to complete his education, focusing on contemporary Chinese history; he feels strongly that as a political activist, there can be no substitute for a solid educational background.

For further information
Black, George, and Robin Munro. *Black Hands of Beijing.* New York: John Wiley & Sons, Inc., 1993.
Unger, Jonathan, ed. *The Pro-Democracy Protests in China: Reports from the Provinces.* Armonk, N.Y.: M. E. Sharpe, Inc., 1991.

—Frederic A. Moritz

Wei Jingsheng

Dissident

(1950 to)

Wei Jingsheng has challenged China's Communist Party as a democracy advocate. The former Beijing zoo electrician personally defied China's leader Deng Xiaoping by continuing to speak out for democracy after Deng closed down Beijing's showcase of outspoken essays and posters, the so-called Democracy Wall, in spring 1979.

Wei Jingsheng was born in 1950 and grew up in Anhui Province, the privileged son of a Communist Party official. The young Wei graduated from the prestigious Affiliated Middle School of People's University. As a member of the Beijing Red Guard leadership, he joined in the nationwide youth rebellion against bureaucracy and participated in Chairman Mao's purge of the Communist establishment. Wei later recalled, "As the youngest in the leadership, I saw it clearly, all the cruelties, which totally destroyed my previously conceived impressions of the Communist Party."

Later, while serving in the military, he met peasants from all over the country, an experience that encouraged him to challenge the tenets of communism. After leaving military service Wei eventually became an electrician and took a job at the Beijing zoo. In 1978, as Deng Xiaoping rose to power, Wei emerged as a symbol of disillusionment among a generation of Red Guard veterans who had spent their youth joining Mao's attacks on bureaucracy.

A stretch of construction wall near a busy commercial district in Beijing attracted nationwide attention as Democracy Wall, a place where people put up posters to voice their criticism of the political system. As informal publications became the most popular mode of disseminating ideas, Wei became a major figure of dissent through the unofficial journal *Exploration*, which he founded in January 1979. Wei mounted a poster entitled "The Fifth Modernization" on Democracy Wall, asserting that without democracy, the four modernizations of Maoist doctrine (in industry, agriculture, defense, and science) would fail. In spring 1979 the government suppressed Democracy Wall and arrested several activists, including Wei Jingsheng. In prison Wei continued to challenge Deng Xiaoping by sending him letters in which he discussed democracy and its prospects in China, human rights, Tibetan autonomy, foreign policy, and economic and social reform.

Wei served fourteen years of a fifteen-year term; he was released six months early in September 1993, when China sought international support for its bid to host the 2000 Olympic Games. He was detained again on April 1, 1994, less than a month after meeting with the U.S. assistant secretary of state for human rights. In December he was sentenced to fourteen more years in prison for "conspiring with hostile foreign organizations and individuals" to subvert China's government. Only after Deng Xiaoping's death in February 1997 was Wei finally released, on condition he leave China for the United States in November 1997. He has been nominated for the Nobel Peace Prize four years in a row (1994–1997).

For two decades Wei Jingsheng has defied China's leaders, often from within prison walls. Democracy, he has said, will not come without taking risks.

For further information
Wei Jingsheng. *The Courage to Stand Alone.* New York: Viking Press, 1997.
Wu, Harry, and Carolyn Wakeman. *Bitter Winds: A Memoir of My Years in China's Gulag.* New York: John Wiley and Sons, 1995.

—Frederic A. Moritz

Wiesel, Elie

Author and humanitarian

(1928 to)

A prominent international speaker on human rights issues, Elie Wiesel is the author of more than thirty books, many of them fueled by the horrors of his own experiences in concentration camps during World War II. In 1986 he was awarded the Nobel Peace Prize for his efforts to bear witness to the suffering of the victims of the Holocaust.

Wiesel was born on September 28, 1928, in the Transylvanian village of Sighet, now part of Romania. The only son of a close-knit Jewish family, he spent his childhood immersed in religious studies. Toward the end of World War II, the Jews of Sighet were rounded up and deported to Nazi death camps in Poland. With his parents and three sisters, fifteen-year-old Elie was taken first to Auschwitz, where the family was separated. His mother and youngest sister, Tzipora, were murdered in the gas chambers, while Elie and his father were marched from camp to camp until the end of the war, ultimately arriving at Buchenwald. His father was killed there, three months before the camp was liberated by American troops in the spring of 1945.

After the war Wiesel was sent to a French orphanage, where he stayed until he began studies at the Sorbonne in Paris in 1948.

His literary career was launched in 1955, when Nobel laureate Francois Mauriac encouraged Wiesel, then working as a journalist, to write about the atrocities he had witnessed during the war. *Night*, a brief memoir of what he experienced at Auschwitz and Buchenwald, was published in 1958 to great critical acclaim. On the heels of this success, Wiesel continued to write both fiction and nonfiction on themes derived from the Holocaust, including *Dawn* (1961), *The Accident* (1962), and *The Gates of the Forest* (1966).

Throughout his career Wiesel has defined himself primarily through his Jewish identity. He has written several books on Jewish folklore and theology, strongly supported the state of Israel, and worked to publicize the persecution of Jews in the Soviet Union and Ethiopia. His work in these fields, as well as his tireless efforts as an educator about the Holocaust, led to his 1978 appointment as the chair of the United States Holocaust Memorial Council by President Jimmy Carter. Serving as chair until 1986, Wiesel was a driving force in the creation of the U.S. Holocaust Memorial Museum in Washington, D.C.

Wiesel has garnered numerous awards and honors, including a Congressional Gold Medal from President Ronald Reagan, the Presidential Medal of Freedom from President George Bush, and the rank of Grand Officer in the French Legion of Honor. He has used his access to government leaders to advocate for the victims of war, famine, and ethnic and religious oppression across the world. Most recently he has worked on behalf of the victims of war in the former Yugoslavia.

In awarding him the 1986 Nobel Peace Prize, the Nobel committee cited Wiesel's legacy as a moral leader, whose personal experiences of the inhumanity of Hitler's concentration camps have been transformed into a compelling and influential voice for peace and human dignity.

For further information
Wiesel, Elie. *The Gates of the Forest.* Translated by Frances Frenaye. New York: Holt, Rinehart and Winston, 1966.
Wiesel, Elie. *Night.* Translated by Stella Rodway. New York: Hill & Wang, 1960.

—Rebecca Sherman

Williams, Jody

Political activist

(1950 to)

Working from her Vermont farmhouse, peace activist Jody Williams helped lead the International Campaign to Ban Landmines (ICBL), a loosely linked alliance of more than one thousand nongovernmental organizations, to a stunning achievement on the international stage: a 1997 treaty signed by 120 nations prohibiting the manufacture, sale, use, and stockpiling of landmines.

Born on October 9, 1950, Jody Williams grew up in Brattleboro, Vermont, one of five children of a county judge and a housing project supervisor. She acquired a taste for advocacy in the schoolyard, defending her deaf older brother from the taunts of other children. Her activist bent was solidified as a college student at the University of Vermont during the Vietnam War. After graduating with a master's degree in international studies from Johns Hopkins University, Williams became the coordinator for the Nicaraguan-Honduras Education Project, bringing U.S. decision-makers to Central America to see the destructive effects of U.S. policies in the region. She later worked as the associate director for Medical Aid to El Salvador.

Her work in Central America familiarized her with the sufferings of landmine victims. An estimated twenty-six thousand people are killed or maimed each year by some of the one hundred million landmines buried in seventy countries around the world. In November 1991, Williams signed on with the Vietnam Veterans of America Foundation (VVAF) to coordinate a campaign to lobby against the use of landmines. A year later the VVAF was joined by five other humanitarian groups to form the steering committee of the International Campaign to Ban Landmines.

As the coordinator for the ICBL, Williams worked from her home without an office or staff, using the Internet to link an increasing number of nongovernmental organizations together to form a grassroots coalition with surprising lobbying power. In 1996 Williams and the ICBL persuaded the governments of several countries to meet with humanitarian groups to discuss details of a possible landmine ban.

The discussion was electrified by Canadian Foreign Affairs Minister Lloyd Axworthy, who called upon the nations attending to reconvene in Ottawa to approve a treaty banning the production, use, and sale of antipersonnel mines. A year later, representatives of more than

120 nations met in Ottawa to sign a treaty drafted in cooperation with the ICBL. For their work in bringing governments and humanitarian groups together to create the antilandmine treaty, Williams and the ICBL shared the 1997 Nobel Peace Prize.

Though the refusal of the United States, China, Russia, and a handful of other states to sign the document cast a shadow over their achievement, Williams and the ICBL were hailed for their success at using revolutionary Internet-based diplomacy to quickly effect radical reforms. Since receiving the Nobel Peace Prize, Williams has stepped down as coordinator of the ICBL; however, she continues to work full-time to ensure that all the nations that signed the landmine treaty go on to ratify it. The historic landmine ban is expected to save countless lives, and its unorthodox mixture of grassroots activists and government negotiators may well serve as a model for future humanitarian campaigns.

For further information

Baldauf, Scott. "Nobel Laureate's Long Trip from Vermont Farm to Fame." *Christian Science Monitor*, October 14, 1997.
Roberts, Shawn, and Jody Williams. *After the Guns Fall Silent: The Enduring Legacy of Landmines*. Atlantic Highlands, N.J.: Highlands Press, 1995.

—Rebecca Sherman

Wu, Harry

Human rights activist
(1937 to)

Harry Wu, an American citizen born in Shanghai, has drawn both praise and criticism for his daring challenge to China's system of forced labor camps. Wu, who spent nineteen years in Chinese labor camps, has embarrassed both Chinese and American governments in his efforts publicize the Laogai system, which he has called "China's Gulag."

Harry Wu was born Wu Hongdu on February 8, 1937, in Shanghai, China. He was arrested in 1960 and served a nineteen-year sentence of "reform through labor" on a charge of stealing about twenty dollars. Wu has said he was really arrested for criticizing China's support of the Soviet invasion of Hungary.

After his release in 1979, Wu taught English and math at the Shanxi College of Economics and Finance. He left China in 1985 for the United States, where he became a citizen and took a position as visiting scholar in the civil engineering department at the University of California, Berkeley.

Wu returned to China without incident three times, twice in 1991 and once in 1994. In April 1994 he visited the remote northwestern Xinjiang province. He uncovered evidence of at least twenty-one forced labor camps, with tens of thousands of prisoners working to reclaim desert for cotton and grain production.

In June 1995 Wu and an American companion attempted to enter China through the northwestern region of Xinjiang but were caught and arrested at the border. The arrests made Wu a cause célèbre among human rights campaigners, as well as a serious irritant in Chinese-American relations. The companion was released after a few days, but the Chinese government held Wu in prison for sixty-six days before expelling him. Wu's arrest and imprisonment brought China's prison labor issues into the spotlight. While in prison in China, Wu became the subject of Congressional speeches, editorial comment, and radio talk show argument in the United States. Wu's wife, Ching Lee, worked tirelessly to keep his name in the news. She traveled throughout the United States and to London, Geneva, and Paris, pinning yellow ribbons on former British Prime Minister Margaret Thatcher and U.S. Senators Bob Dole and Newt Gingrich, among others.

On August 24, 1995, a People's Court in Wuhan announced the results of a four-hour trial: a fifteen-year prison sentence for stealing state documents and revealing them to outsiders. The sentence was altered to expulsion and Wu was sent to the United States, thus reducing tension with Washington over the handling of an American citizen.

The controversy made Harry Wu an important figure in the push for human rights in China, but he came under attack from defenders of China and others who accused him of destructive behavior. After Wu's 1995 arrest in Xinjiang, former U.S. Ambassador to China James Lilley described Wu on national television as someone with a "martyr complex." Still it was undeniable that the human rights campaigner's daring approach made China's forced labor system a major human rights issue on the international scene.

For further information

Wu, Harry, and Carolyn Wakeman. *Bitter Winds: A Memoir of My Years in China's Gulag.* New York: John Wiley and Sons, 1995.
Wu, Harry, and George Vecsey. *Troublemaker: One Man's Crusade Against China's Cruelty.* New York: Times Books, 1996.

—Frederic A. Moritz

José Zalaquett (Courtesy of José Zalaquett).

Zalaquett, José
Lawyer and human rights campaigner
(1942 to)

Zalaquett served as chair of Amnesty International's International Executive Committee and was instrumental in the National Commission for Truth and Reconciliation in Chile. In the 1990s, he has advised similar commissions on three continents and elaborated the principles of a responsible ethics of reconciliation.

José Zalaquett was born on March 10, 1942, to a middle-class family in Santiago, Chile. As a law student, he joined left-wing movements that supported Marxist presidential candidate Salvador Allende in 1970. After Allende was deposed in a military coup on September 11, 1973, Zalaquett founded the human rights department of the church-based Committee for Peace, later renamed the *Vicaría de la Solidaridad*. This was Chile's most important human rights organization during the years of dictatorship from 1973 to 1990.

Zalaquett was imprisoned in 1975 and 1976; on the second occasion he was forced into exile. He lived in France and the United States, and during this period he served as chair of Amnesty International's International Executive Committee (1979–1982). His interest in issues of justice and reconciliation after periods of dictatorship was awakened in 1984 when he was sent as an Amnesty observer to the trials of the Argentine junta leaders. He concluded that even though some of the leaders were convicted, this would have little benefit unless the new government could give a convincing account of what happened during the military regime. That is, in some situations, "truth" can be more important than "justice." He returned to Chile in 1986 and since then has worked as a consultant on human rights issues for various international organizations.

As one of the eight members of the Chilean National Commission on Truth and Reconciliation (1990–1991), he contributed to a report documenting the fate of some 2,300 victims of political killings and disappearances. The commission proposed many measures of reparation, rehabilitation, and compensation, most of which were implemented by the democratic government.

In his many lectures and articles, he has worked out a model based on the work of the nineteenth-century German sociologist Max Weber that draws a distinction between an "ethics of principles," or what is ideal, and an "ethics of responsibilities," what is necessary. Principles are very much the core of human rights activism. However, Zalaquett argues that society as a whole has to deal responsibly with the many forces at work and the interests at stake. Where the transition from dictatorship to democracy is swift, as in Argentina, meting out criminal justice is feasible enough. But in many countries the change is very slow or is the result of a fragile truce struck between military and civilian parties; situations such as these nearly always preclude the punishment of those responsible for past abuses.

As more and more nations are faced with the thorny issues of justice and reconciliation, Zalaquett's work presents inspiring and clearheaded models. Nations in transition need "the courage to forego easy righteousness," Zalaquett argues, and must "learn how to live with real-life restrictions, but to seek nevertheless to advance one's most cherished values day by day."

For further information

Collier, Simon, and William F. Slater. *A History of Chile, 1808-1994* (Cambridge Latin American Studies, No. 82). Cambridge: Cambridge University Press, 1996.
Ratner, Steven R., and Jason S. Abrams. *Accountability for Human Rights Atrocities in International Law: Beyond the Nuremberg Legacy*. Oxford: Clarendon Press, 1997.

—Daan Bronkhorst

PART FOUR

Contemporary Human Rights Issues

Prison bars on Death Row in the Georgia State Penitentiary (CORBIS/Owen Franken).

CHAPTER EIGHT

Contemporary Human Rights Issues

Introduction

In these essays, which explore some of the most common human rights violations in the contemporary world, we are reminded of the worst aspects of our global community. Companies in both developing and developed nations exploit their labor forces, women are beaten in their homes, and government officials abuse their power to limit the judiciary and the press. Human rights abusers act with impunity despite laws that states are morally and legally obliged to honor. Families send their children into armies and bonded labor, or sell their daughters as sex workers. Companies and governments sell arms to militaries and armed opposition groups, weapons that are often used to kill civilians. In our times, characterized by internal conflicts and wars, civilians suffer most. They become homeless and displaced within and outside of their nation's borders, and they are the prey of indiscriminate landmines. Those who do not want to partake in war, conscientious objectors, have little choice in some countries. In addition to investigating the details of these violations, this chapter cautiously celebrates the hard-won gains to combat human rights violations and to make particular violations legal offenses, as well as suggests what challenging work remains to improve human rights protection.

The issues covered in this chapter could not be exhaustive and still fit on these pages; they were chosen to collectively represent the myriad challenges faced by the modern human rights community. The entries highlight the complex nature of human rights protection and promotion, such as the debate over whom is entitled to receive asylum, the arguments made by proponents of female genital mutilation, the differing opinions on the age a child is old enough to fight a war, and the legal intricacies involved in extraditing criminals.

Through investigating contemporary human rights violations and the inspiring efforts to oppose them, it becomes clear that rights are interconnected, indivisible, and nonhierarchical. Human rights issues are not defined by the wealth or geography of a nation. Homelessness occurs worldwide, as does rape. While developed nations may have fewer landmines and refugees, and their citizens may enjoy greater political and press freedom than in developing countries, human rights are blind to nationality, ethnicity, gender, age, sexual orientation, or religion. Issues such as police brutality, self-determination, and discrimination based on sexual preference or HIV/AIDS status are of equal relevance in Uganda as they are in the United States. While respect for human rights varies from nation to nation and fluctuates over time, human rights shouldn't be left or picked up at any airport or border.

Human rights issues overlap. Militaries, including armed opposition groups, recruit child soldiers and mistreat prisoners. Rape can be a form of genocide. Human rights activists are served the death penalty, disappeared, detained, or executed for defending their rights and the rights of others. Children are subject to bonded labor, slavery, and trafficking. And when they are poor, homeless, displaced, or living with HIV/AIDS, children are even more vulnerable. Females young and old suffer gender-related abuses; in some nations they are afforded fewer political rights or denied access to health care, education, and freedom of movement.

Many of the human rights issues point to the disparity of wealth in a world that values cultural, social, and economic richness of all people's lives. Cultural rights, self-determination, indigenous rights, and the right to development are all related to the economic majority's lack of respect for the inherent rights and freedoms of indigenous peoples and linguistic, ethnic, and religious minorities.

What mitigates indignation about human rights abuses is recognition of the tireless work to raise awareness on the issues, to change policy and practices, and ultimately to stop the abuses. These pages recount the countless and often nameless individuals and organizations who promote and protect human rights. Child labor activists in Nepal, publishers in Vietnam, and civilian deminers in Angola work to defend human rights, and ultimately to protect human security—often at their own personal risk. (Chapter 7 chronicles the lives and pursuits of some fearless human rights activists.)

The many individuals and groups around the world, with their steadfast endeavors to effect change, infuse vitality into human rights that to a great extent have existed primarily on paper. For example, the intergovernmental organization, the International Committee of the Red Cross, works to promote and protect the rights of prisoners, the detained, and it also defends medical neutrality. International nongovernmental organizations (NGOs) such as Human Rights Watch conduct systematic investigations of human rights abuses worldwide, holding governments accountable if they transgress human rights.

This chapter details many significant initiatives by the United Nations on a wide variety of human rights questions, such as the drafting of a Declaration on Indigenous Rights and supporting efforts to form an International Criminal Court. The UN has appointed special *rapporteurs* on issues such as child soldiers, the independence of judges and lawyers, and torture. Specialized bodies such as UNICEF make pleas against female genital mutilation and the UN High Commission on Refugees works to deal with the world's massive refugee population. The initiatives surveyed in these entries cry for more support.

While the UN is sometimes criticized for ineffectiveness or for simply not doing enough, this chapter also demonstrates how often we look to it to stop human rights abuses. Without the political will of the world's nations that constitute the UN, its bodies cannot be agents of lasting change. The Universal Declaration of Human Rights (UDHR), while imperfect, is a revolutionary notion. The following essays show that human rights, as defined in the UDHR and a growing number of human rights declarations and treaties, are violated daily. But they also demonstrate the inextinguishable struggle for justice, freedom, human rights, and dignity.

—Carol Devine

AIDS/HIV

Human rights concerns surrounding acquired immunodeficiency syndrome (AIDS) are both political and medical. Discrimination based on actual or suspected infection with the human immunodeficiency virus (HIV) is an especially pressing concern. Other human rights standards important in the context of HIV/AIDS are education, including access to information about HIV; health, including the right to equal access to means of prevention of HIV; privacy, including the right to keep medical tests secret; and freedom from sexual exploitation and violence.

AIDS was first identified in 1981. Initially, little was known about how the disease spread, which resulted in people with AIDS (PWAs) often being the targets of fear and discrimination. It was subsequently discovered that AIDS spreads in a variety of ways, including unprotected sexual intercourse and the sharing of needles by intravenous drug users. In the industrialized world one of the populations most profoundly affected by the disease was homosexual men. Fear of AIDS has provided an excuse for homophobia and has fed into hate crimes and other human rights violations of homosexuals. Worldwide, nearly twelve million people have died from AIDS, and thirty million more are living with AIDS or HIV. Approximately ten million of these PWAs are between ten and twenty-four years old. Sixteen thousand people are newly infected with HIV every day. If no cure is found, the thirty million people who currently have HIV could be dead within ten years.

Discrimination based on actual or suspected HIV infection is a violation of international law norms. Despite this, in 1989 an HIV-positive Dutch citizen was denied entry into the United States to speak at an AIDS conference in San Francisco. Currently, PWAs are not allowed to immigrate into the United States, although the attorney general may waive that regulation if the person has family already in the United States. PWAs entering the United States to visit or attend conferences are no longer restricted. Often PWAs also suffer job and housing discrimination due to their illness, although this has been outlawed; in the United States, for example, it is covered under the 1990 Americans with Disabilities Act.

Each year doctors learn more about treating and preventing AIDS. Nonetheless, almost six million people were infected with HIV in 1997 alone. In 1996, for the first time, deaths from AIDS decreased in the United States, due to new treatment discoveries. This is not true in the rest of the world: two-thirds of AIDS deaths occur in sub-Saharan Africa and the number continues to rise. In Botswana and Zimbabwe one-quarter of the adult population has AIDS; by the year 2005, 1.2 million adults in Zimbabwe will die from AIDS. In Malawi the average life expectancy prior to the AIDS epidemic was fifty-one; now it is thirty-seven. As a result of these adult deaths, there are now eight million orphans living in sub-Saharan Africa.

Although AIDS was at one time believed to be a "gay disease" or "drug addicts' disease," one segment of society that is particularly vulnerable to HIV today is young people: approximately one-third of people with AIDS are between ten and twenty-four years old. Pregnant teens are also at risk: in Zimbabwe 30 percent of pregnant fifteen- to nineteen-year-olds are HIV positive. Another group that is especially susceptible is young prostitutes. In some cases prostitutes' clients mistakenly believe that young girls cannot carry HIV and are therefore "safe." This contributes to the abduction of younger and younger girls for prostitution. Unfortunately, children are actually more vulnerable to AIDS than adults. In Uganda it is believed that prostitutes under the age of nineteen test HIV positive three times as often as adult prostitutes. In Cambodia 30 percent of sex workers under nineteen are infected; in Thailand 50 per cent are HIV positive.

In 1996 the United Nations created UNAIDS, a joint venture of the United Nations Children's Fund, the United Nations Development Program, the United Nations Population Fund, and the United Nations Educational, Scientific, and Cultural Organization, along with the World Health Organization and the World Bank. The goals of UNAIDS are to coordinate action by many AIDS organizations, analyze information about AIDS to determine the best policies for prevention and treatment, advocate among various governments and nongovernmental organizations to implement AIDS policies, and gather and examine information on the global AIDS epidemic. It is hoped this will help end the spread of AIDS and make treatment available in all countries.

For further information

Mann, Jonathan, and Daniel J. M. Tarantola, ed. *AIDS in the World II.* New York: Oxford University Press, 1996.

Gordenker, Leon, et al. *International Cooperation in Response to AIDS.* Herndon, Va: Books International, Inc, 1995.

—Jo Lynn Southard

Armed Opposition Groups

Armed opposition groups are combatants in a relatively new type of conflict, fought by one or more armed groups or factions against each other and/or the government. These groups are responsible for a significant number and wide variety of human rights abuses.

Since the end of the Cold War, the map of state relations, conflicts, and arms control has changed considerably. Formerly, wars were mainly fought by two opposing conventional forces. In recent years there has been a proliferation of noninternational conflicts, often of an ethnic or religious character. The collapse of state institutions and the increased availability of small arms have also fueled abuses of human rights of civilians in internal conflicts.

All violations of human rights during conflicts—whoever commits them—are unacceptable breaches of basic standards of humane behavior. Armed opposition groups have the international legal obligation to respect fundamental rights, just like government armies do. All parties to the conflict are bound by the provisions of the four Geneva Conventions, which prohibit torture and ill-treatment, hostage taking, and deliberate and arbitrary killing of persons taking no active part in the hostilities. In the dozens of armed conflicts being fought around the world, there is an obvious need for increased protection of individuals. Human rights groups such as Amnesty International have informed the international community about abuses by armed opposition groups in Burundi, Kosovo, Algeria, and India, to name a few.

Attacks on civilians by armed opposition groups are nowhere more prevalent than in Burundi, a small country in eastern Africa. Government forces and armed opposition groups in Burundi are divided largely on ethnic lines, Hutu and Tutsi. Both the government and the armed opposition groups have been responsible for slaughtering tens of thousands of civilians in reprisal attacks. An estimated one hundred thousand Burundian civilians have been killed since 1993 as a direct result of the civil war.

Kosovo, a province in the former Yugoslavia inhabited mainly by ethnic Albanians, endures a brutal conflict that began in early 1998. While the Kosovo Liberation Army (KLA) and other armed opposition groups reportedly fight to end the discrimination against Kosovo Albanians, they also are guilty of human rights abuses, including taking hostages and killing civilians.

Armed conflicts remain an unfortunate reality. The International Committee of the Red Cross (ICRC) and Amnesty International recognize this reality and urge armed groups to ensure forces under their control abide by basic humanitarian principles. They recommend that those in positions of power—such as heads of armed groups, political leaders, and the judiciary—end human rights abuses and use the Geneva Convention Article 3 as a minimum standard to protect civilians during civil war. The ICRC also works to train combatants and government forces to spare noncombatants by respecting the rules of war.

International efforts are being made to initiate peace processes in countries such as Burundi where armed opposition groups are responsible for severe human rights abuses. Efforts for peace, as well as disarming and demobilizing combatants, and urging those involved in armed struggles to abide by humanitarian law, are important steps toward building cultures where human rights are respected.

For further information
Amnesty International. "Burundi: Armed Groups Kill Without Mercy." *Amnesty International AFR*, August 16, 1996.
Zartman, William, ed. *Elusive Peace: Negotiating an End to Civil Wars.* Washington, D.C.: Brookings Institution, 1995.

—Carol Devine

Asylum

The principle of asylum, guaranteed by the Universal Declaration of Human Rights, requires that governments provide a place of safety and protection to refugees from other countries. Issues surrounding the rights of individuals to seek asylum and the responsibility of states to provide it are central ones to the human rights movement.

A refugee is a person who, "owing to a well-founded fear of being persecuted for reasons of race, religion, nationality, membership of a particular social group, or political opinion, is outside" the country of citizenship and either can not return home or is fearful of doing so (Convention Relating to the Status of Refugees, 1951). Throughout history, people have faced the necessity of fleeing their homes to seek safety in other countries. The Greeks and the Romans had established areas for refugees, and places of asylum are noted in the Bible. Displacement of large populations has continued to the present. It is important to note that historically, a refugee's legal right extended only to the request for asylum, not a guarantee that it would be granted.

One of the earliest documents in international law dealing with refugees was the Charter of the International Military Tribunal at Nuremberg, which defined forced deportation as a crime against humanity and prosecuted Nazi leaders for pursuing this policy during the Third Reich. Indeed, it was the effort to assist persons fleeing Nazi Germany and the Soviet Union during World War II that evolved into the United Nations High Commission for Refugees (UNHCR). UNHCR operates under the 1951 Convention Relating to the Status of Refugees and its 1967 Protocol.

Currently, several issues are debated regarding refugees and the right to seek asylum. First is the question of *non-refoulement*, or the right of a refugee not to be returned to a home country engaging in persecution. The policy of *non-refoulement* is controversial because, in practice, it undermines the principle that an asylum seeker is not guaranteed sanctuary. Second is the issue of so-called economic refugees. These are refugees fleeing to another country in order to achieve a higher standard of living; some argue that, strictly speaking, these people should simply be considered migrants.

Finally, in recent years the issue of gender persecution has arisen. Gender has not traditionally been associated with asylum; nonetheless, more and more women are fleeing their home countries to escape female genital mutilation, forced marriages, or the Islamic restrictions on women's freedom of movement known as purdah. In June 1996, after a sixteen-month detention, Fauziya Kassindja was granted asylum in the United States. Kassindja had fled her

A Karenni refugee camp, Thailand (CORBIS/Howard Davies).

home in Togo three years earlier to escape genital mutilation and a forced marriage to a polygamist. Although gender had been recognized as a basis for persecution in a few cases prior to this—most notably in Canada—the Kassindja case was the first U.S. case to recognize gender persecution as a basis for granting asylum.

UNHCR estimates that almost six million refugees have applied for asylum in the last decade. The number of applications peaked in 1993 and has fallen somewhat since then. Nonetheless, there is no indication that the refugee problem and, therefore, questions of asylum, are going to disappear anytime soon.

For further information

Bernstein, Anne, and Myron Weiner. *Migration and Refugee Policies: An Overview.* Boca Raton, Fla: C.R.C. Press, 1999.

Goodwin-Gill, G. *The Refugee in International Law.* Oxford: Oxford University Press, 1985.

—Jo Lynn Southard

Bonded Labor

Bonded labor, also known as debt bondage, is a form of debt servitude in which a person works to pay off a debt owed to the employer. The terms of such arrangements are usually so biased in the employer's favor that the bonded laborer, far from settling his or her debt, becomes even more indebted with the passage of time. This allows the debt holder to further consolidate control over the bonded laborer, whose very person becomes the property of the employer as security on the debt. Under these exploitative conditions, the human rights abuses associated with bonded labor have led activists to describe it as a contemporary form of slavery. Though the practice is explicitly prohibited by several major human rights protocols and is illegal according to the laws of many of the nations in which it occurs, enforcement of such laws has proved difficult.

Unlike the historic practice of indentured servitude, to which it is related, bonded labor agreements do not usually specify a period of time during which the debtor will work to settle the outstanding debt. Instead, bonded laborers are paid extremely low wages against which the employer deducts interest on the debt, enormously inflated food and housing costs, and other unilaterally imposed fines or punishments. Persons who enter bonded labor arrangements to pay off a small sum of money then owe progressively greater amounts as their debt bondage perpetuates itself. Security on the debt may pass from one family member to another and from generation to generation, such that very young children may be forced into bonded labor to pay off the debts of their parents.

While adult bonded labor is widespread in countries across Asia, Africa, and Latin America, it is child bonded labor that has attracted the most attention. A specialized agency of the United Nations, the International Labour Organization (ILO), and a host of NGOs are the sponsors of a wide range of initiatives designed to halt the use of child bonded labor, particularly in South Asia where it is most prevalent. In India, where estimates suggest that as many as fifteen million children are held as bonded laborers, children may enter into debt bondage by inheriting a parent's debt, or they may simply be sold to an employer in exchange for a loan to the parent. In a pattern that is repeated around the region, low-caste and indigenous children are particularly at risk because of their parents' poverty, lack of education, and low social status. Some human rights interventions target the use of child bonded labor in particular industries, such as the silk industry in India and the handwoven carpet industry in Pakistan, Nepal, and India. Other interventions target children from vulnerable communities, such as the Dumagat people of the Philippines or the Kamaiya of Nepal.

As part of the ILO's campaign to eliminate the most intolerable forms of child labor, several nations including India, Pakistan, the Philippines, Nepal, and Bangladesh have instituted or strengthened laws prohibiting child bonded labor. However, the sincerity of some governments' commitment is in question, as law enforcement seems more interested in harassing labor and human rights activists than in prosecuting those employers who hold their workers in debt bondage. The ILO plans to introduce a new international convention to further combat the practice of bonded labor. Meanwhile, a growing international movement, sparked in part by the 1995 murder of child labor activist Iqbal Masih, encourages consumers in industrialized nations to shun products made by child bonded labor.

For further information
"The Flourishing Business of Slavery." *The Economist*, September 21, 1996.
Human Rights Watch Children's Rights Project and Human Rights Watch/Asia. *The Small Hands of Slavery: Bonded Child Labor in India.* New York: Human Rights Watch, 1996.

—Rebecca Sherman

Child Soldiers

The use of children as soldiers has increased dramatically in recent decades. Today it is estimated that more than 300,000 children under the age of eighteen—some as young as six years old—serve in government armies and armed opposition groups. This practice is in violation of numerous human rights norms, as it puts children at risk for a wide variety of abuses.

In the past both boys and girls have served as support staff and soldiers for Cambodia's Khmer Rouge, for rebel groups in Uganda during the 1970s, and during the civil war in El Salvador in the 1980s. According to the group Human Rights Watch, children participated in thirty-three conflicts in 1996—in twenty-six of these, children under the age of fifteen were used as soldiers.

Armies use children for the same reasons they should not: children are more easily manipulated than adults, they often do not understand the implications of war or killing, and they are the most "disposable" to do dangerous jobs such as minesweeping. Children are coerced or conscripted into armies or join "voluntarily" out of fear or poverty. The increased availability of small arms makes it physically more practical for children to fight.

The recruitment of children under the age of fifteen and their participation in hostilities is forbidden by the 1997 Additional Protocols to the Geneva Convention. The UN Convention on the Rights of the Child (CRC) Article 38 stipulates, "Parties shall refrain from recruiting any person who has not attained the age of fifteen into their armed forces." Today most states agree the current minimum age of fifteen for recruitment of soldiers is too low. The International Red Cross, the Red Crescent Movement, and key UN agencies have been working to abolish soldiers under the age of eighteen. In 1994 the UN established a Working Group to draft an optional protocol to the CRC, raising the minimum age from fifteen to eighteen. While the majority of states agree on eighteen as the minimum age, the United States, Korea, Israel, and the United Kingdom are among those who argue that eighteen is too high. No consensus has been reached.

Demobilization and rehabilitation of child soldiers is an onerous task. They usually suffer grave social, emotional, and physical problems and are often the last group of concern for a state that is in the midst of war or has recently ended one. UNICEF and other agencies have begun to tackle the job of demobilization, rehabilitation, and family reunification of former child soldiers in Angola, Rwanda, and Sierra Leone. In southern Sudan, at the

A young guerrilla in El Salvador (CORBIS/Owen Franken).

request of two rebel movements, Rädda Barnen (Swedish Save the Children) has begun a program to assist child soldiers.

The movement to ban the use of child soldiers is growing. National campaigns have formed and in 1998 a new initiative, the Coalition to Stop the Use of Child Soldiers, was launched by Human Rights Watch in conjunction with other nongovernmental agencies to mobilize public opinion and political will to ban the military recruitment and participation in armed conflict of children under the age of eighteen.

Efforts to ban the use of child soldiers reaffirm the principle that children should be allowed to be children and condemns an intolerable practice. All recommendations push for their immediate disarmament and the provision of the assistance for their long path to reintegration into civil society.

For further information

Amnesty International. "Old Enough to Kill but Too Young to Vote." Draft Protocol to the Convention on the Rights of the Child on the Involvement of Children in Armed Conflicts. AI Index: IOR/51/01/98. London, 1998.

United Nations. *Study on the Impact of Armed Conflict on Children (the Machel Study)*. UN Doc. A/51/306, August 26,1996.

—Carol Devine

Conscientious Objection

Conscientious objection is defined as a refusal to perform military service based on a sincerely held belief that war is morally or ethically wrong. Conscientious objectors (COs) may oppose all forms of war and violence or may oppose certain types of war, like nuclear or chemical warfare. Selective objectors oppose a particular war as "unjust." Whether their opposition to war is based upon religious or secular convictions, COs are denied the right to freedom of conscience in those countries with a compulsory military draft that offer no civilian alternative to military service or that offer punishingly harsh conditions to anyone seeking such an alternative.

The earliest attempts to formalize the rights of COs coincided with the massive military conscriptions of World War I. In the United States, where Christian pacifist churches like the Society of Friends (Quakers) had long preached opposition to war, some attempts were made to legally accommodate conscientious objectors on religious grounds. Though still required to perform military service, religious COs could serve as unarmed noncombatants. But these provisions left no legal options for COs who objected to war on political or secular grounds, or for those whose consciences forbade any participation in military service. Several thousand of these were court-martialed and imprisoned and some remained in prison for years until freed by a presidential pardon in 1933.

Following World War II the leaders of the international peace movement pressed governments to protect their citizens' civil liberties and right to freedom of conscience by making provisions for COs to be legally exempted from military service. This campaign has met with mixed success. The United Nations Human Rights Commission (UNHRC) recognizes the right to conscientious objection as part of the freedom of thought, conscience, and religion defined in Article 18 of the Universal Declaration of

Human Rights, but more than forty countries with military conscription still do not provide any alternative to armed service. COs who fail to comply with military service orders in these countries face imprisonment, and Amnesty International considers them to be prisoners of conscience.

While growing numbers of nations have abandoned military conscription or have adopted liberal policies regarding COs, many countries still persecute COs. In Greece, where no alternative civilian service exists, more than five hundred men have been imprisoned by military courts for their refusal to join the military. Most of these men are Jehovah's Witnesses, whose religious beliefs expressly forbid any form of military service. In Turkey, where it is a crime to "alienate people from the military," Osman Murat Uelke was prosecuted for "trickery to avoid military service" on the grounds that conscientious objection was not an acceptable concept.

As conscientious objection from military service gains greater recognition as a basic human right, attempts have been made to extend the concept of conscientious objection to other situations where citizens may object to government mandates; for example, health care practitioners may object to certain medical procedures and duties—like euthanasia or abortion—on religious or ethical grounds. While it remains to be seen whether these efforts to expand the scope of conscientious objection will garner international recognition, they do offer compelling proof that the peace movement has succeeded in making conscientious objection a potent symbol of the right to freedom of conscience.

For further information
Moskos, Charles C., and John Whiteclay Chambers, eds. *The New Conscientious Objection: From Sacred to Secular Resistance.* Oxford: Oxford University Press, 1993.
Seeley, Robert A., ed. *Handbook for Conscientious Objectors.* Philadelphia: Central Committee for Conscientious Objectors, 1981.

—Rebecca Sherman

Cultural Rights

Cultural rights are concerned with creating and ensuring the conditions that allow people to participate in and contribute to the cultural life of their communities. Described as the requirements for human dignity and development, cultural rights were originally understood as the rights of individuals to share in education, information, science, and art. But cultural rights have been more recently understood as the rights of peoples—usually ethnic, linguistic, or religious minorities—to freely practice their own culture as a community. Current debates about cultural rights are driven by the unresolved tension between those who argue that human rights can only exist at the level of the individual (the conventional

A member of the Ladakhi ethnic group in Tibet (UN/DPI/F. Charton).

Western understanding of rights) and those who say that groups of people can collectively be the object of human rights protections.

Cultural rights were established in 1948 by the Universal Declaration of Human Rights. Specific cultural rights are represented in two articles of the declaration: Article 26, on the right to education, and Article 27, on copyright protection and the right to participate in cultural life. These rights were elaborated upon and introduced into the formal body of international law by the International Covenant on Economic, Social and Cultural Rights (ICESCR) created in 1966 by the United Nations General Assembly.

The effort to translate the ideals promoted by the ICESCR from prescriptions into action has met with some difficulties. Many international legal experts believe that cultural rights like the right to education are of minor importance compared to the urgency of civil and political rights like freedom from torture. Others have declared that economic, social, and cultural rights are not human rights at all, but unenforceable demands that governments pursue an idealistic—and by no means unanimously shared—model of social justice.

In the past decade a vocal group of Asian nations including Singapore, Malaysia, and Indonesia has argued that the Western emphasis on civil and political rights reflects a cultural bias not shared by the developing nations of Asia, Africa, and Latin America. As developing nations demand a greater voice in determining the international standards of conduct, they draw renewed attention to the concepts of economic, social, and cultural rights, which they claim hold greater urgency for the citizens of impoverished countries.

This attention has coincided with a new conceptualization of cultural rights to include the rights of minority groups. The focus on the rights of a minority community, rather than on the rights of individual persons belonging to a minority, has come under considerable criticism. Critics argue that laws promoting the interests of a cultural minority grant unfair special privileges, sparking sometimes virulent resentment among members of the majority culture. The increasing reluctance of the English-speaking provinces of western Canada to grant special status to French-speaking Quebec—and Quebec's threat to secede if Canada does not provide adequate protection to Francophone culture—illustrate both the hazards and the importance of cultural rights in a multicultural society. A related issue is whether the granting of cultural rights to a community may disable protections for individual rights, particularly in cases where the community observes cultural customs that may violate the human rights of some of its members, as in exclusionary caste systems or female genital mutilation. Though these dilemmas hamper efforts to define or enforce a common standard for cultural rights, it is clear that, as ethnic violence increases around the world, finding solutions to the issues raised by cultural rights will be of primary importance.

For further information
Boutros-Ghali, Boutros. *The United Nations and Human Rights 1945–1995.* New York: United Nations Department of Public Information, 1995.
Shapiro, Ian, and Will Kymlicka, eds. *Ethnicity and Group Rights.* New York: New York University Press, 1997.

—Rebecca Sherman

Death Penalty

The death penalty is generally conceived of as the supreme legal sanction, inflicted only against perpetrators of the most serious crimes. The human rights community has traditionally held a stance against the death penalty for a wide variety of reasons: critics argue that the death penalty is inhuman and degrading; that it is inappropriately applied and often politically motivated; and that rather than reducing crime, the viciousness of the punishment only serves as an inspiration to further violence.

Historically the death penalty has existed all around the world. Only since the beginning of the twentieth century has the death penalty been rejected by a growing number of people and states.

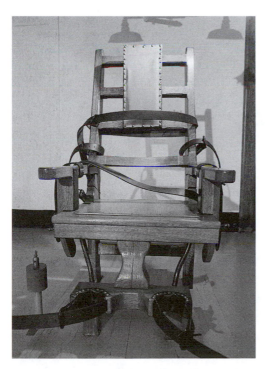

The electric chair at the Virginia State Penitentiary (CORBIS/Bettmann).

International law discourages but does not prohibit it. Article 6 (paragraphs 2 and 5) of the International Covenant on Civil and Political Rights states that "sentence of death may be imposed only for the most serious crimes in accordance with the law in force at the time of the commission of the crime . . . . Sentence of death shall not be imposed for crimes committed by persons below eighteen years of age and shall not be carried out on pregnant women." Regarding the nonreintroduction of the death penalty, the American Convention on Human Rights (Article 4.3) is the most explicit instrument, since it provides that "[t]he death penalty shall not be reestablished in states that have abolished it."

Although the death penalty is not entirely prohibited, several legal instruments have been brought into existence that seem to pave the way for total abolition. The Second Optional Protocol to the International Covenant on Civil and Political Rights (1991) aims at the abolition of the death penalty, by virtue of which thirty-three states have decided to abolish this punishment within their jurisdiction. It is in the European system that the trend has gone the furthest. The Convention for the Protection of Human Rights and Fundamental Freedoms now has a Protocol No. 6 Concerning the Abolition of the Death Penalty. This was adopted in 1982 by the Council of Europe's Committee of Ministers.

According to data presented at the 1998 session of the Sub-Commission on Prevention of Discrimination and Protection of Minorities, fifty-four states have abolished the death penalty and fifteen others have done the same except in times of war. Twenty-seven additional states no longer apply the sentence, although it has not been made illegal. Finally, ninety-seven states maintain the death penalty in their legal systems. According to 1996 Amnesty International figures, China, the Ukraine, the Russian Federation, and Iran had the highest number of executions, accounting for 92 percent of the year's total. Although the execution of people under age eighteen is prohibited by international law, five nations have been accused by Amnesty International of continuing the practice—Iran, Pakistan, Saudi Arabia, the United States, and Yemen.

A death penalty carried out unlawfully comes under the competence of the Special Rapporteur on Summary and Arbitrary Executions elected by the UN Commission on Human Rights. The UN Secretary General, when apprised of impending executions that may not conform to the above-mentioned safeguards, can use his best endeavors, as he did in vain in 1986 with an appeal for the life of James Terry Roche. Roche was later executed in the United States for murder committed when he was seventeen.

Among NGOs, Amnesty International has taken a leading role in pursuing abolition of the death penalty worldwide. The group argues that the death penalty is "an act of violence and violence tends to provoke violence. The imposition and infliction of the death penalty is brutalizing to all who are involved in the process." In 1998 Amnesty International protested the execution of Karla Faye Tucker in Texas, issuing a scathing critique of the Texas jus-tice system, accusing it of "a litany of grossly inadequate procedures which fail to meet minimum international standards for the protection of human rights."

Apart from humanitarian and philosophical concerns, the most striking argument against the death penalty seems to be the fact that, as euphemistically stated by successive United Nations studies, "the deterrent effect of the death penalty is, to say the least, not demonstrated." However, the debate is still lively, as supporters of the death penalty remain firmly convinced that the punishment is a necessary and effective method of controlling crime.

With respect to the death penalty, the challenges ahead are still numerous, but the most fundamental goes beyond the legal sphere—nations must grapple with whether or not "an-eye-for-an-eye" is the doctrine best suited to bring about justice.

For further information
Rodley, Nigel S. *The Treatment of Prisoners Under International Law*. Paris and Oxford: UNESCO and Clarendon Press, 1987.
Schabas, William A. *The Abolition of the Death Penalty in International Law*. Cambridge: Cambridge University Press, 1997.

—Baptiste Rolle

Detention

Detention occurs when a person is deprived of his or her personal liberty and confined to a space, usually a jail cell, prison, hospital, or home. Detention differs from imprisonment in that detainees, unlike prisoners, have not been convicted of a criminal offense. The tremendous vulnerability of detainees to human rights abuses, and the threat that detentions pose to the basic right to liberty, have led to strict international laws governing the use of detention. Nevertheless many governments routinely ignore the international restrictions on the use of detention, and reports issued by many human rights organizations suggest that human rights abuses related to detention are prevalent around the world.

Detailed regulations on detention were established by the International Covenant on Civil and Political Rights (ICCPR, 1966) and the regional European Convention on Human Rights (1950), the American Convention on Human Rights (1969), and the African Charter on Human and People's Rights (1981). These regulations prohibit arbitrary detention, which is defined as any deprivation of personal liberty not justified by and conducted according to previously existing laws. In nations that do not have or do not enforce adequate legal controls over their police or military, arbitrary detention becomes a potent weapon to punish, coerce, or intimidate citizens.

Detention may be used to hold persons who have been accused of committing a crime but have not yet been tried in a court of law for the offense. The ICCPR sets certain conditions for the appropriate use of pretrial detention: a detained person must be immediately informed of the charges against him or her, must be promptly brought before a judicial power, and should be brought to trial within a reasonable amount of time. However, lack of resources, inefficient or overburdened judicial systems, and in some cases, deliberate government foot-dragging make excessive lengths of pretrial detention a human rights issue in many countries where detainees may wait more than two years before standing trial.

Administrative detention, in which a country's legal system specifically allows persons to be detained without charge or trial, is a controversial practice in several countries. For example, according to Israeli law, the government may hold persons indefinitely if evidence suggests that they pose a danger to state security. Several hundred Palestinians from Israel and the Occupied Territories—and in recent years a handful of Jews as well—have been held incommunicado in administrative detention for months or even years without charge or trial. In many cases no credible evidence links the detainees to any terrorist activity, leading Amnesty International and other monitoring groups to conclude that Israel, which ratified the ICCPR in 1991, detains prisoners of conscience for the peaceful expression of their beliefs.

The United States has also been the target of criticism for its use of administrative detention to confine refugees seeking asylum. The Immigration and Naturalization Service (INS) may detain illegal immigrants and candidates for asylum indefinitely. Contrary to the explicit conditions established by the ICCPR, which the United States ratified in 1992, INS detainees not convicted of any crime may be imprisoned in local jails alongside convicted criminals. The publicity surrounding abuses of detention even in Western democracies suggests that the movement to enforce international standards of conduct regarding detention, most recently reiterated in a 1988 United Nations statement on the protections due detained or imprisoned persons, will continue to gain momentum in the future.

For further information
Amnesty International U.S.A. Staff. *Amnesty International Report 1998*. New York: Amnesty International U.S.A., 1998.
Boutros-Ghali, Boutros. *The United Nations and Human Rights 1945–1995*. New York: United Nations Department of Public Information, 1995.

—Rebecca Sherman

Development

Development has traditionally been defined as a process promoting economic growth. But in recent years the international community has pioneered a new understanding in which the aim of development is not merely to produce better results in the leading economic indicators but to improve the quality of life in every sphere of meaningful activity: economic, social, cultural, and political. Using these expanded criteria for successful development, the United Nations issued a landmark Declaration on the Right to Development in 1986, establishing development as a basic human right and demanding that other human rights concerns be integrated with development programs.

Human rights played a tenuous role in the early international development programs created after World War II. Under the Marshall Plan (1948–51), the United States provided billions of dollars in development aid to reconstruct the economies of postwar Europe and encourage European nations to resist communism. In the 1950s and 1960s U.S. aid to the impoverished nations of postcolonial Asia, Africa, and Latin America frequently bypassed struggling local populations, instead enriching corrupt authoritarian—but anticommunist—regimes. Meanwhile, multilateral development agencies like the World Bank and the United Nations Development Program encouraged large industrial projects that provided few benefits to the poor but destabilized indigenous cultures, caused environmental degradation, or siphoned local wealth to Western business interests.

The 1970s marked the beginning of a major change in attitudes toward development. Most sweeping was the rise of the concept of "sustainable development." Born out of a growing concern for the harmful consequences of industrial development to local ecosystems, sustainable development proposed a more holistic model that balanced the potential economic benefits of a project against its ecological costs. Expanding views also encouraged an increasing attention to the social and cultural changes wrought by development. Where previous theories treated development as a phenomenon in isolation, whose effects could be calculated solely in economic terms, advocates of the holistic approach to development viewed economic activity as only one element of a complex, interconnected system.

Not surprisingly, one effect of these development theories was to increase awareness of the human rights implications of development work. Organizations like the World Bank began to place more emphasis on aiding vulnerable populations, while the United States under President Jimmy Carter (1977–1981) tried to link development aid to the recipient nation's human rights record, threatening to end development aid to repressive regimes like Argentina's military junta.

The Declaration on the Right to Development issued by the UN General Assembly signaled another significant shift in approaches to development. The declaration defined development as a human-centered process that should ideally enlarge the choices of individuals and communities while respecting the principles of self-determination, equity, and nondiscrimination. In trying to translate these principles into concrete action, the international community faces the difficult task of bridging the chasm between "developing" and "developed" nations, a task made more complicated by increasing globalization and the dominant economic power of multinational corporations. More than ever, providing the basic human rights called for in the Universal Declaration of Human Rights—such as access to employment and an adequate standard of living—will require international cooperation and a commitment to pursue sustainable and fair development policies.

For further information
Sachs, Aaron. *Eco-Justice: Linking Human Rights & the Environment* (Worldwatch Paper, 127). Washington, D.C.: Worldwatch Institute, 1995.
World Commission on Culture and Development. *Our Creative Diversity: Report of the World Commission on Culture and Development.* Paris: UNESCO, 1995.

—Rebecca Sherman

Disappearances

The term "disappearance" describes the secret arrest, detention, or abduction of a person by government officials or groups acting with the approval or knowledge of the government. The practice of disappearance is a direct violation of several key principles of human rights, outlined in the Universal Declaration and other instruments.

The term *desaparecido* (disappeared) was first coined in the 1960s in Guatemala to label the state-sponsored kidnapping, torture, and murder of antigovernment forces. In the 1960s, '70s, and '80s, disappearances were also reported in Argentina, Chile, El Salvador, and Uruguay. In these and other countries, relatives of the disappeared organized in an attempt to locate the missing and to raise awareness of the issue. The first and most famous of these organizations was the Mothers of the Plaza in Argentina. In the late 1970s these mothers and their allies began demonstrating weekly in the Plaza de Mayo. They were instrumental in raising international awareness of the practice of disappearance.

In 1980 the United Nations established the Working Group on Enforced or Involuntary Disappearances. In the past two decades the Working Group has investigated more than fifty thousand individual disappearances. In 1992 the United Nations General Assembly adopted the Declaration on the Protection of All Persons from Enforced Disappearance, which stated that enforced disappearance is an offense to human dignity and that no state should practice nor allow enforced disappearances. The Working Group is responsible for monitoring compliance with the declaration; in its 1997 report, the group noted that state conformity with the declaration has been slow.

Although the term *desaparecido* was coined in response to the large number of disappearances in Latin America, disappearances have been reported all around the world; in fact, the Working Group is investigating disappearances in seventy countries. For example, they are currently researching more than 450 disappearances in the Philippines since 1970. Afghanistan, Cambodia, Equatorial Guinea, Ethiopia, Morocco, Sri Lanka, Turkey, and Uganda have all been accused of the systematic use of disappearance. In addition, while some professions are targeted more than others—politicians, journalists, and human rights advocates, for example—people from all walks of life have been disappeared.

Although disappearance is widely considered a violation of human rights law, few perpetrators are punished for the crime. First, few countries have implemented laws specifically addressing disappearance, as called for in the declaration. Second, disappearances frequently occur in the context of civil war or unrest. When conflicts cease, perpetrators may go unpunished because general amnesty is granted in conjunction with peace accords. Finally, even when no such amnesty is granted, new governments, hoping to put the civil unrest behind them, frequently grant pardons to those convicted of causing disappearances. The issue of impunity—exempting those who cause disappearances from punishment for their crimes—is becoming especially important as more and more proof of disappearance becomes available.

The Working Group, along with a variety of NGOs, is calling for the implementation of national laws against disappearance, as mandated by the Declaration, as well as international legal norms naming forced disappearance as a violation of international human rights law.

For further information
Bouvard, Marguerite Guzman. *Revolutionizing Motherhood: The Mothers of the Plaza de Mayo.* Wilmington, Del.: Scholarly Resources, Inc., 1994.
Carlson, Eric Stener. *I Remember Julia: Voices of the Disappeared.* Philadelphia: Temple University Press, 1996.

—Jo Lynn Southard

Extradition

Extradition is the official surrender of fugitive offenders from one state to the jurisdiction of another, for the purpose of criminal prosecution or the execution of a sentence. This procedure is part of a broader framework of international cooperation in criminal matters. It is related to human rights for two reasons: first, it helps to achieve international cooperation in the punishment of perpetrators of human rights violations; second, an extradition carried out without due process violates international human rights norms.

Historically, international cooperation on the subject of fugitives dates back to the beginning of formal diplomacy. In 1833 Belgium was the first nation to pass extradition legislation, which outlined the circumstances and methods through which extradition might occur. At first extradition involved primarily political refugees. However, this trend evolved such that extradition procedures now cover "common" criminals, rather than refugees.

The sources of contemporary extradition law may be found in multilateral or bilateral treaties (such as the European Convention on Extradition of 1957), as well as in national extradition policies. There is no worldwide extradition convention. The duty to extradite exists only if a treaty has established the obligation thereof. In the absence of a treaty, the domestic law of the state in question may solely determine whether extradition is permitted and under what conditions.

There are, however, certain substantive principles that can be found in most extradition instruments. For example, the double-criminality rule requires that a person may be extradited only if the act that she or he allegedly committed is a crime under both of the involved states' laws. Another important rule is the specialty rule, which forbids the state seeking extradition (called the requesting state) to punish the person to be extradited for any offense committed prior to the extradition, other than the offense for which he was extradited.

Concurrently, most extradition treaties provide for a number of exceptions to the obligation to extradite. Some states (e.g., Germany, the Netherlands, and France) refuse to extradite their own nationals. It was for this reason that Libya refused to extradite two of its nationals allegedly responsible for the explosion of an airplane over Lockerbie, Scotland. Extradition may also be denied if the offense for which it is requested is punishable by death in the legislation of the requesting state. Humanitarian considerations (due to the age or health of the person to be extradited, for example) may also lead a state to refuse extradition. Likewise, states may refuse to extradite someone for political offenses—although the definition of political offenses raises many problems, as it varies from state to state. Finally, the discrimination clause, contained for the first time in the European Convention on Extradition of 1957, forbids extradition if the request is motivated by the individual's race, religion, or political opinion.

It is also worth mentioning that some treaties (such as the Geneva Conventions of 1949 and its First 1977 Additional Protocol) provide for *aut dedere aut judicare*, which means "to prosecute or to extradite." This obligation is the procedural consequence of the principle of universal jurisdiction, which allows a state to try a person regardless of his or her nationality or where the offense was committed. Universal jurisdiction also exists under customary international law in relation to certain international crimes, such as genocide or crimes against humanity.

In 1998 controversy raged over the fate of former Chilean dictator General Augusto Pinochet, who was arrested in London while recuperating from surgery. Spain issued an international warrant for Pinochet's arrest and requested that he be extradited to Madrid to stand trial for genocide, torture, and terrorism, specifically crimes committed against Spanish nationals under his regime. As of this writing, the procedure is still pending. But regardless of the outcome, the arrest itself was hailed as the dawn of a new era in international cooperation in the prosecution of human rights violators.

With the current development of international criminal law—through the creation of ad hoc and permanent international criminal courts—and an increased willingness on the part of the international community to prosecute human rights offenses, it is evident that the problem of extradition will continue to be of importance.

For further information

Gilbert, Geoff. *Aspects of Extradition Law* (International Studies in Human Rights, Vol. 17). The Hague; Boston, Mass.: Martinus Nijhoff, 1991.

Meron, Theodor, ed. *Human Rights in International Law: Legal and Policy Issues.* Oxford: Clarendon Press, 1984.

—Baptiste Rolle

Extrajudicial Executions

The carrying out of an execution without prior fair trial and without respect for fundamental judicial guarantees is shocking for those concerned with human rights. The concept of extrajudicial executions (also called summary or arbitrary executions) has been addressed by a variety of international legal instruments. According to author Nigel S. Rodley, "Most simply, summary or arbitrary executions are officially sanctioned murder."

Extrajudicial executions first began to be perceived as problematic with the development and acceptance of the rule of law as the basis for liberal democracy, subsequent to the French and American Revolutions (see Part 1). Summary executions obviously infringe on the right to life, but also on the presumption of innocence and the right to a fair trial. The factors conducive to extrajudicial executions are as varied as the states that engage in the practice—some causes include the absence of a democratic political process, the existence of a state of emergency, the lack of judicial independence, or the existence of secret police or paramilitary groups. Extrajudicial executions are not isolated acts; the practice is, unfortunately, very widespread. For example, in UN Doc. E/CN.4/1998/68/Add.1, of December 1997, eighty-seven countries are listed as having participated in extrajudicial executions.

Several human rights instruments prohibit extrajudicial executions. Article 6.1 of the International Covenant on Civil and Political Rights provides that "[n]o one shall be arbitrarily deprived of his life." The Principles on the Effective Prevention and Investigation of Extra-Legal, Arbitrary, and Summary Executions, adopted by the Economic and Social Coucil (ECOSOC) in 1989, constitute standards for implementing this article of the covenant. Governments are to guarantee effective protection to groups or individuals in danger of such execution. Moreover, the principles require a thorough, prompt, and impartial investigation of all suspected cases of summary or arbitrary executions. In times of war, the Geneva Conventions of 1949 and its protocols also provide for judicial guarantees that can reduce the occurrence of extrajudicial executions.

In 1982 the UN Commission on Human Rights designated the first Special Rapporteur on Summary or Arbitrary Executions. He is charged to examine the questions related to summary or arbitrary executions and to report annually to the commission. His reports usually denounce violations and the responsible governments with precision.

The challenge of the future fight against extrajudicial executions is not the establishment of new legal standards, because many solid ones exist. Rather the international community must achieve better implementation and enforcement of existing rules.

For further information

Amnesty International USA. *Getting Away with Murder: Political Killings and Disappearances in the 1990s.* New York: Amnesty International, 1993.

Rodley, Nigel S. "United Nations Non-Treaty Procedures for Dealing with Human Rights Violations." In *Guide to International Human Rights Practice*, edited by Hurst Hannum. Philadelphia: University of Pennsylvania Press, 1994.

—Baptiste Rolle

Female Genital Mutilation

Female genital mutilation (FGM) is the name given to the surgical operation in which part, or all, of the external female genitalia is removed; it is also known as female circumcision. Those who denounce FGM say that it is a violent human rights abuse against women, while proponents say that it is an important cultural tradition that must be preserved.

It is estimated that 80 to 135 million females around the world have undergone FGM, usually between the ages of four and twelve, and at present there are some two million girls at risk each year. The practice occurs in Africa, the Middle East, parts of Asia, and in immigrant communities in Europe and North America. In its mildest form, the clitoris is partially or totally removed. In the most extreme form, called infibulation, the clitoris, labia minora, labia majora, and the urethral and vaginal openings are cut away. The vagina is then stitched or held together, leaving a small opening for menstruation and urination. Cutting and restitching may be necessary for childbirth and sexual intercourse. The operation is commonly performed by untrained practitioners, with no form of anesthetic, and cutting instruments include broken glass, tin lids, scissors, or

Maake women in Lesotho, participating in a female circumcision ceremony (UN Photo187052/J. Isaac).

unsterilized razors. In addition to causing intense pain, the procedure carries with it a number of health risks such as pelvic infections, hemorrhaging, obstructed labor and childbirth, and the spread of HIV.

Typical arguments supporting FGM are that it will reduce promiscuity, increase cleanliness, and enhance femininity. In cultures where FGM is common, marriage prospects are higher for a woman who has undergone the procedure. In some communities it is believed that the clitoris will eventually hang down between a woman's legs unless it is removed. All of the reasons are cultural and traditional and are not rooted in any religious texts.

Frequently there is opposition to outside intervention in communities where FGM is practiced. Western interference can be seen as cultural imperialism, and some ask the rhetorical question, "What right do others have to criticize our way of life?" Some supporters of FGM point to Western practices that they find immoral, such as giving up children for adoption, sending parents to elderly homes, or conducting abortions. Another barrier to foreign involvement is that family members, friends, and relatives apply pressure on young women to undergo FGM, and view the issue as an entirely private family matter.

Nevertheless, the issue of FGM has garnered increasing global attention over the past several years. Nongovernmental organizations like Amnesty International are conducting research and campaign work on FGM. The U.S. government has taken steps to criminalize FGM in America and now considers asylum applications in light of FGM practices in the country of origin. In April 1997 the heads of three UN agencies—the World Health Organization, the United Nations Population Fund, and the United Nations Children's Fund—issued a joint plea for the eradication of FGM, saying it would be a major step forward in the promotion of human rights worldwide.

For further information
Hosken, F. *The Hosken Report: Genital and Sexual Mutilation of Females.* Lexington, Mass.: Women's International Network, 1993.
Walker, Alice, and Pratibha Parmar. *Warrior Marks: Female Genital Mutilation and the Sexual Blinding of Women.* New York: Harcourt Brace & Company, 1993.

— Robert Wilkinson

Gender-Related Persecution

Gender-related persecution is the oppression of women because of their gender. It includes a variety of gender-specific human rights infringements, including forced pregnancy, forced abortion, and female genital mutilation, as well as offenses that are chiefly directed at women, such as rape and domestic abuse.

The earliest human rights protections afforded to women came in the context of their roles as mothers or future mothers; women were not supposed to do heavy labor, work in mines, or work at night. After years of agitation, women's suffrage came into effect in most European countries and North America during the early twentieth century (1920 in the United States). In 1945 the Charter of the United Nations went into effect, and for the first time the human rights of women were afforded equal status with the human rights of men.

Although women's human rights were, therefore, technically part of international law, it was the Convention on the Elimination of All Forms of Discrimination Against Women (CEDAW) in 1979 that standardized women's human rights. CEDAW addresses the human rights of women in several different contexts, covering women's private and public lives; it has been ratified by more than 160 countries, but not the United States. The greatest drawback to CEDAW is the large number of reservations submitted by CEDAW signatories. These reservations allow members to exempt themselves from implementing some of the most fundamental aspects of CEDAW, including the elimination of discrimination in political life, equal citizenship rights, full legal capacity, and the elimination of discrimination in marriage and family.

Although women have made significant gains, they still make up a disproportionate number of the world's poor, illiterate, victimized, and marginalized. Globally, their political participation remains small. And while women in some parts of the world enjoy increasing freedom every day, fundamentalist regimes elsewhere persecute women, imposing gender-based restrictions on every aspect of their daily lives. In Afghanistan, which as of this writing is controlled by Islamic extremists called the Taliban, women are not allowed to go to work or attend school; they are only allowed to leave their houses when covered from head to toe and accompanied by a man, and they are forbidden from wearing white socks or shoes that make noise. Women who violate the edicts risk harassment, arrest, and severe beatings.

At the 1995 United Nations Women's Conference in Beijing, China, delegates identified poverty as the single greatest obstacle to ending gender-based persecution. Among the other issues addressed by the conference were the education of women and girls, violence against women, political rights, economic rights, women in war zones, medical and health issues, the environment, and the rights of the girl child. In recent years women have organized internationally around several other gender persecution issues. Among these are the fight to recognize gender persecution as a basis for granting asylum; the struggle to prosecute wartime rape as a crime against humanity; the effort to understand domestic violence as a form of torture; and the attempt to reconcile cultural and religious traditions with women's human rights.

While conventions and declarations provide moral and political force to women's human rights, and while governments must continue to demand an end to gender persecution, among the most significant advances made in recent years is increased international organizing and coalition-building by and among women. Today it is women themselves who direct the elimination of gender persecution by demanding, defining, and defending their human rights.

For futher information
Neft, Naomi, and Ann D. Levine. *Where Women Stand: An International Report on the Status of Women in 140 Countries, 1997–1998.* New York: Random House, 1997.
Tomasevski, Katarina. *Women and Human Rights.* London: Zed Books, 1993.

—Jo Lynn Southard

Genocide

Genocide is the deliberate destruction of a national, ethnic, racial, or religious group. The word is from the Greek *genos*, which means race or tribe, and the Latin *cide*, which means killing, and was coined by jurist Raphael Lemkin in response to the Holocaust.

While there have been numerous incidents of genocide throughout human history, the international community first acknowledged a legal concept for this phenomenon in 1948, when the United Nations General Assembly approved the Convention on the Prevention and Punishment of the Crime of Genocide. This convention, also known as the Genocide Convention, states that the following acts, when "committed with intent to destroy, in whole or in part, a national, ethnic, racial or religious group," constitute genocide: killing members of the group; causing serious bodily or mental harm to members of the group; deliberately inflicting conditions of life calculated to bring about the physical destruction of the group; preventing births within the group; and forcibly transferring children of the group to another group.

Closer analysis of the Genocide Convention reveals key elements of its role in international law. Genocide is distinct from other grave international crimes such as "crimes against humanity" or "war crimes" because it is criminal both in peace and war. The convention affirms that genocide is not an internal matter, even if committed by a government on its own territory, but an international one. And the convention clarifies that the destruction of a partic-

Rows of human skulls, on display at the Tuol Sleng Museum of Genocidal Crimes, a former Khmer Rouge torture prison in Phnom Penh, Cambodia (CORBIS/Chris Rainier).

ular group is not genocide per se: the term is only applicable if the "intent to destroy" the group is demonstrated. In other words, the individuals must be targeted because they were members of that particular group if the act is to be considered genocidal.

One modern example of genocide occurred in 1994 in Rwanda, where 500,000 to one million members of the Tutsi minority (and some moderate Hutus) were deliberately exterminated. Human rights abuses were committed on a massive scale, including the rape and sexual mutilation of women, which left them physically unable to reproduce. The International Criminal Tribunal for Rwanda (ICTR) was established to try those involved in the killings, and in 1998 (fifty years after the Genocide Convention was approved) it handed down the first conviction for genocide by an international court. It was also the first time that sexual violence was found to be an act of genocide, because it was "committed with the intent to destroy" a particular group.

The United Nations and nongovernmental organizations around the world are currently working on the establishment of a permanent International Criminal Court (ICC). At present the principal judicial organ of the United Nations is the International Court of Justice, whose jurisdiction is restricted to states only. The ICC would be the first permanent global court that could try any individuals, without geographical or chronological limits, for war crimes, crimes against humanity, and genocide, and possibly deter future genocidal massacres.

For further information

Kuper, Leo. *The Prevention of Genocide*. New Haven, Conn., and London: Yale University Press, 1985.
Cigar, Norman. *Genocide in Bosnia: The Policy of Ethnic Cleansing*. College Station, Texas: Texas A&M University Press, 1995.

—Robert Wilkinson

Girl Children

A preference for boy children is deeply entrenched, to some degree, in nearly every country in the world. Therefore, while the human rights of women and the human rights of children have been addressed by the international community, the human rights of the girl child is a relatively new concern. Because they are usually at home, hidden from public view, it has been easy to overlook the human rights of girls.

In many parts of the world, the sex ratio is artificially skewed in favor of boy children. Recently, the number of males has increased and the number of females has decreased in China, India, Pakistan, and South Korea. In some cases, girl children are so devalued that they are abandoned or killed at birth. Female infanticide—the

intentional killing of girl babies—has been widely documented in China and India, and is believed to be common in other Asian countries. Current technology allows women to know the gender of their fetuses before birth, and in many parts of the world, female fetuses are several thousand times more likely to be aborted than males.

If they are allowed to live, girl children often receive little food and no health care or education—all of which are violations of the girls' human rights. Because girls are less often educated than boys, two-thirds of the world's illiterate adults are women. In many countries girls are more likely to become ill, but less likely to be taken to a doctor than their male counterparts. Discrimination against girl children manifests itself in a variety of more subtle ways as well. In some cultures, for example, although girl children may not be denied an education, they often receive less attention in school and are steered into stereotypical areas of study.

Cultural practices are currently an important human rights issue for girl children. In many parts of the world, girl children are under the complete and total control of their fathers. A father may treat his daughter however he sees fit—even kill her—and no one, not even the government, will interfere. In many Asian and African countries, fathers arrange their daughters' marriages: if it benefits the family, girls may be married as young as nine years old. Female genital mutilation, early marriage, and systematic seclusion (called purdah) are all practices that are damaging to girl children but are also cultural traditions.

Discrimination against girl children is so deeply ingrained on an international level that it was nearly left out of the UN Convention on the Rights of the Child (CRC). The convention was nearly opened for signature in 1990 containing only male pronouns: "she" and "her" had to be added at the last minute. Given this, it is perhaps not surprising that the convention often does not speak to the special needs of girl children. For example, it does not address female genital mutilation, son preference, or early marriage—practices that impact girls more than boys.

Currently, a variety of movements throughout the world are promoting a convention aimed specifically at the rights of girl children. This convention would blend protections from the women's and children's conventions, as well as addressing issues that are currently overlooked by both treaties.

For further information
Tomasevski, Katarina. *Women and Human Rights.* London: Zed Books, 1993.
United Nations. *The World's Women 1995: Trends and Statistics.* New York: United Nations, 1995.

—Jo Lynn Southard

Homelessness

Adequate housing is widely agreed upon to be a basic human right, but it is believed that more than 100 million people in the world today are homeless. Some homeless are refugees or internally displaced persons (IDPs), some have been forcibly evicted from their homes, and some are unable to find and keep shelter for economic or other reasons. If the number of people living in inadequate and unsafe housing is included, the total rises to almost 1.2 billion. This issue, therefore, affects one-quarter of the world's population.

The right to housing has been a part of human rights law since the founding of the United Nations in 1945. Article 25 of the Universal Declaration of Human Rights, adopted by the General Assembly in 1948, states that everyone has the right to a standard of living adequate for health and well-being, and that this standard includes housing. The issue is discussed further in the International Covenant on Economic, Social and Cultural Rights. Promotion of housing—along with other economic and social rights—has lagged behind the promotion of civil and political rights.

In the United Nations, the Committee on Economic, Social, and Cultural Rights has determined that the right to housing is legally guaranteed under the covenant; a major function of the committee is to oversee governmental compliance. In addition, from 1992 to 1995, a Special Rapporteur

A homeless child on the streets of São Paulo, Brazil (UN Photo/Claudio Edinger).

on Housing operated under the mandate of the committee. Two of the specific issues the committee and the rapporteur have addressed in recent years are refugees and displaced persons, and forced evictions.

There are currently approximately fifteen million refugees worldwide, usually forced to leave their countries of citizenship because their human rights are in jeopardy. Civil and ethnic wars have also resulted in twenty-five to thirty million more IDPs—people who are displaced within their own countries. Natural disasters also create refugees and displaced persons. According to international human rights standards, the countries to which refugees flee are responsible for providing decent housing to all people within their borders. Nearly two-thirds of these refugees are in Asia and Africa, creating huge strains on the resources in those areas.

In 1997 the United Nations expanded protection from forcible eviction. Of special concern are residents who are evicted in connection with international events, such as the Olympic Games. It was alleged in 1996 that thousands were evicted in Atlanta to make way for Olympic structures. In Korea, more than 700,000 people were evicted in Seoul as the country prepared for the 1988 Olympics. In addition, Brazil, Israel, Nigeria, and the Philippines have been accused in recent years of participating in wide-scale forced evictions. Where previously, only governments were restricted from forcibly evicting people from their homes, now governments are held responsible for monitoring the private sector as well.

In June 1996 a global plan of action, produced by the World Conference on Human Settlements II, expanded governments' responsibilities to foster their citizens' right to housing. As with many other human rights issues, a great deal of the work is done by NGOs in individual countries; nonetheless, strong international backing is vitally important to these organizations. There is still some resistance by Western nations to the notion of economic rights, such as housing. However, as non-Western states gain more influence over human rights standards, housing and other economic, social, and cultural rights will grow in prominence.

For further information
Glasser, Irene. *Homelessness in Global Perspective.* New York: G. K. Hall, 1994.
Huth, Mary Jo, and Talmadge Wright, eds. *International Critical Perspective on Homelessness.* New York: Praeger Publishing, 1997.

—Jo Lynn Southard

Human Rights Activists

Members of human rights groups, lawyers, journalists, relatives who protect victims, and others who act to uphold human rights often become victims themselves. Human rights activists, also known as human rights defenders, have been silenced by threats, imprisonment, disappearance, torture, and death. Recognition of the precarious nature of the work of human rights activists is imperative if they are to be protected in their struggles.

All human beings, including those who defend rights, are guaranteed basic rights under the Universal Declaration of Human Rights of 1948 and international treaties such as the International Covenant on Civil and Political Rights. Rights afforded to all citizens, such as the freedom of thought, conscience, and religion, the right to meet and assemble, and the right to form and join trade unions, are especially relevant to human rights activists.

However, governments often fail to protect activists, despite the national and international laws intended to safeguard them. Cases of violations are shockingly widespread. In March 1997 both the translator and publisher of the 1995 Human Rights Watch report on human rights violations in Turkey were accused of "defaming and belittling the state military and security forces" by the Turkish government. Ertu Rul Kurkau and Ay Enur Zarakolu were found guilty of defamation and were sentenced to ten months in prison and a fine. The punishment meted out to human rights defenders can be extreme. In Honduras, Ernesto Sandoval Bustillo, president of the Human Rights Committee (CODEH) for the region of Santa Rosa de Copan, was executed without trial in February 1998.

For over a decade, a working group of the UN Commission on Human Rights has been negotiating a draft declaration on the rights of human rights defenders which would reaffirm and strengthen the rights of those who work towards the elimination of human rights violations. Obstructions by governments during these negotiations are proof of the challenges in adopting such a declaration. In 1997 Cuba and China proposed wording that restricted defenders to defending only their own rights. Another challenge was a refusal by some governments to recognize the rights of groups to financial resources in the defense of human rights.

On March 4, 1998, the draft declaration was finally adopted by consensus. The final text must still be approved.

Fifty years after the adoption of the Universal Declaration of Human Rights, human rights are violated around the world every day. Continued efforts to fortify the legitimacy and protection of those who struggle to realize these fundamental rights are necessary so human rights violators will continue to be challenged.

For further information
Amnesty International. *Human Rights Defenders: Breaching the Walls of Silence.* Amnesty International Report IOR 40/07/96.
Lawyers Committee for Human Rights. *Protecting Human Rights Defenders: Toward a Strong Declaration on Human Rights Defenders.* New York: Lawyers Committee for Human Rights, January 1998.

—Carol Devine

Independent Judiciary

A judiciary is composed of all the judges who sit on the courts of a given country. Maintaining the independence of the judiciary is an important human rights issue because in order for justice to be served, judges must base all decisions purely on the law, allowing no other external influences from governments, businesses, organizations, or individuals. Judges should not stand to gain or lose anything from their decisions, nor fear retaliation for unpopular legal opinions.

Judicial independence in many countries around the world stems largely from the development of the judiciary in England. Until the late 1600s the king or queen could remove judges from office with no justification required. Growing concern over fairness in taxes, punishments, and individual rights led to the formulation of laws that protected the independence of judges. By 1700, judges could not be dismissed as long as they conducted their duties in accordance with the law.

Judicial independence is a cornerstone for the protection of human rights in any society, as true justice cannot be administered without it. Today there exists an international standard for state judiciaries, set out in the Basic Principles on the Independence of the Judiciary, which was adopted by the UN General Assembly in 1985. These principles explicitly state that judges must be selected impartially and must decide cases based on law and the facts of the case, without improper inducements, pressures, or interference.

Countries that do not measure up to the standards delineated in the basic principles fall under close scrutiny by the international community. In 1994 the UN Commission on Human Rights noted the "link . . . between the weakening of safeguards for the judiciary . . . and the gravity and frequency of violations of human rights" and established a Special rapporteur, a type of investigator, on the Independence of Judges and Lawyers. The rapporteur meets with governments, nongovernmental organizations, and intergovernmental organizations to report on the state of judicial independence.

In one typical example, the government of Bahrain's judiciary allowed the imprisonment of a prominent human rights lawyer, Ahmad Al-Shamlan, in 1996 without charge or trial. It was suspected that he was incarcerated because of his advocacy for human rights victims. The rapporteur intervened, using the documentation of the case to show that there was no legal basis for his imprisonment and that the government had openly applied pressure to the judiciary. Shortly thereafter Al-Shamlan was released with no charges brought against him. The rapporteur documented and publicized the flaws in the Bahraini legal system, which allows judges to be influenced by factors outside the law. In situations such as these, the UN continues its monitoring of the situation, with the ultimate aim of meeting all the standards set by international norms.

In the 1990s there has been increasing worldwide agreement on implementing international standards, as evidenced by regional judicial conferences in Asia, Latin America, Africa, and Europe. While each country is different, it appears that judges around the globe vigorously support the protection of free and fair courts for all.

For further information
American Bar Association. *An Independent Judiciary: Report of the ABA Commission on Separation of Powers and Judicial Independence.* American Bar Association, 1997. American Judicature Society. "Judicial Independence: An Introduction." *Judicature* 80, 4 (1997).

—Robert Wilkinson

Indigenous Peoples

The particular human rights concerns of indigenous peoples have only been recognized in recent years. Representatives of these groups have identified many common goals, such as the right to religions, languages, educational institutions, possession or use of indigenous lands and natural resources, and self-determination.

At present there are approximately four thousand indigenous groups, with a population of 200 to 350 million people, living in more than seventy countries of the world. The many indigenous peoples that populate the globe include the Mayans of Guatemala, the Saami of northern Europe, the Hmong of Laos, the Kuna of Panama, the Aborigines and Torres Strait Islanders of Australia, and the Inuit and Aleutians of the circumpolar region.

Indigenous communities are defined as those with a historical continuity tied to precolonization land and the societies that developed on their territories. They have retained social, cultural, economic, and political characteristics that are distinct from those of the other segments of the national population. Often their native language is different from that of the rest of society. Self-identification is seen as a crucial factor for recognizing an indigenous group. Although they may or may not comprise a numerical minority, they typically form a nondominant sector of society—it is often this minority status that makes it easy, even tempting, for states to violate their human rights.

Indigenous peoples have some protection under international law. The most prominent treaty is the Convention Concerning Indigenous and Tribal Peoples in Independent Countries, known as the International Labour Organization (ILO) Convention 169, which was adopted in 1989. (The convention has been somewhat controversial, as no indigenous people participated in its writing.) The World Bank has also recognized that indigenous peoples have a right to special protection and has developed an operational directive that

defines policies and procedures that will uphold the rights of indigenous peoples. And in Latin America, the Inter-American Commission on Human Rights proposed an American Declaration on the Rights of Indigenous Peoples in 1997.

Indigenous rights only became internationally recognized within the last three decades and are increasingly garnering attention from the international community. In the 1920s a group of American Indians approached the League of Nations in Geneva to raise the issue of indigenous rights, but this initiative produced little or no results. In 1948 the Bolivian government attempted to create a body in the UN to study the problems of indigenous populations, but again the effort did not come to fruition. In 1970 human rights experts in the UN agreed that the rights of indigenous peoples had been ignored for too long and appointed a Special Rapporteur to study the problems of indigenous peoples.

In 1982 the UN established a Working Group on Indigenous Populations (WGIP) which has conducted studies, organized seminars, and acted as a focal point for representatives of indigenous peoples around the world. The WGIP has been drafting a Universal Declaration of Indigenous Rights, which if adopted in its present form, could be a landmark document for indigenous rights. NGOs such as Survival International, Anti-Slavery International, and the Minority Rights Group are heavily involved in the indigenous rights movement. As a symbolic gesture to recognize the rights of indigenous people, the UN has declared 1995–2004 the International Decade of the World's Indigenous People.

For further information
Anaya, S. James. *Indigenous Peoples in International Law*. Oxford: Oxford University Press, 1996.
Barsh, R. L. "Indigenous Peoples in the 1990s: From Object to Subject of International Law?" *Harvard Human Rights Law Journal*, vol. 7 (Spring 1994).

—Robert Wilkinson

Internally Displaced Persons

In recent years a staggering number of people have been forced to leave their homes due to ethnic, religious, and political persecution, human-made disasters, or disruption of law. The world's internally displaced persons (IDPs) population outnumbers the global refugee population. An estimated fifteen million persons have fled across international borders (refugees) whereas at least thirty million persons have fled their homes but cannot or choose not to leave their own countries. International concern about the crisis of IDPs and the inadequate assistance they receive has grown in the last decade.

According to the UN High Commission for Refugees (UNHCR), Africa has approximately sixteen million displaced persons. Sudan, enduring the longest civil war on the continent, has four million displaced persons. Other countries with at least a million displaced include Iraq and Bosnia-Herzegovina.

The definition of IDP has been submitted to the UN Commission on Human Rights as "persons . . . who have been forced to flee their homes or places of habitual residence suddenly or unexpectedly as a result of armed conflict, internal strife, systematic violations of human rights or natural or man-made disasters, and who have not crossed an internationally recognized State border." Thus, IDPs fall beyond the scope of the 1951 Convention on Refugees and the 1967 Protocol.

The Commission on Human Rights is not mandated to protect or assist IDPs although on occasion they have provided help, such as in Afghanistan in 1994 when Pakistan closed the border to fleeing Afghans. The International Committee of the Red Cross (ICRC) and nongovernmental organizations assist IDPs, yet the needs of the displaced are greater than their resources alone. Governments are fundamentally responsible for IDPs but often lack the capacity and will to assist them.

The most pressing human rights concern for IDPs is for their physical safety. IDPs remain in their country and are not specifically protected by law or one humanitarian body. Increasingly, civilians are being deliberately displaced for the purpose of "ethnic cleansing."

In 1992 Dr. Francis Deng was appointed as representative of the UN Secretary-General on the question of IDPs. His investigations show a discrepancy in the way the international community treats IDP and refugee populations—for example, in Burundi and Sudan, refugees received superior international protection and assistance. Deng's recommendations include development of legal standards and improvement of physical security for IDPs, particularly for women and children. He suggests that either the commission have an enlarged mandate or that a new UN agency be created to collaborate with organizations working with IDPs.

In 1995 the ICRC held a conference in Geneva to examine the legal protection of IDPs, the cooperation of concerned agencies, and ways to avert population movements in the future. Other concerned parties consider regional solutions. A conference in Egypt in 1992 resulted in the Declaration on the Protection of Refugees and Displaced Persons in the Arab World. In 1996 a seminar on Refugees, Migrants, Displaced and Stateless Persons, held in Nepal by the South Asia Forum for Human Rights, recommended a South Asia Protocol/Charter for protection of such persons.

Human rights are imperative for the security and dignity of internally displaced persons and for their freedom of movement and voluntary return home. Governments, the UN, and concerned agencies must accelerate their coordination to improve the assistance to IDPs, tackle the root causes of displacement, and search for durable solutions, or their survival will continue to be at stake.

For further information
International Committee of the Red Cross. *Internally Displaced Persons*. Geneva: Conference Report, 1996.
United Nations High Commission for Refugees. *The State of the World's Refugees 1997-98: A Humanitarian Agenda*. Geneva: United Nations, December 1997.

—Carol Devine

Landmines

Landmines are a relatively new but very serious issue for human rights activists, due to their widespread use and indiscriminate nature. Of the several types of landmines in existence, the type of greatest concern is the antipersonnel landmine. These small explosive devices are scattered over some seventy countries, and they are currently deployed in dozens of armed conflicts around the world. Some of the countries that are most affected by landmines include Nicaragua, Sudan, Afghanistan, Angola, Bosnia-Herzegovina, Cambodia, and Somalia.

Landmines were first developed just after World War I, primarily to defend against the tank, but soon they were designed to explode in response to human contact. Landmine use accelerated rapidly after World War II—over 400 million have been deployed—including sixty-five million since the 1980 Convention on Conventional Weapons, which was intended to limit the use of landmines. As instruments of warfare, antipersonnel landmines are unique in their repercussions. They are "victim activated" and indiscriminate, so the vast majority of victims are innocent civilians. Landmines cannot recognize any ceasefire agreements and continue to maim unsuspecting people decades after the fighting has stopped or after frontlines have changed. The United Nations has calculated that the average antipersonnel landmine costs between $3 and $30, while the cost of clearing a mine may be as high as $1000. Peace-building activities and the return of displaced peoples are put in jeopardy by uncleared landmines, and victims of landmines are often unable to find employment, provide for their families, go to school, or reintegrate into society.

In response to these problems, nongovernmental organizations (NGOs) such as Handicap International, the Mines Advisory Group, and Norwegian People's

Aid have been working on the rehabilitation of victims, mine clearance, and mine awareness programs. Programs for psychosocial assistance as well as physical rehabilitation are in operation in several countries. Expatriate and local teams are being trained in the disposal of landmines, and awareness programs in landmine safety and first aid are aiming to reduce the risk of landmine injuries in the years to come.

In 1997 a study commissioned by the International Committee of the Red Cross (ICRC) to investigate the military effectiveness of antipersonnel landmines was conducted by military experts from the Americas, Europe, Africa, Asia, and the Middle East. One of the major conclusions was that antipersonnel landmines have historically had little or no effect on determining the outcome of a conflict. In fact, employing antipersonnel landmines posed a "risk to one's own forces and the loss of tactical flexibility."

The scale of the problem initiated a worldwide campaign to ban antipersonnel landmines in 1991, launched by human rights and medical organizations. Consequently, in December 1997, 127 states signed the Convention on the Prohibition of the Use, Stockpiling, Production and Transfer of Anti-Personnel Mines and on Their Destruction, also known as the "Ottawa Treaty." While this convention will not immediately end the use of these weapons, it is seen as a positive step toward the eventual eradication of the antipersonnel landmine epidemic.

For further information
The Arms Project of Human Rights Watch and Physicians for Human Rights. *Landmines: A Deadly Legacy.* New York: Human Rights Watch, 1993.

Roberts, Shawn, and Williams, Jody. *After the Guns Fall Silent: The Enduring Legacy of Landmines.* Washington, D.C.: Vietnam Veterans of America Foundation, 1995.

—Robert Wilkinson

Medical Neutrality

Medical neutrality is the principle that medical personnel are obliged to provide impartial medical assistance to all victims of a conflict. Questions of access to health care in wartime and of protection for those who provide it are vital human rights concerns and are addressed in a wide variety of human rights instruments.

The obligation to heal without discrimination dates back to the Hippocratic Oath (fourth century BC). Physicians throughout history have been considered to have special skills that demand respect.

A Canadian medic working for the United Nations examines an elderly woman in Cambodia (UN/DPI/J. Isaac).

The context of war has required not only that medical personnel honor neutrality in the provision of treatment, but that combatants honor the independence and neutrality of care providers.

The Geneva Conventions, a series of international treaties first conceived in 1864, require that all war-wounded should receive care and that medical services should be provided without reprisal by belligerents. The protocols extend protection to civilians affected by armed conflict. Protocol II, Article 9 stipulates that "medical and religious personnel shall be respected and protected and shall be granted all available help for the performance of their duties."

Medical neutrality, as defined in the Geneva Conventions of 1949 and their Additional Protocols of 1977, is particularly relevant today as it is flagrantly violated worldwide. Many states are engaged in conflicts whose actors abuse medical personnel and civilians: hospitals are bombed, doctors and nurses are threatened, coerced, or killed, and health care is given prejudicially.

Medical personnel and independent humanitarian organizations that provide medical assistance in war zones—such as the International Committee of the Red Cross (ICRC) and *Médecins sans Frontières* (MSF, known in the United States as Doctors Without Borders)—are constantly challenged by violations of medical neutrality. In Kabul, Afghanistan, in 1997, the ICRC, MSF, and other Afghan and expatriate medical personnel protested the denial of health services to women and the restrictions placed on women health workers.

The healthcare workers publicly insisted that medical personnel not be forced to discriminate against women and suspended their services in protest.

Gross violations of medical neutrality have also occurred during the recent war in Chechnya, a republic in the western part of Russia. In 1995 Chechen rebels occupied a functioning hospital, disrupted medical services, killed hostages, and used physicians and patients as human shields. In December 1996 in Chechnya, six International Red Cross field hospital workers were executed in their beds.

Today, violations of medical neutrality are met by strong protests to governments, rebels, and the international community. Medical workers who protest abuses of medical neutrality by suspending services often create the moral dilemma of denying medical attention to some innocent victims of a war. The long-term effect of such sanctions can only be analyzed over time.

A new initiative has been undertaken in an attempt to safeguard medical neutrality. The Johannes Wier Foundation for Health and Human Rights, supported by members of the international medical community, has called for a United Nations Special Rapporteur on medical neutrality. The new rapporteur would monitor medical workers' freedom from arrest and torture as well as patients' access to medical treatment without discrimination on the basis of nationality, religion, or ethnic origin in war zones or situations of political tension. Such a position could put additional pressure on the abusers of medical neutrality to follow laws and could demand accountability for violations.

For further information
Physicians for Human Rights. *Medicine under Siege in Former Yugoslavia, 1991–1995*. Boston, 1995.
Summary of the Geneva Conventions of August 12, 1949, and their Additional Protocols. Geneva: ICRC Publications.

—Carol Devine

Police Brutality

Police brutality occurs whenever police officers abuse their power by using excessive force against civilians. The category encompasses acts of violence and acts that violate human dignity, including unjustified police shootings of civilians, beatings and chokings of suspects in custody, and methods of inflicting physical or psychological suffering on detainees. Police brutality is one of the most widely reported human rights abuses; in a recent Amnesty International annual report, more than one hundred nations on five continents were cited for incidents of police brutality. The vast majority of these countries lack effective procedures for investigating individual complaints of police brutality, leading human rights organizations to demand that police forces around the world be held to a higher standard of accountability.

Although the problem of police brutality has undoubtedly existed for as long as the existence of professional police forces, it was not formally addressed as a human rights issue until relatively recently. In 1979 the United Nations General Assembly adopted a Code of Conduct for Law Enforcement Officials, calling on police to "uphold the human rights of all persons." Limiting the acceptable use of force to the most extreme circumstances, it also explicit-ly prohibits law enforcement officials from engaging in "any act of torture or other cruel, inhuman or degrading punishment," making no exception for acts committed under orders or under the threat of public emergency. Threats to public safety or national security are frequently used to attempt to justify police brutality. In Turkey, for example, an armed Kurdish insurrection in the east was used to justify extraordinary violence by Turkish police against civilians around the country—violence so condoned by the Turkish judicial system that even members of Turkey's Parliament have been the victims of police brutality.

While police brutality may be perceived as a problem primarily in countries with repressive governments, some liberal Western democracies have an equally troubling record of failing to prevent or punish acts of police brutality. In the past decade both Amnesty International and Human Rights Watch have reported significant numbers of complaints about police violence in the United States, particularly violence against members of racial minorities. Beatings, chokings, and the excessive and sometimes fatal use of firearms were frequently reported. Complaints were also raised about the alarming lack of accountability in police departments across the United States, allowing police officers repeatedly accused of human rights abuses to go without punishment and frequently without investigation.

The rage and frustration experienced by communities affected by police brutality was fatally dramatized in 1992 in Los Angeles, when rioters burned parts of Los Angeles in response to a white jury's acquittal of police officers videotaped while beating African-American motorist Rodney King. In another well-publicized brutality case in 1997, police officers in New York City savagely beat Haitian immigrant Abner Louima and subsequently attempted to cover up their actions—starkly illustrating the warnings of several human rights organizations who had reported increasing incidents of police brutality during Mayor Rudolph Guiliani's administration. While activists in the United States and around the world have had some success in raising awareness of police brutality as a serious human rights issue, it still remains to be seen whether experiments to increase police accountability, like those now taking place in cities like New York and Los Angeles, will be able to effectively address the problem.

For further information
Dudley, William, ed. *Police Brutality*. San Diego, Calif.: Greenhaven Press, 1991.
Human Rights Watch Staff. *Shielded from Justice: Police Brutality and Accountability in the United States of America*. New York: Human Rights Watch, 1998.

—Rebecca Sherman

Press, Freedom of

The right to free access of information, which is the basis for freedom of the press, is a universally accepted human right. However, many states place restrictions on the press, ranging from limitations of journalistic independence to publication licensing laws. Every week, journalists, editors, and publishers are threatened, harassed, attacked, banned, imprisoned, and killed.

Restrictions on the press are not new. They were written into state constitutions long ago, such as in the Bangladesh constitution of 1861. Those who most vigorously uphold the rights of the press are often the press themselves. In 1948 the World Association of Newspapers began defending and promoting press freedom. Organizations such as the U.S.-based Committee to Protect Journalists (CPJ) and the France-based *Reporters sans Frontières* (RSF) were created in the 1980s to monitor cases of restrictions on the press and to campaign on behalf of journalists in danger. Freedom of the press was permanently enshrined in human rights law by Article 19 of the Universal Declaration of Human Rights (see Part 2).

Many state constitutions—and even the Universal Declaration—contain limitations of rights and freedoms (e.g., in the interest of "national unity," "morality," or "public order"). Some argue that restrictions of the press during times of civil disorder or war are justified, such as during the war in the former Yugoslavia in the early 1990s. Although there are problems in the interpretation of what specifically constitutes a threat to public order, there are clear examples of when "the press" should be restricted in the defense of human rights for others. For example, in Rwanda in 1994, the media was used openly and extensively to call for genocide of Tutsis and moderate Hutus.

Restrictions on the press and crimes against journalists are extremely common, particularly in nondemocratic states. Currently, Nigeria, Colombia, Burma, Ethiopia, and Peru are some of the worst violators of journalists' rights and press freedom. Restriction on the press in democratic states such as the United States and England exist but are far less prevalent. According to the CPJ, at least twenty-six journalists were murdered in fourteen countries in 1997, and 129 journalists were imprisoned in twenty-four countries because of their work. According to CPJ's Executive Director William Orme, in politically troubled nations the independent press frequently becomes the de facto opposition to government.

Another organization promoting freedom of expression is the British group, Article 19, which takes its name from Article 19 of the Universal Declaration. Article 19 and more than thirty other organizations are part of International Freedom of Expression eXchange (IFEX) which links groups worldwide, such as Russia's Glasnost Defense Foundation and the Pacific Islands News Association. IFEX's Action Alert Network produces rapid action updates on international press freedom violations in order to effect change.

A hopeful case amidst the many tragic cases of violations of press freedom is the August 1998 amnesty of prominent dissident Doan Viet Hoat, following a major campaign for his release. A sixty-four year-old Vietnamese academic and journalist, he was sentenced in 1990 to fifteen years imprisonment for publishing an underground magazine, *Dien Dan Tu Do* (Freedom Forum). His release illustrates the influence of international pressure.

Standing firmly against restrictions on press are members of the press who courageously and continuously defend their right to seek and publish information despite risks. Their colleagues and human rights organizations together act to protect them and the human right to free information.

For further information
Committee to Protect Journalists. *Attacks on the Press in 1997: A Worldwide Survey by the Committee to Protect Journalists.* New York, 1997.
"International PEN President Homero Aridjis Receives Death Threats." Action Alert, International Freedom of Expression eXchange (IFEX) Clearing House, August 28, 1998.

—Carol Devine

Prisoners

Broadly speaking, there are three main types of prisoners: common law prisoners, political prisoners, and prisoners of war. Common prisoners are persons detained by the state for having committed a crime against the common law in force in that state, whereas political prisoners have committed offenses aimed against the state or having a political character. Prisoners of war may be defined as combatants who have fallen into the hands of the enemy. Protecting prisoners against ill-treatment and monitoring the conditions of their detention have been important human rights tasks because prisoners are among the most vulnerable groups for potential abuse by authorities.

After the horrors of World War II a new sense of how states must behave vis-à-vis their population emerged. Two of the most significant documents to discuss the treatment of prisoners are the Third and Fourth Geneva Conventions of 1949, the former dealing with prisoners of war, and the latter with the civilian population. (Civilian internees enjoy a similar protection to that granted to prisoners of war.) Many subsequent human rights instruments—though not solely adopted for the protection of prisoners—also provide fundamental safeguards for their treatment. Torture and other forms of ill-treatment are prohibited, as are extrajudicial executions, disappearances, and other misconduct that can particularly affect prisoners.

There are many additional guidelines related to the rights of prisoners or detainees. For example, the Standard Minimum Rules for the Treatment of Prisoners adopted in 1955 by the First United Nations Congress on the Prevention of Crime and Treatment of the Offenders deal solely with the conditions of detention, emphasizing rehabilitation and restraint of a prisoner rather than retribution and deterrence. This document has been followed by many others, notably the Body of Principles for the Protection of all Persons under Any Form of Detention or Imprisonment (General Assembly, 1988). This Body of Principles tries to protect all detainees from abuses such as arbitrary detention, coercive interrogation, and other ill-treatment. The focus is on safeguarding the physical safety of detainees, on the importance of access to the outside world, and on independent supervision of the conditions of detention.

The UN Commission on Human Rights as well as the Sub-Commission on Prevention of Discrimination and Protection of Minorities and its Working Group on the Administration of Justice have been discussing issues related to prisons in general, such as the conditions of detention, judicial guarantees like habeas corpus procedures, and the death penalty, among many others. The International Committee of the Red Cross (ICRC) intervenes on behalf of prisoners of war and interned civilians. The ICRC visits prisoners and, if necessary, tries to convince the authorities to fully respect the rights granted by the Geneva Conventions of 1949. There are also many nongovernmental organizations working in the field for the protection of prisoners. For example, prisoners are a major focus of Amnesty International, which monitors and denounces abuses committed by authorities.

Unfortunately, it is never enough. The two components of the protection of prisoners (treatment and material conditions of detention) still require a lot of thought and action. In this respect an interesting related issue is the privatization of prisons, which is taking place around the world. Prisoner advocates have expressed concern about the possible consequences this may have on the conditions of detention and the treatment of prisoners. The UN Sub-Commission on Prevention of Discrimination and Protection of Minorities has decided to study this question in the future.

For further information
Richardson, Genevra. *Law, Process and Custody: Prisoners and Patients (Law in Context)*. Chicago: Northwestern University Press, 1993.
Rodley, Nigel S. *The Treatment of Prisoners Under International Law*. Paris and Oxford: UNESCO and Clarendon Press, 1987.

—Baptiste Rolle

Rape

Rape is sexual intercourse achieved by the use of force or coercion and without the victim's consent. Its targets are overwhelmingly female. Rape has only recently come to be recognized as a human rights issue of international concern, as it has been used as an instrument of terror and genocide in conflicts in Rwanda and the former Yugoslavia.

Rape is committed in times of peace and war, in private homes and in public institutions. Rape perpetrated in wartime has been a violation of international law since the earliest codification of the laws of warfare. However, like peacetime rape, it is an often overlooked crime. For example, the Charter of the International Military Tribunals at Nuremberg after World War II did not mention rape as a crime against humanity.

The recent conflict in the former Yugoslavia has spotlighted rape as a deliberate military tactic; it is estimated that twenty thousand to fifty thousand women were victims of systematic rape in that war. For the first time, the International Criminal Tribunals for Rwanda and the former Yugoslavia have said they will address rape as a human rights violation. This region is not particularly unique, however; in recent years mass rapes in military conflict have been reported in Afghanistan, Bangladesh, Burundi, Cambodia, Liberia, Peru, Rwanda, Somalia, and Uganda.

Judicial systems deal with rape in a variety of ways. Until recently in most countries, it was legally impossible for a husband to rape his wife. Now the majority of countries technically outlaw marital rape; however, the laws are only enforced in a handful of states. In some countries a woman who reports being raped can be jailed herself for committing adultery. In other situations one or two eyewitnesses are required in order to prosecute a rapist. Under some legal systems a rapist is only held responsible if the woman becomes pregnant; often he may escape prosecution if he marries his victim. Women are also particularly vulnerable to rape when they are incarcerated—and the word of a convict is rarely believed over that of her jailer.

Rape is one of the world's most underreported crimes. It is estimated that in some parts of the world fewer than five percent of rapes are reported. It is also believed that in a majority of cases the rapist is known to the victim and that many of the victims of rape are children and adolescents. International enactments against rape have struggled to address the issue. Most mentions of rape in war categorize it as a crime against honor. Whose honor—the victim's, her family's, or her country's—is not clear. In virtually no setting is rape understood as a crime based on gender. Even the Convention on the Elimination of All Forms of Discrimination Against Women does not highlight rape as a gender-based hate crime. Recently, however, international law has begun to recognize rape as a crime committed because of the victim's gender.

Although human rights treaties generally do not address rape directly, rape may be analyzed as a human rights violation under existing laws. Most often, rape is defined as part of a genocide campaign, torture, a war crime, or a crime against humanity. The establishment of an International Criminal Court may provide long-needed protection for victims of rape.

For further information
Human Rights Watch. *The Human Rights Watch Global Report on Women's Human Rights*. New York: Human Rights Watch, 1995.
Davies, Miranda, ed. *Women and Violence*. London: Zed Books, 1995.

—Jo Lynn Southard

Self-Determination

Self-determination is one of the most controversial contemporary human rights issues. While the fundamental principle of self-determination, which declares the right of peoples to choose their leaders and paths of development, is the first article of the two UN Covenants, application of the right is selective and the definition disputed. Self-determination has been described as "one of most confused expressions in the lexicon of international law." Some legal scholars argue that self-determination is mythical and exists as a principle but not a legal right, whereas others say it has achieved historical legitimacy over the last half-century.

The origin of self-determination can be traced to the 1776 American Declaration of Independence and the 1789 French Declaration of the Rights of Man and the Citizen. Both declarations articulated the inherent right of peoples to choose their own government or form of government. V. I. Lenin of the then-USSR proclaimed annexation of territories to be a violation of the "self-determination of peoples" and Woodrow Wilson, U.S. president during World War I, said the principle of self-determination is an element of peace.

After World War II the concept of self-determination was applied in the context of the decolonization process. In 1960 the UN General Assembly adopted its Declaration on the Granting of Independence to Colonial Countries and Peoples (Resolution 1514), stating that by virtue of their right to self-determination, all peoples could "freely determine their political status and freely pursue their economic, social and cultural development." Under these principles, for example, Angola and Mozambique gained their independence from Portugal in 1975.

Collective self-determination has come to imply the rights of the majority to determine their government and development. Today, governments rarely recognize the right to self-determination because in almost all cases it is minority groups who seek it. Indigenous peoples and ethnic minorities—for example in East Timor or in the western Sahara—suffer because of the lack of self-determination, even though the international community acknowledges that many continue to live under colonialism.

Present day struggles for self-determination receive little international legal support even if the moral and political cases are clear. Eritrea, once considered an integral part of the sovereign state of Ethiopia, recently won its independence, but with a dearth of assistance from the international community. Tibetans, whose country has been occupied by China since 1959, fight for self-determination with weak support from only some governments in the UN.

In Australia, the Aboriginal peoples are making small gains in their battle against substandard social and economic conditions and for indigenous ownership of land. The Aboriginal Land Rights Act passed in 1976, giving them inalienable freehold title to Aboriginal reserves in the Northern Territory. Their efforts toward cultural and economic survival and to make their own decisions on land and resources continue.

Critics of the principle of self-determination express concern about the potential creation of a world of states drawn upon ethnically based lines. However, such a fear does not overshadow the reality of human rights violations of dominated peoples and disregard for the principle of self-determination. Whether colonized peoples seek full independence, autonomy, or the restoration of rights over territory, cultural life, and resources, self-determination is considered the base for the enjoyment of all other human rights and fundamental freedoms.

For further information
Twining, William, ed. *Issues in Self-Determination.* Aberdeen: Aberdeen University Press, 1991.
Coombs, H. C. *Aboriginal Autonomy: Issues and Strategies.* Cambridge: Cambridge University Press, 1995.

—Carol Devine

Sexual Minorities

The term "sexual minorities" refers to the concept of sexual orientation—homosexuality, bisexuality, and transexuality. The term may also be interpreted to address certain practices, such as cross-dressing. Human rights issues of concern to sexual minorities vary widely: in some nations, such as the United States, primary concerns include hate crimes, workplace discrimination, and the right to marry. In other nations, sexual minorities struggle for the legal right to simply exist. Although it is estimated that ten to twenty percent of the world's population falls into the category, no UN human rights instrument currently addresses the issue of sexual orientation.

Prior to World War II, issues relating to sexual minorities were virtually not discussed, although homosexuals were among those targeted for extermination by the Nazis. In the last fifty years lesbian and gay human rights organizations have become involved in international human rights law, seeking protection, for example, under Articles 2, 7, and 12 of the Universal Declaration of Human Rights (see Part 2, Chapter 3). Even so, when lesbian and gay organizations were accredited to participate in the UN World Conference on Human Rights in 1993, it was the first time the UN had invited the participation of groups representing sexual minorities.

Around the world, sexual minorities face discrimination in a variety of arenas. In several Asian countries, for example, homosexual sex is illegal and may result in arrest and imprisonment. According to Amnesty International, sentences for Iranian women convicted of lesbianism include "cleaving in two halves lengthwise, pushing off a cliff, or stoning to death." In Zimbabwe a gay rights exhibit was banned from a 1995 book fair in Harare by the government: when there were protests, President Robert Mugabe declared that homosexuals had no rights. In 1997 an official with the African Reformed Church in Zimbabwe called for homosexuals to be publicly flogged, and that same year Amnesty International undertook the cause of Mariana Cetiner, a prisoner of conscience being held in Romania because she was a lesbian.

Sexual minorities in the United States face discrimination as well; numerous states have anti-gay laws on the books, and in a majority of states, employees can be fired because of their sexual orientation. When a popular U.S. television star, Ellen Degeneres, acknowledged her lesbianism, she was denounced by several religious organizations, and some companies withdrew sponsorship of her show. In 1998 the voters of the state of Maine repealed a gay rights law that had been passed by the legislature. Also in 1998 a young student at the University of Wyoming was tortured and murdered because he was gay.

Discrimination against sexual minorities is rarely discussed in international forums. However, in 1994, the UN Commission on Crime Prevention and Criminal Justice recommended the decriminalization of homosexual activities. Also in 1994, in the case of *Toonen v. Australia*, the UN Human Rights Committee found that the prohibition of discrimination on the basis of sex, as contained in the International Covenant on Civil and Political Rights, includes sexual orientation. At the Fourth World Conference on Women in 1995, delegates considered including sexual orientation as a basis of discrimination in the Platform of Action. Although sexual orientation was ultimately not included, the conference marked one of the first protracted discussions of the issue on an international stage. The High Commissioner for Refugees has also held that a "social group," one of the bases for political persecution, includes lesbians and gay men.

Debate over sexual orientation is held on many levels—religious and cultural, as well as international. With such a variety of local regulations affecting sexual minorities, the leadership of the international community becomes especially important. United Nations agencies have begun to recognize discrimination based on sexual orientation, as have nongovernmental organizations such as Amnesty International. Although progress is slow, promising steps have been made in recent years.

For further information
Adam, Barry D., Jan Willem Duyvendak, and Andre Krouwel, eds. *The Global Emergence of Gay and Lesbian Politics: National Imprints of a Worldwide Movement.* Philadelphia: Temple University Press, 1998.
Hendriks, Aart, Rob Tielman, and Evert Vander Veen, eds. *The Third Pink Book: A Global View of Lesbian and Gay Liberation and Oppression.* Amherst, N.Y.: Prometheus Books, 1993.

—Jo Lynn Southard

Slavery

Slavery, the ownership of one person by another, was one of the very first human rights issues to be regulated through international law. In the late twentieth century the definition of slavery has evolved to include a variety of slavery-related practices, including debt bondage, serfdom, child indenture, and marital and sexual bondage.

During the Congress of Vienna in 1815, it was declared that slavery was repugnant to the values of the civilized international community. Since then, numerous instruments as well as national laws have prohibited slavery. In 1926 the Slavery Convention defined slavery as "the status or condition of a person over whom any or all of the powers attaching to the right of ownership are exercised" (Article 1.1). The same convention also prohibits slave trade. Slavery is illegal in every corner of the world. In 1980 Mauritania was the last nation to criminalize the practice, although it should be noted that in recent years Mauritania (along with the Sudan) has come under fierce criticism by the international community for turning a blind eye to the continued existence of slavery.

The slave trade of black Africans to the Americas until the nineteenth century is probably the most evident and dramatic example of slavery, but it is not the only one. For example, "comfort women" used by the Japanese military during World War II were victims of sexual slavery. And in 1998 the UN Commission on Human Rights condemned the enslavement of children, particularly by the Lord's Resistance Army in Northern Uganda (Resolution 1998/75).

The actions undertaken against slavery are manifold. First, they have taken the form of conventions and international agreements. The Universal Declaration of Human Rights states that "[n]o one shall be held in slavery or servitude; slavery and the slave trade shall be prohibited in all their forms." This prohibition is also present in the International Covenant on Civil and Political Rights (Article 8.1), the European Convention for the Protection of Human Rights and Fundamental Freedoms (Article 4), and the American Convention on Human Rights (Article 6). The International Labour Organization has two noteworthy conventions on this subject: the Convention Concerning Forced or Compulsory Labor of 1930 and the Convention Concerning the Abolition of Forced Labor of 1957. More recently, slavery has been included as a crime against humanity and a war crime under the statute of the new International Criminal Court.

The United Nations has undertaken several discussions and studies on the issue, such as the 1982 UN Commission on Human Rights Report of Benjamin Whittaker. Various organs and forums deal specifically with the topic of slavery, such as the Independent Expert on the Sale of Children and the Working Group on Contemporary Forms of Slavery. The Working Group is a good indicator of the important current issues related to slavery. The following topics are under discussion: systematic rape; sexual slavery and slavery-like practices during armed conflict; traffic in persons and exploitation of others; trans-border traffic in women and girls for sexual exploitation; the role of corruption in the perpetuation of slavery and slavery-like practices; misuse of the Internet for the purpose of sexual exploitation; child domestic workers and child labor; debt bondage and bonded labor; and the sale of children for prostitution and pornography.

For further information
Klein, Martin A., ed. *Breaking the Chains: Slavery, Bondage, and Emancipation in Modern Africa and Asia.* Madison, Wis: University of Wisconsin Press, 1993.
Sawyer, Roger. *Children Enslaved.* London: Routledge, 1988.

—Baptiste Rolle

Torture

Torture—the infliction of severe physical and/or psychological pain for purposes such as coercion, punishment, or gaining information—is universally condemned as a violation of fundamental human rights. Numerous, widely accepted international instruments prohibit the practice, including the International Covenant on Civil and Political Rights, the American Convention on Human Rights, the European Convention for the Protection of Human Rights and Fundamental Freedoms, the Geneva Conventions of 1949, and many others.

The use of torture, especially during interrogations, has been widespread, both historically and geographically. Ancient Greeks were known to have tortured their slaves for information, and the practice has continued throughout history—most notably during papal inquisitions, when Pope Innocent IV sanctioned the torturing of heretics in 1252. Torture has been practiced for different purposes—frequently as a method of gathering information or proof, but also as a punishment or as a way of suppressing political opposition—and in different contexts (in times of armed conflict, for example). In the twentieth century torture methods have gone beyond the physical and into the realm of the psychological, including humiliation and threats, sleep deprivation, and the use of pharmacological agents.

Many different mechanisms exist to combat such practices. The United Nations Committee Against Torture, created by the 1984 Convention, has authority to investigate situations that appear to reveal the existence of a systematic practice of torture in a state. One of the challenges ahead for this organ is to clarify the scope of the definition of torture in the 1984 Convention. There is also a possible overlapping between the work of the Committee and the Special Rapporteur on Torture appointed by the UN Commission on Human Rights. There also exists a Working Group on an Optional Protocol to the Convention Against Torture, working to create a preventive system of periodic visits to places of detention. Nongovernmental organizations like Amnesty International and the World Organization Against Torture help focus international attention on violations and offer assistance to victims. Finally, different regional judiciary (the European and Inter-American Courts of Human Rights) or quasi-judiciary organs (the Inter-American Commission on Human Rights and the European Commission on Human Rights) make an important contribution by developing case law in the fields of human rights.

For instance, the European Court of Human Rights declared the combination of five techniques used by the British authorities during the interrogation of persons in Northern Ireland to be torture: forcing detainees to stand for periods of some hours in a "stress position," leaning against a wall; putting black hoods over the detainees' heads at all times except during interrogation; holding detainees pending interrogation in a room where there was a continuous loud hissing noise; depriving detainees of sleep pending interrogation; and subjecting detainees to a reduced diet during the period of detention.

There is still a lot to be done to combat torture. The most recent attempt—and perhaps the most promising—to diminish the abuses has been the adoption, in July 1998, of the Statute of the International Criminal Court at the Rome Conference. In this context, torture is criminalized and can constitute both a crime against humanity (Article 7 of the statute) and a war crime (Article 8). Of course, the fulfillment of this new hope depends largely on what states will do with the newly adopted statute.

For further information
Amnesty International. *Amnesty International Report on Torture.* New York: Farrar, Strauss and Giroux, 1975.
Forrest, Duncan, ed. *A Glimpse of Hell: Reports on Torture Worldwide.* New York: New York University Press, 1996.

—Baptiste Rolle

Traffic in Women and Girls

Traffic in women and girls refers to the practice of abducting, delivering, or selling women and girls across international borders. Most often, they are forced into prostitution; however, the mail-order bride industry and forcible exportation of women and girls to work in foreign countries are also common. The United Nations estimates that four million girls and women are trafficked internationally every year. Human rights activists are concerned not only with the sale of human beings—a blatant human rights violation—but also with the often-abusive treatment of the women and girls after the sale has occurred.

The first international agreement banning the traffic of women for "immoral purposes" went into effect in 1912. In 1950 the Convention for the Suppression of the Traffic in Persons and the Exploitation of the Prostitution of Others came into effect. Both the Convention on the Elimination of All Forms of Discrimination Against Women (1979) and the Convention on the Rights of the Child (1990) forbid trafficking.

Nonetheless, in recent years trafficking in women and girls has increased and become more organized than ever before. A major cause of the expansion of the industry is the growth of sex tourism. Emerging nations rely on tourism to stimulate their economic growth. One of the most lucrative kinds of tourism consists of men from rich nations traveling to poorer nations to take advantage of the sex business, in which young girls are purchased from their families for use as prostitutes. Sexism and racism intertwine to support sex tourism; sexism that devalues women in general and racism that implies that women in certain cultures are more subservient and available than in others.

Another kind of trafficking is the mail-order bride industry. Here, brokers in poor countries recruit women to marry men in richer countries. Although some of these marriages work out, more often they do not. Many of the women who do marry are mistreated by their husbands, again supported by racism and sexism. Often, husbands will abandon their wives after a short period of time, leaving them without money in a strange country, possibly illegally. Or, the broker may in reality be

A prostitute in Bombay, India, waits in a cage for her next customer (CORBIS/The Purcell Team).

procuring women for prostitution, and there never was a husband waiting at all.

Trafficking in women and children is sometimes not for an overtly sexual purpose. Instead, women and children from poor countries are sent to richer nations to work as maids, nannies, and nurses. Often they are sexually abused; if not, they are usually subjected to inhumane working conditions. They may be literally imprisoned in their employer's home, completely isolated and without means of escape. They may be overworked and physically abused by their employers, or the job offers may be, once again, a ruse for obtaining prostitutes.

Women and children are obtained by traffickers in a variety of ways. In impoverished nations, girls may be sold by their parents. In some cases, women and children are kidnapped or, when recruiters misrepresent the jobs available in other countries, the women may volunteer to go.

Currently, a variety of organizations (e.g., Human Rights Watch) are addressing the trafficking issue. Some are encouraging the United Nations to implement treaties that address sexual exploitation as a violation of human rights. Some groups are targeting sex tourism, while others rescue and rehabilitate women and children who have been abused. All are concerned that existing laws be enforced effectively.

For further information
Human Rights Watch. *The Human Rights Watch Global Report on Women's Human Rights.* New York: Human Rights Watch, 1995.
Kempadoo, Kamala, and Jo Doezema, eds. *Global Sex Workers: Rights, Resistance, and Redefinition.* New York and London: Routledge, 1998.

—Jo Lynn Southard

APPENDIX ONE: TIMELINE

Highlights of the History of Human Rights

450 BCE Publication of ancient Roman laws, the Twelve Tables

400 BCE Plato's *Republic*

AD 476 Fall of the western Roman Empire

565 Emperor Justinian I's *Corpus Juris Civilis* (Body of Civil Law)

1215 Magna Carta (Great Britain)

1628 Petition of Right (Great Britain)

1640s English Civil Wars

1679 Habeas Corpus Act (Great Britain)

1688 The Glorious Revolution (Great Britain)

1689 English Bill of Rights

1690 *Two Treatises of Government* by John Locke

1762 *The Social Contract* by Jean Jacques Rousseau

1774 First Continental Congress (United States)

1775–83 American Revolution

1776 Declaration of Independence (United States)

1776 *Common Sense* by Thomas Paine

1789 Declaration of the Rights of Man and of the Citizen (France)

1789 The U.S. Constitution

1789 Revolution of 1789 (France)

1790 *The Declaration of the Rights of Woman and Citizen* by Olympe de Gouges

1791 Bill of Rights (United States)

1792 *A Vindication of the Rights of Women* by Mary Wollestonecraft

1807 Great Britain abolishes the slave trade

1848 The Declaration of Sentiments sets the agenda for the U.S. women's movement

1848 *Communist Manifesto* by Karl Marx and Friedrich Engels

1863 The Emancipation Proclamation (United States)

1869 *The Subjection of Women* by John Stuart Mill

1914–19 World War I

1917 Declaration of the Rights of the People of Russia

1917 Russian Revolution

1919 Paris Peace Conference ends World War I

1919 International Labor Organization founded

1920 American Civil Liberties Union founded

1920 U.S. women win the right to vote

1920 Opening session of the League of Nations

1927 Slavery Convention (League of Nations)

1939–45 World War II

1941 President Roosevelt gives the "Four Freedoms" address

1942 Declaration of the United Nations

1942 The Atlantic Charter

1945 Charter of the United Nations

1945–46 The Nuremberg Trials

1946–48 The Tokyo Trials

1948 Universal Declaration on Human Rights (United Nations)

1948 Convention on the Prevention and Punishment of the Crime of Genocide (United Nations)

1948 Charter of the Organization of American States

1949 Geneva Conventions

1951 Refugee Convention (United Nations)

1953 European Commission on Human Rights founded

1959 Declaration of the Rights of the Child (United Nations)

1961 Amnesty International founded

1963 Declaration on the Elimination of All Forms of Racial Discrimination (United Nations)

1963 Organization of African Unity founded

1966	United Nations adopts the International Covenant on Civil and Political Rights and the International Covenant on Economic, Social, and Cultural Rights
1967	Declaration on the Elimination of Discrimination against Women (United Nations)
1969	American Convention on Human Rights
1969	Convention on the Elimination of All Forms of Racial Discrimination (United Nations)
1973	International Convention on the Suppression and Punishment of the Crime of Apartheid (United Nations)
1974	United Nations establishes the Working Group on Contemporary Forms of Slavery
1975	Declaration on the Protection of All Persons From Being Subjected to Torture and Other Cruel, Inhuman, or Degrading Treatment or Punishment (United Nations)
1975	Helsinki Accords
1979	Convention on the Elimination of All Forms of Discrimination Against Women (United Nations)
1981	African Charter on Human and People's Rights
1981	Declaration on the Elimination of All Forms of Intolerance and of Discrimination Based on Religion or Belief (United Nations)
1985	United Nations Standard Minimum Rules for the Administration of Juvenile Justice ("The Beijing Rules")
1986	Declaration on the Right to Development (United Nations)
1989	European Torture Convention
1989	Convention on the Rights of the Child (United Nations)
1990	Americans With Disabilities Act
1991	Dissolution of the Union of Soviet Socialist Republics
1992	Declaration on the Protection of All Persons from Enforced Disappearance (United Nations)
1993	UN Security Council establishes the International Criminal Tribunal for the former Yugoslavia
1993	United Nations establishes the Office of the High Commissioner for Human Rights
1994	UN Security Council establishes the International Criminal Tribunal for Rwanda
1995–2000	Decade of Human Rights Education declared by the United Nations.
1998	The International Treaty Conference convenes in Rome to work toward the establishment of an International Criminal Court

APPENDIX TWO:
UNITED NATIONS DOCUMENTS

Contents

Universal Declaration of Human Rights   277

International Covenant on Civil and Political Rights   279

International Covenant on Economic, Social, and Cultural Rights 285

Declaration of the Rights of the Child   289

Declaration on the Elimination of All Forms of Racial Discrimination   290

Declaration on the Elimination of Discrimination against Women   291

Declaration on the Protection of All Persons from Being Subjected to Torture and Other Cruel, Inhuman, or Degrading Treatment or Punishment   293

Declaration on the Elimination of All Forms of Intolerance and of Discrimination Based on Religion or Belief   293

For more human rights instruments, please consult the United Nations Public Information Office, or www.un.org. All documents copyright Office of the United Nations High Commissioner for Human Rights, Geneva, Switzerland.

Universal Declaration of Human Rights

Adopted and proclaimed by General Assembly resolution 217 A (III) of December 10, 1948.

Preamble

Whereas recognition of the inherent dignity and of the equal and inalienable rights of all members of the human family is the foundation of freedom, justice and peace in the world,

Whereas disregard and contempt for human rights have resulted in barbarous acts which have outraged the conscience of mankind, and the advent of a world in which human beings shall enjoy freedom of speech and belief and freedom from fear and want has been proclaimed as the highest aspiration of the common people,

Whereas it is essential, if man is not to be compelled to have recourse, as a last resort, to rebellion against tyranny and oppression, that human rights should be protected by the rule of law,

Whereas it is essential to promote the development of friendly relations between nations,

Whereas the peoples of the United Nations have in the Charter reaffirmed their faith in fundamental human rights, in the dignity and worth of the human person and in the equal rights of men and women and have determined to promote social progress and better standards of life in larger freedom,

Whereas Member States have pledged themselves to achieve, in cooperation with the United Nations, the promotion of universal respect for and observance of human rights and fundamental freedoms,

Whereas a common understanding of these rights and freedoms is of the greatest importance for the full realization of this pledge,

Now, therefore,

The General Assembly,

Proclaims this Universal Declaration of Human Rights as a common standard of achievement for all peoples and all nations, to the end that every individual and every organ of society, keeping this Declaration constantly in mind, shall strive by teaching and education to promote respect for these rights and freedoms and by progressive measures, national and international, to secure their universal and effective recognition and observance, both among the peoples of Member States themselves and among the peoples of territories under their jurisdiction.

Article 1

All human beings are born free and equal in dignity and rights. They are endowed with reason and conscience and should act towards one another in a spirit of brotherhood.

Article 2

Everyone is entitled to all the rights and freedoms set forth in this Declaration, without distinction of any kind, such as race, color, sex, language, religion, political or other opinion, national or social origin, property, birth or other status.

Furthermore, no distinction shall be made on the basis of the political, jurisdictional or international status of the country or territory to which a person belongs, whether it be independent, trust, non-self-governing or under any other limitation of sovereignty.

Article 3

Everyone has the right to life, liberty and security of person.

Article 4

No one shall be held in slavery or servitude; slavery and the slave trade shall be prohibited in all their forms.

Article 5

No one shall be subjected to torture or to cruel, inhuman or degrading treatment or punishment.

Article 6

Everyone has the right to recognition everywhere as a person before the law.

Article 7

All are equal before the law and are entitled without any discrimination to equal protection of the law. All are entitled to equal protection against any discrimination in violation of this Declaration and against any incitement to such discrimination.

Article 8

Everyone has the right to an effective remedy by the competent national tribunals for acts violating the fundamental rights granted him by the constitution or by law.

Article 9

No one shall be subjected to arbitrary arrest, detention or exile.

Article 10

Everyone is entitled in full equality to a fair and public hearing by an independent and impartial tribunal, in the determination of his rights and obligations and of any criminal charge against him.

Article 11

Everyone charged with a penal offense has the right to be presumed innocent until proved guilty according to law in a public trial at which he has had all the guarantees necessary for his defense.

No one shall be held guilty of any penal offense on account of any act or omission which did not constitute a penal offense, under national or international law, at the time when it was committed. Nor shall a heavier penalty be imposed than the one that was applicable at the time the penal offense was committed.

Article 12

No one shall be subjected to arbitrary interference with his privacy, family, home or correspondence, nor to attacks upon his honor and reputation. Everyone has the right to the protection of the law against such interference or attacks.

Article 13

Everyone has the right to freedom of movement and residence within the borders of each State.

Everyone has the right to leave any country, including his own, and to return to his country.

Article 14

Everyone has the right to seek and to enjoy in other countries asylum from persecution.

This right may not be invoked in the case of prosecutions genuinely arising from non-political crimes or from acts contrary to the purposes and principles of the United Nations.

Article 15

Everyone has the right to a nationality.

No one shall be arbitrarily deprived of his nationality nor denied the right to change his nationality.

Article 16

Men and women of full age, without any limitation due to race, nationality or religion, have the right to marry and to found a family. They are entitled to equal rights as to marriage, during marriage and at its dissolution.

Marriage shall be entered into only with the free and full consent of the intending spouses.

The family is the natural and fundamental group unit of society and is entitled to protection by society and the State.

Article 17

Everyone has the right to own property alone as well as in association with others.

No one shall be arbitrarily deprived of his property.

Article 18

Everyone has the right to freedom of thought, conscience and religion; this right includes freedom to change his religion or belief, and freedom, either alone or in community with others and in public or private, to manifest his religion or belief in teaching, practice, worship and observance.

Article 19

Everyone has the right to freedom of opinion and expression; this right includes freedom to hold opinions without interference and to seek, receive and impart information and ideas through any media and regardless of frontiers.

Article 20

Everyone has the right to freedom of peaceful assembly and association.

No one may be compelled to belong to an association.

Article 21

Everyone has the right to take part in the government of his country, directly or through freely chosen representatives.

Everyone has the right to equal access to public service in his country.

The will of the people shall be the basis of the authority of government; this will shall be expressed in periodic and genuine elections which shall be by universal and equal suffrage and shall be held by secret vote or by equivalent free voting procedures.

Article 22

Everyone, as a member of society, has the right to social security and is entitled to realization, through national effort and international co-operation and in accordance with the organization and resources of each State, of the economic, social and cultural rights indispensable for his dignity and the free development of his personality.

Article 23

Everyone has the right to work, to free choice of employment, to just and favorable conditions of work and to protection against unemployment.

Everyone, without any discrimination, has the right to equal pay for equal work.

Everyone who works has the right to just and favorable remuneration ensuring for himself and his family an existence worthy of human dignity, and supplemented, if necessary, by other means of social protection.

Everyone has the right to form and to join trade unions for the protection of his interests.

Article 24

Everyone has the right to rest and leisure, including reasonable limitation of working hours and periodic holidays with pay.

Article 25

Everyone has the right to a standard of living adequate for the health and well-being of himself and of his family, including food, clothing, housing and medical care and necessary social services, and the right to security in the event of unem-

ployment, sickness, disability, widowhood, old age or other lack of livelihood in circumstances beyond his control.

Motherhood and childhood are entitled to special care and assistance. All children, whether born in or out of wedlock, shall enjoy the same social protection.

Article 26

Everyone has the right to education. Education shall be free, at least in the elementary and fundamental stages. Elementary education shall be compulsory. Technical and professional education shall be made generally available and higher education shall be equally accessible to all on the basis of merit.

Education shall be directed to the full development of the human personality and to the strengthening of respect for human rights and fundamental freedoms. It shall promote understanding, tolerance and friendship among all nations, racial or religious groups, and shall further the activities of the United Nations for the maintenance of peace.

Parents have a prior right to choose the kind of education that shall be given to their children.

Article 27

Everyone has the right freely to participate in the cultural life of the community, to enjoy the arts and to share in scientific advancement and its benefits.

Everyone has the right to the protection of the moral and material interests resulting from any scientific, literary or artistic production of which he is the author.

Article 28

Everyone is entitled to a social and international order in which the rights and freedoms set forth in this Declaration can be fully realized.

Article 29

Everyone has duties to the community in which alone the free and full development of his personality is possible.

In the exercise of his rights and freedoms, everyone shall be subject only to such limitations as are determined by law solely for the purpose of securing due recognition and respect for the rights and freedoms of others and of meeting the just requirements of morality, public order and the general welfare in a democratic society.

These rights and freedoms may in no case be exercised contrary to the purposes and principles of the United Nations.

Article 30

Nothing in this Declaration may be interpreted as implying for any State, group or person any right to engage in any activity or to perform any act aimed at the destruction of any of the rights and freedoms set forth herein.

International Covenant on Civil and Political Rights

Adopted and opened for signature, ratification and accession by General Assembly resolution 2200A (XXI) of December 16, 1966. Entry into force March 23, 1976, in accordance with Article 49.

Preamble

The States Parties to the present Covenant,

Considering that, in accordance with the principles proclaimed in the Charter of the United Nations, recognition of the inherent dignity and of the equal and inalienable rights of all members of the human family is the foundation of freedom, justice and peace in the world,

Recognizing that these rights derive from the inherent dignity of the human person,

Recognizing that, in accordance with the Universal Declaration of Human Rights, the ideal of free human beings enjoying civil and political freedom and freedom from fear and want can only be achieved if conditions are created whereby everyone may enjoy his civil and political rights, as well as his economic, social and cultural rights,

Considering the obligation of States under the Charter of the United Nations to promote universal respect for, and observance of, human rights and freedoms,

Realizing that the individual, having duties to other individuals and to the community to which he belongs, is under a responsibility to strive for the promotion and observance of the rights recognized in the present Covenant,

Agree upon the following articles:

PART I

Article 1

1. All peoples have the right of self-determination. By virtue of that right they freely determine their political status and freely pursue their economic, social and cultural development.

2. All peoples may, for their own ends, freely dispose of their natural wealth and resources without prejudice to any obligations arising out of international economic co-operation, based upon the principle of mutual benefit, and international law. In no case may a people be deprived of its own means of subsistence.

3. The States Parties to the present Covenant, including those having responsibility for the administration of Non-Self-Governing and Trust Territories, shall promote the realization of the right of self-determination, and shall respect that right, in conformity with the provisions of the Charter of the United Nations.

PART II

Article 2

1. Each State Party to the present Covenant undertakes to respect and to ensure to all individuals within its territory and subject to its jurisdiction the rights recognized in the present Covenant, without distinction of any kind, such as race, color, sex, language, religion, political or other opinion, national or social origin, property, birth or other status.

2. Where not already provided for by existing legislative or other measures, each State Party to the present Covenant undertakes to take the necessary steps, in accordance with its constitutional processes and with the provisions of the present Covenant, to adopt such laws or other measures as may be necessary to give effect to the rights recognized in the present Covenant.

3. Each State Party to the present Covenant undertakes:

(a) To ensure that any person whose rights or freedoms as herein recognized are violated shall have an effective remedy, notwithstanding that the violation has been committed by persons acting in an official capacity;

(b) To ensure that any person claiming such a remedy shall have his right thereto determined by competent judicial, administrative or legislative authorities, or by any other competent authority provided for by the legal system of the State, and to develop the possibilities of judicial remedy;

(c) To ensure that the competent authorities shall enforce such remedies when granted.

Article 3

The States Parties to the present Covenant undertake to ensure the equal right of men and women to the enjoyment of all civil and political rights set forth in the present Covenant.

Article 4

1. In time of public emergency which threatens the life of the nation and the existence of which is officially proclaimed, the States Parties to the present Covenant may take measures

derogating from their obligations under the present Covenant to the extent strictly required by the exigencies of the situation, provided that such measures are not inconsistent with their other obligations under international law and do not involve discrimination solely on the ground of race, color, sex, language, religion or social origin.

2. No derogation from articles 6, 7, 8 (paragraphs 1 and 2), 11, 15, 16 and 18 may be made under this provision.

3. Any State Party to the present Covenant availing itself of the right of derogation shall immediately inform the other States Parties to the present Covenant, through the intermediary of the Secretary-General of the United Nations, of the provisions from which it has derogated and of the reasons by which it was actuated. A further communication shall be made, through the same intermediary, on the date on which it terminates such derogation.

Article 5

1. Nothing in the present Covenant may be interpreted as implying for any State, group or person any right to engage in any activity or perform any act aimed at the destruction of any of the rights and freedoms recognized herein or at their limitation to a greater extent than is provided for in the present Covenant.

2. There shall be no restriction upon or derogation from any of the fundamental human rights recognized or existing in any State Party to the present Covenant pursuant to law, conventions, regulations or custom on the pretext that the present Covenant does not recognize such rights or that it recognizes them to a lesser extent.

PART III

Article 6

1. Every human being has the inherent right to life. This right shall be protected by law. No one shall be arbitrarily deprived of his life.

2. In countries which have not abolished the death penalty, sentence of death may be imposed only for the most serious crimes in accordance with the law in force at the time of the commission of the crime and not contrary to the provisions of the present Covenant and to the Convention on the Prevention and Punishment of the Crime of Genocide. This penalty can only be carried out pursuant to a final judgement rendered by a competent court.

3. When deprivation of life constitutes the crime of genocide, it is understood that nothing in this article shall authorize any State Party to the present Covenant to derogate in any way from any obligation assumed under the provisions of the Convention on the Prevention and Punishment of the Crime of Genocide.

4. Anyone sentenced to death shall have the right to seek pardon or commutation of the sentence. Amnesty, pardon or commutation of the sentence of death may be granted in all cases.

5. Sentence of death shall not be imposed for crimes committed by persons below eighteen years of age and shall not be carried out on pregnant women.

6. Nothing in this article shall be invoked to delay or to prevent the abolition of capital punishment by any State Party to the present Covenant.

Article 7

No one shall be subjected to torture or to cruel, inhuman or degrading treatment or punishment. In particular, no one shall be subjected without his free consent to medical or scientific experimentation.

Article 8

1. No one shall be held in slavery; slavery and the slave-trade in all their forms shall be prohibited.

2. No one shall be held in servitude.

3. (a) No one shall be required to perform forced or compulsory labor;

(b) Paragraph 3 (a) shall not be held to preclude, in countries where imprisonment with hard labor may be imposed as a punishment for a crime, the performance of hard labor in pursuance of a sentence to such punishment by a competent court;

(c) For the purpose of this paragraph the term "forced or compulsory labor" shall not include:

(i) Any work or service, not referred to in subparagraph (b), normally required of a person who is under detention in consequence of a lawful order of a court, or of a person during conditional release from such detention;

(ii) Any service of a military character and, in countries where conscientious objection is recognized, any national service required by law of conscientious objectors;

(iii) Any service exacted in cases of emergency or calamity threatening the life or well-being of the community;

(iv) Any work or service which forms part of normal civil obligations.

Article 9

1. Everyone has the right to liberty and security of person. No one shall be subjected to arbitrary arrest or detention. No one shall be deprived of his liberty except on such grounds and in accordance with such procedure as are established by law.

2. Anyone who is arrested shall be informed, at the time of arrest, of the reasons for his arrest and shall be promptly informed of any charges against him.

3. Anyone arrested or detained on a criminal charge shall be brought promptly before a judge or other officer authorized by law to exercise judicial power and shall be entitled to trial within a reasonable time or to release. It shall not be the general rule that persons awaiting trial shall be detained in custody, but release may be subject to guarantees to appear for trial, at any other stage of the judicial proceedings, and, should occasion arise, for execution of the judgement.

4. Anyone who is deprived of his liberty by arrest or detention shall be entitled to take proceedings before a court, in order that court may decide without delay on the lawfulness of his detention and order his release if the detention is not lawful.

5. Anyone who has been the victim of unlawful arrest or detention shall have an enforceable right to compensation.

Article 10

1. All persons deprived of their liberty shall be treated with humanity and with respect for the inherent dignity of the human person.

2. (a) Accused persons shall, save in exceptional circumstances, be segregated from convicted persons and shall be subject to separate treatment appropriate to their status as unconvicted persons;

(b) Accused juvenile persons shall be separated from adults and brought as speedily as possible for adjudication. 3. The penitentiary system shall comprise treatment of prisoners the essential aim of which shall be their reformation and social rehabilitation. Juvenile offenders shall be segregated from adults and be accorded treatment appropriate to their age and legal status.

Article 11

No one shall be imprisoned merely on the ground of inability to fulfill a contractual obligation.

Article 12

1. Everyone lawfully within the territory of a State shall, within that territory, have the right to liberty of movement and freedom to choose his residence.

2. Everyone shall be free to leave any country, including his own.

3. The above-mentioned rights shall not be subject to any restrictions except those which are provided by law, are necessary to protect national security, public order (ordre public), public health or morals or the rights and freedoms of others, and are consistent with the other rights recognized in the present Covenant.

4. No one shall be arbitrarily deprived of the right to enter his own country.

Article 13

An alien lawfully in the territory of a State Party to the present Covenant may be expelled therefrom only in pursuance of a decision reached in accordance with law and shall, except where compelling reasons of national security otherwise require, be allowed to submit the reasons against his expulsion and to have his case reviewed by, and be represented for the purpose before, the competent authority or a person or persons especially designated by the competent authority.

Article 14

1. All persons shall be equal before the courts and tribunals. In the determination of any criminal charge against him, or of his rights and obligations in a suit at law, everyone shall be entitled to a fair and public hearing by a competent, independent and impartial tribunal established by law. The press and the public may be excluded from all or part of a trial for reasons of morals, public order (ordre public) or national security in a democratic society, or when the interest of the private lives of the parties so requires, or to the extent strictly necessary in the opinion of the court in special circumstances where publicity would prejudice the interests of justice; but any judgement rendered in a criminal case or in a suit at law shall be made public except where the interest of juvenile persons otherwise requires or the proceedings concern matrimonial disputes or the guardianship of children.

2. Everyone charged with a criminal offense shall have the right to be presumed innocent until proved guilty according to law.

3. In the determination of any criminal charge against him, everyone shall be entitled to the following minimum guarantees, in full equality:

(a) To be informed promptly and in detail in a language which he understands of the nature and cause of the charge against him;

(b) To have adequate time and facilities for the preparation of his defense and to communicate with counsel of his own choosing;

(c) To be tried without undue delay;

(d) To be tried in his presence, and to defend himself in person or through legal assistance of his own choosing; to be informed, if he does not have legal assistance, of this right; and to have legal assistance assigned to him, in any case where the interests of justice so require, and without payment by him in any such case if he does not have sufficient means to pay for it;

(e) To examine, or have examined, the witnesses against him and to obtain the attendance and examination of witnesses on his behalf under the same conditions as witnesses against him;

(f) To have the free assistance of an interpreter if he cannot understand or speak the language used in court;

(g) Not to be compelled to testify against himself or to confess guilt.

4. In the case of juvenile persons, the procedure shall be such as will take account of their age and the desirability of promoting their rehabilitation.

5. Everyone convicted of a crime shall have the right to his conviction and sentence being reviewed by a higher tribunal according to law.

6. When a person has by a final decision been convicted of a criminal offense and when subsequently his conviction has been reversed or he has been pardoned on the ground that a new or newly discovered fact shows conclusively that there has been a miscarriage of justice, the person who has suffered punishment as a result of such conviction shall be compensated according to law, unless it is proved that the non-disclosure of the unknown fact in time is wholly or partly attributable to him.

7. No one shall be liable to be tried or punished again for an offense for which he has already been finally convicted or acquitted in accordance with the law and penal procedure of each country.

Article 15

1. No one shall be held guilty of any criminal offense on account of any act or omission which did not constitute a criminal offense, under national or international law, at the time when it was committed. Nor shall a heavier penalty be imposed than the one that was applicable at the time when the criminal offense was committed. If, subsequent to the commission of the offense, provision is made by law for the imposition of the lighter penalty, the offender shall benefit thereby.

2. Nothing in this article shall prejudice the trial and punishment of any person for any act or omission which, at the time when it was committed, was criminal according to the general principles of law recognized by the community of nations.

Article 16

Everyone shall have the right to recognition everywhere as a person before the law.

Article 17

1. No one shall be subjected to arbitrary or unlawful interference with his privacy, family, home or correspondence, nor to unlawful attacks on his honor and reputation.

2. Everyone has the right to the protection of the law against such interference or attacks.

Article 18

1. Everyone shall have the right to freedom of thought, conscience and religion. This right shall include freedom to have or to adopt a religion or belief of his choice, and freedom, either individually or in community with others and in public or private, to manifest his religion or belief in worship, observance, practice and teaching.

2. No one shall be subject to coercion which would impair his freedom to have or to adopt a religion or belief of his choice.

3. Freedom to manifest one's religion or beliefs may be subject only to such limitations as are prescribed by law and are necessary to protect public safety, order, health, or morals or the fundamental rights and freedoms of others. 4. The States Parties to the present Covenant undertake to have respect for the liberty of parents and, when applicable, legal guardians to ensure the religious and moral education of their children in conformity with their own convictions.

Article 19

1. Everyone shall have the right to hold opinions without interference.

2. Everyone shall have the right to freedom of expression; this right shall include freedom to seek, receive and impart information and ideas of all kinds, regardless of frontiers, either orally, in writing or in print, in the form of art, or through any other media of his choice.

3. The exercise of the rights provided for in paragraph 2 of this article carries with it special duties and responsibilities. It may therefore be subject to certain restrictions, but these shall only be such as are provided by law and are necessary:

(a) For respect of the rights or reputations of others;

(b) For the protection of national security or of public order (ordre public), or of public health or morals.

Article 20

1. Any propaganda for war shall be prohibited by law.

2. Any advocacy of national, racial or religious hatred that constitutes incitement to discrimination, hostility or violence shall be prohibited by law.

Article 21

The right of peaceful assembly shall be recognized. No restrictions may be placed on the exercise of this right other than those imposed in conformity with the law and which are necessary in a democratic society in the interests of national security or public safety, public order (ordre public), the protection of public health or morals or the protection of the rights and freedoms of others.

Article 22

1. Everyone shall have the right to freedom of association with others, including the right to form and join trade unions for the protection of his interests.

2. No restrictions may be placed on the exercise of this right other than those which are prescribed by law and which are necessary in a democratic society in the interests of national security or public safety, public order (ordre public), the protection of public health or morals or the protection of the rights and freedoms of others. This article shall not prevent the imposition of lawful restrictions on members of the armed forces and of the police in their exercise of this right.

3. Nothing in this article shall authorize States Parties to the International Labor Organization Convention of 1948 concerning Freedom of Association and Protection of the Right to Organize to take legislative measures which would prejudice, or to apply the law in such a manner as to prejudice, the guarantees provided for in that Convention.

Article 23

1. The family is the natural and fundamental group unit of society and is entitled to protection by society and the State.

2. The right of men and women of marriageable age to marry and to found a family shall be recognized.

3. No marriage shall be entered into without the free and full consent of the intending spouses.

4. States Parties to the present Covenant shall take appropriate steps to ensure equality of rights and responsibilities of spouses as to marriage, during marriage and at its dissolution. In the case of dissolution, provision shall be made for the necessary protection of any children.

Article 24

1. Every child shall have, without any discrimination as to race, color, sex, language, religion, national or social origin, property or birth, the right to such measures of protection as are required by his status as a minor, on the part of his family, society and the State.

2. Every child shall be registered immediately after birth and shall have a name.

3. Every child has the right to acquire a nationality.

Article 25

Every citizen shall have the right and the opportunity, without any of the distinctions mentioned in article 2 and without unreasonable restrictions:

(a) To take part in the conduct of public affairs, directly or through freely chosen representatives;

(b) To vote and to be elected at genuine periodic elections which shall be by universal and equal suffrage and shall be held by secret ballot, guaranteeing the free expression of the will of the electors;

(c) To have access, on general terms of equality, to public service in his country.

Article 26

All persons are equal before the law and are entitled without any discrimination to the equal protection of the law. In this respect, the law shall prohibit any discrimination and guarantee to all persons equal and effective protection against discrimination on any ground such as race, color, sex, language, religion, political or other opinion, national or social origin, property, birth or other status.

Article 27

In those States in which ethnic, religious or linguistic minorities exist, persons belonging to such minorities shall not be denied the right, in community with the other members of their group, to enjoy their own culture, to profess and practice their own religion, or to use their own language.

PART IV

Article 28

1. There shall be established a Human Rights Committee (hereafter referred to in the present Covenant as the Committee). It shall consist of eighteen members and shall carry out the functions hereinafter provided.

2. The Committee shall be composed of nationals of the States Parties to the present Covenant who shall be persons of high moral character and recognized competence in the field of human rights, consideration being given to the usefulness of the participation of some persons having legal experience.

3. The members of the Committee shall be elected and shall serve in their personal capacity.

Article 29

1. The members of the Committee shall be elected by secret ballot from a list of persons possessing the qualifications prescribed in article 28 and nominated for the purpose by the States Parties to the present Covenant.

2. Each State Party to the present Covenant may nominate not more than two persons. These persons shall be nationals of the nominating State.

3. A person shall be eligible for renomination.

Article 30

1. The initial election shall be held no later than six months after the date of the entry into force of the present Covenant.

2. At least four months before the date of each election to the Committee, other than an election to fill a vacancy declared in accordance with article 34, the Secretary-General of the United Nations shall address a written invitation to the States Parties to the present Covenant to submit their nominations for membership of the Committee within three months.

3. The Secretary-General of the United Nations shall prepare a list in alphabetical order of all the persons thus nominated, with an indication of the States Parties which have nominated them, and shall submit it to the States Parties to the present Covenant no later than one month before the date of each election.

4. Elections of the members of the Committee shall be held at a meeting of the States Parties to the present Covenant convened by the Secretary General of the United Nations at the Headquarters of the United Nations. At that meeting, for which two thirds of the States Parties to the present Covenant

shall constitute a quorum, the persons elected to the Committee shall be those nominees who obtain the largest number of votes and an absolute majority of the votes of the representatives of States Parties present and voting.

Article 31

1. The Committee may not include more than one national of the same State.

2. In the election of the Committee, consideration shall be given to equitable geographical distribution of membership and to the representation of the different forms of civilization and of the principal legal systems.

Article 32

1. The members of the Committee shall be elected for a term of four years. They shall be eligible for re-election if renominated. However, the terms of nine of the members elected at the first election shall expire at the end of two years; immediately after the first election, the names of these nine members shall be chosen by lot by the Chairman of the meeting referred to in article 30, paragraph 4.

2. Elections at the expiry of office shall be held in accordance with the preceding articles of this part of the present Covenant.

Article 33

1. If, in the unanimous opinion of the other members, a member of the Committee has ceased to carry out his functions for any cause other than absence of a temporary character, the Chairman of the Committee shall notify the Secretary-General of the United Nations, who shall then declare the seat of that member to be vacant.

2. In the event of the death or the resignation of a member of the Committee, the Chairman shall immediately notify the Secretary-General of the United Nations, who shall declare the seat vacant from the date of death or the date on which the resignation takes effect.

Article 34

1. When a vacancy is declared in accordance with article 33 and if the term of office of the member to be replaced does not expire within six months of the declaration of the vacancy, the Secretary-General of the United Nations shall notify each of the States Parties to the present Covenant, which may within two months submit nominations in accordance with article 29 for the purpose of filling the vacancy.

2. The Secretary-General of the United Nations shall prepare a list in alphabetical order of the persons thus nominated and shall submit it to the States Parties to the present Covenant. The election to fill the vacancy shall then take place in accordance with the relevant provisions of this part of the present Covenant.

3. A member of the Committee elected to fill a vacancy declared in accordance with article 33 shall hold office for the remainder of the term of the member who vacated the seat on the Committee under the provisions of that article.

Article 35

The members of the Committee shall, with the approval of the General Assembly of the United Nations, receive emoluments from United Nations resources on such terms and conditions as the General Assembly may decide, having regard to the importance of the Committee's responsibilities.

Article 36

The Secretary-General of the United Nations shall provide the necessary staff and facilities for the effective performance of the functions of the Committee under the present Covenant.

Article 37

1. The Secretary-General of the United Nations shall convene the initial meeting of the Committee at the Headquarters of the United Nations.

2. After its initial meeting, the Committee shall meet at such times as shall be provided in its rules of procedure.

3. The Committee shall normally meet at the Headquarters of the United Nations or at the United Nations Office at Geneva.

Article 38

Every member of the Committee shall, before taking up his duties, make a solemn declaration in open committee that he will perform his functions impartially and conscientiously.

Article 39

1. The Committee shall elect its officers for a term of two years. They may be re-elected.

2. The Committee shall establish its own rules of procedure, but these rules shall provide, inter alia, that:

(a) Twelve members shall constitute a quorum;

(b) Decisions of the Committee shall be made by a majority vote of the members present.

Article 40

1. The States Parties to the present Covenant undertake to submit reports on the measures they have adopted which give effect to the rights recognized herein and on the progress made in the enjoyment of those rights:

(a) Within one year of the entry into force of the present Covenant for the States Parties concerned;

(b) Thereafter whenever the Committee so requests.

2. All reports shall be submitted to the Secretary-General of the United Nations, who shall transmit them to the Committee for consideration. Reports shall indicate the factors and difficulties, if any, affecting the implementation of the present Covenant.

3. The Secretary-General of the United Nations may, after consultation with the Committee, transmit to the specialized agencies concerned copies of such parts of the reports as may fall within their field of competence.

4. The Committee shall study the reports submitted by the States Parties to the present Covenant. It shall transmit its reports, and such general comments as it may consider appropriate, to the States Parties. The Committee may also transmit to the Economic and Social Council these comments along with the copies of the reports it has received from States Parties to the present Covenant.

5. The States Parties to the present Covenant may submit to the Committee observations on any comments that may be made in accordance with paragraph 4 of this article.

Article 41

1. A State Party to the present Covenant may at any time declare under this article that it recognizes the competence of the Committee to receive and consider communications to the effect that a State Party claims that another State Party is not fulfilling its obligations under the present Covenant. Communications under this article may be received and considered only if submitted by a State Party which has made a declaration recognizing in regard to itself the competence of the Committee. No communication shall be received by the Committee if it concerns a State Party which has not made such a declaration. Communications received under this article shall be dealt with in accordance with the following procedure:

(a) If a State Party to the present Covenant considers that another State Party is not giving effect to the provisions of the present Covenant, it may, by written communication, bring the matter to the attention of that State Party. Within three months after the receipt of the communication the receiving State shall afford the State which sent the communication an explanation, or any other statement in writing clarifying the matter which should include, to the extent possible and pertinent, reference to domestic procedures and remedies taken, pending, or available in the matter;

(b) If the matter is not adjusted to the satisfaction of both States Parties concerned within six months after the receipt by the receiving State of the initial communication, either State shall have the right to refer the matter to the Committee, by notice given to the Committee and to the other State;

(c) The Committee shall deal with a matter referred to it only after it has ascertained that all available domestic remedies have been invoked and exhausted in the matter, in conformity with the generally recognized principles of international law. This shall not be the rule where the application of the remedies is unreasonably prolonged;

(d) The Committee shall hold closed meetings when examining communications under this article;

(e) Subject to the provisions of subparagraph (c), the Committee shall make available its good offices to the States Parties concerned with a view to a friendly solution of the matter on the basis of respect for human rights and fundamental freedoms as recognized in the present Covenant;

(f) In any matter referred to it, the Committee may call upon the States Parties concerned, referred to in subparagraph (b), to supply any relevant information;

(g) The States Parties concerned, referred to in subparagraph (b), shall have the right to be represented when the matter is being considered in the Committee and to make submissions orally and/or in writing;

(h) The Committee shall, within twelve months after the date of receipt of notice under subparagraph (b), submit a report:

(i) If a solution within the terms of subparagraph (e) is reached, the Committee shall confine its report to a brief statement of the facts and of the solution reached;

(ii) If a solution within the terms of subparagraph (e) is not reached, the Committee shall confine its report to a brief statement of the facts; the written submissions and record of the oral submissions made by the States Parties concerned shall be attached to the report. In every matter, the report shall be communicated to the States Parties concerned.

2. The provisions of this article shall come into force when ten States Parties to the present Covenant have made declarations under paragraph 1 of this article. Such declarations shall be deposited by the States Parties with the Secretary-General of the United Nations, who shall transmit copies thereof to the other States Parties. A declaration may be withdrawn at any time by notification to the Secretary-General. Such a withdrawal shall not prejudice the consideration of any matter which is the subject of a communication already transmitted under this article; no further communication by any State Party shall be received after the notification of withdrawal of the declaration has been received by the Secretary-General, unless the State Party concerned has made a new declaration.

Article 42

1. (a) If a matter referred to the Committee in accordance with article 41 is not resolved to the satisfaction of the States Parties concerned, the Committee may, with the prior consent of the States Parties concerned, appoint an ad hoc Conciliation Commission (hereinafter referred to as the Commission). The good offices of the Commission shall be made available to the States Parties concerned with a view to an amicable solution of the matter on the basis of respect for the present Covenant;

(b) The Commission shall consist of five persons acceptable to the States Parties concerned. If the States Parties concerned fail to reach agreement within three months on all or part of the composition of the Commission, the members of the Commission concerning whom no agreement has been reached shall be elected by secret ballot by a two-thirds majority vote of the Committee from among its members.

2. The members of the Commission shall serve in their personal capacity. They shall not be nationals of the States Parties concerned, or of a State not Party to the present Covenant, or of a State Party which has not made a declaration under article 41.

3. The Commission shall elect its own Chairman and adopt its own rules of procedure.

4. The meetings of the Commission shall normally be held at the Headquarters of the United Nations or at the United Nations Office at Geneva. However, they may be held at such other convenient places as the Commission may determine in consultation with the Secretary-General of the United Nations and the States Parties concerned.

5. The secretariat provided in accordance with article 36 shall also service the commissions appointed under this article.

6. The information received and collated by the Committee shall be made available to the Commission and the Commission may call upon the States Parties concerned to supply any other relevant information.

7. When the Commission has fully considered the matter, but in any event not later than twelve months after having been seized of the matter, it shall submit to the Chairman of the Committee a report for communication to the States Parties concerned:

(a) If the Commission is unable to complete its consideration of the matter within twelve months, it shall confine its report to a brief statement of the status of its consideration of the matter;

(b) If an amicable solution to the matter on tie basis of respect for human rights as recognized in the present Covenant is reached, the Commission shall confine its report to a brief statement of the facts and of the solution reached;

(c) If a solution within the terms of subparagraph (b) is not reached, the Commission's report shall embody its findings on all questions of fact relevant to the issues between the States Parties concerned, and its views on the possibilities of an amicable solution of the matter. This report shall also contain the written submissions and a record of the oral submissions made by the States Parties concerned;

(d) If the Commission's report is submitted under subparagraph (c), the States Parties concerned shall, within three months of the receipt of the report, notify the Chairman of the Committee whether or not they accept the contents of the report of the Commission.

8. The provisions of this article are without prejudice to the responsibilities of the Committee under article 41.

9. The States Parties concerned shall share equally all the expenses of the members of the Commission in accordance with estimates to be provided by the Secretary-General of the United Nations.

10. The Secretary-General of the United Nations shall be empowered to pay the expenses of the members of the Commission, if necessary, before reimbursement by the States Parties concerned, in accordance with paragraph 9 of this article.

Article 43

The members of the Committee, and of the ad hoc conciliation commissions which may be appointed under article 42, shall be entitled to the facilities, privileges and immunities of experts on mission for the United Nations as laid down in the relevant sections of the Convention on the Privileges and Immunities of the United Nations.

Article 44

The provisions for the implementation of the present Covenant shall apply without prejudice to the procedures prescribed in the field of human rights by or under the constituent instruments and the conventions of the United Nations and of the specialized agencies and shall not prevent the States Parties to the present Covenant from having recourse to other procedures for settling a dispute in accordance with general or special international agreements in force between them.

Article 45

The Committee shall submit to the General Assembly of the United Nations, through the Economic and Social Council, an annual report on its activities.

PART V

Article 46

Nothing in the present Covenant shall be interpreted as impairing the provisions of the Charter of the United Nations and of the constitutions of the specialized agencies which define the respective responsibilities of the various organs of the United Nations and of the specialized agencies in regard to the matters dealt with in the present Covenant.

Article 47

Nothing in the present Covenant shall be interpreted as impairing the inherent right of all peoples to enjoy and utilize fully and freely their natural wealth and resources.

PART VI

Article 48

1. The present Covenant is open for signature by any State Member of the United Nations or member of any of its specialized agencies, by any State Party to the Statute of the International Court of Justice, and by any other State which has been invited by the General Assembly of the United Nations to become a Party to the present Covenant.

2. The present Covenant is subject to ratification. Instruments of ratification shall be deposited with the Secretary-General of the United Nations.

3. The present Covenant shall be open to accession by any State referred to in paragraph 1 of this article.

4. Accession shall be effected by the deposit of an instrument of accession with the Secretary-General of the United Nations.

5. The Secretary-General of the United Nations shall inform all States which have signed this Covenant or acceded to it of the deposit of each instrument of ratification or accession.

Article 49

1. The present Covenant shall enter into force three months after the date of the deposit with the Secretary-General of the United Nations of the thirty-fifth instrument of ratification or instrument of accession.

2. For each State ratifying the present Covenant or acceding to it after the deposit of the thirty-fifth instrument of ratification or instrument of accession, the present Covenant shall enter into force three months after the date of the deposit of its own instrument of ratification or instrument of accession.

Article 50

The provisions of the present Covenant shall extend to all parts of federal States without any limitations or exceptions.

Article 51

1. Any State Party to the present Covenant may propose an amendment and file it with the Secretary-General of the United Nations. The Secretary-General of the United Nations shall thereupon communicate any proposed amendments to the States Parties to the present Covenant with a request that they notify him whether they favor a conference of States Parties for the purpose of considering and voting upon the proposals. In the event that at least one third of the States Parties favors such a conference, the Secretary-General shall convene the conference under the auspices of the United Nations. Any amendment adopted by a majority of the States Parties present and voting at the conference shall be submitted to the General Assembly of the United Nations for approval.

2. Amendments shall come into force when they have been approved by the General Assembly of the United Nations and accepted by a two-thirds majority of the States Parties to the present Covenant in accordance with their respective constitutional processes.

3. When amendments come into force, they shall be binding on those States Parties which have accepted them, other States Parties still being bound by the provisions of the present Covenant and any earlier amendment which they have accepted.

Article 52

Irrespective of the notifications made under article 48, paragraph 5, the Secretary-General of the United Nations shall inform all States referred to in paragraph 1 of the same article of the following particulars:

(a) Signatures, ratifications and accessions under article 48;

(b) The date of the entry into force of the present Covenant under article 49 and the date of the entry into force of any amendments under article 51.

Article 53

1. The present Covenant, of which the Chinese, English, French, Russian and Spanish texts are equally authentic, shall be deposited in the archives of the United Nations.

2. The Secretary-General of the United Nations shall transmit certified copies of the present Covenant to all States referred to in article 48.

International Covenant on Economic, Social, and Cultural Rights

Adopted and opened for signature, ratification and accession by General Assembly resolution 2200A (XXI) of December 16, 1966. Entry into force January 3, 1976, in accordance with article 27.

Preamble

The States Parties to the present Covenant,

Considering that, in accordance with the principles proclaimed in the Charter of the United Nations, recognition of the inherent dignity and of the equal and inalienable rights of all members of the human family is the foundation of freedom, justice and peace in the world,

Recognizing that these rights derive from the inherent dignity of the human person,

Recognizing that, in accordance with the Universal Declaration of Human Rights, the ideal of free human beings enjoying freedom from fear and want can only be achieved if conditions are created whereby everyone may enjoy his economic, social and cultural rights, as well as his civil and political rights,

Considering the obligation of States under the Charter of the United Nations to promote universal respect for, and observance of, human rights and freedoms,

Realizing that the individual, having duties to other individuals and to the community to which he belongs, is under a responsibility to strive for the promotion and observance of the rights recognized in the present Covenant,

Agree upon the following articles:

PART I

Article 1

1. All peoples have the right of self-determination. By virtue of that right they freely determine their political status and freely pursue their economic, social and cultural development.

2. All peoples may, for their own ends, freely dispose of their natural wealth and resources without prejudice to any obligations arising out of international economic co-operation, based upon the principle of mutual benefit, and international law. In no case may a people be deprived of its own means of subsistence.

3. The States Parties to the present Covenant, including those having responsibility for the administration of Non-Self-Governing and Trust Territories, shall promote the realization of the right of self-determination, and shall respect that right, in conformity with the provisions of the Charter of the United Nations.

PART II

Article 2

1. Each State Party to the present Covenant undertakes to take steps, individually and through international assistance and co-operation, especially economic and technical, to the maximum of its available resources, with a view to achieving progressively the full realization of the rights recognized in the present Covenant by all appropriate means, including particularly the adoption of legislative measures.

2. The States Parties to the present Covenant undertake to guarantee that the rights enunciated in the present Covenant will be exercised without discrimination of any kind as to race, color, sex, language, religion, political or other opinion, national or social origin, property, birth or other status.

3. Developing countries, with due regard to human rights and their national economy, may determine to what extent they would guarantee the economic rights recognized in the present Covenant to non-nationals.

Article 3

The States Parties to the present Covenant undertake to ensure the equal right of men and women to the enjoyment of all economic, social and cultural rights set forth in the present Covenant.

Article 4

The States Parties to the present Covenant recognize that, in the enjoyment of those rights provided by the State in conformity with the present Covenant, the State may subject such rights only to such limitations as are determined by law only in so far as this may be compatible with the nature of these rights and solely for the purpose of promoting the general welfare in a democratic society.

Article 5

1. Nothing in the present Covenant may be interpreted as implying for any State, group or person any right to engage in any activity or to perform any act aimed at the destruction of any of the rights or freedoms recognized herein, or at their limitation to a greater extent than is provided for in the present Covenant.

2. No restriction upon or derogation from any of the fundamental human rights recognized or existing in any country in virtue of law, conventions, regulations or custom shall be admitted on the pretext that the present Covenant does not recognize such rights or that it recognizes them to a lesser extent.

PART III

Article 6

1. The States Parties to the present Covenant recognize the right to work, which includes the right of everyone to the opportunity to gain his living by work which he freely chooses or accepts, and will take appropriate steps to safeguard this right.

2. The steps to be taken by a State Party to the present Covenant to achieve the full realization of this right shall include technical and vocational guidance and training programs, policies and techniques to achieve steady economic, social and cultural development and full and productive employment under conditions safeguarding fundamental political and economic freedoms to the individual.

Article 7

The States Parties to the present Covenant recognize the right of everyone to the enjoyment of just and favorable conditions of work which ensure, in particular:

(a) Remuneration which provides all workers, as a minimum, with:

(i) Fair wages and equal remuneration for work of equal value without distinction of any kind, in particular women being guaranteed conditions of work not inferior to those enjoyed by men, with equal pay for equal work;

(ii) A decent living for themselves and their families in accordance with the provisions of the present Covenant;

(b) Safe and healthy working conditions;

(c) Equal opportunity for everyone to be promoted in his employment to an appropriate higher level, subject to no considerations other than those of seniority and competence;

(d) Rest, leisure and reasonable limitation of working hours and periodic holidays with pay, as well as remuneration for public holidays.

Article 8

1. The States Parties to the present Covenant undertake to ensure:

(a) The right of everyone to form trade unions and join the trade union of his choice, subject only to the rules of the organization concerned, for the promotion and protection of his economic and social interests. No restrictions may be placed on the exercise of this right other than those prescribed by law and which are necessary in a democratic society in the interests of national security or public order or for the protection of the rights and freedoms of others;

(b) The right of trade unions to establish national federations or confederations and the right of the latter to form or join international trade-union organizations;

(c) The right of trade unions to function freely subject to no limitations other than those prescribed by law and which are necessary in a democratic society in the interests of national security or public order or for the protection of the rights and freedoms of others;

(d) The right to strike, provided that it is exercised in conformity with the laws of the particular country.

2. This article shall not prevent the imposition of lawful restrictions on the exercise of these rights by members of the armed forces or of the police or of the administration of the State.

3. Nothing in this article shall authorize States Parties to the International Labor Organization Convention of 1948 con-

cerning Freedom of Association and Protection of the Right to Organize to take legislative measures which would prejudice, or apply the law in such a manner as would prejudice, the guarantees provided for in that Convention.

Article 9

The States Parties to the present Covenant recognize the right of everyone to social security, including social insurance.

Article 10

The States Parties to the present Covenant recognize that:

1. The widest possible protection and assistance should be accorded to the family, which is the natural and fundamental group unit of society, particularly for its establishment and while it is responsible for the care and education of dependent children. Marriage must be entered into with the free consent of the intending spouses.

2. Special protection should be accorded to mothers during a reasonable period before and after childbirth. During such period working mothers should be accorded paid leave or leave with adequate social security benefits.

3. Special measures of protection and assistance should be taken on behalf of all children and young persons without any discrimination for reasons of parentage or other conditions. Children and young persons should be protected from economic and social exploitation. Their employment in work harmful to their morals or health or dangerous to life or likely to hamper their normal development should be punishable by law. States should also set age limits below which the paid employment of child labor should be prohibited and punishable by law.

Article 11

1. The States Parties to the present Covenant recognize the right of everyone to an adequate standard of living for himself and his family, including adequate food, clothing and housing, and to the continuous improvement of living conditions. The States Parties will take appropriate steps to ensure the realization of this right, recognizing to this effect the essential importance of international co-operation based on free consent.

2. The States Parties to the present Covenant, recognizing the fundamental right of everyone to be free from hunger, shall take, individually and through international co-operation, the measures, including specific programs, which are needed:

(a) To improve methods of production, conservation and distribution of food by making full use of technical and scientific knowledge, by disseminating knowledge of the principles of nutrition and by developing or reforming agrarian systems in such a way as to achieve the most efficient development and utilization of natural resources;

(b) Taking into account the problems of both food-importing and food-exporting countries, to ensure an equitable distribution of world food supplies in relation to need.

Article 12

1. The States Parties to the present Covenant recognize the right of everyone to the enjoyment of the highest attainable standard of physical and mental health.

2. The steps to be taken by the States Parties to the present Covenant to achieve the full realization of this right shall include those necessary for:

(a) The provision for the reduction of the stillbirth-rate and of infant mortality and for the healthy development of the child;

(b) The improvement of all aspects of environmental and industrial hygiene;

(c) The prevention, treatment and control of epidemic, endemic, occupational and other diseases;

(d) The creation of conditions which would assure to all medical service and medical attention in the event of sickness.

Article 13

1. The States Parties to the present Covenant recognize the right of everyone to education. They agree that education shall be directed to the full development of the human personality and the sense of its dignity, and shall strengthen the respect for human rights and fundamental freedoms. They further agree that education shall enable all persons to participate effectively in a free society, promote understanding, tolerance and friendship among all nations and all racial, ethnic or religious groups, and further the activities of the United Nations for the maintenance of peace.

2. The States Parties to the present Covenant recognize that, with a view to achieving the full realization of this right:

(a) Primary education shall be compulsory and available free to all;

(b) Secondary education in its different forms, including technical and vocational secondary education, shall be made generally available and accessible to all by every appropriate means, and in particular by the progressive introduction of free education;

(c) Higher education shall be made equally accessible to all, on the basis of capacity, by every appropriate means, and in particular by the progressive introduction of free education;

(d) Fundamental education shall be encouraged or intensified as far as possible for those persons who have not received or completed the whole period of their primary education;

(e) The development of a system of schools at all levels shall be actively pursued, an adequate fellowship system shall be established, and the material conditions of teaching staff shall be continuously improved.

3. The States Parties to the present Covenant undertake to have respect for the liberty of parents and, when applicable, legal guardians to choose for their children schools, other than those established by the public authorities, which conform to such minimum educational standards as may be laid down or approved by the State and to ensure the religious and moral education of their children in conformity with their own convictions.

4. No part of this article shall be construed so as to interfere with the liberty of individuals and bodies to establish and direct educational institutions, subject always to the observance of the principles set forth in paragraph 1 of this article and to the requirement that the education given in such institutions shall conform to such minimum standards as may be laid down by the State.

Article 14

Each State Party to the present Covenant which, at the time of becoming a Party, has not been able to secure in its metropolitan territory or other territories under its jurisdiction compulsory primary education, free of charge, undertakes, within two years, to work out and adopt a detailed plan of action for the progressive implementation, within a reasonable number of years, to be fixed in the plan, of the principle of compulsory education free of charge for all.

Article 15

1. The States Parties to the present Covenant recognize the right of everyone:

(a) To take part in cultural life;

(b) To enjoy the benefits of scientific progress and its applications;

(c) To benefit from the protection of the moral and material interests resulting from any scientific, literary or artistic production of which he is the author.

2. The steps to be taken by the States Parties to the present Covenant to achieve the full realization of this right shall include those necessary for the conservation, the development and the diffusion of science and culture.

3. The States Parties to the present Covenant undertake to respect the freedom indispensable for scientific research and creative activity.

4. The States Parties to the present Covenant recognize the benefits to be derived from the encouragement and development of international contacts and co-operation in the scientific and cultural fields.

PART IV

Article 16

1. The States Parties to the present Covenant undertake to submit in conformity with this part of the Covenant reports on the measures which they have adopted and the progress made in achieving the observance of the rights recognized herein.

2. (a) All reports shall be submitted to the Secretary-General of the United Nations, who shall transmit copies to the Economic and Social Council for consideration in accordance with the provisions of the present Covenant;

(b) The Secretary-General of the United Nations shall also transmit to the specialized agencies copies of the reports, or any relevant parts therefrom, from States Parties to the present Covenant which are also members of these specialized agencies in so far as these reports, or parts therefrom, relate to any matters which fall within the responsibilities of the said agencies in accordance with their constitutional instruments.

Article 17

1. The States Parties to the present Covenant shall furnish their reports in stages, in accordance with a program to be established by the Economic and Social Council within one year of the entry into force of the present Covenant after consultation with the States Parties and the specialized agencies concerned.

2. Reports may indicate factors and difficulties affecting the degree of fulfillment of obligations under the present Covenant.

3. Where relevant information has previously been furnished to the United Nations or to any specialized agency by any State Party to the present Covenant, it will not be necessary to reproduce that information, but a precise reference to the information so furnished will suffice.

Article 18

Pursuant to its responsibilities under the Charter of the United Nations in the field of human rights and fundamental freedoms, the Economic and Social Council may make arrangements with the specialized agencies in respect of their reporting to it on the progress made in achieving the observance of the provisions of the present Covenant falling within the scope of their activities. These reports may include particulars of decisions and recommendations on such implementation adopted by their competent organs.

Article 19

The Economic and Social Council may transmit to the Commission on Human Rights for study and general recommendation or, as appropriate, for information the reports concerning human rights submitted by States in accordance with articles 16 and 17, and those concerning human rights submitted by the specialized agencies in accordance with article 18.

Article 20

The States Parties to the present Covenant and the specialized agencies concerned may submit comments to the Economic and Social Council on any general recommendation under article 19 or reference to such general recommendation in any report of the Commission on Human Rights or any documentation referred to therein.

Article 21

The Economic and Social Council may submit from time to time to the General Assembly reports with recommendations of a general nature and a summary of the information received from the States Parties to the present Covenant and the specialized agencies on the measures taken and the progress made in achieving general observance of the rights recognized in the present Covenant.

Article 22

The Economic and Social Council may bring to the attention of other organs of the United Nations, their subsidiary organs and specialized agencies concerned with furnishing technical assistance any matters arising out of the reports referred to in this part of the present Covenant which may assist such bodies in deciding, each within its field of competence, on the advisability of international measures likely to contribute to the effective progressive implementation of the present Covenant.

Article 23

The States Parties to the present Covenant agree that international action for the achievement of the rights recognized in the present Covenant includes such methods as the conclusion of conventions, the adoption of recommendations, the furnishing of technical assistance and the holding of regional meetings and technical meetings for the purpose of consultation and study organized in conjunction with the Governments concerned.

Article 24

Nothing in the present Covenant shall be interpreted as impairing the provisions of the Charter of the United Nations and of the constitutions of the specialized agencies which define the respective responsibilities of the various organs of the United Nations and of the specialized agencies in regard to the matters dealt with in the present Covenant.

Article 25

Nothing in the present Covenant shall be interpreted as impairing the inherent right of all peoples to enjoy and utilize fully and freely their natural wealth and resources.

PART V

Article 26

1. The present Covenant is open for signature by any State Member of the United Nations or member of any of its specialized agencies, by any State Party to the Statute of the International Court of Justice, and by any other State which has been invited by the General Assembly of the United Nations to become a party to the present Covenant.

2. The present Covenant is subject to ratification. Instruments of ratification shall be deposited with the Secretary-General of the United Nations.

3. The present Covenant shall be open to accession by any State referred to in paragraph 1 of this article.

4. Accession shall be effected by the deposit of an instrument of accession with the Secretary-General of the United Nations.

5. The Secretary-General of the United Nations shall inform all States which have signed the present Covenant or acceded to it of the deposit of each instrument of ratification or accession.

Article 27

1. The present Covenant shall enter into force three months after the date of the deposit with the Secretary-General of the United Nations of the thirty-fifth instrument of ratification or instrument of accession.

2. For each State ratifying the present Covenant or acceding to it after the deposit of the thirty-fifth instrument of ratification or instrument of accession, the present Covenant shall enter into force three months after the date of the deposit of its own instrument of ratification or instrument of accession.

Article 28

The provisions of the present Covenant shall extend to all parts of federal States without any limitations or exceptions.

Article 29

1. Any State Party to the present Covenant may propose an amendment and file it with the Secretary-General of the United Nations. The Secretary-General shall thereupon communicate any proposed amendments to the States Parties to the present Covenant with a request that they notify him whether they favor a conference of States Parties for the purpose of considering and voting upon the proposals. In the event that at least one third of the States Parties favors such a conference, the Secretary-General shall convene the conference under the auspices of the United Nations. Any amendment adopted by a majority of the States Parties present and voting at the conference shall be submitted to the General Assembly of the United Nations for approval.

2. Amendments shall come into force when they have been approved by the General Assembly of the United Nations and accepted by a two-thirds majority of the States Parties to the present Covenant in accordance with their respective constitutional processes.

3. When amendments come into force they shall be binding on those States Parties which have accepted them, other States Parties still being bound by the provisions of the present Covenant and any earlier amendment which they have accepted.

Article 30

Irrespective of the notifications made under article 26, paragraph 5, the Secretary-General of the United Nations shall inform all States referred to in paragraph 1 of the same article of the following particulars:

(a) Signatures, ratifications and accessions under article 26;

(b) The date of the entry into force of the present Covenant under article 27 and the date of the entry into force of any amendments under article 29.

Article 31

1. The present Covenant, of which the Chinese, English, French, Russian and Spanish texts are equally authentic, shall be deposited in the archives of the United Nations.

2. The Secretary-General of the United Nations shall transmit certified copies of the present Covenant to all States referred to in article 26.

Declaration of the Rights of the Child

Proclaimed by General Assembly resolution 1386(XIV) of November 20, 1959.

Whereas the peoples of the United Nations have, in the Charter, reaffirmed their faith in fundamental human rights and in the dignity and worth of the human person, and have determined to promote social progress and better standards of life in larger freedom,

Whereas the United Nations has, in the Universal Declaration of Human Rights, proclaimed that everyone is entitled to all the rights and freedoms set forth therein, without distinction of any kind, such as race, color, sex, language, reli-

gion, political or other opinion, national or social origin, property, birth or other status,

Whereas the child, by reason of his physical and mental immaturity, needs special safeguards and care, including appropriate legal protection, before as well as after birth,

Whereas the need for such special safeguards has been stated in the Geneva Declaration of the Rights of the Child of 1924, and recognized in the Universal Declaration of Human Rights and in the statutes of specialized agencies and international organizations concerned with the welfare of children,

Whereas mankind owes to the child the best it has to give,

Now therefore,

The General Assembly

Proclaims this Declaration of the Rights of the Child to the end that he may have a happy childhood and enjoy for his own good and for the good of society the rights and freedoms herein set forth, and calls upon parents, upon men and women as individuals, and upon voluntary organizations, local authorities and national Governments to recognize these rights and strive for their observance by legislative and other measures progressively taken in accordance with the following principles:

Principle 1

The child shall enjoy all the rights set forth in this Declaration. Every child, without any exception whatsoever, shall be entitled to these rights, without distinction or discrimination on account of race, color, sex, language, religion, political or other opinion, national or social origin, property, birth or other status, whether of himself or of his family.

Principle 2

The child shall enjoy special protection, and shall be given opportunities and facilities, by law and by other means, to enable him to develop physically, mentally, morally, spiritually and socially in a healthy and normal manner and in conditions of freedom and dignity. In the enactment of laws for this purpose, the best interests of the child shall be the paramount consideration.

Principle 3

The child shall be entitled from his birth to a name and a nationality.

Principle 4

The child shall enjoy the benefits of social security. He shall be entitled to grow and develop in health; to this end, special care and protection shall be provided both to him and to his mother, including adequate pre-natal and post-natal care. The child shall have the right to adequate nutrition, housing, recreation and medical services.

Principle 5

The child who is physically, mentally or socially handicapped shall be given the special treatment, education and care required by his particular condition.

Principle 6

The child, for the full and harmonious development of his personality, needs love and understanding. He shall, wherever possible, grow up in the care and under the responsibility of his parents, and, in any case, in an atmosphere of affection and of moral and material security; a child of tender years shall not, save in exceptional circumstances, be separated from his mother. Society and the public authorities shall have the duty to extend particular care to children without a family and to those without adequate means of support. Payment of State and other assistance towards the maintenance of children of large families is desirable.

Principle 7

The child is entitled to receive education, which shall be free and compulsory, at least in the elementary stages. He shall be given an education which will promote his general culture and enable him, on a basis of equal opportunity, to develop his abilities, his individual judgement, and his sense of moral and social responsibility, and to become a useful member of society.

The best interests of the child shall be the guiding principle of those responsible for his education and guidance; that responsibility lies in the first place with his parents.

The child shall have full opportunity for play and recreation, which should be directed to the same purposes as education; society and the public authorities shall endeavor to promote the enjoyment of this right.

Principle 8

The child shall in all circumstances be among the first to receive protection and relief.

Principle 9

The child shall be protected against all forms of neglect, cruelty and exploitation. He shall not be the subject of traffic, in any form.

The child shall not be admitted to employment before an appropriate minimum age; he shall in no case be caused or permitted to engage in any occupation or employment which would prejudice his health or education, or interfere with his physical, mental or moral development.

Principle 10

The child shall be protected from practices which may foster racial, religious and any other form of discrimination. He shall be brought up in a spirit of understanding, tolerance, friendship among peoples, peace and universal brotherhood, and in full consciousness that his energy and talents should be devoted to the service of his fellow men.

Declaration on the Elimination of All Forms of Racial Discrimination

Proclaimed by General Assembly resolution 1904 (XVIII) of November 20, 1963.

The General Assembly,

Considering that the Charter of the United Nations is based on the principles of the dignity and equality of all human beings and seeks, among other basic objectives, to achieve international co-operation in promoting and encouraging respect for human rights and fundamental freedoms for all without distinction as to race, sex, language or religion,

Considering that the Universal Declaration of Human Rights proclaims that all human beings are born free and equal in dignity and rights and that everyone is entitled to all the rights and freedoms set out in the Declaration, without distinction of any kind, in particular as to race, color or national origin,

Considering that the Universal Declaration of Human Rights proclaims further that all are equal before the law and are entitled without any discrimination to equal protection of the law and that all are entitled to equal protection against any discrimination and against any incitement to such discrimination,

Considering that the United Nations has condemned colonialism and all practices of segregation and discrimination associated therewith, and that the Declaration on the Granting of Independence to Colonial Countries and Peoples proclaims in particular the necessity of bringing colonialism to a speedy and unconditional end,

Considering that any doctrine of racial differentiation or superiority is scientifically false, morally condemnable, socially unjust and dangerous, and that there is no justification for racial discrimination either in theory or in practice,

Taking into account the other resolutions adopted by the General Assembly and the international instruments adopted by the specialized agencies, in particular the International Labor Organization and the United Nations Educational, Scientific and Cultural Organization, in the field of discrimination,

Taking into account the fact that, although international action and efforts in a number of countries have made it possible to achieve progress in that field, discrimination based on race, color or ethnic origin in certain areas of the world continues none the less to give cause for serious concern,

Alarmed by the manifestations of racial discrimination still in evidence in some areas of the world, some of which are imposed by certain Governments by means of legislative, administrative or other measures, in the form, inter alia, of apartheid, segregation and separation, as well as by the promotion and dissemination of doctrines of racial superiority and expansionism in certain areas,

Convinced that all forms of racial discrimination and, still more so, governmental policies based on the prejudice of racial superiority or on racial hatred, besides constituting a violation of fundamental human rights, tend to jeopardize friendly relations among peoples, co-operation between nations and international peace and security,

Convinced also that racial discrimination harms not only those who are its objects but also those who practice it.

Convinced further that the building of a world society free from all forms of racial segregation and discrimination, factors which create hatred and division among men, is one of the fundamental objectives of the United Nations,

1. Solemnly affirms the necessity of speedily eliminating racial discrimination throughout the world, in all its forms and manifestations, and of securing understanding of and respect for the dignity of the human person;

2. Solemnly affirms the necessity of adopting national and international measures to that end, including teaching, education and information, in order to secure the universal and effective recognition and observance of the principles set forth below;

3. Proclaims this Declaration:

Article 1

Discrimination between human beings on the ground of race, color or ethnic origin is an offense to human dignity and shall be condemned as a denial of the principles of the Charter of the United Nations, as a violation of the human rights and fundamental freedoms proclaimed in the Universal Declaration of Human Rights, as an obstacle to friendly and peaceful relations among nations and as a fact capable of disturbing peace and security among peoples.

Article 2

1. No State, institution, group or individual shall make any discrimination whatsoever in matters of human rights and fundamental freedoms in the treatment of persons, groups of persons or institutions on the ground of race, color or ethnic origin.

2. No State shall encourage, advocate or lend its support, through police action or otherwise, to any discrimination based on race, color or ethnic origin by any group, institution or individual.

3. Special concrete measures shall be taken in appropriate circumstances in order to secure adequate development or protection of individuals belonging to certain racial groups with the object of ensuring the full enjoyment by such individuals of

human rights and fundamental freedoms. These measures shall in no circumstances have as a consequence the maintenance of unequal or separate rights for different racial groups.
Article 3

1. Particular efforts shall be made to prevent discrimination based on race, color or ethnic origin, especially in the fields of civil rights, access to citizenship, education, religion, employment, occupation and housing.

2. Everyone shall have equal access to any place or facility intended for use by the general public, without distinction as to race, color or ethnic origin.
Article 4

All States shall take effective measures to revise governmental and other public policies and to rescind laws and regulations which have the effect of creating and perpetuating racial discrimination wherever it still exists. They should pass legislation for prohibiting such discrimination and should take all appropriate measures to combat those prejudices which lead to racial discrimination.
Article 5

An end shall be put without delay to governmental and other public policies of racial segregation and especially policies of apartheid, as well as all forms of racial discrimination and separation resulting from such policies.
Article 6

No discrimination by reason of race, color or ethnic origin shall be admitted in the enjoyment by any person of political and citizenship rights in his country, in particular the right to participate in elections through universal and equal suffrage and to take part in the government. Everyone has the right of equal access to public service in his country.
Article 7

1. Everyone has the right to equality before the law and to equal justice under the law. Everyone, without distinction as to race, color or ethnic origin, has the right to security of person and protection by the State against violence or bodily harm, whether inflicted by government officials or by any individual, group or institution.

2. Everyone shall have the right to an effective remedy and protection against any discrimination he may suffer on the ground of race, color or ethnic origin with respect to his fundamental rights and freedoms through independent national tribunals competent to deal with such matters.
Article 8

All effective steps shall be taken immediately in the fields of teaching, education and information, with a view to eliminating racial discrimination and prejudice and promoting understanding, tolerance and friendship among nations and racial groups, as well as to propagating the purposes and principles of the Charter of the United Nations, of the Universal Declaration of Human Rights, and of the Declaration on the Granting of Independence to Colonial Countries and Peoples.
Article 9

1. All propaganda and organizations based on ideas or theories of the superiority of one race or group of persons of one color or ethnic origin with a view to justifying or promoting racial discrimination in any form shall be severely condemned.

2. All incitement to or acts of violence, whether by individuals or organizations against any race or group of persons of another color or ethnic origin shall be considered an offense against society and punishable under law.

3. In order to put into effect the purposes and principles of the present Declaration, all States shall take immediate and positive measures, including legislative and other measures, to prosecute and/or outlaw organizations which promote or incite to racial discrimination, or incite to or use violence for purposes of discrimination based on race, color or ethnic origin.
Article 10

The United Nations, the specialized agencies, States and non-governmental organizations shall do all in their power to promote energetic action which, by combining legal and other practical measures, will make possible the abolition of all forms of racial discrimination. They shall, in particular, study the causes of such discrimination with a view to recommending appropriate and effective measures to combat and eliminate it.
Article 11

Every State shall promote respect for and observance of human rights and fundamental freedoms in accordance with the Charter of the United Nations and shall fully and faithfully observe the provisions of the present Declaration, the Universal Declaration of Human Rights and the Declaration on the Granting of Independence to Colonial Countries and Peoples.

Declaration on the Elimination of Discrimination Against Women

Proclaimed by General Assembly resolution 2263 (XXII) of November 7, 1967.

The General Assembly,

Considering that the peoples of the United Nations have, in the Charter, reaffirmed their faith in fundamental human rights, in the dignity and worth of the human person and in the equal rights of men and women, Considering that the Universal Declaration of Human Rights asserts the principle of non-discrimination and proclaims that all human beings are born free and equal in dignity and rights and that everyone is entitled to all the rights and freedoms set forth therein without distinction of any kind, including any distinction as to sex,

Taking into account the resolutions, declarations, conventions and recommendations of the United Nations and the specialized agencies designed to eliminate all forms of discrimination and to promote equal rights for men and women,

Concerned that, despite the Charter of the United Nations, the Universal Declaration of Human Rights, the International Covenants on Human Rights and other instruments of the United Nations and the specialized agencies and despite the progress made in the matter of equality of rights, there continues to exist considerable discrimination against women,

Considering that discrimination against women is incompatible with human dignity and with the welfare of the family and of society, prevents their participation, on equal terms with men, in the political, social, economic and cultural life of their countries and is an obstacle to the full development of the potentialities of women in the service of their countries and of humanity,

Bearing in mind the great contribution made by women to social, political, economic and cultural life and the part they play in the family and particularly in the rearing of children,

Convinced that the full and complete development of a country, the welfare of the world and the cause of peace require the maximum participation of women as well as men in all fields,

Considering that it is necessary to ensure the universal recognition in law and in fact of the principle of equality of men and women,

Solemnly proclaims this Declaration:

Article 1

Discrimination against women, denying or limiting as it does their equality of rights with men, is fundamentally unjust and constitutes an offense against human dignity.

Article 2

All appropriate measures shall be taken to abolish existing laws, customs, regulations and practices which are discriminatory against women, and to establish adequate legal protection for equal rights of men and women, in particular:

(a) The principle of equality of rights shall be embodied in the constitution or otherwise guaranteed by law;

(b) The international instruments of the United Nations and the specialized agencies relating to the elimination of discrimination against women shall be ratified or acceded to and fully implemented as soon as practicable.

Article 3

All appropriate measures shall be taken to educate public opinion and to direct national aspirations towards the eradication of prejudice and the abolition of customary and all other practices which are based on the idea of the inferiority of women.

Article 4

All appropriate measures shall be taken to ensure to women on equal terms with men, without any discrimination:

(a) The right to vote in all elections and be eligible for election to all publicly elected bodies;

(b) The right to vote in all public referenda;

(c) The right to hold public office and to exercise all public functions.

Such rights shall be guaranteed by legislation.

Article 5

Women shall have the same rights as men to acquire, change or retain their nationality. Marriage to an alien shall not automatically affect the nationality of the wife either by rendering her stateless or by forcing upon her the nationality of her husband.

Article 6

1. Without prejudice to the safeguarding of the unity and the harmony of the family, which remains the basic unit of any society, all appropriate measures, particularly legislative measures, shall be taken to ensure to women, married or unmarried, equal rights with men in the field of civil law, and in particular:

(a) The right to acquire, administer, enjoy, dispose of and inherit property, including property acquired during marriage;

(b) The right to equality in legal capacity and the exercise thereof;

(c) The same rights as men with regard to the law on the movement of persons.

2. All appropriate measures shall be taken to ensure the principle of equality of status of the husband and wife, and in particular:

(a) Women shall have the same right as men to free choice of a spouse and to enter into marriage only with their free and full consent;

(b) Women shall have equal rights with men during marriage and at its dissolution. In all cases the interest of the children shall be paramount;

(c) Parents shall have equal rights and duties in matters relating to their children. In all cases the interest of the children shall be paramount.

3. Child marriage and the betrothal of young girls before puberty shall be prohibited, and effective action, including legislation, shall be taken to specify a minimum age for marriage and to make the registration of marriages in an official registry compulsory.

Article 7

All provisions of penal codes which constitute discrimination against women shall be repealed.

Article 8

All appropriate measures, including legislation, shall be taken to combat all forms of traffic in women and exploitation of prostitution of women.

Article 9

All appropriate measures shall be taken to ensure to girls and women, married or unmarried, equal rights with men in education at all levels, and in particular:

(a) Equal conditions of access to, and study in, educational institutions of all types, including universities and vocational, technical and professional schools;

(b) The same choice of curricula, the same examinations, teaching staff with qualifications of the same standard, and school premises and equipment of the same quality, whether the institutions are co-educational or not;

(c) Equal opportunities to benefit from scholarships and other study grants;

(d) Equal opportunities for access to programs of continuing education, including adult literacy programs;

(e) Access to educational information to help in ensuring the health and well-being of families.

Article 10

1. All appropriate measures shall be taken to ensure to women, married or unmarried, equal rights with men in the field of economic and social life, and in particular:

(a) The right, without discrimination on grounds of marital status or any other grounds, to receive vocational training, to work, to free choice of profession and employment, and to professional and vocational advancement;

(b) The right to equal remuneration with men and to equality of treatment in respect of work of equal value;

(c) The right to leave with pay, retirement privileges and provision for security in respect of unemployment, sickness, old age or other incapacity to work;

(d) The right to receive family allowances on equal terms with men.

2. In order to prevent discrimination against women on account of marriage or maternity and to ensure their effective right to work, measures shall be taken to prevent their dismissal in the event of marriage or maternity and to provide paid maternity leave, with the guarantee of returning to former employment, and to provide the necessary social services, including child-care facilities.

3. Measures taken to protect women in certain types of work, for reasons inherent in their physical nature, shall not be regarded as discriminatory.

Article 11

1. The principle of equality of rights of men and women demands implementation in all States in accordance with the principles of the Charter of the United Nations and of the Universal Declaration of Human Rights.

2. Governments, non-governmental organizations and individuals are urged, therefore, to do all in their power to promote the implementation of the principles contained in this Declaration.

Declaration on the Protection of All Persons from Being Subjected to Torture and Other Cruel, Inhuman, or Degrading Treatment or Punishment

Adopted by General Assembly resolution 3452 (XXX) of December 9, 1975.

Article 1

1. For the purpose of this Declaration, torture means any act by which severe pain or suffering, whether physical or mental, is intentionally inflicted by or at the instigation of a public official on a person for such purposes as obtaining from him or a third person information or confession, punishing him for an act he has committed or is suspected of having committed, or intimidating him or other persons. It does not include pain or suffering arising only from, inherent in or incidental to, lawful sanctions to the extent consistent with the Standard Minimum Rules for the Treatment of Prisoners.

2. Torture constitutes an aggravated and deliberate form of cruel, inhuman or degrading treatment or punishment.

Article 2

Any act of torture or other cruel, inhuman or degrading treatment or punishment is an offense to human dignity and shall be condemned as a denial of the purposes of the Charter of the United Nations and as a violation of the human rights and fundamental freedoms proclaimed in the Universal Declaration of Human Rights.

Article 3

No State may permit or tolerate torture or other cruel, inhuman or degrading treatment or punishment. Exceptional circumstances such as a state of war or a threat of war, internal political instability or any other public emergency may not be invoked as a justification of torture or other cruel, inhuman or degrading treatment or punishment.

Article 4

Each State shall, in accordance with the provisions of this Declaration, take effective measures to prevent torture and other cruel, inhuman or degrading treatment or punishment from being practiced within its jurisdiction.

Article 5

The training of law enforcement personnel and of other public officials who may be responsible for persons deprived of their liberty shall ensure that full account is taken of the prohibition against torture and other cruel, inhuman or degrading treatment or punishment. This prohibition shall also, where appropriate, be included in such general rules or instructions as are issued in regard to the duties and functions of anyone who may be involved in the custody or treatment of such persons.

Article 6

Each State shall keep under systematic review interrogation methods and practices as well as arrangements for the custody and treatment of persons deprived of their liberty in its territory, with a view to preventing any cases of torture or other cruel, inhuman or degrading treatment or punishment.

Article 7

Each State shall ensure that all acts of torture as defined in article 1 are offenses under its criminal law. The same shall apply in regard to acts which constitute participation in, complicity in, incitement to or an attempt to commit torture.

Article 8

Any person who alleges that he has been subjected to torture or other cruel, inhuman or degrading treatment or punishment by or at the instigation of a public official shall have the right to complain to, and to have his case impartially examined by, the competent authorities of the State concerned.

Article 9

Wherever there is reasonable ground to believe that an act of torture as defined in article 1 has been committed, the competent authorities of the State concerned shall promptly proceed to an impartial investigation even if there has been no formal complaint.

Article 10

If an investigation under article 8 or article 9 establishes that an act of torture as defined in article 1 appears to have been committed, criminal proceedings shall be instituted against the alleged offender or offenders in accordance with national law. If an allegation of other forms of cruel, inhuman or degrading treatment or punishment is considered to be well founded, the alleged offender or offenders shall be subject to criminal, disciplinary or other appropriate proceedings.

Article 11

Where it is proved that an act of torture or other cruel, inhuman or degrading treatment or punishment has been committed by or at the instigation of a public official, the victim shall be afforded redress and compensation in accordance with national law.

Article 12

Any statement which is established to have been made as a result of torture or other cruel, inhuman or degrading treatment or punishment may not be invoked as evidence against the person concerned or against any other person in any proceedings.

Declaration on the Elimination of All Forms of Intolerance and of Discrimination Based on Religion or Belief

Proclaimed by General Assembly resolution 36/55 of November 25, 1981.

The General Assembly,

Considering that one of the basic principles of the Charter of the United Nations is that of the dignity and equality inherent in all human beings, and that all Member States have pledged themselves to take joint and separate action in co-operation with the Organization to promote and encourage universal respect for and observance of human rights and fundamental freedoms for all, without distinction as to race, sex, language or religion,

Considering that the Universal Declaration of Human Rights and the International Covenants on Human Rights proclaim the principles of nondiscrimination and equality before the law and the right to freedom of thought, conscience, religion and belief,

Considering that the disregard and infringement of human rights and fundamental freedoms, in particular of the right to freedom of thought, conscience, religion or whatever belief, have brought, directly or indirectly, wars and great suffering to mankind, especially where they serve as a means of foreign interference in the internal affairs of other States and amount to kindling hatred between peoples and nations,

Considering that religion or belief, for anyone who professes either, is one of the fundamental elements in his conception of life and that freedom of religion or belief should be fully respected and guaranteed,

Considering that it is essential to promote understanding, tolerance and respect in matters relating to freedom of religion and belief and to ensure that the use of religion or belief for ends inconsistent with the Charter of the United Nations, other relevant instruments of the United Nations and the purposes and principles of the present Declaration is inadmissible,

Convinced that freedom of religion and belief should also contribute to the attainment of the goals of world peace, social justice and friendship among peoples and to the elimination of ideologies or practices of colonialism and racial discrimination,

Noting with satisfaction the adoption of several, and the coming into force of some, conventions, under the aegis of the United Nations and of the specialized agencies, for the elimination of various forms of discrimination,

Concerned by manifestations of intolerance and by the existence of discrimination in matters of religion or belief still in evidence in some areas of the world,

Resolved to adopt all necessary measures for the speedy elimination of such intolerance in all its forms and manifestations and to prevent and combat discrimination on the ground of religion or belief,

Proclaims this Declaration on the Elimination of All Forms of Intolerance and of Discrimination Based on Religion or Belief:

Article 1

1. Everyone shall have the right to freedom of thought, conscience and religion. This right shall include freedom to have a religion or whatever belief of his choice, and freedom, either individually or in community with others and in public or private, to manifest his religion or belief in worship, observance, practice and teaching.

2. No one shall be subject to coercion which would impair his freedom to have a religion or belief of his choice.

3. Freedom to manifest one's religion or belief may be subject only to such limitations as are prescribed by law and are necessary to protect public safety, order, health or morals or the fundamental rights and freedoms of others.

Article 2

1. No one shall be subject to discrimination by any State, institution, group of persons, or person on the grounds of religion or other belief.

2. For the purposes of the present Declaration, the expression "intolerance and discrimination based on religion or belief" means any distinction, exclusion, restriction or preference based on religion or belief and having as its purpose or as its effect nullification or impairment of the recognition, enjoyment or exercise of human rights and fundamental freedoms on an equal basis.

Article 3

Discrimination between human being on the grounds of religion or belief constitutes an affront to human dignity and a disavowal of the principles of the Charter of the United Nations, and shall be condemned as a violation of the human rights and fundamental freedoms proclaimed in the Universal Declaration of Human Rights and enunciated in detail in the International Covenants on Human Rights, and as an obstacle to friendly and peaceful relations between nations.

Article 4

1. All States shall take effective measures to prevent and eliminate discrimination on the grounds of religion or belief in the recognition, exercise and enjoyment of human rights and fundamental freedoms in all fields of civil, economic, political, social and cultural life.

2. All States shall make all efforts to enact or rescind legislation where necessary to prohibit any such discrimination, and to take all appropriate measures to combat intolerance on the grounds of religion or other beliefs in this matter.

Article 5

1. The parents or, as the case may be, the legal guardians of the child have the right to organize the life within the family in accordance with their religion or belief and bearing in mind the moral education in which they believe the child should be brought up.

2. Every child shall enjoy the right to have access to education in the matter of religion or belief in accordance with the wishes of his parents or, as the case may be, legal guardians, and shall not be compelled to receive teaching on religion or belief against the wishes of his parents or legal guardians, the best interests of the child being the guiding principle.

3. The child shall be protected from any form of discrimination on the ground of religion or belief. He shall be brought up in a spirit of understanding, tolerance, friendship among peoples, peace and universal brotherhood, respect for freedom of religion or belief of others, and in full consciousness that his energy and talents should be devoted to the service of his fellow men.

4. In the case of a child who is not under the care either of his parents or of legal guardians, due account shall be taken of their expressed wishes or of any other proof of their wishes in the matter of religion or belief, the best interests of the child being the guiding principle.

5. Practices of a religion or belief in which a child is brought up must not be injurious to his physical or mental health or to his full development, taking into account article 1, paragraph 3, of the present Declaration.

Article 6

In accordance with article 1 of the present Declaration, and subject to the provisions of article 1, paragraph 3, the right to freedom of thought, conscience, religion or belief shall include, inter alia, the following freedoms:

(a) To worship or assemble in connection with a religion or belief, and to establish and maintain places for these purposes;

(b) To establish and maintain appropriate charitable or humanitarian institutions;

(c) To make, acquire and use to an adequate extent the necessary articles and materials related to the rites or customs of a religion or belief;

(d) To write, issue and disseminate relevant publications in these areas;

(e) To teach a religion or belief in places suitable for these purposes;

(f) To solicit and receive voluntary financial and other contributions from individuals and institutions;

(g) To train, appoint, elect or designate by succession appropriate leaders called for by the requirements and standards of any religion or belief;

(h) To observe days of rest and to celebrate holidays and ceremonies in accordance with the precepts of one's religion or belief;

(i) To establish and maintain communications with individuals and communities in matters of religion and belief at the national and international levels.

Article 7

The rights and freedoms set forth in the present Declaration shall be accorded in national legislation in such a manner that everyone shall be able to avail himself of such rights and freedoms in practice.

Article 8

Nothing in the present Declaration shall be construed as restricting or derogating from any right defined in the Universal Declaration of Human Rights and the International Covenants on Human Rights.

FURTHER READING

For additional suggestions on further reading and research, please see specific
Nongovernmental Organizations (Chapter 6), Individuals (Chapter 7), or Issues (Chapter 8).

Alston, Philip, ed. *Human Rights Law*. New York: New York University Press, 1996.

Amnesty International Staff. *The Amnesty International Handbook*. Alameda, Calif.: Hunter House, 1991.

Amnesty International USA Staff. *The Amnesty International Report*. New York: Amnesty International USA, annual.

Baxi, Upendra, ed. *Inhuman Wrongs and Human Rights: Unconventional Essays*. New Delhi: Har-Anand Publications, 1994.

Beetham, David, ed. *Politics and Human Rights*. Cambridge, Mass.: Blackwell Publishers, 1995.

Bohlman, Otto. *Human Rights Watch World Report 1998*. New Haven, Conn.: Yale University Press, 1998.

Brzezinski, Zbigniew. *Power and Principle*. New York: Farrar, Straus, and Giroux., 1983.

Buergenthal, Thomas. *International Human Rights in a Nutshell*. Second ed. St. Paul, Minn.: West Publishing, 1995.

Council of Europe. *Collected Texts, European Convention on Human Rights*. Strasbourg, 1977.

De Varennes, Fernand. *Language, Minorities and Human Rights*. Boston, Mass.: Martinus Nijhoff, 1996.

Eide, Asbjørn, Catarina Krause, and Allan Rosas, eds. *Economic, Social, and Cultural Rights: A Textbook*. Boston, Mass.: Martinus Nijhoff Publishers, 1995.

Eide, Asbjørn, et al, eds. *The Universal Declaration of Human Rights: A Commentary*. Cambridge, Mass: University of Scandinavia Press North America, 1992.

Falk, Richard A. *Human Rights and State Sovereignty*. New York: Holmes and Meier Publishers, 1981.

Forsythe, David P. *Human Rights and World Politics*. Lincoln, Nebr.: University of Nebraska Press, 1989.

Gearty, Conor, and Adam Tomkins, eds. *Understanding Human Rights*. New York: Mansell, 1996.

Gibson, John S. *Dictionary of International Human Rights Law*. Lanham, Md.: Scarecrow Press, 1996.

Hamlin, D.W. *A History of Western Philosophy*. London: Viking, 1987.

Hasan, Ashraful. *Human Rights Dilemmas in Contemporary Times: Issues & Answers*. Bethesda, Md.: Austin & Winfield, Publishers, 1998.

Heffernan, Liz, ed. *Human Rights: A European Perspective*. Dublin, Ireland and Portland, Ore: The Round Hall Press, 1994.

Henkin, Louis. *The Age of Rights*. New York: Columbia University Press, 1996.

Humana, Charles. *World Human Rights Guide*. New York: Oxford University Press, 1992.

Hurst, Hannum, ed. *Guide to International Human Rights Practice*. Philadelphia: University of Pennsylvania Press, 1994.

Ishay, Micheline R., ed. *The Human Rights Reader: Major Political Writings, Essays, Speeches, and Documents from the Bible to the Present*. New York and London: Routledge, 1997.

Keck, Margaret E., and Kathryn Sikkink. *Activists Beyond Borders*. Ithaca, N.Y.: Cornell University Press, 1998.

Kenny, Anthony, ed. *The Oxford History of Western Philosophy*. Oxford: Oxford University Press, 1994.

Konvitz, Milton, ed. *Judaism and Human Rights*. New York: W.W. Norton and Co., 1972.

Lampe, Gerlad E. *Justice and Human Rights in Islamic Law*. Washington, D.C.: International Law Institute, 1997.

Laqueur, Walter, and Barry Rubin, eds. *The Human Rights Reader*. New York: New American Library, 1990.

Magill, Frank N. *Great Events From History, II. Human Rights Series, Volume 2, 3, 4, 5*. Pasadena, Calif.: Salem Press, 1992.

Maxwell, John A., and James J. Friedberg, eds. *Human Rights in Western Civilization: 1600 to the Present*. Dubuque, Iowa: Kendall/Hunt, 1994.

McNeill, William. *The Rise of the West: A History of the Human Community*. Chicago and London: The University of Chicago Press, 1963.

Mendelsohn, Oliver, and Baxi Upendra, eds. *The Rights of Subordinated Peoples*. Oxford: Oxford University Press, 1997.

Meron, Theodor, ed. *Human Rights in International Law: Legal and Policy Issues*. Oxford: Clarendon Press, 1984.

Meyer, William H. *Human Rights & International Political Economy in Third World Nations: Multinational Corporations, Foreign Aid & Repression*. Westport, Conn.: Greenwood Publishing, 1998.

Mills, Kurt. *Human Rights in the Emerging Global Order: A New Sovereignty?* New York: St. Martin's Press, 1998.

Newman, Frank C., and David S. Weissbrodt. *International Human Rights: Law, Policy, and Process*. Second ed. Cincinnati, Ohio: Anderson Publishing, 1996.

Perry, Michael J. *The Idea of Human Rights*. Oxford: Oxford University Press, 1998.

Pollis, Adamantia, and Peter Schwab, eds. *Human Rights: Cultural and Ideological Perspectives*. New York: Praeger Publishers, 1979.

Poulter, Sebastian. *Ethnicity, Law & Human Rights*. Oxford: Oxford University Press, 1998.

Ratner, Steven R., and Jason S. Abrams. *Accountability for Human Rights Atrocities in International Law*. Oxford: Oxford University Press, 1998.

Scruton, Roger. *A Short History of Modern Philosophy*. London and New York: Routledge, 1996.

Snider, Don M., and Stuart J. Schwartzstein, eds. *The United Nations at Fifty: Sovereignty, Peacekeeping, and Human Rights.* Washington, D.C.: Center for Strategic and International Studies, 1995.

Steiner, Henry, and Philip Alston. *International Human Rights in Context: Law, Politics, and Morals.* Oxford: Oxford University Press, 1996.

Tobin, Jack. *Guide to Human Rights Research.* Cambridge, Mass.: Harvard Law School, Human Rights Program, 1994.

Weiss, Thomas G., and Leon Gordenker, eds. *NGOs, the United Nations, and Global Governance.* Boulder, Colo.: Lynne Rienner Publishers, Incorporated, 1996.

Whalen, Lucille. *Human Rights: A Reference Handbook.* Santa Barbara, Calif.: ABC-CLIO, 1989.

INDEX

Note: Page numbers in **boldface** indicate extended discussion of topic. Those in *italics* indicate illustrations.

A

Abacha, Sani, 214
abolitionists, 38
Aboriginal Land Rights Act of 1976 (Australia), 268
Aborigines, Australian, 258, 268
abortion, 96, 99
  of female fetuses, 253
  fetal legal personality, 82
  forced, 250
  privacy vs. family-life rights issue, 90
  pro-choice vs. pro-life issue, 78
absolute rights, 68, 114, 115
absolutism, 33
  defined, 15n.1
  English checks on, 15, 17, 18, 22
  Enlightenment challenge to, 22, 23, 25
  French monarchy, 23
  Hobbes as theorist of, 19
ACHR. *See* African Charter on Human and People's Rights
ACLU. *See* American Civil Liberties Union
acquired immunodeficiency syndrome. *See* AIDS/HIV
Action Alert Network, 265
activists. *See* human rights activists
ADL. *See* Anti-Defamation League
administrative detention, 243
adoption, 96
adultery, 267
affirmative action. *See* positive discrimination
Afghanistan, 130, 135, 212
  disappearances, 246
  internally displaced persons, 259
  landmines, 260
  mass rapes, 267
  medical neutrality violations, 262
  persecution of women, 251, 262
AFL. *See* American Federation of Labor
Africa, 125, 127, 129
  AIDS deaths, 232
  bonded labor, 236
  child soldiers, 237-38
  disappearances, 246
  displaced persons, 259
  female genital mutilation, 249
  Rwandan war crimes, 145, 147
  slave trade, 271
  U.S. development aid, 244
  See also Organization of African Unity; *specific countries*
Africa Fund, The, **150**
African Americans
  police brutality against, 264

voting rights, 29
African Charter on Human and People's Rights (1981), 71, 76, 113, 140-41, 243
African Commission for Human and People's Rights, 177
African Court of Human and People's Rights (proposed), 141
African National Congress, 198-99
African Reformed Church, 269
AFSC. *See* American Friends Service Committee
agape, 12
aging, rights of, 108
AI. *See* Amnesty International
AIDS/HIV, **231-32**
air pollution, 90
Aké: The Years of Childhood (Soyinka), 214
Albanians, 233
Aleutians, 258
Alexander the Great, 6
Algeria, 233
Allende, Salvador, 225
Alves da Silva, Darly, 202
Alves Pereira, Darci, 202
Amazonian rainforests, 202
amendments, U.S. constitutional, 29
American Bill of Rights (1791). *See* Bill of Rights, American
American Civil Liberties Union, **150**
American Committee on Africa, 150
American Convention on Human Rights (1969), 143, 241, 243, 271
American Declaration of the Rights and Duties of Man, 60n.1
American Federation of Labor, 44
American Friends Service Committee, **151**
American Indians, 259
American Jewish Congress, 62
American Law Institute, 62
American Revolution, 22, 25, 26-29
  as economic protest, 27-28
  as French Revolution antecedent, 30
  immediate causes, 27-28
  intellectual antecedents, 26
  legacy of, 28-29, 248, 268
Americans with Disabilities Act of 1990, 232
Americas Watch. *See* Human Rights Watch
Amin, Idi, 141
Amnesty International, **151-52**, 180, 206, 250, 270
  on abuses by armed opposition groups, 233
  Benenson, Peter, 184-85

on conscientious objection, 239
  on detention abuses, 243
  execution statistics, 242
  homosexual rights, 269
  MacBride, Sean, 196, 197
  police brutality report, 263
  prisoner protections, 266
  on torture violations, 121, 272
  Zalaquett, José, 225, 226
ANC. *See* African National Congress
ANCYL. *See* Youth League of the ANC
Andrey Sakharov Foundation, 185
Anglicanism, 17, 18
  Tutu, Archbishop Desmond, 217-18
Angola, 150, 237, 260, 268
Anthracite Coal Strike (1902), 44
antiapartheid movement. *See* apartheid
anti-Communism, 92
Anti-Defamation League, **152-53**
Anti-Dühring, The (Engels), 47
Antigone (Sophocles), 6-7
antipersonnel landmines. *See* landmines
anti-Semitism, 195, 217
  Anti-Defamation League, 152-53
  by Nazis, 52, 53, 54-55, 76, 94
Anti-Slavery International, 258
Antokoletz, Daniel Victor, 204
Antokoletz, Maria Adela de, 180, 204
AOHR. *See* Arab Organization for Human Rights
apartheid, 180, 190, 191, 198, 199, 217, 218
apostasy, 98
apostolic succession, 31
appeal, right of, 4-5
Arab Organization for Human Rights, **153-54**
arbitrary executions. *See* extrajudicial executions
arbitration, 44
Argentina
  Carter administration and, 186-87, 244
  disappearances, 180, 203-4, 206, 216, 226, 245
  military junta trials, 226
  Mothers of Plaza de Mayo, 203-4, *203*, 245
  Perez Esquivel, Adolfo, 206-7
  Timerman, Jacobo, 216-17
Aris, Michael, 182
aristocracy, 8, 20, 23
Aristotle, 3, 5, 6
armed opposition groups, **232-34**
  child soldiers, 237-38

disappearances, 246
  homelessness, 255
  internally displaced persons, 255, 259-60
  landmines, 260
  rape as military tactic, 267
Armenia, 50, 205
armies. *See* military service
Arouet, François-Marie. *See* Voltaire
arranged marriage, 80, 253
arrest, freedom from arbitrary, 82, 85-87
art confiscation, 111
Article 1 (UDHR), 66, **74-75**
Article 2 (UDHR), 66, **76-77**, 83, 106, 109, 269
Article 3 (UDHR), 66, **77-79**, 82, 85, 115
Article 4 (UDHR), 66, **79-80**, 114, 115, 270, 271
Article 5 (UDHR), 66, 67, 68, 78, 79, **80-81**, 86
Article 6 (UDHR), 66, 78, **81-82**
Article 7 (UDHR), 66, 68, 76, 82, **82-84**, 269
Article 8 (UDHR), 67, 82, **84-85**
Article 9 (UDHR), 78, 82, **85-87**, 115
Article 10 (UDHR), 82, **87-88**
Article 11 (UDHR), 82, **88-89**, 115
Article 12 (UDHR), 66, **89-90**, 269
Article 13 (UDHR), 78, 86, **90-92**, 103, 114, 115
Article 14 (UDHR), 90, 91, **92-93**, 136
Article 15 (UDHR), 85, **93-95**
Article 16 (UDHR), **95-96**, 106
Article 17 (UDHR), **96-98**, 114
Article 18 (UDHR), 68, 78, 93, **98-99**, 238-39
Article 19 (British organization), 265
Article 19 (UDHR), 67, 78, **99-100**, 103, 114, 115, 264, 265
Article 20 (UDHR), 64, 67, 95, **100-102**
Article 21 (UDHR), 86, 94, **102-3**, 115
Article 22 (UDHR), 66, 67, **103-5**
Article 23 (UDHR), 66, 67, 103, **105-6**, 106, 107
Article 24 (UDHR), 66, 67, 103, **106-7**
Article 25 (UDHR), 66, 67, 78, 103, 105, **107-8**, 254
Article 26 (UDHR), 66, 67, 68, 103, **108-10**, 115, 240
Article 27 (UDHR), 66, 67, 103, **110-11**, 240
Article 28 (UDHR), 66, **111-12**

Article 29 (UDHR), 17, 68, 75, 78, 79, 86, 99, 100, **112-14**, 115-16
Article 30 (UDHR), 79, **114-16**
arts, 110
Asharites, 131
Asia, 125, 127, 129
  bonded labor, 236
  disappearances, 246
  female genital mutilation, 249
  homosexual sex illegality, 269
  human rights cultural bias charge, 240
  U.S. development aid, 244
  See also specific countries
Asia Watch. *See* Human Rights Watch
Asquith, Herbert, 40
assembly, freedom of peaceful, 64, 100-102
association, freedom of, 67, 95, 100-102, 106
  defined, 101
asylum, **234-35**
  administrative detention and, 243
  female genital mutilation and, 250
  gender persecution and, 234-35, 251
  lack of international sanctuary guarantee, 136, 234
  Lawyers Committee for Human Rights, 170
  right to seek, 90, 91, 92-93, 136, 234
  See also refugees
Ataturk, Kemal, 130
Athenian democracy, 3, 4, 5, 6, 102
Atlantic Charter (1941), 54
atrocities
  African civil wars, 142
  World War II, 52, 53-55, 60, 74, 119
  See also Holocaust; war crimes
Augustine of Hippo, Saint, 13
Augustus (Octavian), emperor of Rome, 8, 9
Aung San Suu Kyi, **181-82**, *181*
Auschwitz, 222
Australia, 61, 258, 268
Austria, 25, 31, 45, 50
Austro-Hungarian Empire, 49, 50, 51
authoritarianism, 52, 127, 128, 129
Averroes, 131
Avicenna, 131
Axis Rule in Occupied Europe (Lemkin), 195
Axworthy, Lloyd, 223

B
Baden, Max von, 49
Bahrain, 257
bail, excessive, 18
Baker, Eric, 184
Balkans. *See* Yugoslavia (former)
Bangladesh, 236, 264, 267
banishment. *See* exile
baptism, 13
barons, 15, 16

Barre, Siad, 141-42
Basket Three (Helsinki Accords), 122
Bataan Death March, 53
Bebel, August, 45
Begin, Menachim, 187
Belgium, 246
Belo, Bishop Carlos Filipe Ximenes, 181, **182-83**, 207, 208, 209
Benenson, Peter, 151, 180, **184-85**
Bentham, Jeremy, 33, 34-35
Biafra, 194, 214
Bible, 11, 12, 13, 14
Bill of Rights, American (1791), 26, 29
Bill of Rights, English (1689), 17-18, 26, 27
Bill of Rights, International. *See* International Bill of Rights
birth, as inception of rights, 78, 82
birthrates, 51
bisexual rights, 71, 90, 96, 269-70
Body of Principles for the Protection of All Persons under Any Form of Detention or Imprisonment (1988), 266
Bolivia, 258
Bolshevik Revolution (1917), 48
Bonafini, Hebe de, 180, 204
Bonafini, Omar and Raúl, 204
bonded labor, 27, 79-80, **235-36**, 270, 271
Bonded Labour Liberation Front (Pakistan), 200
Bonner, Elena, **185**, 212
book publishing, 13, 25
Bosnia-Herzegovina, 103, 135, 145
  genocide, 195
  internally displaced persons, 146, 259
  landmines, 260
  refugees, 136
  war crimes tribunal, 146, 190, 191
Boston Tea Party (1773), 27
Botswana, 232
brain death, 82
Brazil, 202, 255
Bread for the World, **154**
B refugee status, 136
Britain. *See* Great Britain
British Bill of Rights. *See* Bill of Rights, English
broadcasting licenses, 100
brothels, 80
brotherhood, 11, 74
Brzezinski, Zbigniew, 124
Buchenwald, 222
Buddhism, 191-92
Burke, Edmund, 33-34
Burma, 181-82, 264
Burton Benjamin Award, 159
Burundi, 136, 147, 233, 259, 267
Bush, George, 124, 222
BW. *See* Bread for the World

C
CAHR. *See* Chinese Association for Human Rights

Cambodia, 136, 232, 237, 246
  landmines, 260
  mass rapes, 267
Cambodian Human Rights and Development Association, **154-55**
Camp David accords, 187
Canada
  Francophone culture rights, 240
  Helsinki Accords, 121
  International Centre for Human Rights and Democratic Development, 165-66
capitalism
  early laissez-faire doctrine, 33
  property rights, 97
  socialism vs., 45
  See also laissez-faire doctrine
capital punishment. *See* death penalty
Caracalla, emperor of Rome, 9
Carr, E. H., 62
Carter, Jimmy, 122, 155, 180, **186-87**, *186*, 210, 222
Carter, Rosalynn, 155, 186, 187
Carter administration, **122-24**, 186-87, 244
Carter Center, The, **155**, 187
Cassin, René, 61, **187-88**
Cassiodorus, 12n.2
caste systems, 240
Catherine the Great, empress of Russia, 25
Catholicism. *See* Roman Catholic Church
Catt, Carrie Chapman, 39
CCS. *See* Committee of Concerned Scientists
CEDAW. *See* Convention on the Elimination of All Forms of Discrimination Against Women
censorship, 100
Center for Human Rights, 134
Center for the Study of Human Rights, **155-56**
Central America. *See* Latin America
CERD. *See* Convention on the Elimination of All Forms of Racial Discrimination
Cetiner, Mariana, 269
CFC. *See* Committee for Children
Chadwick, Edwin, 35
charity, 12, 35
Charlemagne, 13
Charles I, king of England, 16, 19
Charles II, king of England, 20n.7
Charter 77 (Czechoslovakia), 193
Chechnya, 262
Chico Mendes Extractive Reserve, 200
child abuse prevention, 157
child custody, 10, 87, 90
child labor, 40-41, 42-43, 45, 46, 80
  bonded, 236, 270, 271
  Masih activism against, 199-200, 236

child pornography, 80, 271
children
  abuses against girls, 251, 253-54, 273-74
  AIDS/HIV vulnerability, 232
  contemporary exploitation of, 79, 80, 271
  death penalty prohibition, 241, 242
  free expression vs. protection of, 100
  health and social assistance rights, 107, 143
  human rights protections. *See* children's rights
  legal personality, 82
  prostitution of, 271
  as rape victims, 267
  rights to conceive and raise, 96
  Roman allowances for, 9
  Roman legal status, 10
  schooling provisions, 35, 42, 46, 47, 108-10
  as soldiers, 236-38, 271
  war victims, 197-98
children's rights, 80, 90
  girl children, 254
  legal personality, 82
  NGOs for, 156, 157
  social welfare rights, 107, 108
  UN convention on, 80, 90, 134, 137, 175, 237, 254
  UN Study on Impact of Armed Conflict on, 198
  See also child labor
Children's Watch International, **156**
child soldiers, **236-38**, 271
Chile, 135, 217
  disappearances, 245
  Human Rights Commission member, 61
  Pinochet extradition controversy, 247
  Zalaquett, José, 225-26
Chilean National Commission for Truth and Reconciliation, 225, 226
China
  Carter administration policy, 122
  executions rate, 242
  Fang Lizhi, 180, 188-89
  female infanticide, 253
  Human Rights Commission member, 61
  human rights defenders' rights, 256
  Human Rights in China, 161, 189
  human rights protests, 101, 180, 188, 189
  Tibetan human rights, 191-92, 268
  Wang Dan, 180, 220
  Wu, Harry, 224-25
Chinese Association for Human Rights, **156-57**
Ching Lee, 225
CHRDA. *See* Cambodian Human Rights and Development Association
Christianity, 11, 12-13
  day of rest, 106
  Latin American nonviolence movement, 206

Christianity, (*continued*)
 Roman Empire, 10-11
 See also church-state
 relations; Judeo-Christian
 tradition; Roman
 Catholic Church; *specific
 denominations*
CHRNAS. *See* Committee on
 Human Rights of the
 U.S. National Academy
 of Sciences, National
 Academy of Engineering
 and Institute of Medicine
Churchill, Winston, 137-38
church-state relations
 American separate entities,
 28
 England's established
 church, 17, 18
 Enlightenment views, 24
 God's sovereignty, 11, 13
 Islamic, 130-31
 monarch's religion as state's,
 15n.1
 UDHR Article 18 on,
 98-99
cinema licenses, 100
circumcision. *See* female
 genital mutilation
citizens' groups. *See* NGOs
citizenship rights, 93-95
 Roman, 8-9
 United States, 29
city-states, 4, 6
Civic Forum
 (Czechoslovakia), 193
civil and political rights, 70
 acceptance of covenant on,
 120
 defined, 66, 104
 refugee movements and,
 92-93
 UDHR Articles 2-21 on,
 66-67, 76-103
 Western capitalist focus on,
 63, 104-5, 125
 See also International
 Covenant on Civil and
 Political Rights
Civil Constitution of the
 Clergy (1790; France),
 31-32
civilians
 armed opposition group
 attacks on, 233
 forced internal
 displacement, 259
 humanitarian law, 81, 115
 medical neutrality, 262
 police brutality against,
 263-64
civil law, 8, 13, 88
 marriage-like agreements,
 96
civil wars. *See* armed
 opposition groups
class
 American colonial social
 mobility, 27
 laissez-faire doctrine and,
 34
 Magna Carta and, 15-16
 power in British
 Parliament, 20, 30
 Roman political power, 8
 See also aristocracy; middle
 class; nobility
classless society, 47
class struggle, 46

Claudius, emperor of Rome,
 10
Clayton Antitrust Act of 1914,
 44
Clemenceau, Georges, 50
Clement of Alexandria, 13
Clinton, Bill, 147, 220
clitorectomy. *See* female
 genital mutilation
Coalition to Stop the Use of
 Child Soldiers, 238
coal strike of 1874-75, 44
Code of Conduct for Law
 Enforcement Officers
 (1979), 263
coeducation, 110
Coeur d'Alene mines (Idaho),
 44
Cold War, 62, 63-64, 70, 71
 defections, 91, 92-93
 freedom of expression
 negotiations, 77, 100
 human rights movement
 and, 121-22, 123, 138-39
 property rights and, 96-97
 UDHR vote abstentions,
 63-64, 120-21
 U.S. development aid, 244
collective rights. *See* group
 rights
collective self-determination,
 268
collectivism, 52, 63, 97
Colombia, 136, 264
colonialism, 49, 51, 71, 97
 decolonization, 112, 127-
 29, 140, 150
 human rights as legacy of,
 124-25
 self-determination, 268-69
colonies and territories, 77
Columbia University, Center
 for the Study of Human
 Rights, 155-56
Combination Acts of 1799
 and 1800 (Great Britain),
 42
comfort women, 271
commerce. *See* trade
*Commission Européenne du
 Droits de l'Homme. See*
 European Commission
 on Human Rights
Commission of Inquiry into
 Public Violence and
 Intimidation (1991). *See*
 Goldstone Commission
Commission on Crime
 Prevention and Criminal
 Justice (UN), 270
Commission on Human
 Rights (UN), 61, 63, 64,
 100, 120, 129, 134, **135**,
 160
 Committee and Special
 Rapporteur on Torture,
 272
 on conscientious objection,
 238-39
 Dayton Accords, 146
 definition of internally
 displaced persons, 259
 draft declaration on rights
 of human rights
 defenders, 256
 enslavement of children,
 271
 independence of judges and
 lawyers investigation, 257
 members, 61, 188

slavery study, 271
 Special Rapporteur on
 Summary or Arbitrary
 Executions, 248
 unlawful executions, 242
Commission on the Status of
 Women (UN), 61
Committee Against Torture
 (UN), 137, 272
Committee and Special
 Rapporteur on Torture
 (UN), 272
Committee for Children, **157**
Committee for Human Rights
 (Soviet Union), 212
Committee for Peace (Chile),
 226
Committee for Peasant Unity
 (Guatemala), 200, 201
Committee of 100 for Tibet,
 206
Committee of Concerned
 Scientists, **157**, 189
Committee of Ministers
 (Council of Europe), 138,
 144
Committee on Economic,
 Social, and Cultural
 Rights (UN), 136
Committee on Human Rights
 (UN). *See* Human Rights
 Committee
Committee on Human Rights
 of the U.S. National
 Academy of Sciences,
 National Academy of
 Engineering and Institute
 of Medicine, **158**
Committee on the
 Elimination of All Forms
 of Discrimination Against
 Women (UN), 136-37
Committee on the
 Elimination of Racial
 Discrimination (UN),
 136
Committee to Protect
 Journalists, **158-59**, 264,
 265
Common Sense (Paine), 28
Commonwealth v. Hunt (1842),
 44
Communism, 46-47, 76
 asylum rights and, 92
 China, 188-89, 220, 221-22
 Czechoslovakia, 192-93
 drafting of Universal
 Declaration of Human
 Rights and, 63
 Marxism, 43, 45-47
 Poland, 219
 post-World War II
 expansion, 138
 Soviet Union, 52, 185
 See also Cold War; socialism
Communist Manifesto (Marx
 and Engels), 46, 47
communitarianism. *See* group
 rights
compulsory education, 108
compulsory hospitalization, 85
CONADEP. *See* National
 Commission on
 Disappeared Persons
concentration camps, 52, 54,
 222
conception, as inception of
 rights, 78, 82
Concilium Plebis, 8

Concordat of 1801 (France),
 32
Congo, Democratic Republic
 of the, 157
Congress, U.S., 28-29
Congressional Gold Medal,
 222
Congressional Human Rights
 Caucus (U.S.), 191-92
Congress of Vienna (1815),
 270
conscience
 conscientious objection,
 238-39
 freedom of, 98-99, 238
 as humankind attribute, 74
conscientious objection, 99,
 238-39
conscription, 238-39
Constitution, U.S., 26, 28-29
 as Declaration of Human
 Rights influence, 62
constitutional government, 26
 inception, 16
 Lockean ideas, 19-20
 Montesquieu ideas, 24
Constitution of the
 International Labor
 Organization, 53n.21
consul, 8
Consultative Assembly
 (Council of Europe), 138
consumer goods, 20
Continental Congress, 27-28
contract law, 82
Convention Against Torture
 (1984), 134, 137, 272
Convention Concerning
 Forced or Compulsory
 Labor (1930), 271
Convention Concerning
 Indigenous and Tribal
 Peoples in Independent
 Countries (1989), 256
Convention Concerning the
 Abolition of Forced
 Labor (1957), 271
Convention for the Protection
 of Human Rights and
 Fundamental Freedoms,
 death penalty protocol,
 241
Convention for the
 Suppression of the Traffic
 in Persons and of the
 Exploitation of the
 Prostitution of Others
 (1951), 80, 273
Convention on Conventional
 Weapons (1980), 260
Convention on the
 Elimination of All Forms
 of Discrimination Against
 Women (1979), 77, 80,
 83, 134, 137
 ban on trafficking, 273
 on educational rights, 109-
 10
 rape and, 267
 signatory reservations, 251
Convention on the
 Elimination of All Forms
 of Racial Discrimination
 (1969), 77, 83, 129, 134,
 137
Convention on the Prevention
 and Punishment of the
 Crime of Genocide
 (1949), 55, 134, 147, 195,
 252

Convention on the Prohibition of the Use, Stockpiling, Production and Transfer of Anti-Personnel Mines and on Their Destruction (1997), 261

Convention on the Rights of the Child (1989), 80, 90, 134, 137, 175
  near exclusion of girls' special needs, 254
  prohibition of child military recruitment, 237
  prohibition of trafficking in girls, 273

Convention People's Party (Ghana), 129

Convention Relating to the Status of Refugees (1951), 92, 93, 234

copyrights, 111, 240

Corinthians, 12

Cornwallis, Lord, 28

Corpus Juris Civilis, 8

COs. *See* conscientious objection

Costa Lopes, Martinho do, 183

Costa Rica, 142

Council of Europe, 71, 132, **137-39**, 139, 144, 145
  death penalty protocol, 241
  NGOs and, 152

courts. *See* judiciary; specific courts

courts, human rights, **144-48**

CPJ. *See* Committee to Protect Journalists

CRC. *See* Convention on the Rights of the Child

crimes against humanity, 89, 119, 148
  forced deportation as, 234
  genocide vs., 252
  jurisdiction, 247
  Nuremberg and Tokyo trials, 55
  rape as, 251, 267
  Rwanda and Balkan tribunals, 145-47
  slavery as, 271
  torture as, 272

criminal justice
  death penalty, 241-42
  detention use, 243
  due process rights, 87-89, 115
  extradition, 246-47
  innocence presumption, 82, 88-89, 248
  liberty deprivations, 86-87
  prisoners, 265-66
  privacy rights, 90
  rape disposition, 267
  See also legal rights

Croat war criminals, 146, 190, 191

Cromwell, Oliver, 20n.7

Cromwell, Richard, 20n.7

cross-dressing, 269

cruel, inhuman, or degrading treatment
  protections from, 18, 78, 79, 80-81, 86
  as absolute right, 115
  death penalty as, 241
  police brutality as, 263

CSCE. *See* Helsinki Accords

CSHR. *See* Center for the Study of Human Rights

Cuba, 256

cultural bias, 240

cultural property, 111

cultural relativism, 23

cultural revolution (China), 189

cultural rights, 110-11, **239-40**
  reconciliation with women's rights, 251

cultural traditions
  discrimination against girl children, 253-54
  human rights and, 125-27, 130-31, 240

Curie, Marie, 36

CWI. *See* Children's Watch International

Cyprus, 6

Czechoslovakia, 48, 50, 122, 138
  Havel, Vaclav, 180, 192-93

Czech Republic, 192, 193

D

Dag Hamarskjold Prize, 194

Dahl, Robert, 129

Dai Quing, 189

Dalai Lama, 180, **191-92**

Dalindyebo, Jongintaba, 198

Daniel, 13

days of rest, 106

Dayton Accords, 146

death, right to, 78

death penalty, 11, 20, **241-42**
  arguments against, 242
  Council of Europe ban, 71
  Draconian, 5
  extradition denial in face of, 247
  extrajudicial, 248-49, 256, 266
  and right to life, 71, 78-79
  UDHR Article 5 applications, 81

death row, 81

death squads, 209

debt bondage. *See* bonded labor

Decade of Human Rights Education (1995-2004), 74, 110

Declaration of Geneva (1924), 109

Declaration of Human Rights (1948). *See* Universal Declaration of Human Rights

Declaration of Independence (1776; U.S.), 28, 62, 268

Declaration of Philadelphia (1944), 53

Declaration of Rights of Man and the Citizen (1789; France), 26-27, 29-30, 31, 32, 34, 36, 86
  as self-determination influence, 268
  as Universal Declaration of Human Rights influence, 62

Declaration of Rights of the People of Russia (1917), 120n.2

Declaration of the Rights of Woman and the Citizen, The (de Gouges), 36

Declaration of the United Nations (1942), 53

Declaration on Democracy (1978), 140

Declaration on the Granting of Independence to Colonial Countries and Peoples (1960), 268

Declaration on the Protection of All Persons from Being Subjected to Torture and Other Cruel, Inhuman, or Degrading Treatment or Punishment (1975), 121

Declaration on the Protection of All Persons from Enforced Disappearance (1992), 245, 246

Declaration on the Protection of Refugees and Displaced Persons in the Arab World (1992), 260

Declaration on the Right to Development (1986), 244, 245

Declaratory Act of 1766 (Great Britain), 27

decolonization, 112, 127-29, 140, 150
  self-determination and, 268

defections, 91, 92-93

de Gaulle, Charles, 188

Degeneres, Ellen, 269-70

deism, 21, 24, 32

de Klerk, F. W., 198, 199

democracy
  Athenian, 3, 4, 5, 6, 102
  developing nations and, 128-29
  direct vs. representative, 102-3
  free exchange of information and, 99-100
  guarantees of, 86
  human rights and, 99
  secular, 98

Democracy Salon (China), 220

Democracy Wall (Beijing), 221

demonstrations. See protests and demonstrations

Deng, Francis, 259

Deng Xiaoping, 189, 221

Denmark, 54-55

deportation, 234

derogations test, 115-16

desaparecido (disappeared), coining of term, 245

despotism, 23

detention, **242-44**
  freedom from, 85-87, 243
  police brutality and, 263
  preventive detention laws, 127
  torture and, 272
  See also disappearances

developing nations
  assembly rights and, 102
  child labor issue, 80, 236
  cultural differences, 126-27
  developed countries' aid to, 104, 112
  development theories, 244-45
  economic, social, and cultural rights focus, 104, 112, 125, 127-29, 240
  group and family focus, 126-27

human rights policies, 123, 128-29, 240
  property rights concerns, 97
  Third World Foundation of North America, 174-75
  traffic in women and girls, 273-74
  U.S. development aid, 244
  WHO assistance, 143-44
  See also specific areas and countries

development, **244-45**, 268

dhimmis, 136

Diana Database. *See* Project Diana: Online Human Rights Archive

dictatorships. *See* authoritarianism

Diderot, Denis, 22, 23, 24, 25

Dien Dan Tu Do (Vietnamese publication), 265

Diocletian, emperor of Rome, 13

diplomacy, 246

direct democracy, 102

direct discrimination, 83

"dirty war" (Argentina), 203, 216, 217

disabled people
  Nazi extermination policy, 54, 76
  rights of, 76, 108

disappearances, **245-46**, 266
  Argentina, 180, 203-4, 206, 216, 226, 245

discrimination
  AIDS/HIV, 231
  definitions of, 83
  extradition clause, 247
  against girl children, 253-54
  gender bias remedies, 106, 251
  protections against, 82-84
  against sexual minorities, 269-70

disease control, 51
  AIDS/HIV, 231-32

displaced persons. See internally displaced persons; refugees

Dissenters, 18

dissidents
  asylum and, 92-93
  China, 188-89, 220, 221-22
  Czechoslovakia, 192-93
  freedom of movement and, 86, 91
  one-party state suppression of, 129
  Soviet Union, 185, 212
  torture of, 272
  Vietnam, 265
  See also political prisoners

District of Columbia, 29

divine link, 11

"divine right of kings," 15

divine will, 6

divorce
  Enlightenment sanction, 23
  religious restrictions, 99
  Roman, 10

Doan Viet Hoat, 265

Doctors Without Borders USA, 121, **159-60**, 180, 193, 194, 262

Dole, Bob, 225

domestic service, 41, 274

domestic violence, 68, 81, 250, 251

double-criminality rule (extradition), 247
Draco, 5
draft. *See* conscription
drought, 93
due process, 82, 87-89, 115
   extradition and, 246-47
   extrajudicial executions and, 248-49
Dumagat, 236
duties, 27
Duvalier, Jean-Claude, 216
DWB. *See* Doctors Without Borders USA

E
Easter Rising (1916), 196
East India Company, 27
East Timor, 181, 182-83, 207-8, 268
ECHR. *See* European Commission on Human Rights
ECJ. *See* European Court of Justice
Economic and Social Council (UN), 61, 136, 177, 248
economic refugees, 234
economic, social, and cultural rights, 63, 70, **122-27**
   acceptance of covenant on, 120
   asylum seeking and, 93
   cultural rights, 110-11, 239-40
   defined, 67, 104
   developing states and, 104, 112, 125, 126-29, 240
   development as, 244-45
   homelessness and, 254-55
   implementation, 104
   self-determination and, 268
   UDHR Articles 22-27 on, 66, 67, 122-27
   See also International Covenant on Economic, Social, and Cultural Rights
economy
   as American Revolution cause, 27-28
   development aims, 244
   laissez-faire, 19n.6, 21, 22-23, 34, 41
   nineteenth-century women's plight, 37-39, 41
   political power to protect assets, 20
   post-World War I disruptions, 43, 51, 52
   pre-revolutionary French problems, 30-31
   slavery and, 9
   state's role in, 63
   See also wealth
ECOSOC. *See* Economic and Social Council
ecosystems. *See* environmental concerns
Ecumenical Movement of Peace and Justice, 206
education
   British reforms, 35
   coeducational vs. same-sex, 110
   Enlightenment reforms, 19, 22, 24, 25
   gender role stereotypes and, 110

human rights definitions of, 108-9
   on individual rights, 35
   individual rights focus and level of, 128
   right to, 67-68, 69, 108-9, 112
   of Roman women, 10
   universal right to free, 46, 47, 108-10
   women's limited opportunities, 37, 251, 253
Edward I, king of England, 16
egalitarian society, 34
Egypt, 130, 187
   Saadawi, Nawal El, 210-11
Einstein, Albert, 189
elderly, rights of the, 108
elections, 102-3
electric chair, *241*
elementary education, compulsory, 108
El Salvador, 135, 187
   child soldiers, 237, *237*
   disappearance, 245
   Romero, Oscar, 180, 209-10
emergency, state of, 115, 248
Emory University, 155
employment, right to free choice of, 67, 105, 106
Encyclopedia (Diderot), 22, 24, **25**
Engels, Friedrich, 45, 46, 47
England. *See* Great Britain
English Bill of Rights (1689). *See* Bill of Rights, English
English Civil War (1640s), 16-17, 19, 20
Enlightenment, 18-21, 22-25, 34
   Encyclopedia, 22, 24, 25
   immediate significant impact of, 22
   legacy of, 24-25, 26, 28, 29, 74, 75, 93
   liberalism and, 36
environmental concerns, 90, 93, 96, 97
   Amazonian rainforest, 202
   development aid and, 244
   Nigerian indigenous lands, 213
epistemology, 33
equality
   as basis of human relations, 74
   Burke's view as "monstrous fiction," 34
   gender, 95, 106
   improvement of Roman women's status, 10
   of rights within marriage, 95, 106
   Roman male citizens, 8
   suffrage rights, 102, 103 (*see also* voting rights)
   three legal approaches to, 83
   UDHR Article I on, 74-75
   UDHR Articles 2-7 on, 66, 67, 76-84
   of women's human rights status, 250-51 (*see also* Convention on the Elimination of All Forms of Discrimination Against Women)
   work conditions, 105-6

equal opportunity, 76
"equal pay for work of equal value," 105, 106
Equatorial Guinea, 246
Eritrea, 268
Essay Concerning Human Understanding (Locke), 33
established religion. *See* church-state relations
Estates-General (France), 31
Ethiopia, 141, 246, 264
   Eritrean independence, 268
ethnic cleansing, 91, 259
ethnic groups
   armed conflict among, 233
   cultural rights, 110-11, 239-40
   diversity of Roman citizens, 9
   genocide against, 252-53
   self-determination, 268-69
   Society for Threatened Peoples, 174
   See also indigenous peoples
EU. *See* European Community
eugenics, 54, 96
Europe
   death penalty, 241
   human rights organizations, 137-40
   labor reform, 40-43
   post-World War II development aid to, 244
   racist marches, 101-2
   refugee movements, 92-93
   student protests, 101
   World War II displacements, 53, 92-93
   See also specific countries and organizations
European Commission on Human Rights, 71, 81, 86, 87, 97, 113, **139-40**, 144, *272*
European Community. *See* European Union
European Convention for the Protection of Human Rights and Fundamental Freedoms, 271
European Convention on Extradition (1957), 246, 247
European Convention on Human Rights (1953), 85, 105, 138-39, 140, 144, 196
   detention regulation, 243
European Council of Ministers, 140
European Court of Human Rights, 81, 84, 139, **144-45**, *272*
European Court of Justice, 139, 145
European Economic Community. *See* European Union
European Parliament, 139, 140, 182, 194
European security conference (1972), 121
European Social Charter, 106
European Torture Convention (1989), 81
European Union, 101, 139, 140, 145
euthanasia, 78
evidence, rules of, 89

executions. *See* death penalty; extrajudicial executions
exile, protection from, 85-87
Exploration (Chinese dissident journal), 221
exposure. *See* infanticide
expression, freedom of, 53, 60, 66-67, 78, 86, 99-100
   hate speech issue, 77
   libel laws and, 34
   limitations justification, 100, 114, 115, 264
   See also press, freedom of
extradition, **246-48**
extrajudicial executions, **248-49**, 256, 266
extraordinary measures test, 115

F
factory workers, 40, 41, 43
fair trial, right to, 18, 82, 87-88
   criminal trial rights, 88-89
   extrajudicial executions contravening, 248
   pretrial detention limits, 243
Falklands War, 204, 206
family
   educational rights, 108
   as institution, 19
   interests of child vs. parental rights, 90
   living standard rights, 107
   non-Western traditions, 127
   personal life rights, 89, 90
   privacy rights, 89-90
   right to found, 95-96
   son preference, 253, 254
famine, 93, 154
Fang Lizhi, 180, **188-89**
Farabi, 131
farming, 27
fascism, 52, 81, 100, 101
FDR Library (Hyde Park, N.Y.), 160
fear, freedom from, 53, 60
Federation Internationale des Ligues des Droits de L'Homme. See International Federation of Human Rights Leagues
female genital mutilation, 210, 231, 234, 235, 240, *249*, **249-50**, 253, 254
female infanticide, 253
feminism, 42, 68, 81; *See also* women's rights
fetal rights, 78, 82
FIDH. *See* International Federation of Human Rights League
Fifteenth Amendment, U.S. (1870), 29
Final Act of the Helsinki Meeting of the Conference on Security and Cooperation in Europe. *See* Helsinki Accords
"final solution." *See* Holocaust
First Continental Congress, 27
first generation rights, 19, 66
FMG. *See* female genital mutilation
forced evictions, 255, 50
forced labor, 79

forced labor, (*continued*)
China, 224, 225
conventions against, 271
defined, 80
Soviet Union, 52
traffic in women and girls, 273, 274
foreign policy, idealist vs. realist, 122-23, **124**, 186
Foundation for Communal Work, 198
Four Freedom Awards, 160
Four Freedoms, 53, 60, 100, 160
Fourteen Points, 47, 49-50
Fourteenth Amendment, U.S. (1868), 29
France
and American Revolution, 28, 30
Cassin, René, 187-88
Enlightenment, 22-25, 30
extradition limitations, 247
government, 23-24
Human Rights Commission member, 61
Kouchner, Bernard, 180, 193-94
labor movement, 42-43
social contract, 20-21
women's employment, 41
women's rights, 36, 37, 38
See also Declaration of the Rights of Man and the Citizen; French Revolution
franchise. *See* voting rights
Frank, Anne, 55
Frank, Leo, 152
Franklin and Eleanor Roosevelt Institute, **160**
fraternity, 74
freedom
cultural values and, 111
Engels view of, 47
as first-generation rights emphasis, 19n.6
Islamic philosophy on, 131
as natural right, 19, 21, 24
UDHR Article I on, 74-75
See also laissez-faire doctrine; liberty, right to; specific freedoms by key word
Freedom of Information and the Press subcommission (UN), 61
Free France, 188
freeman, 15-16
free markets, 23, 34, 97-98
free will, 47
FRELIMO (Front for the Liberation of Mozambique), 197
French Academy of Science, 36
French Red Cross, 194
French Revolution, 18, 21, 25, 29-32
Burke critique of, 34
influences and causes, 30-31
legacy of, 31-32, 248
women's rights advocate, 36
FRETILIN (Revolutionary Front for an Independent East Timor), 207
Front for the Liberation of Mozambique. *See* FRELIMO

fugitive offenders. *See* extradition
Fund for Free Expression, 163

G
Gabriel, Peter, 176
Gaer, Felie, 123-24
Galsworthy, John, 167
Gandhi, Indira, 127
Gandhi, Mohandas, 182, 207
gay rights, 71, 76, 90, 96, 269-70
AIDS/HIV, 231
Geitling v. High Authority (1960), 139
gender-related persecution, **250-51**
asylum rights, 234-35, 251
contemporary issues, 251
denial of health services, 262
girl children, 253-54
rape as, 266-67
sexual minorities, 269-70
sexual slavery, 271
traffic in women and girls, 273-74
See also gay rights; women's rights
General Assembly (UN), 61, 129, 134, 135
Code of Conduct for Law Enforcement Officers, 263
continuing elaboration of UDHR principles, 71-72
Decade of Human Rights Education proclamation, 74
Declaration on the Granting of Independence to Colonial Countries and Peoples, 268
Declaration on the Protection of All Persons from Enforced Disappearance, 245
Declaration on the Right to Development, 244, 245
international judicial standard, 257
International Law commission, 147
Nuremberg Principles ratification, 66
passage of UDHR as nonbinding resolution, 62, 64, 65, 66, 70, 120, 188
"Right to Development" proclamation, 104, 112
Universal Declaration of Human Rights ratification, 55
general will, 21
Geneva, 21
Geneva Conference on Indigenous Population (1992), 213
Geneva Conventions, 136, 145-46
on child soldier recruitment, 237
on medical neutrality, 262
on prisoners of war, 265, 266
on "prosecute or extradite" obligation, 247
on torture, 271

on treatment of prisoners, 265
Geneva Declaration (1924), 109
genocide, 89, 145, 147, 148, **252-53**
coining of term, 180, 195, 252
rape and, 267
universal jurisdiction, 247, 252
See also Holocaust
Genocide Convention (1949). *See* Convention on the Prevention and Punishment of the Crime of Genocide
gentry, 20
George III, king of Great Britain, 28
George V, king of Great Britain, 40
Georgia (republic), 136
Germany
denationalization, 94
extradition limitations, 247
Hegelian thought and, 45
labor movement, 41-42
Nuremberg trials, 55, 147, 195, 234
World War I reparations, 48-49, 50, 52
See also Holocaust; Nazis; World War II
Gesellschaft für bedrohte Völker. See Society for Threatened Peoples
GfbV. *See* Society for Threatened Peoples
Ghana, 128, 129
Gingrich, Newt, 225
girl children, 251, **253-54**
traffic in, 273-74
Glasnost Defense Foundation, 265
Glorious Revolution of 1688 (Britain), 17, 18, 20
God, 75
deist view of, 21, 24
as highest authority, 13, 17
and human dignity, 98
as Islamic ultimate authority, 130, 131
Judeo-Christian view of, 11-12
monarchy and, 15, 24
Goering, Hermann, 55
Golden Rule, 14
"Golden Rule, The" (Rockwell), *1*
Goldman Environmental Prize, 213
Goldstone, Richard J., **190-91**
Goldstone Commission (1991), 190, 191
Gompers, Samuel, 44
Gonne, Maud, 196
goodness, 21, 24
Gorbachev, Mikhail, 122, 185, 212
Gouges, Olympe de, 36
government
ancient Greek, 4-5, 7
Aristotelian advocacy of mixed, 5
authority derivation, 28
citizenship rights, 94
class power interests, 8
consent-of-governed basis, 28-29

English constitutional inception, 16
Enlightenment beliefs, 23-24, 25
general will of, 21
Islam and, 130, 131
laissez-faire policy, 21, 34-35
military juntas, 126, 127, 128, 129
opportunities for criticism of, 34-35
participation right, 102-3
press criticism, 34, 35, 265
protection of property by, 20
Roman, 8
self-determination rights, 268-69
separation of powers, 19-20, 23, 24, 26, 28-29
social reform policies, 35, 38, 40, 42
U.S. constitutional inception, 28-29
utilitarian evaluation, 34
See also state; voting rights; *specific types of government*
governmental organizations, 69, 119, **133-44**
Grande, Rutillo, 209
Great Britain
American Revolution, 27-28
Anglophilia of Voltaire and Montesquieu, 22
Benenson, Peter, 184-85
Bill of Rights, 17-18, 26, 27
colonialism model, 127
Falklands War, 204, 206
government-initiated social reform, 35, 40, 42
Human Rights Commission member, 61
independent judiciary, 256-57
Irish nationalism, 196, 197, 272
labor movement, 36-37, 40-41, 42-44, 46
laissez-faire economic theory, 23
natural rights theory, 19-20, 21, 33-34
Pinochet extradition controversy, 247
press freedom, 264-65
rights and legal tradition, 15-18, 19, 21, 26, 86
self-determination policy and, 49
societal changes, 35
trading wealth, 20
universal suffrage movement, 36-40
utilitarianism, 34-35
woman suffrage, 38, 38, 39, 40
Great Charter of Liberties. *See* Magna Carta
"greatest good" evaluation, 34
Greece
Communist threat to, 138
conscientious objector imprisonment, 239
military coup (1967), 128
war with Turkey, 205
Greece, ancient, 3-7, 10, 102, 234, 272
greed, 46

Group Areas Act (South Africa), 190
group rights, 63, 126-27
    Islamic concept of freedom as, 131
    minority cultural rights, 110, 240
    See also economic, social, and cultural rights
Guatemala, 135, 136
    disappearances, 245
    indigenous peoples, 181, 200-201, 258
    Menchú, Rigoberta, 181, 200-201
guilds, 31
Guiliani, Rudolph, 264
Guinea, 128
Gusmo, Xanana, 207
Gypsies, 54, 76

H

Habeas Corpus Act of 1679 (Britain), 26
habeas corpus right, 26, 115
Habitat for Humanity, 180, 187
Hague Congress, 138
Hague Court. See International Court of Justice
Haile Mariam Mengistu, 141
Haiti, 136
Handicap International, 260
happiness, pursuit of, 28
hate crimes, 153, 267, 269
hate speech, 77
Havel, Vaclav, 180, 192, 192-93
health care, 46, 78, 107-8
    AIDS/HIV, 231, 232
    Doctors Without Borders, 159-60, 194
    medical neutrality, 230, 261-62
    Physicians for Human Rights, 171-72
    World Health Organization, 143-44
"Health for All by the Year 2000" campaign, 143
Health Organization of the League of Nations, 143
Hegel, George Wilhelm Friedrich, 45, 46
Hellenistic age, 6, 7
Helsinki Accords (1975), 121-22
Helsinki Watch. See Human Rights Watch
Henry I, king of England, 15
Hesiod, 4
Hidden Face of Eve: Women in the Arab World (Saadawi), 210-11
High Commissioner for Human Rights. See Office of the High Commissioner for Human Rights
High Commissioner for Refugees. See United Nations High Commissioner for Refugees
Hillel, 12
Himmler, Heinrich, 54
Hinduism, 98
Hippocratic Oath, 261
historical evolution, 45-46

historiography, 45
Hitler, Adolf, 50, 52, 53, 54, 138
HIV. See AIDS/HIV
Hmong, 258
Hobbes, Thomas, 18, 19, 20
holidays, right to, 106, 107
Holocaust, 53-55, 76, 92, 180, 195
    as genocide, 252
    Wiesel, Elie, 222, 223
Holocaust Memorial Museum (Washington, D.C.), 222
holy periods, 106
homelessness, **254-55**, 259-60
homosexuality
    AIDS/HIV, 231, 232
    ancient Greek society, 6
    human rights issue, 71, 90, 96, 269-70
    Nazi persecution, 76, 269
Honduras, 256
Honorary Council of the Latin American Servicio Paz y Justicia, 206
honor, right to protect, 89
hostage crisis (Iran), 122
house arrest, 85
House of Commons, British, 20, 23, 34
House of Lords, British, 20, 34
housing rights, 254, 255
HRC. See Human Rights in China
HRI. See Human Rights Internet
HRW. See Human Rights Watch
Huguenots, 30
humanitarian law, 81, 89, 115, 136
humankind
    as basis for human rights, 65, 66, 74, 75, 77, 98
    Encyclopedia's focus on, 25
    as innately good, 24
    innate value of, 11-12
    Islamic view of, 131
human rights
    absolute, 114, 115
    American and English Bill of Rights as key documents, 26
    American Revolution legacy, 28-29, 248, 268
    antidemocratic aspects of, 99
    as birthright, 75
    Communism and, 46-47
    concept overview, 66-69
    contemporary global movement, 71-72, 119-32
    contemporary issues, 229-74
    English tradition, 15-18
    Enlightenment legacy, 24-25, 26, 28, 29, 74, 75, 93
    first generation rights, 19, 66
    guaranteed to activists, 255-56
    history of theory, 3-55
    humanity as basis, 65, 66, 74, 75, 77, 98
    as international concern, 47 (see also international law)
    in Islamic states, 130-31
    Judeo-Christian contributions, 11-12, 13

League of Nations legacy, 51
    limitations tests, 19, 77, 113-16, 264
    modern definition, 28
    modern movement. See human rights movement
    natural law and, 7, 18, 19-20, 22, 33
    natural rights and, 21-22, 23
    positive vs. negative, 67
    and protection of others,' 78, 100, 112-16
    raising awareness of, 70
    rape as violation of, 267
    remedy for violations, 84-85
    responsibilities and, 113
    as secular concept, 98
    self-determination and, 48
    self-evident. See inalienable rights
    socialist agenda, 45
    vs. duty to state. See state
    woman suffrage legacy, 39
    women's earliest protections, 250
    World War II documents, 53, 60, 100
    See also group rights; individual rights; Universal Declaration of Human Rights; specific rights
human rights activists, **255-56**
    biographies, 179-226
Human Rights Commission (UN). See Commission on Human Rights
Human Rights Committee (UN), 66, 84, 270
human rights defenders. See human rights activists
Human Rights Division (UN), 61
Human Rights in China, **161**, 189
Human Rights Information and Documentation Systems International Secretariat, **161-62**, 172
Human Rights Internet, **162**
human rights movement, 71-72, 119-32
    activists, 179-226, 255-56
    awareness campaign, 137
    courts, 144-48
    enforceability problem, 129-32
    governmental organizations, 133-44
    Helsinki Accords, 121-22
    historical background, 119-20
    idealism vs. realism, 122-23, 124
    nongovernmental organizations, 149-77 (see also NGOs)
    ongoing controversies, 124-32
    See also Universal Declaration of Human Rights
Human Rights Watch, 121, **162-63**, 171, 189, 230
    campaign against child soldiers, 237, 238

campaign against traffic in women and girls, 274
    police brutality reports, 263
    on Turkish human rights violations, 256
Human Rights Youth in Action Award, 200
Hume, David, 33
Humphrey, John, 61-62, 64
hunger strikes, 40, 185
HURIDOCS. See Human Rights Information and Documentation Systems International Secretariat
Husak, Gustav, 193
Hutu, 147, 233, 252, 264

I

IACHR. See Inter-American Commission on Human Rights; Inter-American Convention on Human Rights
Ibo, 194
ICBL. See International Campaign to Ban Landmines
ICC. See International Criminal Court
ICCPR. See International Covenant on Civil and Political Rights
ICDC. See UNICEF International Child Development Centre
ICESCR. See International Covenant on Economic, Social, and Cultural Rights
ICHRDD. See International Centre for Human Rights and Democratic Development
ICRC. See International Committee of the Red Cross
idealism
    economic, social, and cultural rights seen as, 240
    in foreign policy, 122-23, 124, 186
IDPs. See internally displaced persons
IFEX. See International Freedom of Expression Exchange
IGC. See Institute for Global Communications
IHRLG. See International Human Rights Law Group
IIHR. See Inter-American Institute of Human Rights
Ijma, 130, 131
Ijtihad, 130, 131
ILC. See International Law Commission
ILO. See International Labour Office; International Labor Organization
immigration, 43, 93, 94
    administrative detention, 243
    AIDS/HIV prohibitions, 231
    Immigration and Naturalization Service (U.S.), 243

Immigration and Refugee
  Services of America, 176
imperialism. *See* colonialism
inalienable rights
  conflicts among, 33
  Declaration of
    Independence on, 28
  liberty as, 86
  Locke on, 33
  Talmud on, 14
  UDHR Article I on, 74-75
"Inaugural Address of the
  Working Men's
  International Association"
  (Marx), 46
indentured servitude, 27, 236
independence movements. *See*
  self-determination
Independent Expert on the
  Sale of Children, 271
independent judiciary, 87-88,
  256-57
India, 215, 233
  child bonded labor, 236
  female infanticide, 253
Indigenous Initiative for
  Peace, 201
indigenous peoples, **257-59**
  development programs and,
    244
  rights activists, 200-201,
    202
  self-determination seekers,
    268-69
indirect democracy, 102-3
indirect discrimination, 83
individual rights
  absolute, 68, 114, 115
  in ancient Greece, 4-7
  cultural rights as, 240
  development level and, 128-
    29
  Enlightenment focus on,
    25, 30
  inalienable, 14, 28, 33, 74-
    75, 86
  laissez-faire doctrine and,
    19n.6, 21, 35, 41
  limited monarchy and, 19
  minority group rights vs.,
    240
  in natural law
    reconsideration, 33
  social, economic, and
    cultural rights and, 104,
    110, 127
  state's interests vs., 6-7, 8,
    63, 68, 99, 112-16, 127,
    130, 132
  UDHR focus on, 66-69
  violation remedies, 84-85
  vs. Islamic state, 130-31
  vs. monarchical power, 17
  Western emphasis on, 127
  See also civil and political
    rights
Indonesia, 182, 183, 187, 207-
  8, 240
industrialization
  American, 44
  British, 33, 35, 40
  multilateral development
    aid for, 244
infanticide, 6, 10
  female, 253
infant mortality prevention,
  107
influenza epidemic, 51

information, free exchange of.
  See expression, freedom
  of; press, freedom of
inheritance rights, 10, 46, 47
inheritance tax, 9
innocence, presumption of,
  82, 88-89, 248
Innocent III, pope, 16
Innocent IV, pope, 272
Institute for Global
  Communications, **163-
  64**
Institute for the Study of
  Genocide, **164-65**
Institute of Medicine, 158
integrity, judicial, 88
intellectual property, 111, 240
International Society for
  Human Rights, **169-9**
Inter-American Bar
  Association, 62
Inter-American Commission
  and Court of Human
  Rights, 81, 84, 143
Inter-American Commission
  on Human Rights, **165**,
  258, 272
Inter-American Convention
  on Human Rights (1978),
  78, 81
Inter-American Court of
  Human Rights, 142
Inter-American Development
  Bank, 142, 202
Inter-American Institute of
  Human Rights, 142-43
Inter-American Treaty of
  Reciprocal Assistance
  (Rio Treaty), 142
Inter-Enterprise Strike
  Committee (Poland), 219
internally displaced persons,
  53, 146, 254, 255, **259-60**
International Bill of Rights,
  60, 61, 65, 133-34, 153
International Campaign to
  Ban Landmines, 180,
  223-24
International Centre for
  Human Rights and
  Democratic
  Development, 165-66
International Commission of
  Jurists, 184, 196-97
International Commission on
  Missing Persons, 146
International Committee of
  the Red Cross
  armed opposition groups,
    233
  internally displaced persons,
    259, 260
  landmine effectiveness
    study, 261
  medical neutrality, 230
  prisoner of war
    interventions, 230, 266
  war zone medical assistance,
    262
  See also International Red
    Cross
International Confederation
  of Disabled Soldiers, 187-
  88
International Congresses on
  Women's Rights and
  Feminine Institutions
  (1889), 39
International Convention for
  the Suppression and

Punishment of the Crime
  of Apartheid (1976), 199
International Council of
  Churches in the United
  States of America, 173
International Court of Justice,
  94, *117*, 253
International Covenant on
  Civil and Political Rights,
  61, 65, 78, 80, 81, 86, 87,
  97, 98-99, 100, 193, 241,
  243, 248, 270, 271
  activists' rights guarantees,
    255
  on article limitations, 113
  as operational and legally
    binding, 120, 133-34
International Covenant on
  Economic, Social, and
  Cultural Rights, 61, 65,
  193
  on homelessness, 254-55
  as operational and legally
    binding, 120, 129, 133,
    134
  problems implementing
    ideals of, 240
International Criminal Court,
  147-48, 191, 231, 247,
  253, 267
  criminalization of slavery,
    271
  criminalization of torture,
    272
International Criminal
  Tribunal for Rwanda, 252
International Decade of the
  World's Indigenous
  People (1995-2004), 259
International Federation of
  Human Rights Leagues,
  166-67
International Freedom of
  Expression Exchange,
  159, 265
international governmental
  bodies. *See* governmental
  organizations; *specific
  groups*
international human rights law
  courts, 144-48
  cultural and scientific rights,
    111
  foundation of, 64-65
  historical background,
    32, 47, 51
  individual rights focus,
    67, 68
  judicial standard, 257
  monitors and violations
    remedies, 84-85
  public vs. private
    distinction, 68, 113
  sexual minorities rights, 269
  See also international law
International Human Rights
  Law Group, **167**
internationalism, 48-51, 112
international judicial standard,
  257
International Labour
  Organization, 53n.21,
  106, 107, 177, 200, 219
  on child bonded labor, 236
  indigenous and tribal
    peoples convention, 258
  slavery conventions, 271
International Labour Office,
  51

International Ladies Garment
  Workers Union, 44
international law
  death penalty, 241
  exile prohibition, 85
  genocide, 195, 252
  HIV-infection
    discrimination, 231
  humanitarian, 81, 89, 115,
    136
  rape as gender-based crime,
    267
  refugee status, 134, 136, 170
  right to democratic
    government, 103
  self-determination, 268
  slavery, 270
  sovereignty concept and,
    77, 94
  UDHR principles seen as
    binding, 129, 132
  universal jurisdiction, 247
  wartime rape, 267
  See also international human
    rights law
International Law
  Commission, 147
International League for
  Human Rights, 123-24,
  189
International League for the
  Rights and Liberation of
  Peoples, 206
International Military
  Tribunals, 55, 234, 267
international order, right to,
  111-12
International Peace Bureau,
  196, 197
International PEN, **167-68**,
  214
International Police Task
  Force (UN), 146
International Red Cross, 64,
  205
  armed opposition groups,
    233
  opposition to child soldier
    recruitment, 237
  wartime medical care, 262
  See also International
    Committee of the Red
    Cross
International Religious
  Liberty Association, **168**
International Society for
  Human Rights, **168-69**
International Television Trust,
  177
international treaties, 100
International Treaty
  Conference (1998), 147
International War Crimes
  Tribunal for Rwanda and
  the Balkans, **145-47**, 190,
  191
International Women's Rights
  Action Watch, **169**
International Women's
  Suffrage Alliance, 39
International Year for
  Indigenous Populations
  (1993), 201
International Year of the
  Refugee (UN), 176
interregnum (England), 20n.7
Inuit, 258
Iran
  Carter administration
    policy, 122, 187

Iran, (*continued*)
  death penalty rate, 242
  human rights fact-finding,
    135
  lesbian punishment, 269
Iraq, 130, 194, 259
Ireland, 272
  abortion and divorce
    restrictions, 99
  MacBride, Sean, 196-97
  Robinson, Mary, 208-9
*I, Rigoberta Menchú, An Indian
  Woman in Guatemala*
  (Menchú), 201
Irish Centre for European
  Law, 208
Irish Republican Army, 196
IRLA. *See* International
  Religious Liberty
  Association
Isaiah, Book of, 12
ISG. *See* Institute for the
  Study of Genocide
ISHR. *See* International
  Society for Human
  Rights
Islam, 11, 98, 120n.1, **130-31**
  day of rest, 106
  restrictions on women, 210-
    11, 234, 251
  Saadawi, Nawal El, 210-11
Israel, 187, 217, 243, 255
Italy, 42, 52, 119
IWRAW. *See* International
  Women's Rights Action
  Watch

J
Jacobins, 30
James II, king of England, 17,
  20
Japan, 51, 53, 55, 119, 271
Jefferson, Thomas, 28, 62
Jehovah's Witness, 239
Jesus Christ, 10, 12, 13, 14
Jews. *See* anti-Semitism;
  Holocaust; Judaism
Job, 11
jobs. *See* work, right to;
  workdays and hours
Johannes Wier Foundation
  for Health and Human
  Rights, 262
John, king of England, 15-16
John Humphrey Freedom
  Award, 183
John Paul II, pope, 191
Joseph II, emperor of Austria,
  25
journalism. *See* press, freedom
  of
Judaism, 11-12, 14
  Anti-Defamation League,
    152-53
  day of rest, 106
  See also anti-Semitism;
    Holocaust
Judeo-Christian tradition, 11-
  14, 15, 98
  Islamic tradition and, 130
  as Western common
    denominator, 125-26
  See also Christianity;
    Judaism
judicial executions. *See* death
  penalty
judiciary
  human rights courts, 144-
    48

and human rights
    violations, 85
  independence of, 87-88,
    256-57
  partiality of, 100
  precedence adherence, 8
  U.S. system, 29
"June Days" (1848), 42
jury trial, right to, 18
justice
  economic, social, and
    cultural rights
    implementation based on,
    104
  independent judiciary, 87-
    88, 256-57
  Judaic emphasis on, 12
  Platonic utopian, 5
  See also criminal justice;
    judiciary; legal rights
Justinian, emperor of Rome, 8

K
Kamaiya, 236
Karadzic, Radovan, 146
Kassindja, Fauziya, 234-35
Keating, Charles, 216
Khmer Rouge, 237
kidnapping. *See*
  disappearances
King, Rodney, 264
Kirkpatrick, Jeane J., 123n.6
Kissinger, Henry, 124
Knights of Labor, 44
Koran, 120n.1, 130, 131
Korea, 253, 255
Kosovo, 145, 233
Kosovo Liberation Army, 233
Kouchner, Bernard, 180, **193-
  94**
Kuna, 258
Kurds, 194, 263
Kurkau, Ertu Rul, 256

L
labor
  American colonial shortage,
    27
  health and safety
    protections, 42, 45, 46,
    105
  industrialization wage
    effects, 35
  women's nineteenth-
    century opportunities,
    38-39, 41
  women's World War I
    employment, 39
  See also bonded labor; child
    labor; forced labor;
    slavery
labor movement, 23, 35, 40-
  44
  and British Reform acts, 36-
    37
  children's conditions, 42-43
  European legacy, 42-43
  Marxism and, 46
  Polish Solidarity, 219
  socialism and, 45, 43
  unionization rights, 105,
    106
  United States, 43-44
  woman suffrage and, 38
Lafayette, Marquis de, 30, 34
LAHRA. *See* Latin America
  Human Rights
  Association
laissez-faire doctrine, 34-35
  Enlightenment, 22-23

liberal individualism and,
    19n.6, 21, 34, 35, 41, 97-
    98
  negative social effects, 33,
    35, 41
  nineteenth-century
    women's plight, 37-38
  on private control of
    resources, 98
  socialist criticism of, 45
  social reforms and, 35
  See also capitalism
land distribution, 31
landmines, 180, 223-24, **260-
  61**
Laogai system (China), 224
Laos, 258
Laski, Harold, 62
Latin America, 125, **126**, 129
  bonded labor, 236
  disappearances, 245
  Ecumenical Movement for
    Peace and Justice, 206
  human rights activists, 180
  indigenous people rights,
    258
  U.S. development aid, 244
  See also Organization of
    American States; *specific
    countries*
Latin America Human Rights
  Association, **169-70**
Latin language, 12-13
Lauterpacht, Hersch, 62
law
  American, 26
  antidiscrimination, 84
  English, 15-18, 26
  equality before, 82-84
  extradition, 246, 247
  extrajudicial executions,
    248-49
  functions of, 82
  "greatest good" evaluation,
    34
  Greek, 4
  humanitarian, 81, 89, 115
  Islamic, 130-31
  just interpretation and
    application of, 87
  labor workdays and hours,
    42-43, 46
  libel, 34
  nature vs., 7
  precedent, 8
  rape, 267
  religious origins, 99
  retroactive criminality
    prohibition, 89, 115
  Roman, 7-8, 10, 13
  written codes, 4, 7
  See also international human
    rights law; international
    law; judiciary; justice;
    legal rights
law of reason. *See* natural law
Laws, The (Plato), 5
laws of war. *See* humanitarian
  law
Lawyers Committee for
  Human Rights, **170-71**,
  176
LCHR. *See* Lawyers
  Committee for Human
  Rights
League of Nations, 48, 49-51,
  50, *50*, 187, 205, 258
  human rights legacy, 51
  refugee resettlement, 205
  Slavery Commission, 79

Lebanon, 61
Lech Walesa Institute, 219
legal aid, 87
legal personality, right to, 81-
  82
legal precedent, 7
legal rights
  of appeal, 4-5
  of habeas corpus, 26, 115
  procedural guarantees, 82,
    87-89, 115
  UDHR Article 6 on, 81-82
  UDHR Article 7 on, 82-84
  UDHR Article 8 on, 67,
    84-85
  UDHR Article 9 on, 85-87
  UDHR Article 10 on, 87-
    88
  UDHR Article 11 on, 88-
    89
legislator, 4
leisure. *See* rest and leisure
Lemkin, Raphael, 180, **195**,
  252
Lenin, V. I., 46, 268
Lenin International Prize for
  Peace, 197
Lenin Shipyard strike of 1980
  (Gdansk), 219
lesbian rights, 71, 90, 96, 269-
  70
Leviathan (Hobbes), 19
lex aeterna. See natural law
libel laws, 34
liberalism
  human rights basis, 19
  and laissez-faire doctrine,
    19n.6, 21, 34, 35, 41, 97-
    98
  and natural rights, 32-33
  nineteenth-century middle
    class, 36-37
  and self-determination
    rights, 49
  and social and economic
    justice, 35
  socialism vs., 45
  in thirteen American
    colonies, 27
Liberia, 267
liberty, right to, 24, 25, 77-79
  as basis of human relations,
    74
  as inalienable right, 28, 33,
    86
  nature as source, 19
  protection of another's, 78
  three key limitations to, 85-
    87
Libya, 247
life, right to, 19, 77-79
  as absolute right, 115
  definition of "life," 78
  extrajudicial executions
    infringing on, 248
  as inalienable right, 28, 33
  judicial execution
    exemption, 71
  See also death penalty
Lilley, James, 225
limited monarchy, 19-20
Linea Fundadora (Argentina),
  204
Li Shuxian, 188
literacy, 42
living standard. *See* standard of
  living
Livingston, Sigmund, 152
Lloyd George, David, 40, 50

Locke, John, 18, 19-20, 26, 30, 33
Lockerbie (Scotland) airplane explosion, 247
Lord's Resistance Army (Uganda), 271
Los Angeles riots (1992), 263-64
Louima, Abner, 264
Louis XIV, king of France, 30
Louis XV, king of France, 25
Louis XVI, king of france, 30
Louise Weiss European Parliament Prize, 194
love, Christian, 12
"love thy neighbor," 11

M

Maastricht Treaty, 145
MacBride, John, 196
MacBride, Sean, **196-97**, 196, *196*
MacBride Principles (1984), 197
MacBride Round Table, 197
Machel, Graca, **197-98**, 199
Machel, Samora, 197, 198
Magna Carta (1215), 15-16, 18, 26, 62, 86
Mahler, Halfdan, 143
mail-order brides, 273-74
Malaysia, 240
Manchester (England), 41
mandate system, 49, 51
Mandela, Nelson, 148, 180, 190, 198, **198-99**, 218
Man Died, The: Prison Notes of Wole Soyinka, 214
manumission, 9-10
Mao Zedong, 189, 221
marches. *See* protests and demonstrations
Marcos, Ferdinand, 128
marriage
    ancient Greece, 6
    arranged, 80, 253
    bondage, 270
    child brides, 253, 254
    forced, 234-35
    gender equality, 19, 95, 96, 106
    mail-order bride industry, 273-74
    rape within, 267
    right to, 95-96
    Roman Empire, 10, 13
    same-gender, 96, 269
    as social contract, 19
    wife's servile status, 80
Marshall Plan, 244
martyrs, 13
Marx, Karl, 45, 46
Marxism, 43, 45-47
Mary II. *See* William III and Mary II, king and queen of England
Maryland, 28
Masih, Iqbal, 181, **199-200**, 236
Massachusetts, 28
masses, fears of, 33-34
maternal health, 107
Mauriac, François, 222
Mauritania, 270
Mayans, 258
MDM. *See Médecins du Monde*
Médecins du Monde, 194
Médecins sans Frontières USA.
    See Doctors Without Borders USA

media
    definitions of, 100
    See also expression, freedom of; press, freedom of
medical care. *See* health care
medical neutrality, 230, **261-63**
Menchú, Rigoberta, 181, **200-201**
Menchú Tum, Jauna, 201
Mendes, Chico, **202-3**
mercenaries, 15
Metternich, Prince, 45
Middle Ages, 13
middle class
    Enlightenment, 20, 24, 25
    individual rights focus, 128
    liberalism philosophy, 36-37, 45
    social welfare role, 35, 36-38, 42
Middle East, 153-54
    Arab women, 210-11
    female genital mutilation, 249
    peace accord, 187
    See also Islam; *specific countries*
military juntas, 126, 127, 128, 129
    Argentina, 203-4, 206, 216-17, 226, 244
military service
    child soldiers, 236-38, 271
    conscientious objection, 99, 238-39
    French compulsory, 32
    Roman citizenship and, 9
    standing army, 17
Mill, John Stuart, 33, 35, 49
Mines Advisory Group, 260
mining strikes, 44
minorities, 110
    cultural rights as rights of, 110, 239-40
    indigenous peoples, 258-59
    self-determination seekers, 268-69
    sexual, 71, 90, 96, 269-70
    Societies for Threatened Peoples, 174
minorities treaties (World War I), 64, 76, 98
Minority Rights Group, 258
minors. *See* children; children's rights
missing persons, 82 (*see also* disappearances)
Missionaries of Charity, 215
Mladic, Ratko, 146
Mobutu Sese Seko, 128, 147
monarchy
    absolute, 15, 23
    authority based on natural law, 18, 19
    English limitations, 15, 16-18, 19, 20, 21
    enlightened, 23-24
    God's rule over, 17
    limited, 19-20
    monasteries, 12-13
Montesquieu, 22, 23, 25, 28
morality
    cultural variation argument, 23
    in foreign policy, 122-24
    God as highest source of, 11
    human rights and, 28
    law and, 4

Platonic universal, 5
    of slavery, 24
    state vs. universal, 7
Morgan, J. P., 44
Morgenthau, Hans J., 124
Morocco, 246
Mosaic Law, 14
Moscow State University, International Center, 160
Mothers of Plaza de Mayo, **203-4**, *203*, 245
movement, freedom of, 78, 86, 90-92, 114
    Islamic women's restrictions, 234
    people with AIDS and, 231-32
    state of emergency and, 115
Movement for the Survival of the Ogoni People, 213
Mozambique, 150, 197-98, 268
Mozambique National Resistance. *See* RENAMO
Mugabe, Robert, 269
multinational corporations, 245
Muslims. *See* Islam
Mussolini, Benito, 52

N

Namibia, 197
Nansen, Fridtjof, 181, **204-5**
Nansen International Office for Refugees, 205
Nansen Medal, 198, 205
"Nansen passport," 205
Napoleon Bonaparte, 31, 32
nation. *See* state
National Academy of Engineering, 158
National Academy of Sciences, 158
National Assembly (France), 31
National Association of Human Rights Workers, **171**
National Commission on Disappeared Persons, 204, 206
National Council of Maubere Resistance, 207
nationalism
    Enlightenment basis for, 93
    Hegelian "world spirit" and, 45
    See also self-determination
nationality, right to, 85, 93-95
    genocide and, 252-53
    See also citizenship rights; self-determination
nationalization, 127-28
National League for Democracy (Burma), 181, 182
National Organization of Children of Mozambique, 198
national self-determination. *See* self-determination
National Socialist Party. *See* Nazis
Native Americans, 259
NATO, 139, 145
natural disasters, 255, 259
natural law
    critiques of, 32-35

God the "watchmaker" concept, 21
individual rights in context of, 33
philosophes' focus on, 25
rights based on, 18, 19-20, 22, 33
Roman concept of, 9
slavery as contrary to, 24
Stoic concept of, 6
natural rights, 18-22, 26
    critiques of, 33, 34
    as Declaration of Independence basis, 28
    as European revolutionary impetus, 30, 31
    impact on human rights, 21-22, 23
    liberalism and, 32-33
    separation of powers and, 26
nature, 7, 19, 75
Nazis, 52-55
    Argentina and, 217
    art confiscation, 111
    denationalization, 94
    eugenics, 54, 96
    forced deportations, 234
    genocide, 180
    groups persecuted by, 54, 76, 269
    See also Holocaust
negative rights, 67
neo-imperialist, 70
Nepal, 236
Netherlands, 247
New Deal, 63, 70
New Deal Network (Internet), 160
New England, 17
New International Economic Order, 97, 112
newspapers. *See* press, freedom of
New Testament, 12, 14
New York City, police brutality, 264
NGOs (nongovernmental organizations), 60, 69, 119, 120-21, 122, **149-77**, 196, 230
    housing rights, 255
    indigenous rights movement, 258
    initiative against child soldiers, 238
    initiatives against child bonded labor, 236
    landmine problems, 260-61
    prisoner protection, 266
    torture violations, 272
Nicaragua, 260
Nicholson Medal for Humanitarian Service, 189
Nigeria
    Biafran civil war, 194, 214
    forced evictions, 255
    press freedom violation, 264
    Saro-Wiwa, Ken, 180, 212-13
    Soyinka, Wole, 214
Nineteenth Amendment, U.S. (1920), 29
Nixon, Richard M., 124
Nkrumah, Kwame, 128, 129
Nobel Peace Prize
    Amnesty International, 152
    Aung San Suu Kyi, 182
    Cassin, René, 187, 188

Nobel Peace Prize, (*continued*)
   Dalai Lama, 192
   MacBride, Sean, 196, 197
   Mandela, Nelson, 198, 199
   Menchú, Rigoberta, 181,
      200, 201
   Nansen, Fridtjof, 205
   Perez Esquivel, Adolfo, 206
   Ramos-Horta, Jose, 207,
      208
   Sakharov, Andrey, 185, 211,
      212
   Mother Teresa, 215
   Tutu, Desmond, 180, 218
   Walesa, Lech, 180, 219
   Wiesel, Elie, 180, 222, 223
   Williams, Jody/ICBL, 180,
      224
nobility, 20, 30-31
noise pollution, 90
nonconformists, 30
nongovernmental
   organizations. *See* NGOs
non-refoulement policy, 92,
   234
nonviolence, 192, 199, 204,
   206-7
non-Western traditional
   societies. *See* developing
   nations; indigenous
   peoples; *specific areas,
   countries, and groups*
Norris-LaGuardia Act of
   1932, 44
North Atlantic Treaty
   Organization, 139, 145
Northern Ireland, 197, 272
Norway, 204-5
Norwegian People's Aid, 260
nuclear disarmament, 196,
   211, 212
*nullum crimen, nulla poena sine
   lege*, 89
Nuremberg trials, 55, 147,
   195, 234
Nyere, Julius, 128, 129

O

OAS. *See* Organization of
   American States
OAU. *See* Organization of
   African Unity
occupational health and safety,
   42, 45, 46, 105
Oceania, 125
Octavian (Caesar Augustus), 8,
   9
Office of the High
   Commissioner for
   Human Rights (UN),
   123, **134**, 135, 270
   Robinson, Mary, 181, 208,
      209
Ogoni, 181, 212-13
OHCHR. *See* Office of the
   High Commissioner for
   Human Rights
older people, rights of, 108
Old Testament, 11, 12, 13
oligarchy, 3, 5, 27, 46
Olympic Games, 255
OMCT. *See* World
   Organization Against
   Torture
one-party states, 127, 129
Open Sore of a Continent, The
   (Soyinka), 214
opinion, freedom of, 99-100
Opinión, La (Argentine
   newspaper), 216

*Organization Mondiale Contre
   La Torture*. *See* World
   Organization Against
   Torture
Organization of African Unity,
   132, **140-42**, 152, 172
Organization of American
   States, 60n.1, 78, 132,
      142-43, 170
   Inter-American
      Commission on Human
      Rights, 165
organized labor. *See* labor
   movement
Origen, 13
Orme, William, 265
Ottawa Treaty (1997), 261
Ottoman Empire, 48
Owen, David, 145

P

Pacific Islands News
   Association, 265
pacifism, 196, 238
paid holidays, right to, 106,
   107
Paine, Thomas, 28, 65
Pakistan, 259
   child labor, 199-200, 236
   executions of minors, 242
   Islamic law, 130
   male-tilted sex ratio, 253
   Masih, Iqbal, 181, 199-200,
      236
Palestinians, 243
Panama, 258
Pankhurst, Emmeline, 40
Paris Commune of 1871, 42
Paris Peace Conference
   (1919), 49
Paris Peace Treaties (1945),
   100
Paris Peace Treaty (1814), 79
parlements (France), 23
Parliament, British
   colonial taxation, 27
   commissions on social
      conditions, 35
   gentry's gained power in,
      20, 30
   inception, 16
   monarchy limitations by,
      16-18, 19, 21
   Montesquieu's praise for, 23
   mutual checks in, 34
   social reforms, 42
patents, 111
paterfamilias, 10
patricians, 8
Paul, Alice, 39, 40
Paul, Saint, 12, 14, 31n.12
pax Romana, 9
Peace and Justice Network
   (Latin America), 206
Peace and Reconciliation
   Commission (South
   Africa), 180
PeaceNet, 163, 164
PEN. *See* International PEN
pensions, 108
perestroika, 185, 212
Perez de Cuellar, Javier, 183
Perez Esquivel, Adolfo, **206-7**
Perón, Isabel, 216
persecution
   asylum from, 93, 234-35
   See also gender-related
      persecution; genocide;
      Holocaust

Persian Letters (Montesquieu),
   224
personal development, 109
personal life. *See* privacy
Peru, 264, 267
Petition of Right of 1628
   (Britain), 16-17, 26
petition rights, 18
Philip II, king of France, 15
Philippines, 128
   child bonded labor, 236
   disappearances, 246
   forced evictions, 255
   Human Rights
      Commission, 61, 100
philosopher-kings, 5
philosophes, 22, 23, 24, 25, 30
philosophical societies, 35
PHR. *See* Physicians for
   Human Rights
Physicians for Human Rights,
   171-72
physiocrats, 30
Pinochet, Augusto, 247
piracy, 79
Pius II, pope, 209
Place, Francis, 42
Plastic People of the Universe
   (Czech rock group), 193
Plato, 5, 5, 6, 13
Plavsic (Bosnian president),
   146
plebians, 8
Poland
   Lemkin, Raphael, 180, 195
   Nazi racial theories, 54, 76
   self-determination, 48, 50
   Walesa, Lech, 180, 218-19,
      219
police, 68, 114
   UN international task
      force, 146
police brutality, **263-64**
polis, 6
Polish Minority Treaty (1919),
   50
political dissent. *See* dissidents
political parties, 34
   one-party states, 127, 129
   outlawing of, 127
political prisoners, 121, 265
   Africa, 150
   Argentina, 216-17
   China, 224-25
   journalists as, 265
   Soviet Union, 185, 212
   See also torture
political refugees, 92
political rights. *See* civil and
   political rights
political tracts, 35
politics. *See* government
Politicus (Plato), 5
poll tax, 29
polyarchy, 129
Ponnamperuma, Cyril, 174-75
popular sovereignty, 23, 25
   Latin America, 126
population displacements. *See*
   internally displaced
   persons; refugees
Portugal, 268
positive discrimination, 84
positive rights, 67
poverty, 3, 10, 33, 35, 251
Powderly, Terence Vincent, 44
Prague Spring of 1968, 192-
   93
Preamble (UDHR), 70-71,
   73-74

precedent, legal, 8
pregnancy
   AIDS/HIV infection, 232
   death penalty prohibition,
      241
   forced, 250
   related rights, 78, 90, 96,
      107
   See also abortion
Presidential Medal of
   Freedom, 222
press, freedom of, 19, 99-100,
   264-65
   Committee to Protect
      Journalists, 158-59
   as first-generation right,
      19n.6.
   as government critic, 34,
      35, 265
   International PEN, 167-68
   violations of, 264-65
Press Freedom Awards, 159
Prevention of Discrimination
   and the Protection of
   Minorities
   subcommission (UN), 61
preventive detention laws, 127
preventive medicine, 107,
   143-44
primitive people, 21
Principles on the Effective
   Prevention and
   Investigation of Extra-
   Legal, Arbitrary, and
   Summary Executions
   (1989), 248
printing presses, 25, 35
prisoners, 81, 230, **265-66**
   forced labor by, 80
   political, 121, 150, 185,
      216-17, 265
   rape of, 267
prisoners of war, 53, 54, 81,
   205, 265
*Prisoner Without a Name, Cell
   without a Number*
   (Timerman), 217
prison privatization, 266
privacy, right to, 78, 87, 89-90
   AIDS/HIV testing, 231
private organizations. *See*
   NGOs
pro-choice groups, 78
procreation rights, 96; *See also*
   abortion; family;
   pregnancy
progression
   history as, 45, 46
   Holocaust as repudiation of
      belief in, 53
Project Diana: Online Human
   Rights Archive, **172-73**
pro-life groups, 78
propaganda, 100
property rights, 19, 21
   capitalist vs. collective, 63,
      97
   Communist forfeiture of,
      47
   contract law, 82
   developing nations and, 97
   English protection, 20, 27
   French Revolution and, 30,
      31
   as inalienable, 33
   middle-class liberal
      concerns, 36, 45
   slavery and, 79
   UDHR Article 17 on, 96-
      98

property rights, (*continued*)
  women's restrictions, 10
proportionality test, 114, 115
proselytizing, 98-99
prostitution, 41
  AIDS/HIV, 232
  as akin to slavery, 80, 271
  traffic in women and girls,
    273, 273-74
Protestant Church of
  England. *See*
  Anglicanism
protests and demonstrations
  labor movement, 42
  Mothers of the
    Disappeared, 203-4
  rights, 101-2
  rights limitations, 114
  woman suffrage, 40
  See also strikes
Proudhon, Pierre-Joseph, 45
Prussia, 31, 45
psychological abuse, 81
psychological torture, 272
public debt, 30
public health, 35, 107
public hearings, 87, 89
public services, access rights
  to, 102
purdah, 234, 251, 253
Puritanism, 17, 28
pursuit of happiness, 28

Q

Quakers, 151, 238
Quebec (Canada), 240
Quiché Indians, 181, 200-201

R

racism, 101-2
  genocide, 252-53
  Nazi theories, 54, 76, 96
  sex tourism, 273
Rädda Barnen, 238
railroad strikes, 44
rainforest, 202
Ramos-Horta, Jose, 181, 183,
  207-8
rape, 148, 250, 251, 252, **266-
  67**, 271
Raphael, 5
rationalism, 34
Reagan, Ronald, 187, 222
Reagan administration, 123n.6
realism, 122-23, 124
realpolitik, 122
reason
  as distinguishing
    humankind, 75
  Enlightenment, 24, 93
  Stoic, 6
Recamier, Max, 194
Red Crescent Movement, 237
Red Cross. See French Red
  Cross; International
  Committee of the Red
  Cross; International Red
  Cross
redress of grievances, 18
Reebok Foundation, 176, 200,
  220
*Reflections on the Revolution in
  France* (Burke), 34
reform. *See* social reform
Reform Acts of 1832, 1867,
  and 1884 (Great Britain),
  36-37
Refugee Convention (1951).
  See Convention Relating
  to the Status of Refugees

refugees
  administrative detention of,
    243
  Bosnian, 136
  children, 197, 198
  definition of, 234
  economic, 234
  homeless, 254, 255
  international laws on status
    of, 136, 170
  League of Nations
    resettlement, 205
  Nansen's work with, 181,
    205
  nationality deprivation, 94
  OAU activity, 140
  rights of, 53, 91, 92-93, 234
  United States Committee
    for Refugees, 175-76
  See also asylum; internally
    displaced persons
registered partnerships, 96
relationships, rights to, 89, 90,
  95-96
religion
  conversion, 98-99
  day of rest, 106
  English rights, 18
  Enlightenment views on,
    19, 23, 24-25
  French persecutions, 30
  genocide, 252-53
  zealotry, 131
  See also church-state
    relations; *specific religions*
religion, freedom of, 53, 60,
  68, 78
  conscientious objection,
    238, 239
  Declaration of
    Independence on, 28
  NGOs on, 168
  UDHR Article 18 on, 98-
    99
Religion in Communist-
  Dominated Areas. *See*
  Research Center for
  Religion and Human
  Rights in Closed Societies
RENAMO (Mozambique
  National Resistance), 197
Reporters sans Frontières, 264
*Report on the Sanitary Condition
  of the Laboring Population of
  Great Britain* (Chadwick),
  35
representative democracy,
  102-3
Republic (Plato), 5
republicanism, 23, 31-32
republics, 21
Republika Srpska, 146
reputation, right to protect, 89
Research Center for Religion
  and Human Rights in
  Closed Societies, 173
residence, freedom of, 90-92
responsibilities, rights and,
  113
rest and leisure, right to, 106-
  7
Restoration (1660; England),
  17
return, right to, 91-92
revolution
  justifications, 21, 28, 31, 65
  See also American
    Revolution; French
    Revolution

Revolutionary Front for an
  Independent East Timor.
  See FRETILIN
RFK Human Rights Awards,
  173-74
Rhodesia. *See* Zimbabwe
rights. *See* group rights;
  human rights; individual
  rights; natural rights;
  Universal Declaration of
  Human Rights; *specific
  rights*
Rights of Man (France). *See*
  Declaration of Rights of
  Man and the Citizen
"Right to Development"
  proclamation (1986), 104,
  112
Rigoberta Menchú Tum
  Foundation, 201
Rio Treaty, 142
riots, labor, 44
Robert F. Kennedy Center for
  Human Rights, **173-74**
Robinson, Mary, 134, 181,
  208-9, 208, *208*
Roche, James Terry, 242
Rockwell, Norman, *1*
Rodley, Nigel S., 248
Roger Baldwin Medal of
  Liberty, 170
Roman Catholic Church, 17,
  18, 28
  bans on *Encyclopedia*, 25
  East Timor, 182-83, 207
  Latin American activism,
    206, 209-10
  papal inquisitions torture,
    272
  Platonic views and, 13
  resistance to French
    republicanism, 31-32
  Mother Teresa, 215-16
  Voltaire's attacks on, 24
Roman Empire, 7-11, 14, 234
  Christian legacy of, 12-13
Romania, 269
Roman law, 7-8, 10, 13
Romero, Oscar, archbishop of
  San Salvador, 180, **209-10**
Roosevelt, Eleanor, 57, 63,
  100
  Commission on Human
    Rights chairmanship, 61,
    120, 188
  Franklin and Eleanor
    Roosevelt Institute, 160
  on simplicity of rights
    declaration, 64
  as UDHR Articles 22-28
    advocate, 104
  on UDHR as "living
    instrument," 72
  and UDHR as nonbinding,
    62, 129
Roosevelt, Franklin D., 53, 60,
  63, 100, 160
Roosevelt, Theodore, 44, 160
Roosevelt Institute. *See*
  Franklin and Eleanor
  Roosevelt Institute
Roosevelt International
  Disability Award, 160
Roosevelt Study Center
  (Netherlands), 160
Rousseau, Jean-Jacques, 18,
  20-21, 22, 28, 30
Royal Dutch Shell, 213
Rural Workers Union of
  Brazil, 202

Russia (former Soviet Union)
  Bolshevik Revolution, 48
  Bonner, Elena, 185
  Chechen medical neutrality
    violations, 262
  collectivism, 52, 63, 97
  death penalty rate, 242
  Helsinki Accords, 122
  Human Rights
    Commission member, 61
  human rights issues, 140
  movement restrictions, 91
  Sakharov, Andrey, 211-12
  Soviet bloc, 63-64, 91, 120,
    121, 139
  Stalinism, 52, 185
  Universal Declaration of
    Human Rights, 63-64,
    77, 120
  World War I casualty rate,
    51
  World War II casualties, 53,
    54
  World War II refugees, 234
  See also Cold War
Russia (imperial), 25, 45
Rwanda
  child soldiers, 237-38
  genocide, 195, 252, 264,
    267
  mass rapes as tactic, 267
  refugees, 136
  war crimes tribunal, 145,
    147, 190, 191

S

Saadawi, Nawal El, 180,
  210-11
Saami, 258
SACC. *See* South African
  Council of Churches
Sadat, Anwar, 187
SADC. *See* Southern African
  Development
  Community
Said, Abdul Aziz, 125-26, 130
Sakharov, Andrey, 185, **211-
  12**, *211*
Sakharov Prize for Freedom
  of Thought, 182
same-gender marriage, 96,
  269
same-sex education, 110
sanctuary, 136, 234
Sandoval Bustillo, Ernesto,
  256
Saro-Wiwa, Ken, 181, **212-
  13**, 214
Sato, Eisaku, 197
Saudi Arabia
  execution of minors, 242
  Islamic law, 130
  UDHR vote abstention,
    63-64, 120
schooling. *See* education
"School of Athens" (Raphael),
  5
science
  Enlightenment, 24, 36
  human rights NGOs, 157-
    58
  right to share benefits of,
    110
scientific property, 111
Sean MacBride Peace Prize,
  197
Secondat, Charles-Louis de.
  See Montesquieu
Second Continental Congress,
  28

second generation rights, 66
Second Treatise (Locke), 26
Secretariat (UN), Human
  Rights Division, 61
secret ballot, 102
secular democracy, 98
Security Council. See United
  Nations
security of person, right to,
  77-79
self-determination, 71, **268-69**
  development and, 245
  East Timor, 208, 268
  post-World War I, 48, 49,
    50, 168
  post-World War II, 127,
    267
  Tibet, 192, 268
Senate, Roman, 8
Seneca, 7
separation of powers, 19-20,
  23, 24, 26, 28-29
Serbia. See Yugoslavia (former)
serfdom, 79, 270
servitude, UDHR Article 4
  ban, 79-80; See also
  slavery
sex ratio, 253
sex tourism, 273, 274
sexual bondage, 270, 271,
  273-74
sexual minorities, 71, 90, 96,
  269-70; See also
  homosexuality
sexual orientation. See sexual
  minorities
sexual violence, 148, 250, 251
  rape as, 266-67
  Rwandan genocide, 252
Sgarlata v. Commission (1965),
  139
Shamlan, Ahmad Al-, 257
Shariah, 130, 131
Shaw, Anna Howard, 39
Shell Oil Corporation, 213
Shultz, George, 124
Sierra Leone, 237
sine manu, 10
Singapore, 240
slave revolts, 10
slavery, **270-71**
  ancient Greece, 6, 10
  contemporary forms, 79-80,
    235-36, 270, 271
  Enlightenment
    condemnation, 23, 24, 25
  Judeo-Christian tradition
    and, 12, 14
  prohibition as absolute
    right, 114, 115
  Roman Empire, 9-10, 14
  UDHR Article 4 ban, 67,
    79-80
  U.S. abolishment of, 29
  U.S. female abolitionists, 38
Slavery Convention (1926),
  79, 270
slave trade, 20, 271
  UDHR Article 4 ban, 79-
    80, 270, 271
Slovak Republic, 193
smallpox, 143
Smith, Adam, 21, 23, 34-35
social conditions
  ancient Greece, 6
  British technological
    improvements of, 35
  Communist classless
    society, 47

industrialization effects, 33,
  35, 40-41
post-World War II
  reconstruction, 63
See also class; economic,
  social, and cultural rights;
  social welfare
social contract, 18-22, 28
Social Contract, The
  (Rousseau), 21
socialism, 45-47
  group and economic rights
    emphasis, 125
  internationalism, 48
  labor movement and, 43, 45
  self-determination and, 49
  Universal Declaration of
    Human Rights and, 63
  woman suffrage and, 38
  See also Communism
social justice. See equality;
  justice
social mobility, 27
social order, right to, 111-12
social reform. See social
  welfare
social rights. See economic,
  social, and cultural rights
social security. See social
  welfare
social welfare
  as Islamic commitment, 131
  labor movement, 40, 42, 44
  natural law critiques and, 35
  nineteenth-century, 35, 38,
    42
  post-World War II
    reconstruction, 63
  right to, 103-5, 106, 107-8
  Roman, 9
  state provisions, 132
  U.S. New Deal, 63, 70
societal evolution, 45, 46
Society for Threatened
  Peoples, **174**
Society of Friends. See
  Quakers
soldiers. See military service
Solidarity (Polish labor
  union), 219
Solon, 4-5
Somalia, 142, 194, 260, 267
son preference, 253, 254
Sophists, 4, 6
Sophocles, 6-7
South Africa, 140, 142, 148
  Africa Fund, 150
  Goldstone, Richard J., 190-
    91
  Mandela, Nelson, 198-99
  Tutu, Desmond, 217-18,
    180
  UDHR vote abstention, 64,
    120
South African Anglican
  Church, 218
South African Constitutional
  Court, 190, 191
South African Council of
  Churches, 218
South America. See Latin
  America
South Asia, 236
South Asia Forum for Human
  Rights, 260
Southern Africa, 150, 142
Southern African
  Development
  Community, 148
sovereignty, 70, 77, 94

of God, 11, 13
popular, 23, 25, 126
See also international law;
  state
Soviet bloc, 63-64, 91, 120,
  121, 139
Soviet Union. See Russia
Soyinka, Wole, **213-14**
Spain, 247
Sparta, 6
Spartacus, 10
Special Committee of the
  International
  NonGovernmental
  Organizations on Human
  Rights, 196
specialty rule (extradition),
  247
speech, freedom of. See
  expression, freedom of
Sri Lanka, 140, 246
Stalin, Joseph, 52, 120, 122,
  185
Standard Minimum Rules for
  the Treatment of
  Prisoners (1955), 265
standard of living
  development and, 244, 245
  homelessness, 254-55
  refugee movement and, 234
  right to, 107
standing army, 17
state
  asylum rights, 92-93
  children's rights, 80
  citizenship rights, 94
  common interests, 113
  death penalty, 241-42
  extradition, 246-48
  failure to protect human
    rights activists, 256
  forced evictions, 255
  foreign policy ideology,
    122-24
  freedom of movement,
    90-92
  God's authority vs., 11, 13,
    17
  government participation
    rights, 28-29, 102-3 (see
    also voting rights)
  "greatest good" doctrine, 34
  human rights compliance
    monitors, 84-85
  human rights expectations,
    67-68
  human rights limitations,
    68, 113-16
  human rights recognition as
    authority prerequisite, 65
  human rights standards, 69-
    70
  human rights violations
    remedies, 84-85
  individual duties to, 63,
    112-14, 115
  individual vs., 6-7, 8, 63, 68,
    99, 112-16, 127, 130, 132
  international judicial
    standard, 257
  Islamic traditions, 130-31
  marriage entitlements and
    regulations, 95, 96
  positive vs. negative rights
    and, 67
  press criticism, 34, 35, 265
  press restrictions, 264-65
  religion and. See church-
    state relations

role in combating
  discrimination, 83-84
role in social, economic,
  and cultural welfare, 63,
  67, 104, 127
sovereignty concept, 70, 77,
  94
See also government
state churches. See church-
  state relations
State Department, U.S., 146-
  47
statelessness, 85, 94
Stauder v. City of Ulm (1979),
  139
Stoicism, 5-6, 7
Stork v. High Authority (1959),
  139
strikes, 43, 44, 52
Stuart monarchy, 17, 20n.7
student protests, 101, 180,
  188, 189, 194, 220, 221
Study on the Impact of Armed
  Conflict on Children
  (UN), 197, 198
Sub-Committee on the
  Prevention of
  Discrimination and
  Protection of Minorities
  (UN), 135, 266
Subjection of Women, The
  (Mill), 33
Sudan, 237-38, 259, 260, 270
Sudetenland, 50
suffrage. See voting rights
summary executions. See
  extrajudicial executions
Sunday schools, 42
Sunnah, 130, 131
Supreme Court, U.S., 29
Survival International, 258
sustainable development, 244
sweatshops, 44, 45
Swedish Save the Children,
  238

T

Taliban, 251
Talmud, 14
Tambo, Oliver, 198
Tanzania, 128
taxation
  American colonial protest,
    27-28
  British Parliament and, 17
  French rigidity, 30
  Magna Carta restrictions,
    15
  progressive income tax, 46
  Roman citizenship and, 9
Tea Act of 1773, 27
technological advances, 35
television licenses, 100
Tenzin Gyatso, 180, **191-92**
Teresa, Mother, 180, **215-16**
territories and colonies, 77
terrorism, 115, 247, 267
textile factories, 41
Thailand, 232
Thatcher, Margaret, 225
Third World Academy of
  Science, 175
Third World Foundation of
  North America, **174-75**
Thirteenth Amendment, U.S.
  (1865), 29
Thorolf Rafto Prize for
  Human Rights, 182
thought, freedom of, 98-99,
  238

Tiananmen Square protests (1989; China), 101, 180, 188, 189, 220
Tibet, 180, 191-92, 206, 268
Timerman, Jacobo, 180, **216-17**
Togo, 235
Tojo, Hideki, 55
Tokyo trials, 55, 147
Toleration Act of 1689 (Britain), 18
Toonen v. Australia (1994), 270
Torres Strait Islanders, 258
torts, 82
torture, **271-72**
  as affront to humankind, 11
  Amnesty International campaign against, 121, 272
  Argentina, 217
  Communist regimes, 46
  definition, 271, 272
  detention and, 86
  domestic violence as, 251
  Enlightenment condemnation, 25
  Greek military dictatorship and, 128
  Guatemala, 200, 201
  Nazi concentration camps, 54
  Physicians for Human Rights, 171-72
  police brutality, 263
  prisoner protection from, 266
  prohibition as absolute right, 68, 115
  prohibition as negative right, 67
  rape as, 267
  UDHR Article 5 ban, 67, 68, 78, 79, 80-81
  UN convention against, 134
  World Organization Against Torture, 177
totalitarianism, 52-53, 119-20
Touré, Sékou, 128, 129
tourism, sex, 273, 274
town meetings, 17
trade
  English duties on colonial imports, 27
  English overseas interests, 20
  free markets, 23, 34, 97-98
trade associations, 42
Trade Union Act of 1875 (Britain), 42
trade unions. See labor movement
traffic in women and girls, 51, **273-74**
Trajan, emperor of Rome, 9
transexuality, 269
trial rights. See fair trial, right to
Triangle Shirtwaist Company fire (1911), 44
tribunals, 88
Trinidad and Tobago, 147
Truth and Reconciliation Commission (South Africa), 218
Tucker, Karla Faye, 242
Tudjman, Franjo, 146
Turkey
  Armenian eviction by, 50

conscientious objector prosecution, 239
disappearances, 246
human rights violations, 256
Ottoman Empire end, 48
police brutality, 263
secularism, 130
war with Greece, 205
Tutsi, 233, 252, 264
Tutu, Desmond, archbishop of South Africa, 180, 183, **217-18**, *217*
Twelve Tables, 8
Twenty-Fourth Amendment, U.S. (1964), 29
Twenty-Third Amendment, U.S. (1961), 29
Two Treatises of Government (Locke), 26
"tyranny of the majority," 99

U

UDHR. *See* Universal Declaration of Human Rights
Uelke, Osman Murat, 239
Uganda, 141
  AIDS/HIV, 232
  child soldiers, 237, 271
  disappearances, 246
  mass rapes, 267
Ukraine, 61, 242
UNAIDS, 232
UN Charter, 70-71, 120, 250
  preamble (1945), 53, 60
unemployment protection rights, 105
UNESCO. *See* United Nations Educational, Scientific, and Cultural Organization
UNHCR. *See* United Nations High Commissioner for Refugees
UNICEF, 143, 198, 231, 237
UNICEF International Child Development Centre, **175**
unions. *See* labor movement
United Kingdom. *See* Great Britain
United Mine Workers, 44
United Nations, **133-34**, 135-37, 152, 230-31
  AIDS action, 232
  background, 50, 52, 53
  charter, 53, 60, 70-71, 120, 250
  children's rights, 80, 90, 134, 137, 175, 237
  creation of, 60, 120
  Decade of Human Rights Education (1995-2004), 74, 110
  detention and imprisonment protections, 243-44
  on development as basic right, 244, 245
  disappearance monitoring, 245
  drafting of Declaration of Human Rights, 61-64, 120 (*see also* Universal Declaration of Human Rights)
  efforts against female genital mutilation, 250

forcible eviction protections, 255
founding aims, 111-12
genocide convention, 134, 147, 195, 252
human rights awareness campaign, **137**
human rights standards, 69
indigenous peoples rights, 258-59
International Year for Indigenous Populations, 201
nonratification of Convention on the Elimination of All Forms of Discrimination Against Women, 251
refugee agency, 92, 135-36, 176
Rwandan and Balkan war crimes tribunals, 145-47, 190, 191
Secretariat Human Rights Division, 61
sexual minorities discrimination recognition, 269, 270
slavery studies, 271
South African sanctions, 199
Study on the Impact of Armed Conflict on Children, 197, 198
torture convention, 121, 134, 137
unlawful executions safeguards, 242
See also General Assembly; *specific bodies*
United Nations Children's Fund, 232, 250
United Nations Congress on the Prevention of Crime and Treatment of Offenders (1955), 266
United Nations Development Program, 232, 244
United Nations Educational, Scientific, and Cultural Organization, 62, 175, 197, 198
  AIDS/HIV, 232
  Cassin, René, 187
  cultural property restitution, 111
  education rights, 108-9, 110
  Menchú, Rigoberta, 201
United Nations High Commissioner for Refugees, **135-36**, 231
  asylum requests, 234, 235
  Nansen, Fridtjof, 181, 205
  on numbers of internally displaced persons, 259
  Refugee Convention, 92, 93, 234
United Nations Population Fund, 232, 250
United Nations Women's Conference (1995). *See* World Conference on Women
United Nations Working Group on Contemporary Forms of Slavery, 79-80
United States
  AIDS/HIV, 231-32
  Bill of Rights, 26, 29
  Carter, Jimmy, 186-87

colonial government, 17
Constitution, 26, 28-29
court system, 8
death penalty, 241, 242
death row conditions, 81
Declaration of Human Rights (1948), 97
Declaration of Independence (1776), 28, 62, 268
detention abuses, 243
development aid by, 244
gender persecution as asylum basis, 234-35
Helsinki Accords, 121
human rights policy, 122-24
labor movement, 43-44
New Deal social welfare, 63, 70
NGOs, 150-53, 155-56, 157-60, 162-65, 170-74, 175-77
police brutality, 263-64
policies against female genital mutilation, 250
press freedom, 264-65
sexual minorities rights, 269
slave trade, 271
student protests, 101
UDHR binding covenants and, 63
woman suffrage, 37, 38-39, 250
World War I casualty rate, 51
See also American Revolution
United States Committee for Refugees, **175-76**
United States Holocaust Memorial Council, 222
Universal Declaration of Human Rights (1948), 57, 59-116, 133, 138, 141, 149, 231
  analysis of, 73-126 (*see also specific articles*)
  Cassin authorship, 187, 188, 61
  concept and categories of rights, 66-69
  continuing rights violations, 256
  covenants as binding, 62-63, 129, 132
  criticism of, 70
  description of, 64-72
  drafting of, 61-64
  enforceable elements, 65-66, 129, 132, 133
  on enforcement mechanisms, 69-70
  guaranteed rights for activists, 255
  historical background, 60, 120-21
  implementation efforts, 120
  nature of, 65-66
  preamble, 70-71, 73-74
  ratification, 55, 120
  Roosevelt Institute activity, 160
  as universal, 70-72
  Western bias of, 63, 70, 125
Universal Declaration of Indigenous Rights (draft), 258
universal jurisdiction principle, 247
universal moral law, 4, 7

universal rights, 7, 28, 30
universal suffrage. *See* voting rights
University of Wyoming, 270
Uruguay, 61, 245
USCR. *See* United States Committee for Refugees
utilitarianism, 33, 34, 35
utopias, 5

V

Van Buren, Martin, 43
Vance, Cyrus, 145
Versailles, Treaty of, 48, 50, 52
Vicaría de la Solidaridad (Chile), 226
Victoria, queen of Great Britain, 38
Videla, Jorge Rafael, 216, 217
Vietnam, 136, 265
Vietnamese boat people, 194
Vietnam Veterans of America Foundation, 223
Villaflor de Vicenti, Azucena, 204
Vincent-Daviss, Diana, 172
Vindication of the Rights of Women, A (Wollstonecraft), 36
violence
   against human rights activists, 256
   against journalists, 264, 265
   peaceful assembly vs., 101-2
   police brutality, 263-64
   sexual, 148, 250, 251, 252, 266-67
   terrorist, 115, 247, 267
   UDHR Article 5 on, 80-81
   See also torture; war
virgins, 12
Voltaire, 21, 22, 23, *23*, 24, 25, 30
voting rights
   Greek males, 4
   Roman citizens, 9
   universal and equal suffrage, 102, 103
   universal suffrage movement, 33, 36-40, 42, 45
   U.S. constitutional amendments, 29
   woman suffrage, 29, 37-40, 250

W

wages, 35, 37, 41, 105, 236
Wahhabis, 130
Walesa, Lech, 180, **218-19**, *219*
Wang Dan, 180, **220**
want, freedom from, 53, 60
war
   child victims, 197-98
   conscientious objection, 99, 238-39
   cultural property restitution, 111
   Engels justification of, 47
   humanitarian law, 81, 89, 115
   landmines, 260-61
   medical neutrality, 261, 262
   as natural condition, 19

noninternational conflicts, 233-34
   as press limitation justification, 264
   prisoners of, 53, 54, 81, 205, 265
   propaganda curbs, 100
   rape as tactic, 267, 271
   slavery-like practices, 271
   UDHR Article 5 application, 81
war crimes, 79, 89
   forced deportation as, 234
   genocide vs., 252
   International Criminal Court, 147-48
   Nuremberg and Tokyo trials, 55, 147, 195
   rape as, 251, 267
   Rwanda and Balkans tribunal, 145-47, 190, 191
   slavery as, 271
   torture as, 272
Washington, George, 30
Watch Committee. *See* Human Rights Watch
wealth
   international redistribution of, 104, 112
   laissez-faire economy creating, 34
   oligarchy and, 3
   political participation and, 4
   private control of, 98
   Roman political power and, 8
Wealth of Nations, The (Smith), 23
Weber, Max, 226
Wei Jingsheng, **221-22**
welfare. *See* social welfare
welfare states, 132
Wells, H. G., 62
western Sahara, 268
Western tradition
   dichotomy with non-Western societes, 126, 127
   human rights outlook, 63, 70, 104-5, 124-26, 127, 129, 132, 240
   Judeo-Christian roots, 11-14, 15, 98, 125-26
   See also specific countries
Westminster model, 127
Whittaker, Benjamin, 271
WHO. *See* World Health Organization
widows, 12
Wiesel, Elie, 180, **222-23**
Willam III and Mary II, king and queen of England, 17
Williams, Jody, 180, **223-24**
Wilson, Woodrow, 47, 48, 49-51, 268
Witness, **176-77**
Wollstonecraft, Mary, 36
women
   abortion controversy, 78
   contemporary exploitation of, 79, 80
   genital mutilation, 210, 231, 234, 235, 240, 249-50
   labor reforms, 42-43, 250

nineteenth-century employment, 41, 42
   rape as human rights issue, 266-67
   traffic in, 51, 273-74
   See also gender-related persecution; pregnancy
women's rights
   as asylum basis, 234-35, 250, 251
   conventions on, 51, 77, 80, 83, 109-10, 134, 137, 251
   current status of, 250-51
   eighteenth-century advocates, 36, 37-39
   Enlightenment hedging, 23
   French exclusions, 32
   French labor movement, 42
   gender equality concept, 106
   girl children's suppression, 253-54
   Greek restrictions, 6, 10
   International Women's Rights Action Watch, 169
   Islamic suppression, 210-11, 234, 251
   in marriage, 19, 95, 106
   Mill support, 33, 35
   Platonic defense of, 5
   Roman measures, 10
   socialist advocacy, 45
   suffrage, 29, 37-40, 250
   United States, 37, 38-39, 250
Women's Social and Political Union, 40
Women's Trade Union League, 62
work, right to, 67, 105-6
workdays and hours, limitations on, 42-43, 46, 106, 107
"Workers of the World Unite!" (Marx manifesto), 46
Working Group on an Optional Protocol to the Convention Against Torture, 272
Working Group on Contemporary Forms of Slavery, 271
Working Group on Enforced or Involuntary Disappearances, 135, 245, 246
Working Group on Indigenous Populations, 258
World Association of Newspapers, 265
World Bank, 232, 244, 258
World Conference on Human Rights (1993), 269
World Conference on Human Settlements II (1996), 255
World Conference on Women (1995), 251, 270
World Health Organization, **143-44**, 232, 250
world hunger, 154
World Organization Against Torture, **177**, 184, 272

"world spirit" (Hegel concept), 45, 46
World War I
   bloodiness of, 61
   conscientious objection, 238
   economic disruptions, 43, 52
   policies following, 48-50, 64, 76, 98, 268
   veterans organization, 187-88
   woman suffrage and, 39
World War II, 52-55
   antecedents, 49, 52
   brutality of, 52, 53-55, 60, 74, 119
   casualties, 53
   "Four Freedoms" and, 53, 60, 100
   Free France government, 188
   as human rights movement impetus, 119, 138, 265
   identity as basis of Nazi persecutions, 76
   Japanese comfort women, 271
   Nazi identity-based persecutions, 54, 76, 269 (*see also* Holocaust)
   postwar development programs, 244
   postwar landmine deployment, 260
   postwar reconstruction, 63, 137-38
   postwar self-determination, 127, 268
   refugees, 53, 92, 234
   as Universal Declaration of Human Rights impetus, 60
   war crimes trials, 55, 147, 195, 234
Wu, Harry, **224-25**

X

Xhosa nation, 198

Y

Yale University, 172
Yeats, William Butler, 196
Yemen, 242
Youth League of the ANC, 198-99
Yugoslavia (former), 140, 264
   creation of, 48
   Human Rights Commission member, 61
   Kosovo abuses, 233
   rape as military tactic, 267
   refugee movement, 91
   war crimes tribunal, 145-47, 190, 191
   See also Bosnia-Herzegovina

Z

Zalaquett, José, *225*, **225-26**
Zarakolu, Ay Enur, 256
Zeno of Citium, 6
Zimbabwe, 150, 197
   AIDS cases, 232
   denial of homosexual rights, 269

CONTRIBUTORS

Daan Bronkhorst is a staff member of the Dutch section of Amnesty International and the author of various books about human rights and refugee issues, including a study on truth commissions, *Truth and Reconciliation: Obstacles and Opportunities for Human Rights* (1995).

Carol Devine is a writer and human rights worker, whose assignments have taken her from Canada to India, the former Soviet Union, Central America, and Rwanda with NGOs, including the Diplomacy Training Program and Médecins Sans Frontières.

Carol Rae Hansen, Ph.D. is an international relations and educational consultant to business, government, and academia in the Washington, D.C. area. She received her Ph.D. in Government (International Relations) from Harvard University.

Frederic A. Moritz is a writer and teacher based in Belfast, Maine who maintains the Web site "American human rights reporting as a global watchdog," (http://www.worldlymind. org/expose.htm). He covered human rights issues for *The Christian Science Monitor* as Asia correspondent (1977-1981).

Baptiste Rolle holds a Master of Arts in Law and Diplomacy from Tufts' Fletcher School of Law and Diplomacy and is currently working at the Legal Division of the International Committee of the Red Cross in Geneva.

Rebecca Sherman is member of the National Writers Union. She writes about cultural issues, human rights, and public health from her home outside Boston, Massachusetts.

Jo Lynn Southard, J.D., LL.M, is a writer and Adjunct Professor at Andover College in Portland, Maine.

Ralph Wilde is an English barrister specializing in public international law, and currently engaged in legal research at Corpus Christi College, Cambridge University, UK. He was formerly the Henry Fellow at Yale University, and a Visiting Scholar at Yale Law School.

Robert Wilkinson is a writer and consultant who has worked with a wide variety of organizations including Save the Children Australia, UNICEF, the Netherlands Red Cross, and the Parliamentary Human Rights Group of British Parliament.